THE MODERN PILGRIM

Liturgia condenda 8

1. Gerard Lukken & Mark Searle, *Semiotics and Church Architecture. Applying the Semiotics of A.J. Greimas and the Paris School to the Analysis of Church Buildings*, Kampen, 1993
2. Gerard Lukken, *Per visibilia ad invisibilia. Anthropological, Theological and Semiotic Studies on the Liturgy and the Sacraments*, edited by Louis van Tongeren & Charles Caspers, Kampen, 1994
3. *Bread of Heaven. Customs and Practices Surrounding Holy Communion. Essays in the History of Liturgy and Culture*, edited by Charles Caspers, Gerard Lukken & Gerard Rouwhorst, Kampen 1995
4. Willem Marie Speelman, *The Generation of Meaning in Liturgical Songs. A Semiotic Analysis of Five Liturgical Songs as Syncretic Discourses*, Kampen, 1995
5. Susan K. Roll, *Toward the Origins of Christmas*, Kampen, 1995
6. Maurice B. McNamee, *Vested Angels. Eucharistic Allusions in Early Netherlandish Paintings*, Leuven, 1998
7. Karl Gerlach, *The Antenicene Pascha. A Rhetorical History*, Leuven, 1998
8. Paul Post, Jos Pieper & Marinus van Uden, *The Modern Pilgrim. Multidisciplinary Explorations of Christian Pilgrimage*, Leuven, 1998

Liturgia condenda is published by the Liturgical Institute in Tilburg (NL). The series plans to publish innovative research into the science of liturgy and serves as a forum which will bring together publications produced by researchers of various nationalities. The motto *liturgia condenda* expresses the conviction that research into the various aspects of liturgy can make a critico-normative contribution to the deepening and the renewal of liturgical practice.

Liturgisch Instituut
P.O. Box 9130
5000 HC Tilburg
The Netherlands

THE MODERN PILGRIM

Multidisciplinary Explorations of Christian Pilgrimage

Paul Post, Jos Pieper & Marinus van Uden

PEETERS

D. 1998/0602/316
ISBN 90-429-0698-7

TABLE OF CONTENTS

List of Illustrations VII

Introduction 1

PART ONE: THE STUDY OF PILGRIMAGE: SITUATION IN RESEARCH, THEORY, METHODS, PROJECTS AND PERSPECTIVES

1. Reasons for Going. A Social Science Perspective on Motives for Pilgrimage 19
2. The "Places of Pilgrimage in The Netherlands" Project. An Orientation 49
3. "God isn't concerned with trivial details," or, Rereading Hobsbawm 89
4. The Miracle of Dokkum and Other Accounts of Distance and Engagement. A Comparison of Local Pastoral Interaction at Holy Places 121

Illustrations: Plate 1-22 144

PART TWO: THE MODERN PILGRIM: EXPERIENCES, MOTIVES AND EFFECTS

5. Transformation and Confirmation. Interviews with Pilgrims to Wittem and Lourdes 157
6. Modern Pilgrimage to Lourdes: Motives and Effects. 173
7. Lourdes: A Place of Religious Transformations? 189
8. Pilgrims to Santiago: A Case-Study of their Spiritual Experiences 205
9. The Modern Pilgrim. A Study of Contemporary Pilgrims' Accounts 221

Illustrations: Plate 23-34 243

Part Three: Contextual Explorations and Perspectives: Sacred Person and Place, Ritual between Tradition and Modernity

10. On Saints. Two Case-Studies Between Belief and Superstition 253

11. Good Times, Bad Times. Devotional Rituals Between Tradition and Modernity 263

12. Ritual Landscape: On Outdoor Liturgy. Processional Parks, Papal Visits, and Popular Rites Associated With Sudden Death 281

Illustrations: Plate 35-46 315

Bibliography 321

Index 363

Notes on the authors 369

LIST OF ILLUSTRATIONS

1. Wittem (The Netherlands, prov. Limburg), cloister and pilgrimage complex (photo: P. Post).

2. Wittem (The Netherlands, prov. Limburg), statue of St. Gerard Majella (from a postcard).

3. Wittem (The Netherlands, prov. Limburg), cult statue of St. Gerard Majella (photo: P. Post).

4. Wittem (The Netherlands, prov. Limburg), cult statue of St. Gerard Majella (photo: coll. P. Post).

5. Wittem (The Netherlands, prov. Limburg), procession in the cloister garden (photo: P. Post).

6. Wittem (The Netherlands, prov. Limburg), café St. Gerardus, near the cloister and pilgrimage complex (photo: P. Post).

7. Banneux, Banneux-Notre-Dame (Belgium) (photo: P.J. Margry, 1993).

8. Banneux, Banneux-Notre-Dame (Belgium) (photo: P.J. Margry, 1993).

9. Dokkum (The Netherlands, prov. Friesland), aerial photograph, St. Boniface spring and processional park, c. 1928 (collection: P. Post).

10. Dokkum (The Netherlands, prov. Friesland), "Restored" processional park, 1994 (photo: P. Post).

11. Dokkum (The Netherlands, prov. Friesland), 12th station of the cross in restored park (photo: P. Post).

12. Dokkum (The Netherlands, prov. Friesland), St. Boniface Chapel (photo: P.J. Margry).

13. "Dokkum: 'n moordstad" (City of his death) (postcard ca. 1990; coll. P. Post).

14. Dokkum (The Netherlands, prov. Friesland), St. Boniface Chapel (photo: coll. P. Post).

15. Dokkum (The Netherlands, prov. Friesland), statue of St. Boniface in the Boniface Chapel (photo: coll. P. Post).

16. Dokkum (The Netherlands, prov. Friesland), pastor Herman Peters by the spring of St. Boniface, 1993 (photo: coll. P. Post).

17. Dokkum (The Netherlands, prov. Friesland), redesigned basin by the Boniface Chapel and park, 1995 (photo: coll. P. Post).

18. Dokkum (The Netherlands, prov. Friesland), programme of the St. Boniface Pilgrimage in 1983; in the background, pilgrims in the Boniface Chapel, August 21, 1983 (photo: P.J. Margry).

19. La Salette (France), pilgrimage complex of Notre-Dame de la Salette (from a 1960s postcard; coll. P.J. Margry).

20. La Salette (France), pilgrimage complex of Notre-Dame de la Salette (from a 1960s postcard; coll. P.J. Margry).

21. La Salette (France), pilgrimage complex of Notre-Dame de la Salette (from a 1960s postcard; coll. P.J. Margry).

22. La Salette (France), procession near the pilgrimage complex (from a 1960s postcard; coll. P.J. Margry).

23. Lourdes (France), Dutch pilgrims (photo: coll. M. van Uden).

24. Lourdes (France), Dutch pilgrims (photo: M. van Uden).

25. Lourdes (France), Dutch pilgrims (photo: M. van Uden).

26. On the way to Santiago, Camino de Santiago (photo: P.J. Margry).

27. Santiago de Compostela (Spain), the cathedral from the Paseo de la Alameda (photo: J. van Herwaarden).

28. Santiago de Compostela (Spain), the statue of St. James (1694), Puerta Santa, cathedral, Plaza de la Quintana (photo: J. van Herwaarden).

29. Santiago de Compostela (Spain), cathedral, portico of the Glory, 12th cent. (coll. P.J. Margry).

30. Heiloo (The Netherlands, prov. Noord-Brabant), sale of devotional items, May-month, pilgrimage grounds of Our Lady of Need (Onze Lieve Vrouw ter Nood) (photo: P.J. Margry, 1983).

31. Laren (The Netherlands, prov. Noord-Holland), St. Jan's Procession (photo: P. Post, 1993).

32. Laren (The Netherlands, prov. Noord-Holland), St. Jan's Procession (photo: P. Post, 1993).

33. Laren (The Netherlands, prov. Noord-Holland), processional banners in the St. Janskerkhof during the celebration of the Eucharist (photo: P. Post, 1993).

34. Laren (The Netherlands, prov. Noord-Holland), festive arch in a street in Laren on the route of the St. Jan's Procession (photo: P. Post, 1993).

35. Tilburg (The Netherlands, prov. Noord-Brabant), painting of Peerke Donders in the Peerke Donders Chapel (photo: P.J. Margry).

36. Barger Oosterveld (The Netherlands, prov. Drenthe), prayer, blessing and offering of pilgrimage candles midway on the procession honouring St. Gerard Majella, near the wayside altar in the processional park, July 1, 1984 (photo: P.J. Margry).

37. Amsterdam (The Netherlands, prov. Noord-Holland), in March 1988 on the Rokin the "Pillar of the Miracle" was erected, consisting of elements from the medieval chapel of the Holy Site, which was demolished in 1908 (photo: P.J. Margry).

38. Amsterdam (The Netherlands, prov. Noord-Holland), Kalverstraat. The Lipstick store is situated on the site of the former "Holy Corner", the spot where the fireplace in which the Miracle of the Sacrament took place was at that time located (photo: P.J. Margry).

39. Panorama of Beek airfield (The Netherlands, prov. Limburg), papal visit, 1985 (photo: Dutch Papal Visit Foundation; ANP).

40. Naarden (The Netherlands, prov. Noord-Holland), flower bed at the site of Tom's accident, 1994 (photo: P. Post).

41. Amsterdam South East (The Netherlands, prov. Noord-Holland), memorial garden for Bijlmer air crash, 1994 (photo: P. Post).

42. Amsterdam South East (The Netherlands, prov. Noord-Holland), memorial garden for Bijlmer air crash, 1994 (photo: P. Post).

43. Marker at the site of young woman's fatal accident, beside Provincial Road N 417 between Hilversum and Hollandsche Rading (The Netherlands, prov. Noord-Holland), 1995 (photo: P. Post).

44. Marker at the site of young woman's fatal accident, beside Provincial Road N 417 between Hilversum and Hollandsche Rading (The Netherlands, prov. Noord-Holland), 1995 (photo: P. Post).

45. Landscape prayer card, 1981 (Collection: P. Post).

46. Naarden (The Netherlands, prov. Noord-Holland), announcement of an open air Christmas celebration, December, 1996 (photo: P. Post).

INTRODUCTION

1. The Paradox of the Crisis in Christian Ritual

Various experts on ritual have pointed to what is termed the "paradox of the crisis in ritual" in Europe and the United States. On the one hand questions are being asked with increasing urgency about the inculturation of Christian rituals. But at the same time, unexpectedly and often outside the sphere of the organized church, on the other hand there is an enormous interest in rituals and symbols. The "traditional" Christian liturgical repertoire seems to be playing a part in this at numerous points. In many places there is a flowering of rituals, public and private, which also – according to research – includes rituals from popular religious culture. For example, it has now become exceptionally busy on the old pilgrimage routes to Santiago de Compostela again. In this context, which is of the utmost importance for theological, liturgical and ritual studies, it is fitting that attention be devoted to the themes of pilgrimages and devotions.

For some years now, from the early 1980s, pilgrimage has figured in the agenda of a research collective in The Netherlands, in which questions relating to it are being raised within the broader framework of an interest in innovation in ritual and the role of traditional liturgy in a modern or post-modern world. Here, as in many branches of ritual studies, one can speak of a dynamic interplay of cultus and culture which leads to creative interaction among new questions, new sources and new techniques and research methods.

This book is conceived as a report to an international forum on this long-running research programme. In this introduction we will briefly summarize the origins, development and context of this pilgrimage research, in order to subsequently, on the basis of that summary, present the objectives and scheme of this book. This introduction will close with some notes on the editorial process, and several acknowledgements.

2. Context: Programme and Projects

2.1. Origins

This book arises from a relatively long history of pilgrimage research in a Dutch theological setting. The roots lie in the theological faculty at Heerlen (Universiteit voor Theologie en Pastoraat, now a division of the Katholieke Universiteit Nijmegen) at the beginning of the 1980s, where religious popular culture was placed on the agenda of the research programmes in a series of theological disciplines and sub-disciplines. The breadth of its foundation among church historians, dogmatists, liturgists, missiologists and pastoral theologians can be seen in the 1982 collection *Volksreligiositeit: uitnodiging en uitdaging.*[1] This trajectory continued around the central theme of the phenomenon of pilgrimage, after the mid-'80s taking the form of an official, broadly structured multidisciplinary research programme, the central focus of which was contemporary Christian pilgrimage.[2] This programme, "Christian pilgrimage, manifestations and functions of a popular-religious phenomenon," had many of the features of a "podium" or "platform" programme, in which a number of researchers, disciplines and traditions could encounter and engage one another. Although since that time the composition of the research group has been constantly changing, from the very beginning two lines of research with continuing researchers/coordinators have functioned as both dominant factors in and a source of continuity for the whole. On the one side there is the track of liturgical studies, in which an historical, European ethnological and anthropological approach has predominated, its work being carried out and coordinated by Paul Post. On the other side there is the social science track, with specific content coming from psychology of religion, its work being carried out and coordinated by Jos Pieper and Rien van Uden. The combination of these two lines appears to have been extremely fruitful, as demonstrated by the many congresses, workshops, symposia, collections, articles and research reports in which the results of their investigations have been presented.

In the early phase, one of the places of pilgrimage upon which the liturgical studies' research focused was Wittem. An extensive historical index was assembled for the site, and the ritual disposition[3] and hymn

[1] Blijlevens, Brants & Henau (1982).
[2] Post & Van Uden (1985).
[3] Post (1989b); (1990c).

culture was also examined.[4] From this entry point, the research broadened out more and more to an analysis of pilgrimage as the focus for understanding popular religious ritual in change. This study was closely linked with important developments in European ethnology and historical sciences which were deeply influencing Dutch liturgical studies precisely during the years when the pilgrimage research programme was beginning. A brief excursus with regard to these will not be out of place here, because to an important degree these developments form the theoretical background for the structuring and development of the research programme and, as it is derived from the programme, this book. At the same time they are the background for the constant interaction of the lines set out by the two disciplines, as mentioned above, and thus for the programme's multidisciplinary character.

2.2. Liturgical Studies: Striking Developments[5]

Especially if we inquire into how the subject of religious popular culture in general and pilgrimage in particular came onto (and periodically returns to) the theological agenda, liturgical development itself forms an important orientation point, not only for theology and liturgical studies but for other disciplines as well. The liturgical reforms that took shape after the Second Vatican Council, particularly in the 1970s and early 1980s, were directly or indirectly an impetus for a good deal of reflection and debate over and around religious popular culture. The special issue of *La Maison-Dieu* from 1975, "Religion populaire et réforme liturgique," is an illustration of this.[6] There was a fierce debate about popular religiosity going on in France and Latin America at that time, and arising from pastoral theology and the social sciences from about 1974, but especially after 1977, the subject of popular belief and popular religiosity assumed a place on the theological agenda.[7] From our perspective today, it is striking that in spite of this special issue of *La Maison-Dieu*, liturgical studies were really to all intents and purposes absent

[4] EVERS (1993).

[5] See for this section: P. POST: Religious Popular Culture and Liturgy. An Illustrated Argument for an Approach, in *Questions liturgiques/Studies in Liturgy* 79, 1-2 (1998) 14-59.

[6] Religion populaire et réforme liturgique, = special issue, *La Maison-Dieu* 122 (1975).

[7] There are various sources where one can find a survey of this debate concerning popular religion, with extensive bibliographies. I will list only: BLIJLEVENS, BRANTS & HENAU (1982); GREINACHER & METTE (1983); RAHNER, et al. (1979).

from this debate. Systematic theologians, pastoral theologians, pastors from parishes and ecclesiastical policy-makers all entered the lists, and so did liberation theologians and "post-modern culture theologians" like Harvey Cox. In Latin America, North America and France the argument proceeded along very diverse tracks within the framework of a discussion over the orientation of ecclesiastical action, chiefly about the boundaries of liturgical renewal, the experience and reception of rituality, the often unappreciated anthropological dimensions of rituality, and also the rediscovery of the dominance of a relatively autonomous, lived faith that, as Jean Delumeau argued, at the very least nuances the channeling strategies of the Church.[8]

It is likewise striking, and in a certain sense has had tragic consequences down to the present, to see how despite some influences from the social sciences, this theological debate stands almost in isolation from other academic disciplines. Theologians show little or no acquaintance with discussions and reflections in adjoining disciplines which were and are occupied with the same problematic. For instance, in German-speaking countries the theological debate had been preceded by an interesting theoretical debate about popular culture and its study in the circles of European ethnology / "Volkskunde".[9] Unfortunately, it was relatively late – in general, after 1985 – before people in other fields became acquainted with the fruits of this debate which took place over the decade from 1967 to 1977. Briefly, and leaving aside nuance and subtleties, in "Volkskunde" or European ethnology the issue was an important wrestling with the object of study. The old established canon of popular culture was being left behind. On the one hand, the canon was problematized (see Hermann Bausinger's apposite slogan, "Probleme statt Fakten"[10]); on the other hand, the canon was being thrown open. In addition to rural areas, the city and the working class now came under the loupe; not only the past was of interest, but also the present. This reconsideration of object and canon concentrated primarily on a fundamental theoretical and critical thinking through of the sustaining concepts of "people" ("Volk") and "culture." In a general sense, as also in the historical disciplines, there was a movement from a normative conception of culture to an interactive concept of culture. By

[8] PANNET (1974); PLONGERON & PANNET (1976); DELUMEAU (1977).

[9] For this debate we will here mention only: BAUSINGER (1971) and FRIJHOFF (1997a).

[10] BAUSINGER (1971); FRIJHOFF (1997a) 130.

"popular culture" one no longer referred primarily to certain segments or layers of the society (elite vs. popular), nor primarily to nations or tribes, but rather to general civilization, the culture that people often unconsciously share with one another. One might here speak of the matrix of the culture. Popular culture is like that part of an oak leaf that survives when the rest moulders away, the supporting structure that determines the contours of the leaf. This broad, generally shared group culture is culture with a small "c", not culture of the "kleine Leute." Study of this popular culture brings regional and social differences in a culture into focus, and is oriented particularly to collective, broad, supporting cultural phenomena that shape daily life.

Another important element in the discussion was the insight that the starting point and presupposition was no longer the continuity of culture, but rather its dynamics and development, or, also, contingency. In many respects, the masks of centuries-old traditions fell away. In the debate it became all the more clear how many assumed continuity theses were constructs.

Now, this aspect of continuity touches particularly on religious popular culture and liturgy. Here, after all, one often finds the development schema of superstition, religion and Christianity employed, whereby elements of religious popular culture can then be cherished or decried (according to one's ecclesiastical or ideological standpoint) as remnants of earlier phases of culture and religion.

"Volkskunde" or European ethnology stands between anthropology and the historical disciplines.[11] We turn now particularly to the historical studies because it was via this channel that modernizing impulses reached liturgical studies. Church history served here as the intermediary. The influential programmatic article by Willem Frijhoff from 1981 with the sketch of a "histoire religieuse" that took the place of the old traditional "histoire de l'Église" can serve as a model for the modernizing agenda of historiography.[12] Some years ago, in a theoretical essay also precisely oriented to religious popular culture, the Belgian historian Jan Art arrestingly laid out this new approach, the opportunities it offers and its perspectives.[13] In historical scholarship, as it has been modernizing itself, scholars have increasingly been raising the most difficult questions

[11] For the academic "cross-border traffic" among these three disciplines, see: FRIJHOFF (1992a) and (1997a).

[12] FRIJHOFF (1981).

[13] ART (1990); PACE (1981).

that historians can ask, namely, those about everyday life. This is such a favourite subject area for them chiefly because in it they can (perhaps!) rise above the hoary opposition between action and structure or the interplay of objective and subjective factors in history. Thus everyday life becomes a beckoning perspective.

Traditional historical research into religious factors in culture, certainly as it has been carried out within the framework of church history, generally avails itself of what can be termed the institutional approach. Religion in everyday life, the sense in which religious popular culture is now being understood, is here approached by investigating what influences a religious institution has in and on daily life. These could be certain pastoral activities, or ecclesiastical prescriptions, etc. Under the influence of the social sciences, research takes a new direction now: the starting point is not a religious phenomenon but rather a general social category, and researchers ask what role religion plays within that framework. Culture, but more pointedly, everyday life, is first broadly and descriptively approached via a group, profession or, most often, a location (a town or city; we are here thinking of the influential work of William Christian, Jr., who defines religious popular culture chiefly as local culture; for him "popular religion" is "local religion"[14]), and then the religious factor is brought into focus within this broad cultural and social context. In addition to new questions, this approach, which offers a much greater opportunity for a contextual descriptive research phase than before, especially demands new sources and new research methods and techniques. In this regard, there is a preference for speaking of "traces." The researcher goes in search of diverse traces of actions and actors. In addition to the traces of elites, one also diligently searches now for traces of "silent groups." It is here of importance to note how, with this new approach, it is chiefly rituals which come under the lense. Historians who work with this new agenda discover how it is precisely through ritual repertories that the researcher can penetrate deeply and decisively into the network of a culture.

This approach to popular culture as, briefly, the particular design of everyday life then comes to be seen with increasing frequency in the context of appropriation processes.[15] This important research perspective,

[14] Christian (1981a); (1981b); (1984); (1989); (1992); (1996).

[15] An outstanding theoretical introduction with regard to appropriation is offered by Frijhoff (1997b).

which can be traced back through Chartier[16] and the Jesuit De Certeau[17], does not focus on how culture and cultural elements are designated from the outside, but defines popular culture as "a specific manner of dealing with culture which is rooted in the social group or community itself".[18] This leads to an essential shift in the accents in research: from top down to bottom up, from vertical to horizontal, from prescribed order to lived practice, in which the central locus is the community in which culture is shaped.

To recapitulate, in the field of historical studies we see an open, broad, contextual and multidisciplinary approach to culture, directed toward everyday life, in which rituality plays a key role. It is here, in this specific programmatic context, that the term "religious popular culture" is preferred, as is in the title of an influential 1986 collection in which Gerard Rooijakkers and Willem Frijhoff had a hand.[19] The subtitle of the collection, "the tension between prescribed order and lived practice," shows us that the earlier dichotomy of "elite" and "popular" had not entirely disappeared. In addition to the term "religious popular culture," there are several other favoured terms, chiefly "religion in everyday life," "everyday religion" and "lived faith," and there have been a number of multidisciplinary conferences held under the title "Religion in everyday life".[20]

It did not take long for this line of research to achieve a prominent place in Dutch liturgical studies. After all, scholars here had for some time been sensitized to academic "cross-border" traffic, and, more particularly, were in search of ways, sources and methodologies for approaching the newly arisen questions about reception and experience. Liturgy was no longer a book, but faith as it was lived and celebrated by people. Moreover, this new wind connected with the growing interest in the fundamental anthropological dimensions of liturgy and in completing the "turn" to the subject. After the mid-1980s, popular religious themes were abundantly present in Dutch liturgical studies. I will mention here only the annual conferences held by those teaching in the field of liturgical studies in The Netherlands. In 1986 the one-day conference was

[16] CHARTIER (1988); cf. CHARTIER (1993).

[17] For DE CERTEAU, see: FRIJHOFF (1997a) 10 (with bibliography in note 20) and FRIJHOFF (1997b).

[18] FRIJHOFF (1997a) 94.

[19] ROOIJAKKERS & VAN DER ZEE (1986).

[20] See BRINGÉUS (1994); LAEYENDECKER, JANSMA & VERHAAR (1990).

devoted to prayer cards[21], in 1991 explicitly to liturgical studies, "Volkskunde" or European ethnology and the study of feast, festival and ritual.[22] I would also mention a Palm Sunday project[23], the festschrift for Herman Wegman in 1990 devoted to the role of "the people" in the liturgy[24], the work of Herman Wegman[25] and Gerard Lukken[26], and also the ongoing national research project with liturgical movements as its unifying theme.[27]

2.3. The Social Sciences: Psychology of Religion

The social science track involves input from the psychology of religion, and focuses on an empirical analysis of pilgrims' conduct in the form of a series of quantitative and qualitative surveys.

Two strands of research meet in the contribution of the psychology of religion to the research programme. First, popular-religious practices are studied as fully valued expressions of the human search for answers to questions of existence and meaning. Second, the effect of these practices is studied within the context of the transforming power of rituals. As pilgrimage is studied for its transforming possibilities, these inquiries necessarily examine the three successive phases in pilgrimage: before, during and after. The first phase involves analysis of the pilgrims' status preceding the pilgrimage: their profile and motives. The second phase involves an analysis of their actual activities and experiences en route and at the place of pilgrimage. Finally, the third phase involves analysis of measurable effects after the completion of the pilgrimage. The focus of the study, then, is on effects with regard to the pilgrims' faith and their attitudes toward it, and their physical and psychological well-being.

In our analysis of pilgrimage as transforming ritual, we avail ourselves of Van Gennep's long-accepted schema: separation, transition and

[21] See: *Jaarboek voor liturgie-onderzoek* 2 (1986) 1-31.

[22] See: *Jaarboek voor liturgie-onderzoek* 7 (1991) 77-184. In this connection, see also the conference devoted to the reception of hymns, *Jaarboek voor liturgie-onderzoek* 3 (1987) 217-273.

[23] POST & PIEPER (1992a); (1992b).

[24] CASPERS & SCHNEIDERS (1990).

[25] See the bibliography in CASPERS & SCHNEIDERS (1990) and: *Jaarboek voor liturgie-onderzoek* 12 (1996) 6-20 and 13 (1997) 213-218.

[26] LUKKEN (1994).

[27] POST (1996b).

incorporation.[28] Attention is then focused on the middle phase, also aptly termed the liminal phase, as elaborated by Victor and Edith Turner in their book *Image and Pilgrimage in Christian Culture.*[29] With regard to this liminal phase, the possibilities for a cognitive reorganization on the part of the pilgrim, based on his or her confrontation with the mythological framework supplied by the pilgrimage ritual, are further examined.

To date, arising from the social science contribution to the programme, there have been four quantitative surveys conducted by means of questionnaires among pilgrims to various pilgrimage places: three preliminary investigations (Wittem, Banneux, Lourdes) and a main investigation (Lourdes). Two surveys were carried out in 1985 among pilgrims to Wittem and Lourdes respectively. In 1987 a similar survey was carried out among pilgrims to Banneux. The aims of these three preliminary investigations were to gain initial insights into the area that was to be investigated and subsequently to design questionnaires for use in a large-scale investigation among pilgrims to Lourdes.

From the outset we accepted, however, that assembling quantitative data concerning pilgrimages is of limited value, and that consequently qualitative data must also be collected. Therefore interviews were held with pilgrims and analyses were made of diaries kept by pilgrims. This qualitative data was used to check the results of the pilot studies, with an emphasis on the in-depth study of the material that had been obtained by the survey.

This double strategy reflects the debate in the social sciences over the pros and cons of quantitative and qualitative methods of research. Within the social sciences – and hence within the psychology and sociology of religion – two methods are available to collect and process research data, the quantitative and the qualitative approaches. Which approach is taken largely depends on the nature of the data the researcher wants to obtain. In the quantitative approach data is collected from a relatively large number of people. However, one may also opt for a qualitative approach, in this case interviews and analyses of diaries. Interviews are conducted with a relatively small number of people, and touching upon other aspects of the phenomenon being researched, in particular those which cannot be dealt with in a poll of the survey type.

Each approach has advantages and disadvantages that need not be discussed here. Our opinion is that one does better by combining both

28 VAN GENNEP (1909).

29 TURNER & TURNER (1978).

methods of research. Large-scale research can yield a framework that can be filled in with the data obtained from qualitative research. Our research on pilgrimages was designed to reflect this view.

2.4. Development

Since its origins in the mid-1980s, a clear growth process can be traced for this programme of pilgrimage research, one which to a not unimportant extent has been connected with the alliances it entered into, and also institutional changes. At first, when the centre of the programme lay in Heerlen, the nearby pilgrimage place for St. Gerard Majella at Wittem was a focus of study, as we have indicated. Later Lourdes and Banneux were added as foci. Still later, when Amsterdam (Meertens Instituut of the Royal Academy of Arts and Sciences) and Tilburg (Liturgical Institute, Tilburg Faculty of Theology) joined Heerlen/Nijmegen as bases for research, Dokkum (the city of St. Boniface) and Santiago de Compostela became still additional foci. Amsterdam itself and La Salette should also be mentioned as subjects for research. In this further development two trajectories in the project can be identified as a sort of second phase.

First and foremost there is the large-scale inventory project which was planned from Amsterdam after 1992.[30] The intention is to produce an exhaustive multi-volume lexicon of all places of pilgrimage in The Netherlands, past and present; as of this date (1997), the first thick volume has appeared.[31] Further, since 1995 pilgrimage research has been a component of the "Festa chori, festa fori" project which is included in the national research programme of the inter-university Liturgical Institute established at Tilburg.[32] The study of liturgical movements within the dynamic of cultus and culture is central to that project. With these initiatives, pilgrimage research has indisputably expanded its horizons. If initially the modern pilgrim, his or her profile, motivation and experience was central, later the context surrounding the pilgrim came more and more under the loupe as well. What is involved, then, is not only the immediate context of the place of pilgrimage, with its specific physical and pastoral aspects, but also the broader process of change in rituals and their practice in modern culture.

30 See in this book Chapter 2.

31 MARGRY & CASPERS (1997).

32 POST (1996b).

It is against this background of tradition and modernity that continuing processes such as folklorization and musealization, and also tendencies in how people define and experience places, persons and things as sacred, are discussed in the research, and thus also in this book. It is our conviction that in wrestling with these issues, modern pilgrimage can be situated in the often complex and startling interplay of cultus and culture. This development of a tradition in research, as it has unfolded through projects in the 1980s and 1990s, is reflected in this book: Part II, specifically focused on the pilgrim, is followed by more broadly structured, contextual discussions in Part III.

A series of books and collections of papers serve as mileposts in the developments which have been sketched here. After the 1982 general collection on popular religion mentioned above[33], we may list in the order of their appearance *Historisch repertorium Wittem* (1986)[34], *Christelijke bedevaarten: op weg naar heil en heling* (1988)[35], *Bij geloof. Over bedevaarten en andere uitingen van volksreligiositeit* (1991)[36], *Bedevaart als volksreligieus ritueel* (1991)[37], *Bedevaart en pelgrimage. Tussen traditie en moderniteit* (1994)[38], *Oude sporen, nieuwe wegen. Ontwikkelingen in bedevaartonderzoek* (1995)[39], and the first volume of the large-scale inventory project (1997).[40]

In any case, this sketch of the context should dispel the impression that in this book we are merely floating along with the tide of interest in popular religious themes in general, and pilgrimage in particular, that is rising everywhere. That said, however, for theological circles this interest must be recognized as being of a relative nature.[41]

3. Objectives and Scheme of the Book

The book which you now have in hand is intended to provide a representative picture of the results achieved in the course of the research

33 Blijlevens, Brants & Henau (1982).
34 Evers & Post (1986).
35 Van Uden & Post (1988).
36 Van Uden, Pieper & Henau (1991).
37 Van Uden & Pieper (1991a).
38 Pieper, Post & Van Uden (1994).
39 Van Uden, Pieper & Post (1995).
40 Margry & Caspers (1997).
41 Cf. the article mentioned in our note 5.

sketched above. In doing so, it will concentrate on both of the central lines mentioned, liturgical studies and psychology of religion. In addition to the results of various surveys of contemporary pilgrimage practice and the previously sketched expansion of the research into the ritual and cultural context in which modern pilgrims find themselves, special attention is also bestowed on the historiographic dimension involved in orienting pilgrimage research, and on its theoretical and methodological aspects. With regard to orientation of the research, Chapters 1 and 2 function as two rather comprehensive balance sheets for pilgrimage research, in which trends, themes, theories and perspectives are inventoried and critically discussed. These two balances were drawn up at two distinct moments in the course of the research programme; Chapter 1 dates from the end of the 1980s, and Chapter 2 from the mid-1990s. A separate and very extensive sketch of the tradition of inventorying places of pilgrimage is closely conjoined with these, and indirectly gives a revealing image by disciplines of how scholars and researchers have dealt with the phenomenon of pilgrimage and pilgrimage places.

The intention of these orientation chapters is chiefly to place the research in a wider context of broadly subdivided academic and scientific activity concerning pilgrimage. It is precisely for research which was and is undertaken especially from the realm of theology or religious studies that such a broad approach and structure appears to be necessary. In our view, people in those fields still have too little recognition of relevant developments in adjoining disciplines. Therefore this book can also be seen as an argument for greater academic "cross-border traffic," and in Part I the theoretical and methodological aspects of this plea are given a foundation and developed. Moreover, in place of intra-, inter- or even trans-disciplinary thinking, a conscious choice has been made here to use the term "multidisciplinary." The basic assumption in doing so is that a multidisciplinary approach is characterized by an effort to become acquainted with the methods of other disciplines, and to make them one's own, in order to be able to handle findings independently oneself and integrate these into a new whole.[42]

[42] Cf. POST: Wetenschappelijk grensverkeer tussen discipline-vorming en ontdisciplinering, in *Jaarboek voor liturgie-onderzoek* 6 (1990) 65-82, here 70, following: S. DE BLAAUW: *Cultus et decor. Liturgie en architectuur in laatantiek en middeleeuws Rome* (Delft 1987) proposition 8. Now see also POST (1995c); (1996b).

From the output produced over the course of about 15 years of this Dutch pilgrimage research – an output which can justly be characterized as rich – a selection has been made which has subsequently been adapted so as to give shape to the objective stated above. The selections provide the materials for three parts, with a total of twelve chapters, in which the interplay of disciplines and approaches emerges chiefly in a series of multidisciplinary explorations.

Part I is – as we have already indicated – the part in which the research is positioned. As well as concrete projects in progress, historiography, theory and method are the central concerns of this section. After a sketch of some fundamental points of discussion in research into religious popular culture in general and pilgrimage in particular, Chapter 1 introduces the Heerlen research into the motivation of the modern pilgrim. At the same time, it enters into the results of the quantitative part of the preliminary investigation with regard to the motivation of pilgrims to Wittem, Banneux and Lourdes in particular. That track will be pursued further in Part II of the book.

The first part of Chapter 2 extensively discusses contemporary trends, themes and the shaping of theories in international pilgrimage research and in the large-scale Dutch inventory project. This chapter offers an extremely well documented sketch of the positioning of international pilgrimage research. This positioning is mapped out critically by disciplines, and various perspectives are evaluated.

A specific and extremely important theoretical aspect is discussed in Chapter 3, namely the issue of tradition, identity and how we deal with the past. After a rereading of Eric Hobsbawm's extremely influential work on the "invention of tradition," an attempt is made to place Hobsbawm in a new perspective, which is in part to say, the perspective which he originally intended. In our eyes, this issue of tradition and how we deal with the past is a fundamental category in the study of ritual such as pilgrimage, labeled as it is as "traditional." In Parts II and III of the book this issue returns again in Chapters 9, 11 and 12.

In Chapter 4 attention is directed toward the processes that play a role in the origin and development of a place of pilgrimage. Here local pastoral interaction is central. An attempt is made to supply a model in which distinct forms of this interaction can be connected with various types of holy places. This exploration is illustrated through the revitalization of Dokkum as the City of St. Boniface, and the classic Marian holy place of La Salette, the birth and development of which is well documented.

In Part II five surveys into the experiences, perceptions, motives and effects of modern pilgrimage are presented. Here the modern pilgrim is always central. Having, as we have said, dealt in Chapter 1 with the quantitative preliminary research regarding the motivation of pilgrims, particularly those going to Wittem, Banneux and Lourdes, Chapter 5 examines the qualitative part of this preliminary investigation. The results of two depth interviews, one with a pilgrim to Wittem and one with a pilgrim to Lourdes, are handled under the heading "transformation and confirmation." Furthermore, the quantitative data obtained earlier is related to this qualitative data.

Chapter 6 introduces a large-scale Lourdes study in which we once again turn our attention to the motivation structure of the pilgrim. In addition, especially the effects that pilgrimage to Lourdes has on the physical and psychological well-being of the pilgrims is discussed. We establish that pilgrimage does have a positive effect on the mental well-being of pilgrims. Particularly feelings of anxiety are reduced.

In Chapter 7, within the context of the same investigation, we pose the question of to what extent pilgrims to Lourdes undergo a religious transformation. This question is framed within an attribution-theoretical perspective.

This search for changes experienced by pilgrims in the realm of religion and spirituality as a consequence of their pilgrimage continues in Chapter 8. In this chapter pilgrims who are walking to Santiago de Compostela are studied, by means of a qualitative research method (their reaction to "trigger-words") to determine how their religious perceptions change on the way and after the completion of the journey.

Chapter 9 likewise concentrates on the pilgrimage routes to Santiago which have again become so busy. It reports on research into pilgrims' diaries, which are so abundantly available, especially in Dutch-speaking areas. Through the careful reading of a selection of these diaries, in the ethnological tradition of literary folkloristics and the personal narrative, an effort is made to create an image of these pilgrims: to what extent can one perhaps speak of a new type of pilgrim, "the modern pilgrim"?

The perspective broadens in Part III. Here a trio of contextual explorations are brought together. Holiness of place and person in the dynamic context of tradition and modernity are central here.

In Chapter 10 the distinction between "faith" and "superstition" is critically illuminated on the basis of a pair of case studies on modern saints' cults. With regard to this distinction, it is proposed that a crucial criterion lies in the question of to what degree belief helps the individual to deal with his or her lot in life in specific situations.

Chapter 11 explores the changes and shifts in context that devotional rites such as pilgrimage undergo in modern urban culture. The famous Silent Procession in Amsterdam is the case study on which the exploration is based.

Lastly, Chapter 12 takes as its point of departure the aspect of landscape and outdoor ritual which is so important for the culture of pilgrimage. After a theoretical orientation (once again), several specific and highly contemporary forms of ritual landscape are discussed: the processional park (where once again Dokkum is discussed), the rites accompanying a Papal visit, and the ritual design after a sudden, unexpected death.

4. Editorial Notes and Acknowledgements

Finally, in this introduction, several notes about how this book came into being. Earlier publications always served as the foundation for the various chapters. The first footnote for each chapter reports which publication or publications this involves. Although all three of us regard ourselves as responsible for the book as a whole, the authors of each chapter are the following: Introduction and Ch. 1: P. Post, J. Pieper & M. van Uden; Ch. 2: P.J. Margry & P. Post; Ch. 3 and 4: P. Post; Ch. 5, 6, 7 and 8: J. Pieper & M. van Uden; Ch. 9: P. Post; Ch. 10: M. van Uden; Ch. 11 and 12: P. Post. (For further information, once again see the first footnote in each chapter.) It should be separately recorded here that P.J. Margry was the co-author of Chapter 2. He was also responsible for a large number of the photographs.

With regard to the editorial method, it should be said that the book is the outcome of a formal editorial process. The diverse contributions were revised in form so that they became chapters in this book. In this process, every effort was made to avoid overlap. Despite the relationships indicated above, each chapter is an independent entity. As much as possible, illustrative material included with earlier publications has also been included here. The content of the various chapters was not, however, revised to incorporate later research or insights. Occasional relevant publications and references to other chapters in this book were, however, included in the notes.

Lastly, we must express our gratitude to Dr. Ch. Caspers, the secretary of the *Liturgia condenda* series, who gave us indispensable editorial support, and the team which bore responsibility for the translation of the Dutch texts which were the foundation for the various chapters. They were, respectively, D. Mader, M.Div. (Rotterdam), for the Introduction and Ch. 1, 2, 3, 4, 11 and 12; A. van Heeswijk, M. Psych., clinical psychologist (Isle of Wight) for Ch. 5, 6, 7, 8 and 10; Dr. M. Meadow and Prof. Dr. A. Fenton (Edinburgh) for Ch. 9.

P. Post, J. Pieper & M. van Uden
Tilburg/Heerlen, April 1998

PART I

THE STUDY OF PILGRIMAGE: SITUATION IN RESEARCH, THEORY, METHODS, PROJECTS AND PERSPECTIVES

1. REASONS FOR GOING
A SOCIAL SCIENCE PERSPECTIVE ON MOTIVES FOR PILGRIMAGE[1]

1. Introduction

In this chapter, we wish to report on an important segment of the "Christian Pilgrimage" multidisciplinary research programme[2], namely, the social science investigation into the current motivations of Dutch pilgrims. At the same time, we want to provide a brief sketch of the theoretical framework for this research. After all, we are, in our opinion, touching here on two most interesting matters. On the one hand, we are concerned here with performing research in the humanities with the assistance of social science methods; on the other hand, we are here dealing with research which is focused on the subject of the pilgrim.

By now, the progress of the various projects which are parts of the research programme has been reported in a number of sources and ways.[3] This is in no less measure true for the social science project which focused particularly on the motives of Dutch pilgrims to Wittem, Lourdes and Banneux.[4] The results and analysis of these inquiries will be central to this chapter, in which we will limit ourselves to the results from the questionnaires.

The underlying reason for this presentation is that in addition to being a valuable contribution to the study of pilgrimage, we also have here an important example of academic cooperation or multidisciplinary research in which the social sciences have been fully involved. It is

[1] J. Pieper, P. Post & M. Van Uden: Beweegredenen. Sociaal-wetenschappelijke peilingen naar bedevaartmotieven, in *Volkskundig Bulletin. Tijdschrift voor Nederlandse cultuurwetenschap* (P.J. Meertens-Instituut van de Koninklijke Nederlandse Akademie van Wetenschappen) 16,2 (1990) 176-202.

[2] Post & Van Uden (1985).

[3] We make reference to only one: Van Uden & Post (1988).

[4] Oosterwijk et al. (1986a); (1986b); Pieper & Van Uden (1988); Oosterwijk, Van Uden & Hensgens (1986); Van Uden & Pieper (1988); Pieper, Oosterwijk & Van Uden (1988); Derks, Pieper & Van Uden (1989).

precisely because of this methodological aspect that we want to preface the actual research report with a sketch of the place and importance of the social sciences in the study of religious popular culture in general, and of pilgrimage in particular. We will do this by offering a short sketch with reference to several previous surveys[5] of the most important developments within this field over the last decade.

2. The Situation in Research into Religious Popular Culture

2.1. The State of Affairs

For a sketch of research into religious popular culture, we can fall back on a series of survey articles which have been published in German ethnological circles in the past few years. In addition to compilations of articles[6], we can here draw particular attention to the sketch of ethnology of religion ("Religiöse Volkskunde") since 1945 which appeared in a recent essay by G. Korff.[7] Although written with special reference to the research situation of the European ethnology ("Volkskunde") in Germany, this article throws a particularly clear light upon the context out of which the above discussed research programme at Heerlen arose. This context is characterized by a number of fundamental developments.

First of all, there is the explicit consideration of all sorts of often hidden scholarly presuppositions or preambles. It is precisely in the study of religious popular culture that a number of ecclesiastical, political and denominational aspects have played (and still play) a role. For instance, ideas regarding the continuity of the non-Christian (in this case, Germanic) past, but also theories about the process of secularization must be taken into account. In regard to the latter, one can by now recognize how research no longer takes place exclusively against a background of a secularization process for which remnant, decline, loss, dilution and loss of meaning are the key words.[8]

A subsequent characteristic of recent developments in the field, closely connected with this, is the fact that people are beginning to give full weight to the historical, regional and social *context*. For instance, pilgrimage is no

[5] See Post (1988b) and (1989a).

[6] Here we list only: Daxelmüller (1988). See our Introduction sub 2.2.

[7] Korff (1987). In addition to this article, two other contributions to this volume deserve mention in this connection: Niederer (1987) and Brückner (1987).

[8] See Post (1989c) 188f.

longer dealt with from a universal perspective, but is placed in a historically and empirically delimited time/place context. As a result of this important perspective, it has become the rule to phrase the questions in terms of *function*. It is now not so much an exhaustive inventory and description of the phenomena which is central[9], but the question of how pilgrimage functioned in the history of piety in a specific period at a specific time. Thus research into pilgrimage forms an important link in investigations which seek to determine to what degree religious conduct and mentalities are determined by ecclesiastical, theological developments on the one hand, and social, economic and political developments on the other. It is at this point that the social sciences are called upon for their assistance – though, it must be admitted, relatively late, and still with considerable hesitation. Furthermore, people have become increasingly conscious of the necessity of adopting a methodology which will build attention for the subject, the bearer of piety, into the investigation. Again, it is research into pilgrimage which provides us with a good example. Studies of the profile and motivation of pilgrims form an important link for the process of testing various kinds of interpretive models which are currently in circulation in pilgrimage studies.

2.2. Profile, Motivation and Interpretative Models

Some pronouncements about the profile of pilgrims are as peremptory as they are vague and diffuse.[10] It is only rather recently that people have begun to further test commonplaces regarding regional and social/economic context. That is an extremely difficult matter for the past. Until the fourth century it appears that pilgrimage was a practice of the elite; after that date, the phenomenon touched all layers of the Christian population. It is really only after the sixth century that we can really get something of an image of the social/economic background of the pilgrims. The first attempt to categorize the pilgrimage population which is known to us is in regard to Tours.[11] For the period from the Middle

[9] See although for the special situation of The Netherlands the article of MARGRY & POST on the large scale Dutch inventory project in this volume. See Chapter 2 in this book and MARGRY & CASPERS (1997).

[10] KORFF (1987) 262ff.

[11] PIETRI (1975); (1977). Out of this source, it appears that the majority of the visitors indeed belonged to "the people" (Luce Pietri uses the word "populaire"), but at the same time, about 30% still belonged to the secular or clerical upper class. Two other figures which also give some indication are that 86% were adults and 75% male.

Ages to our own time, the picture with respect to place and period is also still to be sharply delineated yet, and it appears to be too early for global pronouncements about pilgrims' social/economic origins.

A further step can be taken through research of this type, and the important question of motivations and motives can be posed. Quite generally one here encounters a distinction between primary motives which are religious or assumed to be religious, and non-religious, or secondary, motives. The distinction between primary and secondary motives can already be found among many of the church fathers. The search for something to hold on to, for reconciliation, mediation, salvation and healing can be thought of as among primary motives; escape from workaday life, seeking communal experiences, establishing connections with nature, recreational/touristic aspects ("having a day out") and "magical" aspects can be considered among the secondary motives. On the basis of this classification of motives, typologies of pilgrims are also often developed (cf. for instance, these classifications: pilgrims with a strong popular devotion; those interested in spirituality; militant pilgrims; the sick; youth).

There are still many more sorts of classifications and distinctions among motives in circulation. Thus others have sought to couple the forces which motivate pilgrims with the distinction between individual and communally directed rites, in which they proceed from the proposition that pilgrimage is characterized by the collective perspective within which this ritual must be placed. In addition to the work of V. Turner, that of J. Rémy can be mentioned in this connection.[12] Still others have also sometimes derived classifications from the assumption that either the journey or the eventual goal are of greatest importance to the pilgrims.[13]

Conceptions and pronouncements about the profile and motivations of pilgrims touch directly on the phenomenon of pilgrimage as a whole.[14]

[12] See TURNER & TURNER (1978); RÉMY (1984) esp. 229ff. A citation may illustrate the classification of motives intended here: "Au contraire le pèlerinage structurant implique une histoire communautaire dont le sens commence avant "moi" et s'achève après "moi." Ceci n'exclut nullement l'entremêlement d'objectifs practiques et individuelles." (230).

[13] See summary with literature: POST (1989a) 150ff. See further the extensive bibliography regarding the definitional problems surrounding "pilgrimage," *ibidem* 142ff, and also the special issue of *Social Compass*, "Pilgrimage and Modernity" (36,2 (1989)). Special mention should be made of the following articles from this issue: RÉMY (1989); OSTERRIETH (1989); DELUZ (1989); LOPEZ (1989); LUKATIS (1989); PACE (1989).

[14] For a survey of models for interpretation, see POST (1988b) 12ff, and POST (1989a) 151ff.

This is also where the great importance of a further empirical determination of the profile and motives lies, since many of the models for interpreting the phenomenon of pilgrimage which are currently in circulation proceed implicitly or explicitly from certain ideas about the profile and motivational structure of pilgrims. Thus there is the model which sees pilgrimage as a "left-over" from a non-Christian antecedent which still appeals particularly to the agrarian-oriented margins and unravelling edges of industrialized society. "Left-over" is also heard in the sense of pilgrimage being considered as a remanent of traditional Christian devotion to which people still cling. Interpretation models of this latter type are often connected with an supposed reaction. The reaction can, for instance, be placed within the context of a modern and rational society.[15] In pilgrimage, people are going in search of a "lost era." But the reaction can also be connected with Church renewal and reorganization. In that case, the reference is especially to the movement for liturgical renewal since Vatican II, through which the practices surrounding Christian symbols were rationalized, individualized and became more austere. Here pilgrimage would be a reaction to the new liturgical repertoires which are cold, individualistic and robbed of every form of sensuous appeal. Still other models of interpretation and evaluation address themselves primarily to the broader context of the phenomenon of pilgrimage, and those who promote pilgrimage. Thus some, for instance, trace veiled – or quite open – ecclesiastical or political strategies in pilgrimage, or relate it to the acquisition of power. Authorities promote people's allegiance to themselves through pilgrimage. Such "unmasking" of pilgrimage is encountered especially in function analyses and value appraisals in anthropological literature. In this connection one can refer, for instance, to the research done by the Amsterdam anthropologist M. Bax, who sees pilgrimage functioning as a "devotional regime."[16] For him, the Church is not a relatively passive monolith within which pilgrimage can take place. No, he sees in it rather a complex system of competing religious regimes, intent on expansion and consolidation. From this perspective, pilgrimage is not so much to be considered as more or less spontaneous movement which arises out of the devotion of the believers, but rather as a means to achieve power

[15] See the study by RÉMY (1984).

[16] BAX (1984); (1985a); (1985b); (1985c); (1986a); (1986b); (1986c); (1987a); (1987b). See also summarizing: BAX (1988). In part also: BAX (1989). See now BAX (1995).

and process of competition between the religious regimes. But various strategies – deliberate or not – can also be surmised behind pastoral practice. Here too the profile and motivation of pilgrims play a role, because strategies of this sort are often directed quite expressly toward certain segments of the "church goers," and certain motivational structures are mobilized. "Secondary" purposes, such as travel, tests of endurance, encountering nature, shared experience, etc., are mobilized in order to ultimately be able to reach "primary" values such as church involvement, evangelism (re-evangelization) or revival.

2.3. Perspectives and Problems

Multidisciplinary research, whether broader or specifically concerned with pilgrimage, which further explores piety and which could further test the models of interpretation which we have listed, has only gotten off the ground on a very limited scale. A 1989 special issue of the social science journal *Social Compass* shows how intensive contacts, particularly between anthropologists and sociologists, exist.[17] In the German situation, it is striking how, in research into religious popular culture and pilgrimage, because of the traditional rooting in what is termed "Kulturraum-forschung," input from sociology, economy and geography is especially sought after, and how psychological research, including that in the psychology of religion, and modern surveying methods here are only used slightly.[18] The fact remains that everywhere the attention for the subject of piety elaborated here is the main stimulus for building bridges to the social sciences, and furthermore that attention is centred strongly on ritual.

Beginning with the important step of now fully involving the subject in the research process, researchers discovered both perspectives and problems in this process which crossed academic disciplines. We wish to briefly list three of these perspectives and problems.

– First there is the perspective of a study of the phenomena of religious popular culture which, from historical, regional, and social context analysis, was directed toward aspects such as meaning, function, motives, intentions and effects.

– After having left behind all kinds of presuppositions, hidden or explicit, the researcher must be on the lookout for an often unforeseen

[17] See note 13, above.

[18] Summarized in: KORFF (1987).

cohesion between social and intellectual processes of change and modernization of various sorts. Thus one can, for instance, speak of a "principle of non-competition." It is precisely research into profiles and motives based on social science that can give us an eye for aspects of religious life that do not merge seamlessly into ecclesiastic practice, but which equally neither compete with nor are in conflict with it. We come upon a similar non-competition principle in studies of folk medicine. Steadfast and active parishioners go on pilgrimages, just as people will seek physical and mental healing at the same time in both the regular and alternative medical circuits.

– A third and last element which we wish to list is the fact that despite the appeal to empirical research connected to time and place, there is always still a penchant for structural research which can be discerned. This penchant can take on many shapes: one might think of interest in the "long term," or in certain forms of semiotic research, but also of the morphological approach provocatively formulated by C. Ginzburg, which will again lift certain phenomena situated in a particular place and time above the historical context in an attempt to connect them with one another.[19]

Homing in on the phenomenon of pilgrimage, recently, particularly in the social sciences, we can discover how pilgrimage often is beginning to function as a sort of explanatory model in the analysis of ritual conduct. Now that people have finally shown the door to cliched ideas about the profile and motives of pilgrims, it appears that these selfsame cliches are often being brought back in by another entrance. All sorts of rituals are being interpreted as "pilgrimage," as if there was already complete clarity about the profile and motives of pilgrims, and the effects of pilgrimage. The special issue of *Social Compass* mentioned above offers many striking apposite examples such as Rajneeshpuram (the Baghwan's centre in Oregon, since closed, where the "second world celebration" was held in 1983), Woodstock, Taizé, and German Church Congresses. In the issue of *Social Compass* in question, it is not always clear what the distinction really is between collective rites connected to a certain place, and pilgrimage.[20] In this connection, one can also note rituals which grow in response to disasters, accidents and catastrophes. We can list here the rites at the location of Olof Palme's murder, analyzed by M. Scharfe[21],

[19] See GINZBURG (1989)

[20] See particularly the articles LUKATIS (1989) and PACE (1989).

[21] SCHARFE (1989).

and the analysis of the public rituals after the Hillsborough Stadium disaster in April, 1989, analyzed by D. Gray.[22]

In our view, the connection with the phenomenon of pilgrimage there, intended to clarify things, is made too quickly.[23] We are not arguing here for reopening the discussion over the definition of pilgrimage, nor for a continuous debate about V. Turner's theories regarding pilgrimage rites, but rather for a quantitative and qualitative social scientific investigation into the motivations for and functions of pilgrimage. The many "quest patterns" (e.g., individual vs communal orientation; religious vs non-religious or primary vs secondary motivation; absolution, penitence; healing, miracle; vision, appearance of the saint) or profiles of pilgrims (e.g., pilgrim/traveller, pilgrim/tourist) which are currently in circulation, and the interpretative models based upon these, can only be tested and nuanced through this sort of empirical research. On the basis of empirical preliminary inquiries and research, well-founded working hypotheses can be formulated, which subsequently can be used in qualitative and quantitative research.

Against the theoretical, scientific background which has been briefly sketched here, in the remainder of this chapter we wish to offer an analysis of motives for pilgrimage to three sites, as well as formulate a

[22] See "Bridging the Gap", the "Presidential Address" at the 12th International Congress of Societas Liturgica, York, August 14-19, 1989. Gray is very explicit in his analysis. A somewhat expanded quotation from a lecture given in York may serve to illustrate what is meant by pilgrimage becoming an explanatory model for ritual: "During the days immediately following the tragedy, many thousands of people went "on pilgrimage" to Liverpool's football ground at Anfield. They queued for hours to get in and, once inside, they covered the football pitch with the flowers they had brought with them. They tied scarves and other favours as well as photographs and letters on the goal posts and it's netting, and just walked quietly around the ground. Eye-witnesses have told me that there was little conversation, even in the long wait queuing outside the ground, certainly none of the high spirits or boisterousness of a football crowd. This went on for a whole week, even on the days when it was pouring down with rain. I've already anticipated the interpretation of these phenomena by saying that they went "on pilgrimage". Yet this was what they were doing, surely. They went to "the shrine". That, in the past, had been a jokey title for the football ground, but now it was a reality. There they took their votive offerings and offered something precious. (...) The scarves, together with the pictures and letters gave the football pitch a Lourdes-like atmosphere. It might have been Walsingham for a week". The lecture has been published in *Studia liturgica* 20 (1990) 1-7, quotation p. 3. A French version of the lecture appeared as: Jeter un pont, in *La Maison-Dieu* 179 (1989) 7-14.

[23] We have since become less rigorous in this judgement. Searching for parallel forms of ritual acitivity can put us onto the track of the remarkable dynamism of the postmodern ritual market; see POST (1998).

working hypothesis for subsequent research formulated on the basis of this analysis. Unfortunately, because of the divergence in the ways the inquiries were carried out, at this stage of the international investigation it is not yet possible to offer a comparison with other surveys. The research design and surveying techniques used vary too greatly for that.[24]

3. Research into the Profile and Pilgrimage Motives of Dutch Pilgrims

3.1. Background and Design of the Research

In 1985 two pilot studies among pilgrims to Wittem and Lourdes were carried out within the framework of the "Christian Pilgrimage" research programme described above. In 1987 the same research was carried out among pilgrims to Banneux. These preliminary studies were intended to provide a first insight into the subject to be investigated and to develop a questionnaire for use in a larger-scale research project which was to be conducted among pilgrims to Lourdes some years later. Results of these preliminary studies have since appeared in the form of reports, articles and lectures. From the very beginning, in the long-term planning for the programme, it was assumed that in a second phase of the research emphasis would have to be placed on a further examination of the connection between the motivation for pilgrimage and effects on religiosity and a sense of psycho-social well-being.

Within the social sciences one has, in general, two methods of collecting research data. The strategy to be chosen depends to a great extent on the nature of the data which the researcher wishes to collect. One can choose for a quantitative approach in which, generally in written form through a questionnaire, data is assembled from a relatively large number of persons. This implies survey-like inquiry research, of which, in the case of religion, the two "God in The Netherlands" studies are two previous Dutch examples.[25] When the persons on whom the research is to be based are selected in the proper manner, such research can deliver extremely reliable data, which will be valid for a particular group of people.

[24] Readers are referred to the special issue of *Social Compass* previously mentioned (and in particular, Pace's article) for a first overview, and to overviews in *Anthropology Today* (see, for instance, 4 nr. 6 (1988) 20-23).

[25] Zeegers, Dekker & Peters (1967); Goddijn, Smit & Van Tillo (1979). See now: Dekker, De Hart & Peters (1997).

For the two studies just mentioned above, during the 1960's and 1970's thousands of persons were questioned for each study, but these persons were chosen in such a way that their answers were representative of the religious opinions and practices of all 14 million inhabitants of The Netherlands.

Depending on the subject of the research, one can also choose, however, for a qualitative approach. In this case, a relatively small number of persons are the subject of interviews, in which other aspects of the phenomenon to be investigated can be addressed than is possible in survey research. The advantage of a qualitative approach is the greater depth in the data which one can assemble from it. Both approaches have many advantages and disadvantages, all of which do not have to be discussed here. We will only list two, namely, depth versus reliability. What the one method has as its advantage, the other lacks, and the same is true for disadvantages. This is to say that the qualitative method is relatively unreliable, first because the analysis of the data is to a large degree dependent on the person of the researcher, on his or her expertise and impartiality. A second reason lies in the generally small number of respondents, which means that the researcher increases the risk of having an inadequate sample.

The high reliability of the quantitative method comes at the cost of the depth of the information. As researchers, what do we really know when, as was the case in our pilot study of pilgrims to Lourdes, a certain percentage of respondents (25% before their visit, 40% after) answered the question "What is the state of your health?" with "reasonably good"? We do know that within the group as a whole, a shift has apparently taken place, but we know nothing of substance about what these respondents meant by "reasonably". In interviews this could have been explored more deeply.

The obvious conclusion, then, is that it would be advantageous to combine the two research methods. Large-scale research can provide a skeleton which can be fleshed in with the aid of data from interviews.[26] From the outset, it was the intention to utilize this approach in the research on pilgrimage. This chapter will report on the quantitative approach and offer an analysis of the outline which this provided.

3.2. The Pilgrimages Selected

A choice was made for holding three different surveys among Dutch pilgrims to Wittem, Lourdes and Banneux who travelled to these sites on

[26] See DERKS, PIEPER & VAN UDEN (1989).

"organized" pilgrimages by bus or train. Thus, strictly speaking, the surveys only are representative of these organized bus and train pilgrimages from The Netherlands. By comparisons among the three independent surveys we intended to still be able to sketch a picture which would be representative to some degree of organized pilgrimage from The Netherlands to major pilgrimage sites. This image must ultimately be tested by further investigation. For background in the cases of Lourdes and Banneux, the reader can be referred to the abundant literature available.[27] For Wittem, there is a recent publication which has also come out of the research programme begun at Heerlen.[28]

Wittem is a relatively small pilgrimage site in South Limburg where St. Gerard Majella (1726-1755) is venerated at the Redemptionist monastery, while, in addition, there is also a strong Marian devotion to be found. The Marian devotion appears to have been the determinative factor in Wittem in the previous century, while the great bloom of the cult of St. Gerard Majella can be located primarily in the 1920's, after his canonization in 1904. The pilgrimage season runs from May through October, with the most important celebration being October 16, the feast of St. Gerard Majella. As in the case of all pilgrimage sites, there can be a distinction made between organized (generally by bus) and unorganized pilgrimage. Weekends, and particularly Sunday, are central in the rhythm of pilgrimage. About 200,000 pilgrims come per year.

Lourdes and Banneux are two international centres of Marian devotion. The eight appearances of Mary as the "Virgin of the Poor" to the eleven-year-old Mariette Béco in the Belgian village of Banneux in the diocese of Liège in 1933 was the impetus for a flourishing pilgrimage site upon which, especially after official ecclesiastical recognition of the appearances in 1949, hundreds of thousands converge every year. The accent here lies primarily on the Marian festivals and the two months devoted to Mary, May and October. Traditionally a strong connection bond has existed with sections of The Netherlands, among which Limburg and the flower-bulb producing region between Haarlem and Leiden and other parts of the province of North Holland (especially Volendam) must be mentioned.

The origins and rise of Lourdes three-quarters of a century earlier must be viewed in the light of the same Marian devotion. Here too it was an

[27] For a summary with bibliography, see BEINERT & PETRI (1984) passim (Lourdes: esp. 531f; Banneux: 533f).

[28] EVERS & POST (1986). See now also: EVERS (1993).

appearance of Mary (to Bernadette Soubirous, in 1858) that was the cause. Since the 1870's this site has developed into one of the greatest international pilgrimage centres, to which more than three million pilgrims come every year now, of whom about a half million are ill or handicapped.

4. Survey of Pilgrimage Motivation

4.1. The Wittem Research

Performing the Research and Response

Our data involves Dutch pilgrims who visited Wittem by bus on June 2, 1985.[29] They came from four Dutch provinces: Overijssel, Gelderland, Noord-Brabant and Zuid-Holland. We had previously established contacts with pilgrimage organizers from these areas. The pilgrims were approached through them. Thirty-eight possible reasons for going on a pilgrimage were placed before these pilgrims in the form of a printed questionnaire. With the aid of a five-point scale (very applicable, applicable, don't know, not applicable, absolutely not applicable) respondents could indicate to what degree each reason was applicable for their own pilgrimage. Of the 180 pilgrims approached, 81 filled in the questionnaire. This was a 45% response rate.

Before we enter upon the analysis of the motives, let us characterize the "average" respondent. Our respondent is Roman Catholic (100%), 63 years old and female (82%). She is married or widowed (88%) and has six children. She is a housewife by profession (75%), has completed primary school but not any higher level (62%), and votes for the Christian Democratic Appeal (CDA) (72%). She has been to Wittem more than 10 times (71%), but has also frequently visited other places of pilgrimage (78%). She goes to church in her own parish at least once a week (90%), and feels strong (31%) or very strong (43%) ties to it. Her interest in religious matters (reading about them, listening to and watching radio and television programmes) is great.

Global Analysis of Motives

We will first give an overview of the ten motives which were felt to be most applicable. We rated a motive as applicable when it was chosen as "very applicable" or "applicable."

[29] Detailed data from this research can be found in Oosterwijk et al. (1986a); Van Uden & Pieper (1988).

Table 1. Overview of Motives

		%
1.	On account of St. Gerard Majella	90
2.	To give thanks	87
3.	To implore God's blessing	85
4.	To implore help or assistance	83
5.	To pray for a better world	83
6.	On account of the Virgin Mary	81
7.	To pray for the healing of another person	81
8.	To receive renewed strength	80
9.	To pray for the need and misery in the world	80
10.	To pray for their children or grandchildren	74

What is most striking when we review this list?

(a) The "top ten" motives are all of a strictly religious nature.
(b) St. Gerard Majella, God and Mary are represented in the first ten. Jesus only comes in in 16th place.
(c) The majority of the highest scoring items are concerned with asking for or giving thanks for help and support.
(d) Touristic or recreational motives do not show up in the "top ten."
(e) The same is true for motives which refer to tradition or custom.

Findings after Factor Analysis

For a more precise insight into the interconnections and meaning of the various statements about motives, we must now examine the results of a factor analysis carried out on the data.[30] The result of a factor analysis as it was performed here is that motives which have things in common are brought together in one factor. The precise meanings of the various statements also becomes clearer as one brings them into relation with other items which make up the same factor. The basic assumption is that there is a fundamental concept which underlies the group of motives which belong together, a concept which, as it were, guides the responses coming from these motives. The name given to this concept is based on an interpretation of the motives which are a part of a particular

[30] All of the factor analyses which are discussed in this chapter were carried out with the use of the SPSS programme (NIE et al. (1975)). The procedure followed in establishing the factors for the Wittem research is discussed in the 1986 Wittem report: OOSTERWIJK et al. (1986a) 11.

factor. Each motive has what is termed its *factor loading,* which indicates the degree to which a motive hangs together with the other motives in the factor. Motives with a higher factor loading have more weight in defining the nature of the underlying concept than motives with a lower factor loading. Because there were questionnaires which were not filled in completely, only 40 of the questionnaires were able to be used for the factor analysis. These 40 did, however, appear to be a representative sample of the total group of respondents. The factor analysis yielded eight factors, that we have described as follows.

We have named *Factor 1* as "Comfort in family problems." Such matters as giving thanks, praying for the welfare of children or grandchildren, finding comfort and praying for the healing of others come together in this factor, all in the generally consoling atmosphere of Wittem. In fact, one can distinguish two elements within this factor, which belong together because of the fact that they form one factor: on the one side, consolation (both asking in prayer to receive, and giving thanks for receiving comfort and healing for others), and on the other, the solace provided by the restful atmosphere at Wittem. The peace radiated by Wittem would appear to be an important part of being able to attain relief in the face of the littler problems of life. It is these smaller family problems which bring our older, female pilgrims to ask for help. The pilgrimage site is a place where their concerns can be heard. In this factor there is no room for concerns such as the Church militant or international problems. It is rather a matter of concrete problems, healing for people in one's immediate circle. The point of reference is the family and family life. That about 85% of our respondents should endorse this complex of motivations is understandable when we place it in the light of the high number of children per family (six, on the average).

Factor 2 has been named "God and a better world." In contrast to factor 1, here we are certainly dealing with something wider than family problems. God is the leading figure in two items in this factor. God is, as it were, symbolic for this breadth of concern, and is joined in this factor with matters which rise above individual problems. In the perception of the pilgrims, it is not Jesus, Mary or St. Gerard Majella but precisely God Who is connected with the social dimension of existence, which includes concerns about unemployment. Moreover, such prayers for a better world are joined together with the prayers of many others. Here there is a point of contact with V. Turner, who underscores the sense of community (*communitas*) among the pilgrims as an important characteristic of pilgrimage.[31] The importance which people attach to prayers for a better world yields nothing to the attention given to family problems; this factor was also applicable for 85% of the pilgrims.

Factor 3 contains five items, four of which in any case clearly refer to "recreational motivation." In these items the emphasis lies on the touristic values of Wittem, its location and historic places of interest. In addition, coming into contact with other people during the trip and on arrival in the pilgrimage site plays a role. The motive "because it's just a good thing to do" also fits with this factor, and thus must be seen in light of the other motives. In other words, one must interpret it as meaning, it is good to go to Wittem for typically recreational reasons. With reference to travelling as a group, this played a role for 50% of the respondents. From the character of the other motives in this factor (the beautiful surroundings and the historic sites), it would appear that travelling this way didn't always have to have a specifically religious purpose. All in all, these recreational motives played a role for 38% of our respondents.

Factor 4 is constructed of four items which explicitly refer to the "pilgrimage site as devotional centre," a place where devotion (66%), contemplation (70%) and thanksgiving (80%) were more central than in the pilgrims' own parish church. Of course, this is not so surprising, though the fact that the motive which implies a kind of flight from the parish should belong to this factor is striking: "because I feel increasingly less at home in my own parish." The number of persons who shared this view was not great, but still 19% of our respondents feel increasingly less for their own parish when it comes to contemplation, thanksgiving or devotion.

Three motive statements comprise *Factor 5*. The first two involve personal contacts with the brothers and fathers at Wittem. The third item has bearing on the import of this contact: people hope to be healed. From this we have named this factor "the pastor as source of aid." If we then look at the percentage for whom this was applicable, it becomes clear that this factor does not apply to large numbers. On the average, this factor was only applicable for 31% of the pilgrims.

[31] TURNER & TURNER (1978); and RÉMY (1984).

Factor 6 assembles the motives for the Wittem pilgrimage which specifically involve "Gerard Majella as a source of help." Gerard Majella is preeminently the one to turn to "for protection" (91%), "help and assistance" (88%), and "thanks for favours received" (80%). Of all the motives given, "on account of St. Gerard Majella" is the one which scored highest (97%), which is not surprising since devotion to him is central in Wittem. This is also the factor with the highest average: 89%.

Two motives belong to *Factor 7*, "social/traditional motivation." The first (42%) involves deference to tradition ("because I observe tradition"), and the second (26%) involves yielding to social pressure ("because my husband/wife or other family member wanted me to go"). Averaged, this factor was valid for 34% of the respondents. That means that this complex of motives comes out at the bottom in "applicability," along with Factor 5 (the pastor as a source of aid).

We have called *Factor 8* "penance with Mary and Jesus." It is true that Mary and Jesus are highly regarded by pilgrims to Wittem (89% and 77% regard them as an applicable motive, respectively), but as compared with St. Gerard Majella (Factor 6) their function is different. In contrast to him, Mary and Jesus are seen in the light of expiation.

Applicability of the Factors

We will now consider the way in which the factors are ordered. For this purpose they have been ranked in the order of their average applicability.

Table 2. Interrelation of the Factors

	%	
St. Gerard Majella as source of help	89	
Comfort in family problem	85	a
God and a better world	85	
Penance with Mary and Jesus	72	b
Pilgrimage site as devotional centre	59	c
Recreational motivation	38	
Social/traditional motivation	34	d
Pastor as source of aid	31	

For an overwhelming majority of the respondents, a complex of three motives (a) leads in identifying why they went to Wittem. An average of 89% answered "Gerard Majella as a source of help," and both "comfort in family problems" and "God and a better world" received an 85% endorsement as applicable. At the same time, we find a coincidence of asking help and returning thanks, like two sides of the same medal. This first involves asking and returning thanks through St. Gerard Majella as a mediator, then the family as object of prayer and thanksgiving, and finally it takes the form of prayer for a better world and honour to God. What is striking is that this asking and praying is not purely on behalf of the pilgrims themselves, but is particularly concerned with their children and grandchildren, and with the situation in the world. The micro and macro worlds are thus regarded as of equal importance. Then follows the complex of motives "penance with Mary and Jesus" (b), which still applied to three quarters of our pilgrims. Here two central figures in the Christian tradition are involved with the devotion to St. Gerald Majella. For many this pilgrimage is also a possibility to receive help from Jesus, and even more so, from Mary.

Next, the pilgrimage site as a concentration point for devotion is a reason for going on pilgrimage for 59% of the respondents (c). A small majority apparently have need of a numinous place to permit expression of the above mentioned concerns and thanksgiving. Their own parish is apparently not felt to be a suitable place for this.

The last three groups of motives (d) are all applicable for only about one third of those who filled in the questionnaire. Among them, recreational motivations (38%) were listed just slightly more frequently than social/traditional motivations (34%) and the pastor as a source of aid (31%). First, it is clear that the more extrinsic recreational and social/traditional motives play a significantly smaller role than the strictly religious motives which have been discussed previously. In the second place, one is immediately struck by the relatively slight value which people seem to attach to personal contact with the brothers and fathers at Wittem. The pilgrimage site itself is nearly twice as important (59%) as the "staff" who are present there (31%).

4.2. The Lourdes Research

Performing the Research and Responses

An organized pilgrimage by train, on Saturday, 12 October, 1985, leaving from the Dutch city of Roosendaal to Lourdes was the point of departure for this survey.[32] It was a combination of three pilgrimages: the Third Youth Journey to Lourdes, the 132nd National Pilgrimage and the Limburg Pilgrimage. About 250 young people and about the same number of older people were participating in the journey. For our purposes here, young people are defined as those under 35, and older people as those over 35. After the departure from Roosendaal a number of compartments on the train were visited randomly, in the course of which 78 questionnaires were distributed, equally divided between younger and older people. Of these we received back 71 filled in (91%). This is a high response, which is probably to be credited to the possibility of approaching potential respondents personally.

The respondents' ages varied from 15 to 78. Among them there were 35 older persons and 36 young people. The average age of the younger group was 22; of the older group, 58. About 70% were female. This was true for both the younger and older age groups. In regard to political opinions, there was a striking difference between the two groups. The vast majority of the older people had a preference for a Christian political party, whereas among the young people, as many as 58% felt absolutely no attraction to a political party.

Global Analysis of Motives

In this second study, during their outbound trip the pilgrims received a list of 34 statements of motives. Their answers were subsumed in two categories: applicable ("very applicable" and "applicable") and not applicable ("absolutely not applicable," "not applicable" and "don't know"). When we brought the answers of the younger and older people together in one overview, a very diffuse image was produced. When, on the other hand, we looked at the answers of the two groups separately, clear outlines did become visible. In the following discussion we will first examine the motives of the young people, and then those of the older people. The motives are ranked according to the degree to which they were applicable. We look first at the ten most important motives of the young people (n=36).

[32] Detailed data from this research is to be found in: OOSTERWIJK et al. (1986a); PIEPER, OOSTERWIJK & VAN UDEN (1988); VAN UDEN & PIEPER (1989); PIEPER & VAN UDEN (1990). See Part 2 in this book, especially Chapter 5, 6 and 7.

Table 3. Motives, Young People, Lourdes	
"I'm going to Lourdes…"	%
1. To meet others	89
2. Also to relax	80
3. Out of curiosity	69
4. Because the atmosphere attracts me	66
5. To renew my strength	64
6. Because I enjoy confessing my faith along with others	56
7. To strengthen my faith	56
8. To pray for a better world	53
9. Because of the chance for contemplation	53
10. To pray for the healing of others	50

It is striking that among the young people the most important motives involve meeting others and relaxation. In the list of possible motives which we distributed, there were a number of items of a non-religious nature. Three of these items ("to meet others," "also to relax" and "out of curiosity") came in in the first three places in the "top ten" for younger people.

The ten most important motives for the older people (n=35) produced the following picture:

Table 4. Motives, Older People, Lourdes	
"I'm going to Lourdes…"	%
1. On account of the Virgin Mary	80
2. To renew my strength	74
3. To pray for the need and misery in the world	71
4. To give thanks	69
5. To strengthen my faith	68
6. To pray for the healing of others	65
7. To pray for a better world	65
8. To implore help/assistance	63
9. To implore God's blessing	63
10. Out of thanks for blessings received	61

Among the older people, all of the important motives are of a religious nature. It is clear that non-religious motives are not to be found in their "top ten" of important motivations.

If we now compare the motives of the younger and older pilgrims, the following observations must be made. The three non-religious motives which are the most important for the younger people ("to meet others," "also to relax" and "out of curiosity") only come in at the 21st, 13th and 34th and last place among the older pilgrims. The most important motive among the older people, "on account of the Virgin Mary," only comes in in 17th place among the younger pilgrims. The items which place third and fourth among the older people ("to pray for the need and misery in the world" and "to give thanks") come in in 13th and 15th place among the younger people. In other words: younger people go on pilgrimage for entirely different reasons than older people.[33]

Results of Factor Analysis

Once again, a factor analysis was carried out to provide greater insight into the interconnections and meaning of the various statements about motives. This produced three factors.[34] We have given a name to each factor which reflects our interpretation of the factor as a whole. Moreover, we indicate to what degree the younger and older pilgrims regarded the factor as applicable as a reason for their own pilgrimage.

Factor 1 involves what we have termed "deepening faith." The motives "to learn to pray," "because the preaching is so good there," "to strengthen my faith," "to experience the Church universal" and "for a revival of faith" all belong to this factor. The motives which refer to God ("to honour God") and Jesus ("because the figure of Jesus of Nazareth attracts me") also come to the fore explicitly in this factor. Moreover, in further analysis, a significant connection appears to exist between a high score in factor 1 and agreeing with the statement "my personal faith is directed principally toward God." This underscores the connection between this factor and God. On the average, this factor was applicable for 33% of the young and 30% of the older people.

We have termed *Factor 2* "imploring help and healing." In addition to the motive "to implore help or assistance," this factor also includes "to be healed myself." Further, the motives "because I made a vow" and "because my husband/wife/partner (or someone else) desires it" belong with this factor. Also comprising this factor are a motive related to imploring God's blessing ("to implore God's blessing") and one that brings some-

[33] One can find more information about the differences between younger and older pilgrims in: PIEPER (1988a).

[34] For further details about this factor analysis, see: OOSTERWIJK et al. (1986a) 16ff.

thing into relationship with Mary ("on account of the Virgin Mary"). The motive "out of curiosity" has an inverse relation to this factor: that is to say, pilgrims who scored high on motivations comprising factor 2 usually did not score on the motive "out of curiosity." From further analysis it would seem that pilgrims who agree with the statement "my personal faith is directed most toward Mary" often score high in factor 2. It would thus appear that asking help or healing are primarily connected with Mary. On the average, this factor was applicable for 20% of the young and 53% of the older people.

Factor 3 was called "seeking peace and tranquility together." This factor includes motives which express a certain atmosphere or circumstances: the beautiful surroundings ("because Lourdes is in such a beautiful location"), relaxation ("also to relax"), and meeting other people ("to meet others"). These motives come together in this factor with the motives "because of the chance for reflection" and "to seek peace." This suggests that they cannot be too easily interpreted as recreational motives, but rather appear to have to be understood as motives which create favourable conditions for inner peace and contemplation. On the average, this factor is applicable for 61% of the young and 39% of the older people.

Comparing the percentages of applicability of the various factors, then it is striking that factor 1 (deepening faith) scores relatively low with both the younger and older pilgrims. Further, we see that among the older pilgrims factor 2 (imploring help and healing) scores the highest, while among the young it is factor 3 (seeking peace and tranquility together). Older people scored factor 1 the lowest, and younger people factor 2. The older pilgrims were characterized primarily by seeking help and healing with Mary, the younger by the need to seek rest and tranquility together with others and possibly, through that, to enter into reflection.

4.3. The Banneux Research

Performing the Research and Responses

As with the two previous studies, this involved a survey based on a questionnaire from an organized pilgrimage.[35] The research took place among pilgrims who had come by bus from various parts of The Netherlands: Arnhem/Utrecht, Haarlem, Rotterdam and the bulb-growing area north

[35] Detailed data about this research can be found in: PIEPER & VAN UDEN (1988).

of Den Haag, and Twente. The duration of their trips on the weekend of September 19-21, 1987, varied from group to group. The buses from Arnhem/Utrecht made a one day trip, which left little time for the recreative aspect of pilgrimage. The busses from Rotterdam left Saturday morning for Rolduc in Limburg, and from there went on to visit Hasselt, in Belgium, where the grave of the "Holy Little Father Valentine" ("Heilige Paterke Valentinus") is found. They attended a celebration of the Eucharist that evening in Rolduc. Sunday morning they went on to Banneux, and returned the same evening to Rotterdam. The busses from Twente travelled by way of Den Bosch, where the pilgrims attended a celebration of the Eucharist, with a coffee hour afterward, and then went on to Valkenburg where they were to spend the night. That evening they made a side-trip to attend a prayer service at the "Grotto of Lourdes" at the Cauberg. Sunday morning they left for Banneux, where they reboarded the busses for the return trip to Twente about 3:00 p.m. The busses from Haarlem left for Banneux on Saturday morning, stopping on the way to pick up more passengers from Alkmaar, Amsterdam and Utrecht. These busses went straight through to Banneux, where the pilgrims spent the night, and remained the whole day Sunday. On Monday morning they made a sightseeing tour in Banneux, and then left for home. On the way they stopped for lunch in Vaals and coffee in Maastricht.

In total, we received back 273 of the 457 questionnaires distributed. This return rate of 60% is high for a questionnaire survey among primarily older people. The average age of the respondents to our survey was 62, and 82% of them were women. About three quarters of all the respondents indicated they were housewives. The educational level was rather low; 65% of the pilgrims had not completed any education other than vocational training. Half of the respondents were married, with an additional 30% widows or widowers. With regard to their health, 90% of them reported that it was good or reasonably good. The pilgrims involved in the survey had made many pilgrimages; 79% of the pilgrims had already been on pilgrimage to Banneux before, and 69% had already been there four or more times. Among our respondents, 21% went only to Banneux for pilgrimages, while the rest also went on pilgrimage to other sites. Banneux exercised the greatest attraction on 46% of the subjects, followed by Lourdes at 20%. Further, our respondents were faithful in church attendance: 232 of them went to church at least once a week (87%). Only 10% did not feel ties to a parish. Mary was clearly central in the pilgrims' prayer life: 89% of the people pray to her. God and Jesus were invoked by 31% and 27% respectively. Among other saints mentioned in this connection, the most often named were Joseph and Anthony, with 27% and 26% respectively.

Global Analysis of Motives

The first way of ordering the data with respect to motivation is to reflect the degree to which the respondents regarded a motive as applicable to their pilgrimage. A table with percentages of applicability per motive, in which we rank the ten most important motives, is found below. Respondents chose from a list of 45 possible motives.

Table 5. Motives, According to Degree of Applicability

		%
1.	On account of the Virgin Mary	92
2.	To get Mary's intercession	88
3.	To pray for those close to me	86
4.	To pray for the healing of others	82
5.	To ask for help or assistance	81
6.	To acquire new strength	78
7.	To give thanks	78
8.	To strengthen my faith	77
9.	To pray for a better world	76
10.	To implore God's blessing	74

The most important motives are all religious in nature. Of the trinity of God, Jesus and Mary, the latter plays by far the most important role. In fact, two Marian items come in in the first two places. Motives involving God and Jesus come in between 10th and 21st place. Closely connected with the two Marian items, in third and fourth place come asking for help for others, particularly those who are closest. Recreational and social motives clearly are far down the list. Recourse to Mary with requests for healing and help is central to this pilgrimage.

Results of Factor Analysis

After analyzing the degree to which each motive separately is applicable, by means of a factor analysis it is possible to go deeper into the coherence among various motives.[36] This factor analysis yielded the following

[36] For further details of this factor analysis, see PIEPER & VAN UDEN (1988) 19ff.

eight factors. We begin with the factor which averaged the highest and end with the factor which, on the average, was of the least applicability.

Factor 1, "turning to Mary," which was applicable for an average of 81% of the subjects, comprises that part of seeking help and healing which takes place through Mary. Mary is the most important person to whom the subjects turn for help. It is noteworthy here that people primarily ask Mary's intercession for others, particularly people from their direct environment, the nuclear and extended family.

Factor 2, "turning to Jesus and God," which was applicable for an average of 63%, comprises particularly the items in which Jesus and God come to the fore. First, people turn to Jesus or God in order to enter into contact with them, to confess their faith. Subsequently this contact is also directed toward setting right the wrongs in this world, for instance, solving the problem of poverty.

Factor 3, "contemplation," valid for an average of 52%, alludes to quiet reflection on one's own life. For the type of pilgrims in this study – the more traditional group of pilgrims, relatively old and female – reflection about life primarily takes place within the framework of prayer.

The "recreational motives" in *factor 4* were of importance for a third of the respondents (33%). The motives which belong to this factor all speak for themselves: a beautiful trip, beautiful surroundings, companionship, "getting out for a bit," meeting other people, relaxation, etc.

Factor 5, "help for myself," applicable for an average of 30%, comprises four items ("contact with clergy," "vows made," "for my healing" and "the way I was trained up") which at first glance are difficult to connect with one other. Yet it is possible to explain the construction of this factor. At its core is the search for healing for oneself. This is generally coupled with a vow, to be fulfilled once one receives healing. Further, it appears that in the search for healing, contact with a member of the clergy is sought, a contact which appears to be rooted in tradition ("the way I was trained up").

There are still three more factors, which each consist of one motive, and which were also a reason to go on pilgrimage for only a few. Of these three, "accompaniment" ("to accompany someone") scored the highest:

21%. Then follows "social motivation" ("because a lot of people I know are going"), that was a motive for only 11% of the respondents. The two motives offered, which are more oriented to tradition, are not connected with this social motive. Entirely at the end comes the factor "curiosity" ("out of curiosity"). With regard to this, it must be remarked that this factor is applicable for only a tiny fraction of the pilgrims (4%), and that it is apart from recreational motives. Curiosity seems to be the last thing which may serve as a motive for the respondents.

When we review the degree to which the factors are regarded as applicable, it is possible to reach the following conclusions:

(a) Non-religious motives are clearly of less weight than religious motives. They place fourth, sixth, seventh and eighth.
(b) Within the religious motives, seeking help and healing are more important than deepening faith. In this process, it is primarily Mary who is sought out. There is one exception. Asking for one's own healing is a motive for only 30% of the respondents to go to Banneux. This fits well with the fact that the health situation of the pilgrims is good to reasonably good.

5. Synthesis and Conclusions

In closing, we will try to combine the three surveys described to produce one total picture. In this way we hope that the results of the various surveys will reinforce each other and we can thus get more insight into the profile, on the one hand, and the motivation structure of pilgrims participating in "organized" Dutch bus and train pilgrimages on the other.

What sort of Dutch residents signed up for our bus and train trips to what V. and E. Turner call modern, postindustrial pilgrimage sites?[37] To begin with, a clear distinction can be made between the older and younger pilgrim. In making this distinction we use the possibly somewhat arbitrary demarcation point of 35 years of age. We encountered a group of young pilgrims in the Lourdes research; older pilgrims were found in the Lourdes study as well as in those involving Wittem and Banneux. This does not, however, say that Wittem and Banneux do not attract younger pilgrims, but rather that they make relatively little use of organized bus trips to these locations. The characteristics of the three

[37] See Turner & Turner (1978).

groups of older pilgrims who were investigated show such a great measure of agreement that it seems justified to speak of a homogenous population of older pilgrims who, so far as is possible, visit a whole series of pilgrimage sites. This is also self-reported: they list a whole lot of other pilgrimage sites which they have also visited. Particularly Lourdes, Banneux and Kevelaer are listed together by many. The personal characteristics of this older pilgrim are as follows: his average age is 60 – though it would be better to say "her," as nearly 80% of the pilgrims are women. The overwhelming majority of the respondents are married or have been married. They have had a large number of children. The role most characteristic of the pilgrim is, then, that of a mother and/or grandmother. The educational level is low, often not reaching beyond primary school. Thus it is no surprise that "housewife" is profession the most frequently listed. With regard to a relation to religion and faith, the following image emerges: we are dealing with what, with some caution, can be called the traditional Catholic believer.

The percentage who attend church weekly is extremely high: nearly 90% go to church once a week, while among all Catholics that averages just under 20%. Their parish involvement is high. Their interest in religious matters is equally great. Finally, this traditional faith also expresses itself in their political preference: Christian parties are favoured by a wide margin.

The younger pilgrims have a different profile. They are better educated than their elders and, given their age (their average age is 22), their social position naturally is also very different: married individuals are the exception. In general, political parties do not gain their endorsement. It is striking, however, that among younger pilgrims women are also overrepresented, at 70%.

When we now take a look at the pilgrims' motivational structure, and compare the most important ten motives from the pilgrims to Wittem and Banneux and the older Lourdes pilgrims, it is striking to note that they are as good as identical. What differences do arise are caused by the fact that certain motives – for instance, "on account of St. Gerard Majella" – were included in the questionnaire in only one of the surveys (in this case, Wittem). This means that, in terms of motives, respondents who participated in the Banneux and Wittem research also were to a great extent congruent with the older Lourdes pilgrims.

If we subsequently turn our attention to the results of the various factor analyses, we note that both the Wittem and Banneux studies yielded eight factors. From the Lourdes study a trio of factors were distilled.

On the basis of the meaning and content of these nineteen factors, as described in the foregoing paragraphs, it is possible to compile them into a number of what we shall term basic factors. That is to say, the three separate factor analyses produced similar factors. The choices which we have made in this process of combination, if not already evident, will be tested in subsequent research.

The factors "comfort in family problems" (Wittem), "Gerard Majella as source of help" (Wittem), "imploring help and healing" (Lourdes) and "turning to Mary" (Banneux) all refer back to one basic factor, which we will term imploring help and assistance. This can happen through Mary or through St. Gerard Majella, and has, as its primary object, the nuclear or extended family.

The factors "God and a better world" (Wittem), "deepening faith" (Lourdes) and "turning to Jesus and God" (Banneux) refer back to deepening faith. The primary reason that people turn to God is not to ask for help and strength, but to be closer to God and Jesus. Furthermore, faith is deepened by acts of witness, whether alone or with others. It is striking that the problems of the world also have a place within this deepening of faith.

We would want to bring the factors "pilgrimage site as a devotional centre" (Wittem), encompassing items which refer to devotion, contemplation and thanksgiving, "seeking peace and tranquility together" (Lourdes) and "contemplation" (Banneux) together under the title religious/existential reflection. These involve meditation on life, which is made easier by the special atmosphere of the pilgrimage site: quiet, devotional surroundings and tranquility. For older pilgrims, this reflection on life takes place primarily within the framework of prayer (religious). For the younger people, however, possibilities for relaxation and particularly meeting others (existential) would also seem to be important conditions for beginning this process of reflection. Indeed, the last two elements are connected (though in the Lourdes study, for young and old together, alone) with contemplation.

We would want to add together the factors "the pastor as source of aid" (Wittem), "penance with Mary and Jesus" (Wittem) and "help for myself" (Banneux) into the basic factor of healing-tradition. This term is derived from the characteristic motives which comprise this factor, namely, contact with members of the clergy, being healed, performing vows, doing penance and being trained up traditionally. These are motives which, in our view, point back to the conviction rooted in traditional belief that one finds physical and spiritual healing for oneself at the pilgrimage site. Personal contact with a member of the clergy is important in that process, as it is for confession. At the same time, there exists a connection between this traditional basic motivation and asking for help and assistance. In the Lourdes study in particular, two characteristic motives of the healing tradition (making vows and receiving healing for oneself) are found in the factor "imploring help and healing."

We encounter a recreational factor at both Wittem and Banneux, which in both cases is difficult to present in any other way than under the title of recreation. This is a matter of pilgrimage as a "day out," with eminent characteristics of tourism. It is notable that, among the older pilgrims (Wittem and Banneux), meeting others must be seen in the perspective of tourism. In the Lourdes study this item comes, as we said earlier, in the factor involving reflection, "seeking peace and tranquility together." It is possible that we are here seeing a transitional area between reflection and recreation which has to do precisely with encountering others. Depending, then, on the age of the pilgrim, this encounter with another will have more to do with reflection or with recreation.

There remain four factors, which consist of one or two items each. Of these, the factors "social/traditional motivation" (Wittem) and "social motivation" (Banneux) can be collected under the heading social motivation. Two factors, "accompaniment" (Banneux) and "curiosity" (Banneux), are left over. Thus we have reduced the nineteen factors with which we began to eight basic factors.

In order to determine to what degree the pilgrims regarded these basic factors as applicable to their pilgrimage, we have computed the average of the "applicable" percentages of the factors which comprise each basic factor. This yields the following picture:

Table 6. Basic Factors

		%
1.	Help and assistance	73
2.	Deepening faith	60
3.	Religious/existential reflection	54
4.	Healing-tradition	44
5.	Recreation	36
6.	Social motivation	23
7.	Accompaniment	21
8.	Curiosity	4

Here again it is clear that religious motives precede non-religious motives.

In conclusion, taking into account both the sorts of basic motives and the degree to which they were applicable, we are able to summarize the three preliminary investigations schematically in the following chart. Each circle stands for a basic factor, while the size of the circle reflects its degree of applicability. Furthermore, by the schematic placement of the circles, we have tried to assure that basic factors which have a substantive connection with each other also touch on each other physically.

In this chart, it can clearly be seen that we distinguish between two groups of basic factors, religious and non-religious. However, on the basis of the Lourdes study, one must assume that the dividing line in general is not so hard and fast as this chart suggests. We have commented on this above, in relation to the factors "contemplation" and "recreation." Furthermore, the chart comes across as rather static. With regard to this, it is important to point out that a flesh and blood pilgrim cannot be characterized by reference to any one basic factor alone. Also, someone's motivation can gradually change during the pilgrimage. One can set out for purely recreational reasons, but come to be spiritually touched after arriving at the pilgrimage site. The next time that person may then go on pilgrimage out of the motivation of deepening their faith. This was a process which we regularly encountered in the course of interviews with younger pilgrims.[38]

In the chart, we have placed the "social motivation" factor on the left side, indicating that we see this factor standing in a substantive relationship with the basic factor "healing-tradition," reflecting what was called the social-traditional motive from the Wittem study, with its component "because I observe tradition." Again, because of their substantive content, we have placed the factors "accompaniment" and "curiosity" on the "social" and "recreational" sides of the chart, respectively.

As we have indicated, we offer this chart as a working hypothesis developed on the basis of preliminary investigations. Its usefulness must be tested in the course of further research. Our main investigation, among a large number of older pilgrims to Lourdes, going forward at this time, is one attempt to do this.

[38] DERKS, PIEPER & VAN UDEN (1989).

Chart: *Motivation structure: Wittem, Lourdes, Banneux*

	%		%
Help and assistance	**73**	**Deepening faith**	**60**
Comfort	(W)85	God and world	(W)85
Turning to Mary	(B)81	Turning to God & Jesus	(B)63
Help and healing	(L)37	Deepening faith	(L)32
Gerard Majella as help	(W)89		
Healing-tradition	**44**	**Reflection**	**54**
Pastor as source of help	(W)31	Devotional centre	(W)59
Help for myself	(B)30	Contemplation	(B)52
Penance with Mary & Jesus	(W)72	Peace together	(L)50
RELIGIOUS			
NON-RELIGIOUS			
Social motivation	**23**	**Recreation**	**36**
Social/traditional	(W)34	Recreation	(W)38
Social motivation	(B)11	Recreation	(B)33
Accompaniment	**21**	**Curiosity**	**4**
Accompanying someone	(B)21	Curiosity	(B)4

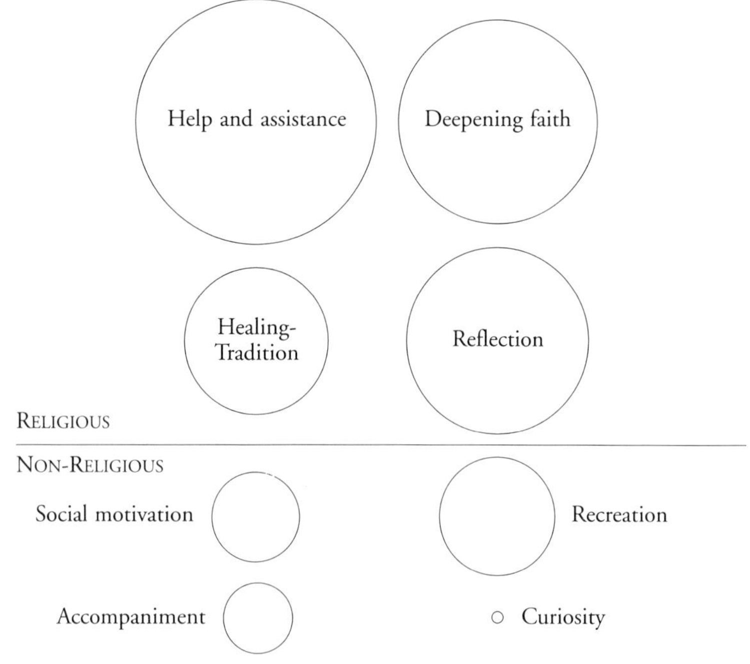

2. THE "PLACES OF PILGRIMAGE IN THE NETHERLANDS" PROJECT

AN ORIENTATION[1]

1. Introduction

The Places of Pilgrimage in The Netherlands (Bedevaartplaatsen in Nederland = BiN) project, an inventory and description of places of pilgrimage in The Netherlands past and present, was initiated in 1993 by the P.J. Meertens Institute. Information about pilgrimage and pilgrimage sites in The Netherlands has been limited and fragmentary. That can be seen in the presentation of various analytical investigations and theories, which rest on weak foundations because of the lack of fundamental data. Basically documentary in purpose, in combination with source and empirical research BiN is intended to broaden knowledge in this field, and thereby generate and stimulate innovative and well-founded research. Focusing attention on Dutch pilgrimage culture fits well with the increasing interest in pilgrimage, pilgrimage sites, appearances and miracles that is to be found in international scientific research.

In addition to a first presentation of the inventory project in this chapter, at the same time we also wish to give an account of the orientation of the BiN project. For this, the project will be related to recent

[1] P.J. Margry & P. Post: Het project "Bedevaartplaatsen in Nederland": een plaatsbepaling, in *Volkskundig Bulletin. Tijdschrift voor Nederlandse cultuurwetenschap* 20,1 (1994) 19-59; = Wallfahrt zwischen Inventarisierung und Analyse. Ein niederländisches Forschungsprojekt in historiographischem und methodologischem Kontext, in *Rheinisch-westfälische Zeitschrift für Volkskunde* 39 (1994 [1995]) 27-65.

In 1997 Volume 1 of the BiN-project appeared: P.J. Margry & Ch. Caspers (eds.): *Bedevaartplaatsen in Nederland. Deel 1: Noord- en Midden-Nederland* (Amsterdam/Hilversum 1997). The volumes 2 (Noord-Brabant) and 3 (Limburg) are in preparation and will be published in 1998 and 1999. See for this Chapter now the Introduction of Volume 1: (1) Wetenschappelijke positionering, 8-11; (2) Opzet en werkwijze van het BiN-project, 12-24; (3) Classificatie van bedevaartplaatsen, 25-33; (4) Historiografie van inventarisatieprojecten, 34-44; (5) Structuur en gebruik van het lexicon, 45-48. Important for the theme of this part of the book are: Thijs (1996) and Margry (1996).

developments in international pilgrimage research, and in particular to the tradition of pilgrimage inventories. This determines the structure of this chapter: to achieve proper placement in the theoretical framework provided by existing research, the way in which general pilgrimage research has developed over the past years must be studied (Part 2)[2]; subsequently we will delve more deeply into the tradition of cataloging pilgrimage sites (Part 3); finally, resting on this background study, the structure and methods of the project will be presented (Part 4). The inventorization project raises a number of questions and problems which must be answered or solved through further research. Because of continuing discussion of the definitions of and terms used for pilgrimage and pilgrimage sites, establishing the scope of the project and setting definitions with regard to existing research is absolutely necessary.

2. Trends in Contemporary Pilgrimage Studies

Interest in the theme of pilgrimage can be classified as follows:

(a) First of all, there is interest in performing ritual acts, the practice of pilgrimage itself: that is to say, the devotional interest of the believers themselves. For some years now there has been evidence from a number of sources of revitalization in pilgrimage. As has so often been the case in the past, this revival is coupled with, among other things, a certain type of apologetic and devotional literature that could be termed "propaganda."

(b) Connected with this is the swelling current of reports by pilgrims themselves which are published and circulated in The Netherlands and Belgium by various means.[3]

(c) This interest is also reflected in popular academic literature. In addition to promotional literature and pilgrims' reports, which are an interesting and (particularly for the study of contemporary developments) often neglected source, there is a stream of general cultural/historical or touristic surveys appearing here and in other countries.[4]

[2] For a survey of the studies which have appeared since 1986, see the bibliography in Pieper, Post & Van Uden (1994) 277-301.

[3] Post (1992b). Cf. Chapter 9 in this book.

[4] For instance, Plechl (1988); Hansen (1991); Wasser (1993); see further footnotes 118 and 121 here and the "Pilgerweg" series of guides from St. Otto Verlag, Bamberg: *Rom* (1984); *Fátima* (1986); *Assisi* (1988); *Umbrien* (1989); *Santiago* (1989); *Jerusalem*

(d) In the fourth place, there is scientific interest. This is the track which will be followed through the rest of this essay, for various academic fields: social sciences, anthropology, historical disciplines and theology and various religious disciplines. The regional historical and/or anthropological studies and inventories of pilgrimage sites which are steadily appearing also belong to this category.[5]

For an image of academic research in The Netherlands and internationally on pilgrimage, to a large extent a sketch of the situation since 1988 can suffice, because a balance sheet for the preceding period has already been drawn up.[6] The years since that date have not witnessed any major change of direction in pilgrimage studies, but it is clear that the developments described in 1988 have further crystallized, or have undergone changes in part.

In the present survey, the emphasis lies on the social sciences, historical disciplines, and the grey area that lies between them.[7] Moreover, the survey is primarily oriented to Western European Christian pilgrimage since the Middle Ages. Particular attention is devoted to a series of collections, often issued in connection with multidisciplinary conferences at national or international levels, which function as boundary markers of a sort for pilgrimage studies. In addition to several Dutch workshops and symposia on the relation of popular culture and pilgrimage, such as those at Heerlen and Amsterdam in 1991 and Nijmegen in 1992, there were important congresses dealing with pilgrimage in general or with certain sub-themes successively in Arezzo and Aachen in 1987, London and Bamberg in 1988 and Krems an der Donau in 1990.[8]

(1990); *Kevelaer* (1992); *Heiliges Land* (1993); and those from the regional "Kleine Pannonia-Reihe": *Wallfahrten zwischen Inn und Salzach* (1976); *Wallfahrten im Bayerischen Oberland* (1977); *Wallfahrten im Passauer Land* (1978); *Wallfahrten in und um München* (1980), edited by the Pannonia Verlag in Freilassing.

[5] See the preceding footnote and notes 118 and 121.

[6] POST (1988b).

[7] Other areas of expertise that are important for pilgrimage studies, such as archaeology, art history, historical geography and literary studies, cannot be discussed within the scope of this chapter. See for art history, geography and literary studies: POST (1994b) with ample bibliograhy (1994c); for (Christian) archaeology there are now the in two volumes the papers of the 12th. international congress of Christian archaeology held in Bonn in 1991: *Akten* (1995).

[8] VAN UDEN & PIEPER (1991); POST (1991c); POST (1992b); WEGMAN (1992); EADE & SALLNOW (1991); *Wallfahrt und Alltag* (1990); FATUCCHI (1990); HERBERS (1988).

In this general survey, "pilgrimage" is the general point of departure[9], although the theme must be placed within a wider context. It is precisely this broadening in connection with developments within the wider frame of research in the field of religious popular culture that is both one of the trends and one of the perspectives that will hereafter come to figure prominently.

2.1. Social Sciences

Within the wide field of the social sciences, the points of concentration are here cultural anthropology and the psychology of religion. The 1989 special "Pilgrimage and Modernity" issue of the international social sciences journal *Social Compass* is exemplary for this, in offering a good insight into the breadth of research into pilgrimage going on within the framework of the social sciences, with marked attention for the historical dimension.[10]

This issue of *Social Compass* also in part enters the field of cultural anthropology, where several interesting developments in pilgrimage studies can be traced. Changes in the way that the ideas of V. Turner are being dealt with, and the effects these changes in turn have, are especially striking. In the scope of this chapter, it is impossible to give a complete picture of the spectrum of anthropological work on pilgrimage, as this involves a range of religious traditions, and many studies of details from many parts of the world. But it is interesting, for instance, to see how G. Hersbach attempted to test what is termed the reaction model in the Dutch situation.[11] Following the work of other researchers, primarily from abroad, expressions of religious popular culture in general and pilgrimage in particular are viewed as protests and compensatory movements in periods of social or ecclesiastical change or renewal (i.e., the Industrial Revolution, Vatican II). Still another approach might be termed "metaphorical." Reader and Walter's collection of essays investigates the phenomenon of non-religious pilgrimage in modern culture

[9] Without resuming the discussion surrounding the definition and terminology of "bedevaart" and "pelgrimage," we would briefly note that in a general sense we will speak of "bedevaart" (here translated "pilgrimage") as much as possible, while theoretically the double "bedevaart/pelgrimage" would be more correct. (For a summary, see BERBÉE (1986), HARTINGER (1992) 99ff). See also sub 3.1.

[10] RÉMY (1989).

[11] See HERSBACH (1992); (1994).

(for instance, to military cemeteries or Elvis's Graceland) from this perspective.[12]

Perhaps the most important research in cultural studies on appearances and visions from the late Middle Ages down to the present – a subject of immense import for pilgrimage studies because it touches upon the origin of many pilgrimage sites and holy places – has been done by the American anthropologist working in Spain, William Christian, Jr. His œuvre is more strongly characterized by quality and an extreme reticence for theoretical pronouncements rather than by quantity and methodological detours.[13] Christian combines high quality source research with a creative handling and analysis of his material and is subsequently able to present it clearly. Here, therefore, Turner plays hardly any role.

The multidisciplinary inventory project carried out in Europe under the leadership of the Americans Mary Lee and Sidney Nolan occupies a place of its own.[14] It is being listed here although the project really involves the confluence of elements from cultural geography, anthropology, comparative religion and historical studies. The Nolans' study is the outcome of a research project which began 12 years ago. Central to the project is a data base which brings together information about 6150 Christian holy places ("shrines") in 16 Western European lands. Initial information was collected by mailing out questionnaires to various dioceses and umbrella organizations involved in organizing pilgrimages. The goal of the project is to describe and interpret the various dimensions of contemporary European pilgrimage, but because the data, arranged by classifications and types and often reduced to numbers, determines and limits the final analysis, typological analysis emphatically overshadows interpretation. Essentially, the book raises questions about the potential and even desirability of inventory projects, and about the correct basis for more diachronic and comparative studies. In part in the light of methodological perspectives raised later in this survey, precisely in view of the Nolans' large-scale project, national or regional pilgrimage inventory projects which are quantitatively more limited but more thorough would seem to merit priority. In the meantime, the Nolans

[12] READER & WALTER (1993). On pilgrimage as metaphor also: BAUMER (1977) 101-106.

[13] See for instance: CHRISTIAN (1981a); (1981b); (1984); (1989); (1992). Now: CHRISTIAN (1996).

[14] NOLAN & NOLAN (1989); see also the review by P. POST, in *Volkskundig Bulletin* 17 (1991) 84f.

themselves have continued along the broader path that they have been following; their project is now focusing on holy places on other continents.

The American/Scotch study of Protestant family reunions by the anthropologist Gwen Kennedy Neville is hardly known in continental Europe.[15] It applies the concept of "pilgrimage" in an exemplary way, and is decidedly more than an interesting case study of American Protestant family rituals. Following particularly in the footsteps of Turner and Geertz, family reunions are analyzed as a "pilgrimage system." In the Protestant context, one can speak of reverse pilgrimage; if the Roman Catholic system is characterized by "travelling outward from home," the Protestant pilgrimage is a "return home" from a diaspora situation. In particular, the general sketch of pilgrimage as a social and cultural process in both Roman Catholic and Protestant contexts is of interest for pilgrimage studies in general. How the Protestant side in The Netherlands will relate to the new interest in pilgrimage is an interesting subject for further research.[16]

The provocative collection *Contesting the Sacred* also comes from the corner of anthropology. The book is a product of the major congress on pilgrimage mentioned earlier which was held in London in July, 1988.[17] The somewhat pretentious introduction is intended to shake up pilgrimage research, and attempts "to set a new agenda for the study of pilgrimage." According to the editors, Eade and Sallnow, the following elements are to adorn this new agenda: first of all, and before all else, pilgrimage is "an arena for competing religious and secular discourses." A very emphatic call is made to leave behind classical but limited models like Turner's, for which concepts such as "liminoid," structure, anti-structure and *communitas* are central[18], as these are experienced as straitjackets. This fits with the postmodern dismissal of all prevailing paradigms. After all, Turner's theory can nowhere really be demonstrated: one always encounters a multiplicity of behaviours and experiences.[19] In particular, the group experience which is so central for Turner often appears to be entirely absent.[20]

[15] NEVILLE (1987) 13ff.

[16] MARGRY (1993a), particularly 193f.

[17] EADE & SALLNOW (1991).

[18] See TURNER & TURNER (1978); see also the critical review of this study by VAN HERWAARDEN (1980). Cf. TURNER (1969).

[19] MORINIS (1992) 8.

[20] See what Morinis has to say about this in his "Introduction" in MORINIS (1992) 1-28, and the German discussion on the definition of "Wallfahrt." For that, see sub 3.1. and footnotes 9, 129 and 131.

There are many questions to be raised about Eade and Sallnow's "agenda." Thus, it could be asked if this agenda is really as new as is suggested. On further examination, and certainly after reading the articles included in the collection, have these writers really distanced themselves from Turner? In other words, isn't there more discontinuity being suggested than is really the case? Is the call for empirical description of the phenomenon of pilgrimage in all its variety really a new agenda?

This agenda was also, and particularly, the subject of criticism by the anthropologist Morinis, who saw Turner's merit as lying in the indicatory and heuristic value of the concepts he employed. Morinis urged, as for instance some European ethnologists had already done, that attention be given to individual pilgrims and their motives.[21] The goal of the pilgrimage, the holy place, is however dropped from the picture by Morinis; he is oriented entirely and exclusively to the "journey," thus, at least for Christian pilgrimage practice, missing the mark.

Likewise more nuanced and less obstreperous than Eade and Sallnow is a short sketch of pilgrimage research that Driessen gave in a recent collection about Islamic pilgrimage practices.[22] Driessen placed more emphasis on continuity in the research. He sees pilgrimage research posing three enduring questions for anthropology (although he also extends this to other disciplines): a) How does the religious aspect relate to the other aspects? b) What does the journey mean for the participants? c) What theoretical approach is most suitable for obtaining insight? It is the absence of precisely the synthesizing, theoretical studies that Turner's work could inform which Driessen laments in current pilgrimage research. According to him, the absence of this dimension has to do with the fact that until recently anthropology was occupied with group cultures, and operated within the boundaries of group experience. For a long time, a sacred journey which, by definition, broke through the boundaries of the group fell outside its field of vision. Now that there are increasing numbers of case studies available, the time is ripe for comparative and synthetic studies. Driessen's call for a new theory is thus diametrically opposed to Eade and Sallnow's rather fashionable "deconstructive" model.

Finally, a few remarks regarding psychology of religion. Within the framework of a programme of research on pilgrimage at the University

[21] MORINIS (1992) 1-28. European ethnologists such as G. Korff, M. Scharfe and H. Gerndt have for some time been occupied with research into motivations. See SCHARFE (1991).

[22] DRIESSEN (1991).

for Theology and Pastoral Care at Heerlen, a number of empirical social science surveys have been carried out since 1986. Popular religious practices such as pilgrimage are studied there as designs for the human search for answers to questions of existence and finding meaning in life. This research has provided more insight into particularly the profile and motives of Dutch pilgrims, and with it, also into the definition of pilgrimage and pilgrimage sites.[23]

2.2. Between Social Science and Historical Disciplines: "Volkskunde" or European Ethnology

"Volkskunde" or European ethnology lies in the academic "grey area" between historical disciplines and social science, and so does the work of Alphonse Dupront. Dupront merits separate mention because of an important collection of essays which appeared in 1987, *Du Sacré*.[24] The book is important methodologically because Dupront, from the position of an historian, enters into dialogue with the social sciences (in particular, anthropology) to search for new ways of analysis and interpretation with regard to various forms of religious experience. The book indicates how important Dupront is for contemporary pilgrimage studies.

With regard to "Volkskunde" or European ethnology, it would seem that pilgrimage is still one of the important elements in the international study of folklore. Apart from the modest contribution of Dutch scolars on the field of European ethnology, it can be said that pilgrimage plays a less prominent role, in contrast to the 1960s and 1970s, in international ethnological studies, which are, as is well known, dominated by German-language work. Würzburg, but also Bonn, Bamberg and Munich, can still continue to be regarded as the important centres of research, and it is still true that the *Jahrbuch für Volkskunde* from the Görres Gesellschaft is an important platform for pilgrimage studies.

While it is true that Turner and other too rigid research models are no longer being used, on the other side it appears that the interchange between historical disciplines and the social sciences has led to thriving, innovative studies such as that by Freitag.[25] From the somewhat emotional

[23] PIEPER, POST & VAN UDEN (1990). In this book: Chapter 1.
[24] DUPRONT (1987); see the review by P. POST in *Volkskundig Bulletin* 15 (1989) 91-95.
[25] FREITAG (1991).

reactions in circles of European ethnology[26] to the "political" pilgrimage study by the historian Rebekka Habermas[27], it appears that people there sometimes still find it difficult to accustom themselves to new theoretical formulations and modern conceptual systems. However, it must be admitted, the content is sometimes also not much more than old wine in new wineskins.

An important part of the pilgrimage research in Germany, Austria and Switzerland still consists of a stream of local and regional folklore and cultural/historical inventories and pilgrimage studies, often varying considerably in quality. Others examine the cultural artifacts of pilgrimage (pennants, prints, pilgrims' badges, etc.). As we will see hereafter in some detail, while inventories occupy a prominent place among them, sadly enough the majority have too weak a scientific foundation to serve as part of the basis for further analytical or comparative research. An exception to this which should be mentioned here, but still an initiative, is the "Kultstätten-Kurzkataloge" from Würzburg.[28] But all told, it appears that European ethnological pilgrimage studies, after the often stimulating debates of the 1980s, share in the more general "crisis" in German "Volkskunde" studies.[29] Perhaps the appearance of retrospective and historiographic (European) ethnological studies synthesizing earlier work can be placed in this light. On the theme of pilgrimage, Hartinger's fine synthesis *Religion und Brauch* and Scharfe's textbook on *Brauchforschung*, for instance, still need to be mentioned.[30]

2.3. Historical Disciplines

It goes without saying that the lion's share of pilgrimage studies can be credited to historical disciplines. In a field this broad, it is particularly difficult to keep pilgrimage in sharp focus. Many studies active in the wide terrain of religious popular culture of the past often yield up direct or indirect contributions to pilgrimage research. In addition to the flood of methodological studies about popular culture (including religious),

[26] See for instance BRÜCKNER (1993b) particularly 92-94.

[27] HABERMAS (1991).

[28] DÖRING et al. (1982).

[29] On this "crisis," see for instance W. BRÜCKNER, in *Bayerische Blätter für Volkskunde* 19 (1992) 193-196; 20 (1993) 84-98, but also the reaction from H. BAUSINGER, *ibidem* 20 (1993) 131-138.

[30] HARTINGER (1992): particularly "Wallfahrtswesen" sub 2.2., 99-121; SCHARFE (1991).

there are various studies on themes such as relics, Eucharist, piety, saints and their cults, models of saintliness, miracles, visions and so forth.[31] The cult of Mary and Marian appearances, subjects so important for pilgrimage studies, are also amply represented.[32]

As was the case with European ethnology, a quick survey of the studies specifically handling pilgrimages establishs that the "classic track" is also dominant here: many source publications and a rich palette of case studies[33] and pilgrimage inventories. The adjective "classic" should also indicate that over the past few years few if any innovative tendencies have been visible in historical pilgrimage research.

With regard to Santiago de Compostela, during these years a separate series of *Jakobus-Studien* – traditional in form – has been started in Germany[34], and there are regular conferences on the subject. In The Netherlands we can point to the thorough study by Jan van Herwaarden in which *The Book of St. James* and *The Pilgrim's Guide* are central.[35] Further, the "classic" track in The Netherlands is represented by Verhoeven's highly professional dissertation on Delft as a goal of pilgrimage.[36]

For all that, however, the perspective in historical pilgrimage studies appears to be shifting toward subjects which are on the interface between historical disciplines, anthropology, sociology and European ethnology. Pilgrimage is being situated in a dynamic force field of processes of appropriation, with attention for the relationship between image and ritual.[37] A fine example, in which Marian pilgrimage is analyzed by an historian, using the tools of social science with input from the perspective

[31] DIERKENS & DUVOSQUEL (1990); HILHORST (1988); ZIKA (1988); DELUMEAU (1989); DINZELBACHER & BAUER (1990); DÜNNINGER (1990); LÄPPLE (1990); BRANDENBARG (1992); VROOM (1992); WYNANDS (1992); WINGENS (1993).

[32] ORSI (1985); R. LAURENTIN: "Bulletin Marial," regularly included in Revue des sciences philosophiques et théologiques (see f.i.: 69 (1985) 611-643, 70 (1986) 101-150); KSELMAN & KSELMAN (1986); BARTOLOTTI & BARTOLOTTI (1988); TURI (1988); ZIMDARS-SWARTZ (1991); recently added to these was an Austrian catalogue listing all the known appearences of Mary over the past two millennia: HIERZENBERGER & NEDOMANSKY (1993).

[33] Santiago de Compostela still scores very highly, but many researchers also focus on Rome or Jerusalem.

[34] HERBERS (1988); GANZ-BLÄTTER (1990); PLÖTZ (1990).

[35] VAN HERWAARDEN (1992).

[36] VERHOEVEN (1992). See now for Amersfoort: THIERS (1994).

[37] See for instance the articles by ROOIJAKKERS, WINGENS and MARGRY in the collection: MONTEIRO, ROOIJAKKERS & ROSENDAAL (1993). See for the fundamental concept of "appropriation" now: FRIJHOFF (1997b).

of the common people and the elite, is the previously mentioned study by Freitag. But the innovative research regarding Germany and France quite frequently comes from foreign – particularly American – universities, as in the studies by Kselman, Sperber, Devlin and Soergel.[38] The historiographic and methodological innovations that play a role in this have been described by Frijhoff.[39]

2.4. Theological and Religious Studies

Now that popular religious expressions have almost entirely disappeared from the agenda in theological and religious studies, studies of pilgrimage have become scarce in those fields. Those working from theological and religious perspectives were working from a relatively isolated position. The theme was viewed almost entirely in the context of popular religion as relevant to pastoral care. The debate over popular and elite culture and definitional questions in the case of pilgrimage thus bypassed many of the researchers involved.

For The Netherlands, one exception to this has been liturgical studies, in which multidisciplinary research on the theme of pilgrimage has taken place. In addition to the liturgical studies component in the Heerlen pilgrimage programme[40], one can also point both to Snoek's study[41] and, in particular, to Caspers's study on eucharistic piety in the late Middle Ages.[42] The situation outside The Netherlands is much less defined by debate and traffic across academic borders, as is reflected by the absence of such forces for renewal in the 1987 special "Pilgrimage and Liturgy" issue of the journal *La Maison-Dieu*, and other sources.[43]

Beyond that, in this international connection one can mention at least one isolated study, that of Hüttl dealing with Church history, in which Church, the common man and royalty are central.[44]

[38] KSELMAN (1983); SPERBER (1984); DEVLIN (1987); SOERGEL (1993). See now: BLACKBOURN (1993), ARETZ (1995) and CHRISTIAN (1996).

[39] FRIJHOFF (1992a).

[40] For a summary, see POST (1992b); (1994b); and our Introduction.

[41] SNOEK (1989).

[42] CASPERS (1992).

[43] See now the recent specials of *Concilium* and *Communio*: *Pelgrimage* (1996) and *Bedevaart en pelgrimage* (1997); cf. LAMBERTS (1997).

[44] HÜTTL (1985).

2.5. Synthesis: Crossing Borders, Subsiding Debate, Broadening Scope and Inventories

If we now place the most important trends, themes and perspectives along side one another, we are led to the following conclusions:

(a) A first observation involves the small amount of traffic across academic borders to be seen from our vantage point. Only a modest amount of multi- or interdisciplinary pilgrimage research exists. The collection which came out of the great London conference[45], with such high aims, is perhaps symptomatic of this; ultimately it was compiled strictly from within the boundaries of cultural anthropology.

(b) Further, it is striking how the discussions and social, ecclesiastical and academic/theoretical debates which to a large degree determined pilgrimage research in the period until about 1985, have since to a great extent died down. One can think of the debate around the dichotomy between popular and elite culture, or the discussion about the definitions and terminology regarding pilgrimage, and about popular religion, once so important in theological circles.

The greatest achievement of the debate around popular and elite culture appears to be a certain consensus about the concept of culture in contemporary cultural studies. This consensus proceeds from a broad and interactive concept of culture, and through that, in an analysis of cultural actions, offers the possibility of comprehending dynamics, the process of change, and particularly dissynchronous and sometimes conflicting appropriations and grants of meaning. Pilgrimage must be placed in a broad cultural force field, on the interface between history, anthropology and European ethnology. This is true not only for general analytical studies, but equally for case studies of pilgrimage sites, and for the inventories of pilgrimage sites which are an extension of them. Adequate attention must be given to these inventories, because new perspectives in research will be stimulated strongly by the increase in factual material available.

Some remarks about the theoretical concepts of Victor Turner also fit within this context of less vocal discussions. Although, from the perspective of theory, to a large degree Turner's thought still determines pilgrimage research done by anthropologists, it is being dealt with more critically. Anthropologists appear to be parting ways from Turner. This

[45] EADE & SALLNOW (1991).

departure can take one of three forms. It can be a call to leave great theoretical models behind completely, or a postmodern argument for small reports on the basis of local "discourses." Closely connected with this is the plea to concentrate particularly on the personal "discourse" of the individual pilgrim in research, and not simply proceed from an amorphous communal depiction.[46] The "farewell to Turner" can also be sounded as a challenge to develop new models to succeed Turner – perhaps in part built on his theories – in which comparative, structural and diachronic aspects can together be given a place. As, among other reasons, the weaknesses of large scale projects such as that of the Nolans seem to indicate, it is precisely here that inventory projects again seem to have a role to play.

(c) The key concept of broadening has already been mentioned. This expansion involves a number of closely interrelated areas, such as an expansion of object, of context, of presentation of the questions, and of sources and methods employed.

First of all there is the important aspect of the definition of pilgrimage. The discussion on this point seems to have relieved the above mentioned debate about definition and terminology. There are researchers who wish to maintain pilgrimage as a metaphor which can be employed broadly.[47] We have already in another context referred the dangers associated with this[48], but there also can be productive applications of a broader – non-religious – use of the idea of pilgrimage.[49] We can also see how, in dealing with the problem of definition, some place the emphasis on the journey (particularly Morinis), while others stress the place (see the key concept of "shrine" in both Christian and the Nolans). Every inventory project, especially, will have to return to this always topical discussion, and have to assume a standpoint related to the current position in pilgrimage research.

A related expansion of the research perspective lies in studies that wish to set their sights on other segments than the traditional ecclesiastical pilgrim or participant in organized pilgrimage. Increasingly scholars are turning their attention to the individual pilgrim, who shuns organized

[46] Aziz (1987).

[47] See, for instance, Abélès (1988); Ellwood (1991); Dayan (1990); Miles (1988); Scharfe (1989).

[48] Pieper, Post & Van Uden (1990). See Chapter 1 in this book. See now however the also broader use of "pilgrimage" in Post (1998).

[49] For instance, Neville (1987).

pilgrimages. It is in this research that the new types of pilgrims come to the fore, too.

These expansions also touch especially on the perspective of contextuality. It is of great importance to place pilgrimage in the context of dynamic cultural processes such as ways of dealing with the past[50], ways of dealing with nature, the search for identity, folklorism, invention of tradition, the tension between tradition and modernity[51], the culture of travelling[52], etc.

As yet, the contours of the new "agenda" and the process of shaping the theoretical framework of future pilgrimage research are being delineated primarily by the expansion we have just sketched, through multidisciplinary projects in which comparative elements, in particular, are also taken into account. One of the most important perspectives for future pilgrimage investigations lies in continuing and increasing the interchange across the boundaries of academic disciplines. It is therefore not without reason that at the moment, the most interesting research is taking place on the interface between the social sciences and historical studies.

But operating on this sort of cutting edge also has its dangers.[53] For instance, there can be a strong inclination to move to a sort of "shameless eclecticism," bringing together bits and pieces of usable insights for a model or theory from all sorts of places, or not too closely observing accepted procedures in disciplines other than one's own, whether it be handling and analyzing statistics in the social sciences or investigating sources in history. The critical reservations we noted with regard to the large-scale American inventory project especially touch on this point.

(d) Lastly, a final observation regarding inventories, by way of a bridge into the next section. We are now able to locate pilgrimage studies which conduct inventories generally in the larger framework of contemporary pilgrimage research. Following from what we have already said regarding them, three general lines can be distinguished. There is the "traditional" and "classic" track of regional and national inventories, especially within ethnological and the historical disciplines. Next, we have the Nolans' large-scale data base project. The call by Eade and Sallnow

[50] READER (1987); POST (1991b); (1991c); (1991d); (1992b).

[51] *Volkskunde zwischen Tradition und Modernisierung* (1991).

[52] BAUSINGER, BEYER & KORFF (1985).

[53] See FRIJHOFF (1992b).

(and also that by Morinis) for empirical research based on case-studies could be seen as a third line. Although phrased in different ways, we see here a search for a solid foundation for new syntheses and new theoretical constructions, and particularly for innovative comparative research in which inventory projects could play an important role.

In the next section we will pause to spend considerable time examining the tradition of pilgrimage inventories itself, and the changing contexts in which these have been conceived and carried out.

3. From Analysis to Inventory and Vice Versa

More pointedly, one might ask how the survey of trends and themes just provided, and particularly the perspective with regard to expansion and multidisciplinary research which has been sketched out, is related to the large segment within pilgrimage research that is oriented toward inventorying and describing pilgrimages and pilgrimage sites. Are the many German and French inventories, the American data bases and now a Dutch project perhaps a sign that points to a crisis in this field of research? After all, when confronted with stagnation or the loss of bearings, one is perhaps more quickly inclined to direct attention on (or to flee into?) the more primary activities of collecting, cataloging and describing.

Our view is that innovative research in the field of pilgrimage can only take place when there is sufficient, processed basic information in hand. One of these instruments and sources is a scientific inventory of places of pilgrimage. In the Nolans' American investigation, one can see just how fatal the lack of such work can be. The position of The Netherlands in their statistical/analytical processing is inaccurate, because both the number of, and the image of Dutch pilgrimage sites employed were entirely incorrect.[54] Especially in social science research, the perimeters of the investigation are not always sound, which results in too wide a spectrum being handled in certain investigations, and there being too little reliance on systematic research.[55] This possibly is a result of an overwhelmingly one-sided approach that, rather than the pilgrimage site, takes the phenomenon of pilgrimage much more as its point of departure.

[54] See Chapter 2 in Nolan & Nolan (1989), in which, because of limited insight into the real Dutch situation, untrustworthy distribution maps and tables are to be found.

[55] Morinis (1992).

A detailed and complete inventory of pilgrimage sites is of fundamental importance not only as the basis for research and analysis, but also as basic material for new views on the phenomena of pilgrimage and pilgrimage sites. In this connection one should recall the shape of Turner's and Morinis's theories, with their emphasis on only one dimension. Likewise, inventory work is necessary within the research framework of casuistry and empiricism. For that reason too it is again important to set up an inventory such as this, taking into account methodological expansion, and working diachronically, up to and including the present.

The problems surrounding the perimeters of the investigation and definitions require that the Dutch BiN-lexicon project can be placed in the perspective of the tradition of catalogues of pilgrimage sites. An account of the widely divergent ways in which pilgrimage sites were and are described – from histories of local cults compiled by pastors through systematic historical, folkloristic or scientific topographies – will be worthwhile, in order to trace developments in the methods applied in inventories over the past centuries. When using certain kinds of works – especially histories produced by pastors – modern research must apply a form of historical criticism. The emphasis on the German language area in the following survey is to be explained by the particularly strong tradition there.

3.1. Inventory Projects In Historical Perspective

Prior to the 20th Century

The oldest descriptive enumerations of pilgrimage sites and holy places were chiefly practical in purpose.[56] Like the *Pilgrim's Guide* to Santiago de Compostela[57], the *Mirabilia Urbis Romae*[58] and guides to the Holy Land[59], they were a functional instrument for offering pilgrims more opportunities for obtaining grace at the venerated holy places. It is only in the 17th century that more general, systematic surveys appear, within the framework of the Counter Reformation and the propagation of

[56] See RICHARD (1981); HERBERS (1988); HOWARD (1980).

[57] For the function of this guide, see the introduction to the Dutch translation: VAN HERWAARDEN (1992).

[58] HUYGENS (1970); see also, for instance, WOODRUFF (1933).

[59] One of the earliest guides, about 685 CE, is: MEEKAN (1958); for guides which were incorporated in travel reports, see further: RÖRICHT & MEISNER (1880); WASSER (1983).

Marian devotion. Although the Jesuit Jakob Gretser categorized all the important Christian pilgrimage sites in his *De sacris et religiosis peregrinationibus libri quatuor*[60], most of the survey works which appeared during this period dealt with Marian holy places. The first was Locrius's work of 1608, followed by Gumppenberg's great *Atlas Marianus* in 1657, with 1200 Marian locations.[61] Not only were there surveys for the whole of the Western Christian world, but there were also regional works such as, for instance, those of Ertl, De Santa Maria and Wichmans compiled for Austria, Portugal and Brabant, respectively.[62] Setting aside the propagandistic element, that it was chiefly Marian pilgrimage sites which received the lion's share of attention in these is also a consequence of the clearly delineated form of the cult. In the light of the "offensive" that the Church was conducting against the diverse forms of "popular," non-Marian devotion, the description of pilgrimage sites of a more "popular" signature was consciously avoided.

After the 17th century, such pilgrimage catalogues are rather scarce until the first half of the 19th century. The limitations placed on devotions, pilgrimages and processions in the German states and imperial Austria contributed to this decline. While it is true that descriptions of pilgrimage sites begin to appear in various works of Church history and Protestant disputational texts, one cannot speak of systematic treatment of pilgrimage sites. Under the influence of the general revival of religion and devotion, a new interest in pilgrimage grew up in the course of the 19th century.[63] On the one hand, this interest was historic and scientific in nature, as reflected in Migne's great *Encyclopédie Théologique*, in which one finds an almost anthropological understanding of pilgrimage sites – Christian and non-Christian, ancient and modern – in the article by De Sivry and Champagnac in volumes 43 and 44.[64] On the other hand, many publications were chiefly propagandistic in character. The most important reasons for the revival in the publication of survey works, again chiefly of Marian pilgrimage sites, were the stream of Marian

[60] Ingolstadt 1606.

[61] LOCRIUS (1608); GUMPPENBERG (1657).

[62] ERTL (1735); DE SANTA MARIA (1707-1723); WICHMANS (1632). In addition there appeared many other more general works, such as: SPINELLUS (1619); MAYR (1655); SPERELLI (1679); RHO & BOVIO (1737); RENATO (1768).

[63] See CHÉLINI & BRANTHOMME (1982) 295-318: "La renaissance des pèlerinages au XIXe siècle."

[64] DE SIVRY & CHAMPAGNAC (1859).

appearances beginning in the first quarter of the 19th century, the elevation of Immaculate Conception to the status of dogma in 1854, and the further centralized stimulation of Marian devotion from Rome. The need for academic foundations – sometimes pseudo-historical – for old, national holy places likewise played a role. Within the publications, the descriptions in the entries for each holy place were more extensive, chiefly in the elaboration of their origin and miracle narratives and historical development. These treatments were almost exclusively written by representatives of the Roman Catholic Church. In addition to general works[65] there particularly appeared national surveys for France[66], Belgium[67], Germany[68], Austria[69], Switzerland[70], and Italy, Spain and Portugal[71]. *Maria's Heiligdommen* was published for The Netherlands and Belgium.[72] Not only national, but also regional surveys appeared, such as the works of the Belgian Friar Minor Schoutens organized by provinces.[73] Protestants also applied themselves to the theme, as in the anti-Papist *Roomsche Feest- en Heilige Dagen* by J.G. Swaving, and the later, more moderately critical consideration of pilgrimages to holy places in The Netherlands and across its borders by the Protestant minister Van der Kemp.[74]

The 20th Century, Prior to World War II

Only around the turn of the century does more distance become possible. A general historical/critical and ethnological/scientific interest in pilgrimage sites was growing. Although this interest initially was especially the province of representatives of the Church, we see how later this kind

[65] For instance: *Pèlerinages célèbres* (1894).

[66] In the second half of the 19th century there was a deluge of such publications in France; we will here list only: HAMON (1861-1867); DE GAULLE (1869).

[67] R[EUME] (1859).

[68] MEHLER (1864) and later the smaller HEIZMANN (1932).

[69] KALTENBAECK (1845); DONIN (1872) and the voluminous book by Pastor A. Hoppe, HOPPE (1913).

[70] VEUILLOT (1893) later followed by: BURGERNER (1864) and CHÈVRE (1898).

[71] ZANELLA (1839-1847); DE LAFUENTE (1889); PIMENTEL (s.a.).

[72] *Maria's Heiligdommen* ([1881]). This was followed by a second part in ([1882]).

[73] SCHOUTENS (1877), and his other volumes on the provinces of Oost- en West-Vlaanderen (1875), Limburg, Antwerpen, Henegouwen, Luik, Namen and Luxemburg.

[74] SWAVING (1824), VAN DER KEMP (1880).

of research is also being carried out by persons and institutions not related to the Church. As a representative of the first we must mention the seven volume standard work written by the Dutch Redemptorist Kronenburg, who produced a unique study of the history of Marian devotion in The Netherlands in his *Maria's Heerlijkheid in Nederland*.[75] The book is still conceived with 19th century breadth, but has a critical approach to older sources remarkable for its time, and presents an almost exhaustive treatment from the beginning to its own day. Few books of comparable thoroughness have appeared. In Germany the Jesuit Stephan Beissel produced various scientific studies, including the 1913 description of Marian pilgrimages with a list of the most important places of pilgrimage in the world.[76] However, as had also been the case for most 19th century material, much else was the work of industrious pastors and amateur historians who often took over existing literature and sources word for word with little critical sense, or consciously distorted it.[77]

This is also still often true for clerical works from the years between the World Wars. Nevertheless, this was a period of transition for inventories of pilgrimage sites. The first representative of this transition was R. Kriss with his investigation of Bavarian pilgrimage sites and their votive usages.[78] But it was particularly the rise of institutes for the study of "Volkskunde" or European ethnology that provided an impulse for new research resting firmly on ethnocartographic methods, in which distribution maps were compiled based on a system of correspondents and questionnaires. The initiative for the compilation of a national atlas of "Volkskunde" ("Atlas der deutschen Volkskunde") appeared in Germany at the end of the 1920s; in the process regional questionnaires were also mailed out.[79] This was also noticed in The Netherlands, but it

[75] KRONENBURG (1904-1914), with: [SCHEEPERS] (1931).

[76] BEISSEL (1913) 299-492, with on pages 374-379 a list of Dutch Marian shrines; see also: BEISSEL (1910).

[77] Aspirations for official recognition often emanate from such works, in which absolutely anywhere might be included as a pilgrimage site. Regarding the dangers of these compilations, see: DÜNNINGER (1982) 172f.

[78] KRISS (1930); this study was reprinted in two volumes in 1953-1955, to which a third volume was added in 1956: "Theorie des Wallfahrtswesens."

[79] The two "Fragebogen" which were circulated in Rhineland in 1931 and 1934 are of importance for pilgrimage research; see COX (1989/90). This article also contains a test publication of the questionnaire. Further, the articles about this area by F. Heckmanns appeared in these years: HECKMANNS (1929) and (1930); QUASTEN (1936).

was only after the Second World War that, as a result of Dutch and Belgian cooperative efforts, the *Volkskunde-atlas van Nederland en Vlaams-België* was published.[80]

Particularly because of personal sensitivities, questions pertaining to religious popular culture, and in particular pilgrimage, rarely appeared in the *Atlas* questionnaires that were regularly distributed by the then "Volkskunde" Commission among their correspondents beginning in the 1920s. It is telling that the only time that such matters were extensively broached in a questionnaire, it happened under the title of "Folk Medicine and Popular Meteorology in Connection with the Veneration of Saints." This questionnaire concentrated on the popular customs surrounding illness and "saint-healers" or "healing saints" for people and animals. The presentation of the data from the questions ultimately appeared in the third installment of the *Volkskunde-atlas*.[81]

After World War II

A new interest in pilgrimage research arose after the Second World War, once again often inspired by the experience of the loss of old "traditional" religious customs in a modern, secularized society. The revitalization that many pilgrimage sites underwent through the thanksgiving pilgrimages after the end of the war once again temporarily brought extra attention to the phenomenon. On the other hand, it appears that the sharp rise in the theft of votive paintings in Germany was also an extra stimulus for research.[82]

The most important project was set up in Austria. There the five volume *Österreichs-Gnadenstätten in Kult und Brauch* was compiled by Gustav Gugitz.[83] It was an innovative work, which, in reaction to the existing pilgrimage studies that generally approached their subject from a religious or art historical angle, instead treated pilgrimage sites according to methods of European ethnology, in a "kultdynamische" manner.[84] The strictly topographic arrangement and the inclusion of religious prints and other images and an extensive bibliography and source listing also made it a model for many European ethnologists. One drawback of "der Gugitz" was, however, that it often stopped short of the present; many

[80] Regarding the origins of this atlas, see: DEKKER (1989a); see also: DEKKER (1989b).

[81] DE MEYER (1968).

[82] BRÜCKNER (1959).

[83] GUGITZ (1955-1958).

[84] See Gugitz's "Vorwort" in Volume 1, VII-XI.

descriptions ended in the 19th, and sometimes the 18th century. Later, in 1971 and 1979, on the basis of a new questionnaire sent out, a cartographic handling of the larger pilgrimage sites appeared in the *Österreichischer Volkskunde-Atlas*.[85]

Germany

In the meantime, in Germany in 1949 the Bavarian Landsstelle für Volkskunde in Munich issued a questionnaire about *Wallfahrtsvolkskunde*. The limited approach is expressed in the fact that this involved only a *Bestandsaufnahme der Votivgaben*. Some years later the Amt für rheinische Landskunde in Bonn tried to follow this up with its own questionnaire.[86]

In the 1970s Germany once again saw an expansion in interest in pilgrimage and pilgrimage sites. There was a need to make a census of all cultus locations by means of systematic projects. These were often multipurpose projects which recorded the wealth of pilgrimage artifacts – votive gifts and paintings, processional objects, images and architecture – at the same time. This interest was not only carried through by academics with a background in history, "Volkskunde" or European ethnology, anthropology or theology, but was supported – often very intensively – by the Catholic Church and, in particular, the dioceses involved. The first concrete steps were taken in 1975 with the creation of a comprehensive and systematic data base of all pilgrimage sites in Bavaria, divided by diocese, at the Institut für Volkskunde at the Bavarian Academy of Sciences. Inspired by Gugitz, they projected a seven volume manual. The project was collectively designed in Munich (Kriss-Rettenbeck) and Würzburg (Brückner).[87] Various questionnaires were sent out, but because of the large number of pilgrimage sites and limited finances, the pilgrimage project ground almost entirely to a halt.[88]

[85] Relating to a double question about "Marien-Gnadenstätten" in the religious "Volkskunde"-questionnaire, treated on page 73 (1971): "Die großen marianischen Gnadenstätten der gegenwart und ihr regelmäßiger Wallfahrtszuzug" and on page 116 (1979): "Die bedeutendsten Wallfahrtsorte Österreichs und Südtirols."

[86] At the end of the 1960s, for the Institut für geschichtliche Landskunde, Klaus Beitl began with an inventory for the Rhineland, on the basis of the 1959 "Wallfahrtsorte" questionnaire for the area of the diocese of Cologne. The project, however, has remained in the initial phase.

[87] For the activities and development of this project, see: *Bayerische Blätter für Volkskunde* 3 (1976) 74-101; 4 (1977) 35-37; 6 (1979) 3-56.

[88] Except for the small Bavarian dioceses of Passau and Eichstätt, which were treated by W. Hartinger and W. Pötzl, respectively.

Through their methodological studies, the pilgrimage research that had become highly developed at Würzburg under the direction of W. Brückner[89] and H. Dünninger[90] soon became the focus for German pilgrimage studies.[91] Various case studies were treated according to methods and techniques of the "Volkskunde" or European ethnology.[92] One rarely, however, encounters studies there which attempt a synthesis.[93]

The projects were an impetus for reflections on the development of new methods and techniques, on the one hand for tracking down old pilgrimage sites by means of pilgrim's badges, devotional and pilgrimage prints, archive material, secondary literature and questionnaires[94], for instance, and on the other hand through better structuring and systematization of the data obtained, and through refinement of the definitions for the conceptual apparatus. Especially with regard to the latter, to this day German research is marked by rather opaque forest of terms, concepts and definitions.

The structuring of the data was advanced by the development of a "Dokumentationsschema" that was composed in Würzburg.[95] It comprises a fixed plan of aspects that are necessary to be able to arrive at a description of pilgrimage and cultus sites which is complete and fulfills the standards of historical and ethnological research, and includes artifacts and the use of visual resources, archive material, etc. This led in 1982 to the appearance of the first initiative, the *Kurzkataloge* of *Kultstätten* for the archdiocese of Freiburg and several dioceses. The organization is scientific, but at the same time is rather sharply confined to the present. Unfortunately this "Zwischenbericht" has never been worked

[89] For his rich œuvre, see: KLOTZ & FIDLER (1990) 93-142.

[90] His most important work in this field is DÜNNINGER (1961/1962).

[91] See, for instance, the interim situation as described in: BRÜCKNER (1982).

[92] For instance, the ethnological ("volkskundliche") pilgrimage studies: BRÜCKNER (1978); (1979); DÜNNINGER (1979).

[93] We are not taking into account the semi-popular survey works regarding this part of Bavaria by Karl Kolb, who operates outside of the project; these include: KOLB (1974); (1976); (1979) and (1980).

[94] In 1978-79, for the "Wallfahrtinventarisation in Bayern bzw. Franken" project, the Institut für deutsche Philologie sent out the "Statistische Erhebung zur Inventarisierung von Wallfahrts- und Andachtsstätten im Regierungsbezirk Unterfranken" questionnaire. It was the intention to produce a "Deutschland-Gugitz" or "Wallfahrts-Dehio" (the "Dehio" is a multivolume, solidly researched German art tour guide) for Bavaria.

[95] DÖRING (1982). Regarding the problems of this inventory research, see: BRÜCKNER (1982).

out into a definitive catalogue.[96] The museum world has also produced a study of images and religious prints from the culture of pilgrimage, in addition to votive gifts.[97]

New pilgrimage projects were also set up in Bonn.[98] Zender's important synthesis of the veneration of saints in the Rhine and Meuse region appeared in 1959.[99] His *magnum opus* offered entirely new insights into the spread of the adoration of saints in the Middle Ages. Despite its innovative approach and the treasure trove of data, the often undifferentiated handling of source materials and its cartographic treatment has often restricted its usefulness for modern research. Various large and small surveys also appeared over the years in regional historical journals.[100]

France, Benelux and Other Countries

In its execution, Zender's geographic research on saints shows similarities with the French tradition, the tone for which was established by the anthropologist Arnold van Gennep with his many thematic studies of cults of "healing saints."[101] Van Gennep set the precedent for primarily French research focused on saints to whom worshippers turned for health problems, considered by region. We here list Leproux's work, or Bensa's fine anthropological study of the Perche-Gouët, with its inventory and analysis.[102]

Marian research once again experienced a flowering in postwar France. A great eight volume work appeared under the title *Maria, études sur la sainte Vierge*, two volumes of which were devoted to descriptions of

[96] In 1983 the impetus was given to revise the catalogue, and the not always too precise data was checked on the spot and amended by two staff members; as a result, a second, revised edition will appear. Several years ago, a new edition of places of pilgrimage in the archdiocese of Freiburg also appeared, and although based on the *Kurzkataloge* and edited by a former staff member, it offers relatively little new information: BROMMER (1990).

[97] This involves the series *Gnadenstätten im Erzbistum München und Freising* from the Diözesan Museum für christliche Kunst des Erzbistums: STEINER (1979) and STEINER & BRENNINGER (1986).

[98] For instance, "Umfrage zur rheinischen Volkskunde, nr. 2: Heiligenverehrung, Prozessionen, Wallfahrt," consisting of 133 questions, most with several parts, sent out by the Amt für rheinische Landeskunde.

[99] ZENDER (1959).

[100] BERGMAN (1953); VAN GILS (1959); (1960); WEBER (1974).

[101] Especially the series of monographs of regional studies of devotions and folklore that begins with: *Le Folklore du Dauphiné* (1932-1933).

[102] LEPROUX (1957); BENSA (1978).

Marian holy places throughout the world.[103] The strength of Rome's campaign to promote Marian devotion could be seen once again in 1954, the Marian Year, when the whole Church was circularized with a letter which called upon people to make Marian holy places better known.[104] In France, this led to the founding of the Centre de documentation des Sanctuaires et Pèlerinages, which published a monthly bulletin with historical, religious and iconographic descriptions of French pilgrimage sites, both those devoted to Mary and to other saints.[105] After the Second Vatican Council an initiative also was taken, under the title Orbis Marianus, to set up a ten part series with descriptions based on "sources sûres" from Vatican Archives of all the "crowned" (miraculous) images of Mary in the world.[106] Likewise, in Spain and Portugal the documentation of Marian pilgrimages and worship set the tone.[107]

Taking an approach that is more or less analogous to that of the French geographical studies of saints, in 1968 Knippenberg published his *Oude pelgrimages vanuit Noord-Brabant.*[108] A year later, working from France, Frijhoff compiled a survey of pilgrimage sites in the Northern Netherlands during the Ancien Régime.[109] Belgium, despite its rich diversity of pilgrimage sites and devotions, remained at the level of incidental treatments of individual pilgrimage sites[110] or general guides[111] that were superficial in nature. Berbée rightly remarks of them, "Neither

[103] DU MANOIR (1949-1971); we refer here to Volume 4, with descriptions of shrines in Europe and Asia, and volume 5 with those in Africa, Asia and the Americas, and a supplement to volume 4.

[104] The three volume work by I. Couturier de Chefdubois appeared the same year: COUTURIER DE CHEFDUBOIS (1954).

[105] Its contemplated activities were also to include a "dictionnaire-atlas" of pilgrimages, maps of shrines for each department of France, and a general bibliography: see the "Présentation" by director J. Ramond in the first issue of *Sanctuaires et pèlerinages. Bulletin du Centre de documentation*, May, 1955. Issue 41, the last (?), appeared in May, 1956.

[106] Of the projected ten volumes, only one appeared: DEJONGHE (1967).

[107] See, for instance, general works such as those by SANCHEZ PEREZ (1943); PÉREZ 1941-1948); and DOS REIS (1967); and regional surveys such as BARREIROS (1931), and QUELHAS BIGOTE (1948). For (Spanish speaking) Latin America: VARGAS UGARTE (1931).

[108] KNIPPENBERG (1968).

[109] FRIJHOFF (1969).

[110] For instance, THYSSEN (1922), and more recently, LANTIN (1971).

[111] For instance, CAUBERGHE (1967), or SLOSSE [ca. 1980].

their terminology nor research methods were characterized by any great analytical consciousness."[112]

In the meantime the first results of the cooperative Volkskunderat Rhein-Maas, established by European ethnologists from The Netherlands, Belgium, Luxembourg and the German Rhineland in 1979, appeared. The book *Wallfahrt im Rheinland* was compiled in 1981 for the first theme, "Pilgrimage."[113] A year later a bibliography of all pilgrimage literature dealing with the Rhine/Meuse region appeared.[114] As a follow-up, in The Netherlands a pilgrimage project inventorying sites in Limburg, the area around Cuyk, Nijmegen and the Peel was carried out. Since then, however, no other work has been done.[115]

Increased attention for the phenomenon of pilgrimage at the beginning of the 1980s did produce two other publications. In 1981 there appeared a sort of promotional work dealing with a number of pilgrimage sites in the Benelux.[116] The following year a descriptive inventory of still-existing pilgrimage sites in the province of North Brabant was published.[117] In other European lands increasing numbers of inventories of pilgrimage sites were rolling from the press.[118]

We will mention only one of these projects here. Together with Thomsen, Brückner's student Daxelmüller published important research into the problems of and the methods to be used in tracing pilgrimage sites of the Middle Ages which have disappeared in areas which became Protestant.[119]

[112] BERBÉE (1986) 173.

[113] PESCH (1981). This book came about as a result of the "Wallfahrt (Prozession) im Rheinland. Vorumfrage zur Bestandserhebung" circulated by B. Heizmann in 1979. This inventory was under the auspices of a collaboration between the ARL and the Volkskunderaad Rhein-Maas. With regard to the realization of this inventory, see A. DÖRING in BRÜCKNER (1982) 251-258. The long-announced "Wallfahrten" section in the *Geschichtlicher Atlas der Rheinlande* will not appear for the present.

[114] *Bibliographie Bedevaart* (1982).

[115] The Commission régionale Wallonne Rhin-Meuse and the Musée de la Vie Wallonne has also compiled an exhaustive questionnaire about "Les pèlerinages en Wallonie," but it too never reached the stage of implementation.

[116] Reference is made here to the appendix that Th.G.A. Hendriksen added to the translation he made of ANTIER (1979): "Supplementary remarks about places of pilgrimage in the Dutch-speaking region and the whole of the Benelux [= Belgium, The Netherlands and Luxemburg], added by the translator" (p. 326).

[117] MARGRY (1982).

[118] For instance, ADAIR (1978); *Santi e Santuari* (1979); HEIM (ca. 1980); PURCELL (1981); MARCUCCI (1983).

[119] DAXELMÜLLER & THOMSEN (1978).

Academic interest in the religious subculture also was growing in the communist countries of Eastern Europe in the 1970s, and it was particularly pilgrimages that appeared to attract wide participation from among the population in Poland and Hungary.[120] All things considered, Germany and Austria remain the most important lands, where there have almost continually been efforts undertaken to compile popular and semi-scientific inventories of pilgrimage sites.[121]

With reference to this diachronic survey, there follow several remarks regarding frequently encountered problems or insufficiencies of a methodological nature from which pilgrimage inventories suffer.

3.2. Problems

Problems of a methodological nature can be identified in most of the inventories. In the first place, under the influence of the strong tradition of organized pilgrimages, or what are termed processional pilgrimages, an approach has grown up that is much more oriented to pilgrimages than to pilgrimage sites. That could clearly be seen in the discussion of definitions which took place among German pilgrimage specialists.[122] But it also appeared there that adequate research perimeters had not yet been established, and that the criteria had to be sharpened to produce a sound inventory.

A second general problem, which is also found through the whole of the 20th century, is associated with the tradition of clergy writing descriptions of pilgrimages. The research and its publication is supported financially, with staff, and/or morally, especially by dioceses and archdioceses. Already, very early in the 20th century, that expressed itself in an emphasis on spiritual considerations, pilgrimage as spiritual experience, and the repression of popular cultural elements.[123]

In Germany almost all of the publications appeared with support, financial or in personnel, from German dioceses. For the most part, the

[120] Bujak & Young (1976); Bangó (1979).

[121] Several examples: Fischer & Stoll (1977/1982); Utz (1981); Läpple (1982); Macher (1981); Schroubek (1985); Wynands (1986); Casel & Steil (1987); Plechl (1988); Brems (1988); Brückner (1989); Pfister & Ramish (1989); Brommer (1990); *Zu Fuss, zu Pferd* (1990); Oberhauser (1992).

[122] See footnotes 9, 129 and 131.

[123] See, for instance, the work compiled by Bishop Christian Schreiber: Schreiber (1928).

authors there also come from clerical circles. This has, in part, resulted in great qualitative differences in the publications. Where the inventories in the archdioceses of Freiburg and the diocese of Aachen were organized in a reasonably scientific manner[124], the content of Schlafke's recent publication for Cologne is weak.[125] Like Pfister and Ramisch's book on the archdiocese of Munich and Freising, in this book the publication is legitimized by referring to the promotional efforts for the veneration of saints emanating from Pope John Paul II. That this is in practice chiefly the veneration of Mary can also be seen in Schlafke's work; it would appear from the major attention given to things Marian, and to sites favoured by the Pope, and the lesser attention for "volkstümliche" pilgrimage sites, that a strategic ecclesiastical choice has been made. The accompanying images reinforce this: there are a lot of quiet architectural studies, but in the full colour photographs there are hardly any expressions of popular devotion to be seen.

Another problem is the limitation imposed on a great number of publications because of economics and marketing principles. Because of the growing market fueled by cultural/historical interest, publishers of books on the subject of pilgrimage slant them strongly in the direction of architecture and art history. One sees that particularly in the more popular publications like the colourful diocesan guides to pilgrimage sites that have appeared in the *Grosser Kunstführer* series from Schnell & Steiner in Munich.[126] But Hansen's great guide to German pilgrimage sites also appeared in 1991 with the subtitle, *Ein Kunst- und Kulturführer*.[127] Such intentions however have the result that attention for Kult and Brauch, and the developmental history of the cultus remains very limited, while on the other hand attention for churches, chapels, altars, sculpture and such things is greater, in particular in the illustrative material. There is little or no case history analysis for each site.

3.3. Taking Stock

All in all, the balance that can be drawn up in the field of pilgrimage inventory and description at the moment is not positive. If we leave

[124] For Freiburg see note 96; for Aachen see WYNANDS (1986).
[125] SCHLAFKE (1989).
[126] FISCHER-WOLPERT (1983); JÖCKLE & GRAMER (1983); see also HOTZ (1983).
[127] HANSEN (1991).

aside works from the Counter Reformation, catalogues of pilgrimage sites only really took shape in the 19th century. They are then shaped by official, ecclesiastical attitudes. On the one hand, they supported the ongoing devotional offensive, and on the other, they formed a legitimation for the pilgrimages which were being revived on all sides. Only at the beginning of the 20th century does a scientific approach have a chance, especially with the *Volkskunde-Atlas* projects in German-speaking countries, The Netherlands and Belgium, although there was a strong emphasis on "healing saints." After the Second World War the inventorying of pilgrimage sites found itself in a broader scientific context. But the ambitious (too ambitious?) projects ground to a halt because of insufficient theoretical foundations and financial problems. The gap which was in part created by this certainly did provide room for dozens of inventories of pilgrimage sites, many commercial, and most of them at a superficial level and often organized from an ecclesiastical perspective in which there was, for instance, no room for "unofficial" devotions. Moreover, this pilgrimage research, even that in folkloristic circles, generally did not run right up to the present day, which means that it is of limited value for social-scientific investigations, for instance.

The following scheme for an inventory of Dutch pilgrimage sites – without any influence on its content from either clerical or market/economic forces – has been drawn up on the basis of the conclusions from the preceding historiographic survey, and the acquaintance it provides with the problems which have confronted individual inventory projects, to enable it to meet the demands of modern scientific research.

4. The Places of Pilgrimage in the Netherlands (BiN) Project

In 1992 it was decided to devote one of the three new lexicographical and data base projects at the P.J. Meertens Institute in Amsterdam – a research institute of the Royal Academy of Sciences and Arts – to the yet almost unexplored field of cataloging and describing pilgrimage sites in The Netherlands. The goal of the project was to be the compilation of an up-to-date data base and the publication of a multi-volume lexicon with descriptions of all historic and modern Dutch pilgrimage sites.

The quality of such a scientific project is to an important degree determined by definitions and specifications that are as clear as possible. It is precisely such inventory projects that run the risk, by not being clear about what does and does not belong in their field of investigation, of becoming imbalanced. In addition to discussing the concepts to be employed, in the following section we will discuss the geographical and chronological perimeters and religious range of the project. That all this is not a simple matter can be seen from the fact that definitions and specifications are still the subject of study, and as a consequence are not entirely settled. This chapter is a presentation of the project, and is particularly situated in the development of multidisciplinary pilgrimage research as that has been sketched out here: going first from analysis to inventory, and subsequently again arriving at a new analysis from the inventorization.[128]

4.1. The Concept "Place of Pilgrimage"

The point of departure for the BiN project are places of pilgrimage ("bedevaartplaatsen"), and the pilgrimages which are directly connected with them. In vernacular Dutch, the terms "pelgrimsoord" and "pelgrimages" are also used for these. There has already been a considerable discussion in Dutch sources about the distinctions between "bedevaart" and "pelgrimage." We do not have to repeat that discussion here, since Berbée has presented a clear and adequate summary of the differences in meaning.[129] Aside from urging that the difference in meaning be kept in mind, there is in fact no classical "pelgrimage" or "pelgrimsoord" within Dutch territory[130], so our further discussion here will relate only to "bedevaart" and "bedevaartplaatsen."

The "place" is primary in the project, and the pilgrimage as an act is derivative. In the literature – and certainly in foreign literature – there are likewise various terms used for what Dutch terms a "bedevaartplaats." Therefore the definition of this concept is generally far from clear. One time the pilgrimages (individual or group) to the site will be the point of reference, and another time the holy place itself, but there is also the attempt to encompass the nature of the site of worship and pilgrimage in the language used.

[128] See now the Introduction in MARGRY & CASPERS (1997); see also our note 1.

[129] BERBÉE (1986); (1987).

[130] Thus this does not include journeys which could be considered "pelgrimages," made by persons who travel *from* The Netherlands through the Christian world *to* the Holy Land, Rome or Santiago de Compostela, for instance.

To some degree this coincides with the discussions that are ongoing over, on one side, Turner's *communitas* thesis and on the other the German controversy over the question of whether pilgrimage must always be viewed in a group context, or whether what happens on an individual basis can also be characterized as pilgrimage.[131] According to the "Würzburger Begriffsdiktatur" one cannot speak of a place of pilgrimage in a case where only individuals come to worship. This standpoint has later been adequately contested.[132] Although the question served a good purpose in stimulating the discussion of pilgrimage, it in fact was a tempest in a teacup, a sort of misunderstanding with regard to the specific meaning in Franken of the questionable word *Wallfahrt*.[133]

For obtaining a picture of the culture of pilgrimage, it is clearer to take the cult object and the whole holy place or sacred space – the place of pilgrimage – as the point of departure, than (as was often the case in Germany) the act of pilgrimage, whether group or individual. The pilgrimage forms only one component of the whole cultus; the holy place itself is after all the centre around which all rotates.[134] In this, we are taking a position diametrically opposed to that of Morinis, who considers the holy place itself, or the goal of pilgrimage in general, is subordinate to the journey which must be undertaken to reach it.[135] The impression exists that in Morinis too the classical (and possibly non-Christian) "pilgrimage" perspective has the upper hand. In opposition to this, for research the anthropologists Eade and Sallnow attach importance to the central holy place.[136]

As a rule, places of pilgrimage are coupled with the veneration of saints or relics. It is not, however, always the case that devotions to saints or relics are indicators of the existence of pilgrimage and pilgrimage sites. There is absolutely no equivalence to be drawn with the devotion to saints in general which is stimulated by the Church and sanctioned through the list of canonized saints and beatified individuals. The forms

[131] See Kriss (1963); Dünninger (1963).

[132] Brückner (1970) and Hartinger (1992) 99-101.

[133] "Wallfahrt" there has the meaning of a processional pilgrimage conducted by a group, and not of a pilgrimage carried out by an individual.

[134] See Post (1988b) 6ff and Hartinger (1992) 102. This is not to say that the activity of pilgrimage itself cannot be taken as a subject: see, for instance, Baumer (1977).

[135] Morinis (1992) 14.

[136] The pilgrimage site is "the very *raison d'être* of pilgrimage, the notion of a holy place;" see Eade & Sallnow (1991) 6-16.

of veneration for saints (often national saints) or holy days (for instance Corpus Christi) prescribed in the cycle of the liturgical calendar certainly can not be reckoned as devotions such as are customary in pilgrimage sites, because of the lack of a tradition of a specific devotion connected to a particular place. By definition, such devotions, and also the daily, private devotions before the image of a saint, or at a Marian chapel or Lourdes grotto, fall outside of the field of investigation for the Dutch inventory project, as they do not necessarily indicate a place of pilgrimage. Devotion to a saint, or the holiness of a place are thus not absolute elements for determining whether a certain place is a pilgrimage site. What then distinguishes a pilgrimage site from the place or location where only the simple adoration of a saint or relic, not connected with pilgrimage, takes place?

The Roman Catholic Church itself does not recognize the existence of "pilgrimage sites;" so far as the Church is concerned, there are only places which are "holy." For this reason, pilgrimage research often speaks of "holy places." In canon 1205 of the new *Codex Iuris Canonici* holy places are defined as places which, through consecration or blessing have been set apart for the celebration of worship or for the burial of the faithful. Among the places which fulfill this definition for the Roman Catholic Church are churches, chapels and private chapels, altars, church yards and cemeteries and shrines (*sanctuaria*).[137] Thus the definition of a "holy place" is wider than that of what we consider a "place of pilgrimage." As used in present Church law, the concept of *sanctuarium*, the shrine which a church or other holy place can be, comes closest to what we understand by "pilgrimage site." The *Codex* of 1983 lists the requirements for a "shrine" (in the sense of a place of pilgrimage) as follows[138]: it must attract numerous believers, for the particular reason of piety, and, in the case of a new shrine, have the approval of Church authorities. For the rest, the concept of *sanctuarium* has passed through a process of development, and was only introduced by the Church as a new definition for a pilgrimage site during the course of the 18th and 19th century.[139] These aspects can be used as a starting point for our definition process, but they are not satisfactory, since they require the fulfillment of a modern definition laid down by the Church itself, in

[137] *Codex Iuris Canonici* [CIC] (1983) can. 1205-1243: "De Locis sacris." See now: VAN DE WIEL (1995).

[138] *CIC*, can. 1230; CARLEN (1987) 46-47.

[139] See CARLEN (1987) 45.

which the place of pilgrimage must meet a number of strict conditions set by the Church. For the purposes of the BiN project, this makes the terms "holy place" or "shrine" on the one hand too wide, and on the other hand too limited, and therefore unsuitable.[140]

No unequivocal terminological canon exists for scientific pilgrimage research. In Germany and Austria it is only in the past few years that "Orte" has come to replace "Fahrten" as the express focus of attention. There too scholars were seeking suitable terms, but for the most part they spoke only of *Wallfahrten* and they refrained from using the term *Wallfahrtsorte.* In the pilgrimage literature there, in addition to the concept of pilgrimage site (*Wallfahrtsort*) one encounters diverse other terms such as sanctuary (*Heiligtum*), cultic site (*Kultstätte*[141]), place of grace (*Gnadestätte*) and devotional site (*Andachtsstätte*). These are terms which were incorporated into pilgrimage research in the 19th century in German-speaking lands, and still exert a powerful influence.[142] In French scholars speak of *lieu cultuel* or *lieu de pèlerinage*, but most frequently use *sanctuaire*; in English "place of pilgrimage," "sanctuary" or "shrine" are used, while anthropologists often have a preference for the more general *lieu sacré* or "holy place." The variation in terms still creates confusion because various inventories divide pilgrimage sites into diverse categories without giving any further definitions.[143]

140 For that matter, *loca sancta*, in its historic Christian sense, as used to characterize the authentic religious sites in the Holy Land and surrounding areas and in Rome, is of equally little use as a term for a pilgrimage site. See MARAVAL (1985). This involves a catalogue of the holy places in the Byzantine section of the Roman Empire, compiled on the basis of contemporary pilgrims' accounts and guides and classical historical sources.

141 The distinction that is made in Germany between *Primär- und Sekundärkulte* (see: DÖRING (1982) is not meaningfully applicable. After all, the "second tier" pilgrimage sites thus characterized, that function as substitute "daughter" sites for important existing places of pilgrimage such as Our Lady of Banneux, Lourdes, Fátima, La Salette, etc., are nothing more than an individual object of adoration, or grow up into a pilgrimage site with its own status and tradition, in the way that in the past the spread of the adoration of Cornelius from Kornelimünster led to the rise of new places of pilgrimage.

142 See, for instance, HERCHENBACH (893).

143 Brückner too found that the terms "grundsätzliche Klärung bedürfen," but he and his colleagues in Bavaria never got around to that. They fell back on old definitions, as in the case of "Gnadenbild," which was designated as "Jenes Kultbild das – wie man im Barok sagte – sich als Wundertätig erwiesen hat." They also fell back on "Gnadenstätten" and "Kultstätten" in place of the general term Wallfahrtsätten in order not to exclude "Kleinkultstätten;" in principle, they wished to include everything that deviated from the normal ("kirchlich liturgische") cultus (see the files "Wallfahrtinventarisation," Institut für Deutsche Philologie, Würzburg).

Particularly in the German terms, the topographic distinction is clear: site or place. That indicates that a specific location is being distinguished. The veneration must be more or less connected with a definite place. Things become more difficult when we look at the other distinguishing terms in the definitions: pilgrimage, holy, cult, grace and devotion. These are all terms which express that which can happen at such a place, in a religious (and specifically Christian) sense: pilgrims come to it, the place is considered as "holy," a cultus can be identified, people can "find" grace and "perform" devotions. The terms are not, however, interchangeable among themselves. As we have already said, more places than cultic sites can be holy; there are many more cultic sites than those to which pilgrims come; while places of grace are still more difficult to define, because that is a subjective term. It is impossible to objectively define what a person experiences as grace. Devotion or pious godliness is, once again, a phenomenon which is found very widely within the normal religious actions of believers.[144] Just as grace can be experienced at other locations besides pilgrimage sites, devotion can take place anywhere. Thus the terms *Gnade-* and *Kultstätte* can also include many more places than pilgrimage sites.

Because of its provisional character, in the Würzburg *Kultstätten-Kurzkataloge* of 1982 the compilers did not feel up to the task of classifying the pilgrimage sites generally under "Wallfahrtsorte," but under the broader "Kult- und Andachtsstätten."[145] Nevertheless they considered *Kultstätte* analogous to *Wallfahrtsstätte* in the narrower meaning, and *Kultort* to *Wallfahrtsort* in the broader. This meant that at one *Ort* (place in the sense of location, a city or town) there could be more than one *Stätten* (place, in the sense of a specific holy place). The same parallel can be seen in The Netherlands: here there can also be multiple places of worship or holy places within the confines of a pilgrimage site or location. This, now, is how we will understand "pilgrimage site:" as the geographically more or less separate sacred space, within which one or more devotional cults take shape.[146] At the same time we opt unambiguously for the term "pilgrimage site" rather than "holy place," or any other term which would have a less clear connotation.

[144] Regarding the problems surrounding these terms, see: DAXELMÜLLER (1988).

[145] DÖRING (1982) 9.

[146] For the sake of clarity, descriptions of the various cult sites located at one pilgrimage site will be handled separately, each under its own name. In everyday speech, however, the name of the village or city is often used to designate the pilgrimage site itself, the sacred space of worship.

4.2. The "Boundary Crossing" Element

Before giving the working definition of a pilgrimage site that we intend to employ in the Dutch inventory project, the transitional aspect of pilgrimage, the degree to which it involves stepping outside boundaries, briefly demands our attention. Pilgrimage is characterized by a devotional going and returning, a "re-placing." The re-placing can not be understood in the limited meaning which Morinis grants it. As we saw, in his view "pilgrimage" can be reduced to only the journey or trip. There is, however, a very serious question whether the "journey" is really the defining element. Rather one can follow Kötting, for whom these essential, successive aspects define a pilgrimage: the leaving of one's own parish, consciously going to a holy place or object of a cultus possessing particular grace, followed by a return home.[147] Although in this description of the "boundary crossing" element, "parish," with its strong ecclesiastical connotations, perhaps could better be replaced by "one's own local environment," a sufficient beginning has already been made here at relativizing the element of journeying.[148] The pilgrimage site is absolutely central, and the likewise distinctive and determinative element of going and returning has its place within it.

4.3. Working Definition

For an institutionalized cultus to be considered as a place of pilgrimage, within the context of the organized BiN project, it must fulfill a number of conditions. In summary, the characteristics to be employed, both more spacious and more specific than has been usual to date, are as follows:

- There is evidence of a tradition, whether continuous or not, of devotional acts which are specifically connected with a particular cult object (a saint or image thereof, relic, spring, other object or a remembered element, as, for instance, a miracle or legend).

[147] KÖTTING (1950) 11.

[148] In judgements about a pilgrimage site, one must take into account the fact that, in addition to pilgrims, there can also be many persons who do not leave their home parish, or their own doorstep, to participate in the cultus. This is not a relatively new element in pilgrimage culture, but something that, it has recently been established, also was true for the Middle Ages (see: VERHOEVEN (1992) 123-126). In fact, the community of pilgrims seems almost always to be a combination of persons from both the local area and outside it. The social circumstances and sensitivity to fluctuations of pilgrimage

- The cultus is connected with a specific, more or less permanent[149] location, or better, a sacred cultic space[150], in which, in the opinion of the visitor, blessing and grace are more present than in other places, whether these other places are consecrated or not.
- Religious feeling is the inspiration for the pattern of acts performed by the visitor at the place.[151]
- There is evidence that the veneration is ritually rooted in time and space, for instance being expressed on particular holy days and specifically connected ritually with worship.[152]
- People come to the place regularly, whether individually or in groups.[153]
- Among these visitors, there must be those whose pattern of religious behaviour displays aspects which are transitional or otherwise transcend conventional boundaries.[154]

sites is accompanied by the fact that places with a broadly spread aura can change into almost entirely local devotions. Likewise it often happens that more or less consciously established devotions have been able to develop into little more than a local cultus. In practice, though, it appears that both forms of cultic practice still continue to be called, and experienced as, real places of pilgrimage.

149 This is linked with the dynamic of localization for places of pilgrimage; because of political or religious reasons, places of pilgrimage sometimes have been transferred to new locations.

150 "Space" is the better term, because on pilgrimage days, for instance, spatial modifications are often introduced into the church, or the cultic space is enlarged to include an area outside the chapel or church (other connected chapels, crosses, processional parks, shops). In the case of larger pilgrimage sites, the pilgrimage space is often permanently separated from its surroundings; on this, see POST (1989b); (1990c).

151 This does not say that there are not visitors who come to a pilgrimage site because of other, and/or subsidiary motivations; the chief motivation, however, should be religious; on this, see PIEPER, POST & VAN UDEN (1990) 194-199 [in this book: Chapter 1]. The chief non-religious factors appear to be recreation (tourism), social motivations (going with others), accompaniment (helping or assisting someone) or curiosity. For the patterns of actions, see BAUMER (1977).

152 Often there is evidence of institutionalization of the devotion by means of confraternities, the printing of special pictures or booklets, and announcement of the pilgrimage by means of posters and articles in the media.

153 Although possibly an unnecessary addition, this has still been included here because of the discussions which have been carried on around definitions. The ritual aspect of the veneration in fact also implies that as a rule pilgrims will come at least once a year, and often on one or more special feast days as well. Apart from that, a fixed day is not strictly necessary: compare BENSA (1978) 9, who suggests that in addition to a ritualized devotion and specific place, a fixed date is also necessary for a devotional cult.

154 This is meant in the sense used by Van Gennep, and thus is related to the "liminal" and "liminoid" from Turner's terminology; see TURNER (1969).

In summary, a pilgrimage site is characterized by veneration of a cult object, as performed by religiously inspired persons and defined through a particular or ritualized devotional tradition, and for which the persons involved have undertaken a specific "journey" at a particular time and to a particular, fixed location, which, through custom and devotion, has come to be considered as sacred.

4.4. Geographic Limits

It has been decided that the project will describe places of pilgrimage in The Netherlands. Given that the approach of European ethnology plays an important role in the research, the primary choice has been to observe the current national boundaries as the geographical limits for the present. By choosing the modern boundaries, the project also links up with comparable research and inventory projects in other countries. From practical considerations and to simplify cooperation with other academic disciplines, as a rule the present national boundaries are also projected into the past. For The Netherlands, this choice has quite a few consequences, in view of the fact that through the Middle Ages and during the *Ancien Régime* the country has undergone considerable changes in its size and the location of its borders. In relation to pilgrimage sites, this factor is still more serious because religious developments in Dutch history led to the removal of pilgrimage shrines to beyond the national boundaries. Because of this peculiar situation, which has fundamentally influenced pilgrimage practices in areas along the borders, it was decided that the historical situation could not be ignored. This means that pilgrimage sites that were previously within the Northern Netherlands, and places that have arisen just over the borders and, so far as the nationality of the pilgrims is concerned, are "fed" primarily from The Netherlands, are also to be included in the project. These pilgrimages to foreign pilgrimage sites, which literally cross borders but fall within the historically determined Dutch "Kultraum," will be listed along with the adjoining Dutch province.[155] Now that the outer boundaries have been indicated, the internal boundaries can be determined.

[155] There is presently consideration being given to including, in the form of an appendix, an enumerative description of the more important, further distant foreign places of pilgrimage that are regularly visited by Dutch pilgrims, such as, for instance, Banneux, Beauraing, Scherpenheuvel, Lourdes, Rome, Jerusalem, Fátima, Santiago de Compostela, Medjugorje, etc.

The places of pilgrimage will not be dealt with alphabetically for the entire country, but separated in three parts: the North and central provinces (1), Noord-Brabant (2) and Limburg (3).[156] This has the advantages of doing greater justice to regional diversity, and of making it easier to consult and compare the data by region. Arrangement according to diocesan boundaries in The Netherlands, such has generally been the practice for Germany, was considered and rejected. The advantages which might accompany such a division (for instance, the distribution of devotional cults by diocese) make little sense here, because the present diocesan lines are relatively new and, moreover, are little known.

4.5. Religious Limits

A "pilgrimage" is a religious (or at least semi-religious) act by a person or group of persons for the purpose of venerating a person or object, and is to be encountered in almost every culture around the world. A place is included here as a pilgrimage site when the pilgrims come to it with a *religiously inspired* devotion for the person or object venerated at the holy place, in the course of which a specific pattern of acts (whether or not a formal ritual) is carried out. It is not yet certain whether we must add the condition that this veneration must stand within the Christian tradition. The understanding of non-Christian devotional locations, such as, for instance, the grave of Comenius in Naarden or the memorial garden for the Bijlmer airplane disaster, is still so limited that the consequences, practical and otherwise, of employing the more open definition are not yet clear.

The distinguishing criterion is, in the first place, to be found in the phrase "religiously inspired," which by definition excludes secular "hero worship" or the particular veneration of writers, sports heros or media stars[157], because in general these lack a religious motivation and a definite location for the adoration determined by tradition. In practice, this will mean that in Europe, and particularly in The Netherlands, the vast

[156] Volume 1 appeared in December 1997; volumes 2 and 3 are planned for 1998 and 1999.

[157] In this, we are not saying that the religious, or semi-religious, plays no role among the practitioners of pop music and their admirers; see: B. VAN DE KAMP: Wat heeft rock & roll toch met religie?, in *Oor* nr. 25/26 (december 1993) 4-7. See now: J. KOENOT: *Voorbij de woorden. Essay over rock, cultuur en religie* (Averbode/Baarn 1996).

majority of pilgrimage sites and devotions will fall within the religious framework of the Roman Catholic Church. Naturally, cults of veneration inspired by the (Eastern) Orthodox Churches, the Protestant tradition and Judaism are by definition within the scope of the project, as elsewhere in Europe Protestant pilgrimages have been identified and described, but there are few if any of these in the Netherlands.

As has been said above, the decision to include a place in the listing is *not* dependent on ecclesiastical approval or disapproval of the devotion or of its status as a pilgrimage site. The formal canonization or beatification of the person venerated, the authentication of the relic, or the authenticity of the miraculous occurrences are likewise not conditions. For the sake of scientific completeness, inclusion of pilgrimage sites which are not officially acknowledged is not an option. Moreover, such pilgrimage sites are at least as important, if not more important, for a thorough analysis of the dynamics of the culture of pilgrimage.

4.6. Limits Regarding Date

The point of departure for this project is to include all the places of pilgrimage which can be traced since the introduction of Christianity in The Netherlands. This means that in regard to time, the choice has been made not to set any limit with respect to the present. On the contrary, from the ethnological perspective it is necessary to describe all modern, active places of pilgrimage. From a strictly historical perspective the omission of pilgrimage sites which no longer exist would be unacceptable, not only because of the possibility for comparative investigations with other countries, but moreover because of the peculiar religious/ecclesiastical development of The Netherlands, and with it, also, of the practice of pilgrimage. Pre-Christian cults, such as may have been practiced among the Roman or Germanic population, thus fall outside the perimeters of the project.

4.7. Tracing and Handling Places of Pilgrimage

After definitional questions, the next necessary step in the project is to arrive at a complete survey of all pilgrimage sites which have ever existed in The Netherlands. For this purpose, already existing surveys of pilgrimage sites are being used, various data banks consulted, and a large number of local studies examined, and, finally, in October 1993 a double questionnaire[158] was sent to parishes and cloisters, and historical associations and local history societies in The Netherlands. By these means, an almost complete survey of pilgrimage sites can be compiled for modern times.

The Middle Ages is the period which will pose the most problems. It will not be possible to assemble a complete list of pilgrimage sites for that era, on the one hand because of the lack of sources, which will mean that many cult devotions will have dropped from sight, and on the other hand because sources in this field often provide information that is unclear, making it difficult to establish whether one is dealing with a *pilgrimage* site.[159] In almost every chapel and church votive offerings and candles were presented before the image of a saint, and other rituals connected with pilgrimage were practiced. For this period, therefore, supplementary research in various published and archival sources and collections of cultural artifacts (badges, medals, *insignia*) will have to be done.[160] Not only for the Middle Ages, but also for the 17th and 18th century, one must exercise caution with regard to reports of pilgrimages. It is precisely in the sources from the Protestant side that "devotions" are often stereotypically characterized as "pilgrimages."

After after the round of research, a rough list comprising about 900 places of pilgrimage has been reduced to 650. A complete, definitive list of places will never be able to be obtained; not only are the Middle Ages only comprehensible in part, but also at a later date certain devotions, for whatever reason, remain hidden from view. None the less, the vast majority of Dutch places of pilgrimage will be able to be described.

4.8. Perspectives

In 1999, the results of the BiN project must be recorded in a three-volume reference work, and be available for research at the Meertens Institute in the form of a realizable electronic data bank and a physical documentation and source collection. They will form the basis for further research in all relevant academic disciplines. It is our intention that, precisely through this bipartite arrangement, further investigations in

[158] "Volkskunde" Questionnaire No. 64 A+B "Bedevaartplaatsen en bedevaarten": Department of European ethnology, Meertens-Institute, Amsterdam).

[159] For the problems and limits of research in this period, see: Dünninger in BRÜCKNER (1982) 177-178.

[160] For the methods to be used in this, see DAXELMÜLLER & THOMSEN (1978) passim.

the field of the culture of pilgrimage, ritual conduct, and also the history of religion and religious popular culture can be stimulated, and the BiN should generate innovative and well-grounded research conclusions. It will make it possible, for instance, to pose questions and perform research diachronically and synchronically, which will permit greater insight into the typologies of cultus and pilgrimage. For this, the strict approach from the perspective of the place of pilgrimage, rather than pilgrimage itself, will offer still greater clarity. The inclusion of modern pilgrimage culture will give the whole an added value, especially for disciplines such as anthropology, European ethnology, theology and ritual and religious studies.

In short, as far as we are concerned, there is no crisis in research. The time is now ripe to fill lacunae in the knowledge of Dutch pilgrimage culture, and thereby promote reinvigorated analytical, diachronic and comparative research. We hope that BiN can begin to provide an important contribution to a stimulating new "pilgrimage agenda" for those working in cultural studies.

3. "GOD ISN'T CONCERNED WITH TRIVIAL DETAILS" OR, REREADING HOBSBAWM[1]

1. By Way of Introduction

Let us begin with the title. Please note, these words about the generous way that God considers things is not a theological or dogmatic pronouncement on my part. They appear in quotation marks, and come from the pen of the pastor at Dokkum. Before presenting the complete passage, which appeared as part of an ongoing controversy in regional newspapers in the northern Netherlands, it is necessary to briefly locate it within its context. This is also done primarily to provide some empirical framework for my further, chiefly theoretical and methodological argument.

1.1. Growth of the Devotion Surrounding St. Boniface's Spring

The letter containing the statement from the pastor at Dokkum stems from 1990, the year of the summer in which Dokkum enjoyed an enormous and apparently sudden flowering as the city of St. Boniface.[2] At the end of the 1980's, within the context of the (to coin a term) "Dokkum promotion" interest was growing for the dilapidated devotional pilgrimage site that had arisen around what is called St. Boniface's Spring, just outside the town centre of Dokkum. This fine example of Roman Catholic devotional landscape dates from the 1920's and '30's, the golden age of the Catholic revival in The Netherlands. In part through the efforts of Titus Brandsma, who mobilized the Frisian clergy

[1] This Chapter is based on two articles: P. Post: "God kijkt niet op een vierkante meter..." of Hobsbawm herlezen, in C. van der Borgt, A. Hermans & H. Jacobs (eds.): *Constructie van het eigene. Culturele vormen van regionale identiteit in Nederland* (= Publikaties van het P.J. Meertens-Instituut, 25) (Amsterdam 1996) 175-200 and P. Post: Rituals and the Function of the Past: Rereading Eric Hobsbawm, in *Journal of Ritual Studies* 10,2 (1996 [1998]) 85-107. See also: P. Post: De creatie van traditie volgens Eric Hobsbawm, in *Jaarboek voor liturgie-onderzoek* 11 (1995) 77-101.

[2] Post (1993); (1997d); see also Chapter 4 and 12 in this book.

in the Frisian diaspora, the spring was the centre for a blooming pilgrimage site.

It is impossible to explore the rich annals of Dokkum as a place of pilgrimage in all their historical, cultural and social/economic complexity.[3] I would lift up one particular aspect, primarily to give some feeling for the waves of interest in the Boniface tradition at Dokkum. Interest in Boniface and Dokkum as a town has known periods of bloom and decline. After the mediaeval period, with a devotion which spread throughout The Netherlands and Germany immediately after Boniface's death, Boniface, along with many other "national" saints – Willibrord chief among them – was rediscovered by Sasbout Vosmeer's missionary Church in the 16th and 17th centuries during the "Dutch Mission." This occurred in a climate that Rogier characterized as being marked by the convergence of three factors: historical realization, national feeling and Catholic piety.[4] In the 19th century there were again initiatives surrounding Boniface and Dokkum between 1874 and 1882. Initially the impetus for these arose from Frisian clergy. In the 1920's and '30's, all this resulted in confraternities, infrastructure, and organized regional and national pilgrimages. As has been said, the Frisian clergy played the central role in this; the name of Titus Brandsma must particularly be mentioned in this regard.[5] The first bicycle pilgrimage to Dokkum took place in 1919. The first pilgrimage of Frisian priests to Dokkum was in 1924. In 1925 Titus Brandsma joined others in establishing the Confraternity of St. Boniface and His Companions, with the goal of "encouraging pilgrimages and the erection of a sanctuary and park by the spring," actually a "dobbe" or basin located outside the town centre. The first National Pilgrimage was in 1926 – the pilgrims were "delivered" by train – and in 1934 the memorial chapel was completed. The next high point was 1954, the 1200 year observance of the murder of Boniface and His Companions. Interest began to wane in the 1960's; the pilgrimage complex of park, stations of the cross and chapel became increasingly dilapidated, and the spring came under the care of the town's Parks Department and became polluted. The devotion to Boniface at Dokkum

[3] For the literature on this subject I refer the reader to an extensive bibliography in POST (1993) 242 note 4, supplemented by JELSMA (1973); VAN MOORSEL (1968); KINGMANS (1994). For insight into the complex function of miracles in this context, see also NIEUWLAND (1991). For a survey with bibliography see POST (1997d); cf. our note 1.

[4] ROGIER (1947) II, 763-767 and 773.

[5] See AUKES (1985). For a good contextual survey, see STRUYKER BOUDIER (1993).

was kept alive by a small group of conservative Catholics, who could count on the support of a core group of about 150 organizers and pilgrims at an annual Boniface anniversary service in August, entirely in Latin. Initiatives to engage in a "Dokkum promotion" got under way in the 1980's, coming from various groups. Boniface and the tradition of pilgrimage played a role in these. With the arrival of a new young pastor in 1984, the parish community once again turned its attention to the Boniface tradition and the material infrastructure. Cooperation with the conservative group who had led the tradition away on their own path during the lean years appeared impossible, and after 1985 the ritual Boniface repertoire was reborn from the parish and residents of Dokkum. The high point is the annual Boniface anniversary festival, now moved back to July again, now coupled with a youth day organized by the youth pastorate. A number of new initiatives came out of this context of renewed interest in Dokkum's Boniface tradition: the parish council provided for a first restoration of the deteriorating chapel, a permanent exhibition mounted on panels was placed in it, plans were laid to promote cultural tourism, and the regional museum began actively laying plans.

The floodgates were opened for this process of recovery through the miraculous healing of a little girl, Nefthys Brandsma (in point of fact, related to Titus), who on the afternoon of Sunday, July 29, 1990, seems to have suddenly have been cured of a stubborn pertussis after she was immersed in the spring. After notices appeared in the press, people from The Netherlands and foreign countries streamed in, and by his own admission, the pastor at Dokkum took on new duties. The town dredged the spring and restored the masonry along its sides. By now, upwards of 20,000 people from in and outside The Netherlands visit the spring each year, Boniface, his spring and his tradition stand have become the subject of abundant interest within the church and outside it, and the complex has since been entirely restored and refurnished, and some are talking about a "Lourdes of the north." Numerous celebrations and activities are organized around the spring every year, and the annual Boniface anniversary draws more than 1200 people.

Elsewhere I have presented a first analysis of the process alluded to,[6] in which a series of cultural circles, their interests and appropriations come together. Thus the parish and church have taken advantage of

[6] POST (1993) and Chapter 4 in this book.

civic efforts, while the local regional museum – not to forget local businessmen and the area's tourist industry – have benefitted from the church's work. Each group or circle has its own agenda, each interest will raise its profile by calling on the riches of the Boniface tradition: the local Roman Catholic parish community, the town of Dokkum, the regional museum with its young, energetic new director. The miracle is that they all join hands so harmoniously around the spring, the miracle and the pastor. All lay claim to the figure of the pastor, the tradition and the events in their own way.

1.2. Two Springs, One Controversy

In the midst of the harmony, however, there is one jarring note. This comes from what I might denote as the "scientific discourse." The regional archivist rose in revolt in the local, regional, and later national press: the rejuvenated Boniface tradition was connected with the wrong spring.[7] From his residence in Amersfoort, a former staff member of the National Institute for Archaeological Investigation, the archaeologist Dr. Herre Halbertsma, joined in the debate. He too is convinced that Catholics, following their emancipation in the last century, returned to the wrong place when they moved to restore the Boniface tradition to its full glory. On the basis of research in ancient records and archaeological test digs, Halbertsma and his supporters assume – apparently correctly – that the "real" spring of St. Boniface was not near the basin (a "Dobbe" in the local dialect), once the pond for a brewery, outside the town centre, but in the town centre itself, on the Market at the place where a small fountain now sometimes spouts tap water next to a small statue of the city's patron saint.[8] A controversy arose in the columns of various regional and national newspapers and magazines. Under the headline "Spring has nothing to do with Boniface," the fiercest and most extensive article appeared in the *Amersfoortse Courant* of August 23, 1990. Among other things, taking his lead from the immersion of Nefthys, the outraged Halbertsma writes there, "Those who know this streamlet in the middle of the Dokkum processional park from having seen it with their own eyes will shudder at the thought that anyone would have

[7] See H. PETERS (ed.): *Dossier "Rondom de Bonifatiusbron. Dokkum 1990-1991, deel 1"* (Dokkum 1993) (collection of press clippings) 69, 73, 79, 80, 81, 89, 93.

[8] See HALBERTSMA (1960/61). See also POST (1997d).

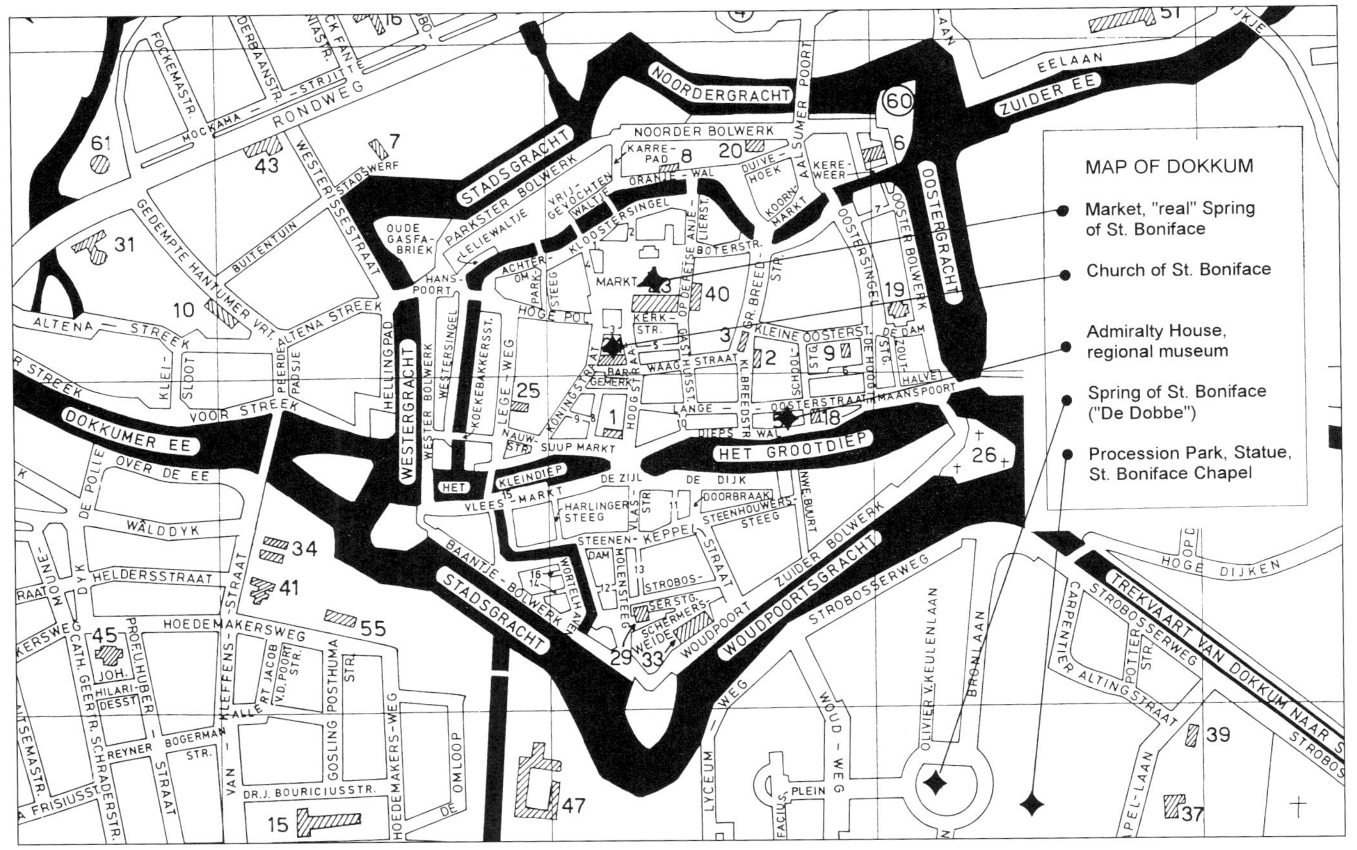
MAP OF DOKKUM
Market, "real" Spring of St. Boniface
Church of St. Boniface
Admiralty House, regional museum
Spring of St. Boniface ("De Dobbe")
Procession Park, Statue, St. Boniface Chapel
NOORDERGRACHT
ZUIDER EE
OOSTERGRACHT
STADSGRACHT
WESTERGRACHT
DOKKUMER EE
HET GROOTDIEP
WOUDPOORTSGRACHT
TREKVAART VAN DOKKUM NAAR

dared do this to a baby, and can only hope that the child's hacking cough has not been replaced by Friesland's specialty of the moment, brought in by diseased muskrats. Quite apart from whether they believe in Boniface miracles or not, Nefthys's God-fearing parents could have spared themselves the trouble of a pilgrimage, because the spring involved has nothing to do with Boniface himself." He subsequently supports this thesis with five columns of historical and archaeological data.

Now, with these introductory notes about Boniface and Dokkum under our belt, I can quote from the letter to the editor of August 30, 1990, from which I have taken my title. The pastor of Dokkum responds to Halbertsma, writing in the middle of the turbulent period in which the miracle is being appropriated by various groups and individuals. "Through his publications in various newspapers, Prof. Halbertsma tries to prove that "his" spring in the Market is the only real one... He has every right to do so. I detect in Dr. Halbertsma a strong sense of an academic scorned. It's a very human emotion. I can imagine feeling something like it myself. And it may well be true that his spring is *the* spring par excellence. But I can sense no feeling for faith and living tradition on his part, and based on his publications it would seem that dealing with people and their experiences is not precisely his strong suit. Seven stories have come in from people who have benefitted from a pilgrimage to the Spring of St. Boniface. I don't know what to think of this, can make no judgements about it, and my faith is not knowing for certain, but trusting, searching and fumbling. How God works in the midst of our human world remains in a large part a mystery; for the rest, I don't think that He is concerned with trivial details when it comes to keeping the tradition of St. Boniface alive."[9]

2. Statement of the Question and Aims: Invention of Tradition

Worship and tradition. Real and living tradition. Stories and history. Effective pilgrimage. Conflicting calls on the past. Science and faith. A flourishing cultus. A miracle. Identities. Two traditions about a spring. Falsification of history. But however we read and analyze the controversy

[9] Letter to the editor, Pastor H. Peters, dated August 30, 1990, in the *Nieuwe Dockumer Courant*, Publieke Tribune column.

from close up, it comes down to this: tradition and calling on the past are the pivotal issues, as is so often the case with developments in or revitalizations of celebrations.

I would now draw your attention to the fact that always, on every occasion on which I have presented the example of Dokkum in lectures, symposia or seminars, the term "invention of tradition" has almost immediately become part of the discussion.

Internationally, in works in the field of cultural studies, from the social sciences to historical research, one encounters the term "invention of tradition" with a certain regularity. By now the concept has become a dominant presence in studies devoted to the formation of theories concerning rituals[10], and in particular in studies which are concerned with the processes by which rituals change or with involvement with tradition and the past, or which are directed toward research into rites and folklorism or folklorization. From this broader context, "invention of tradition" has meanwhile also entered the domain of liturgical studies.[11]

In the terms "invention of tradition," "invented tradition" or "invented traditions," reference is made, explicitly or otherwise, to the collection *The Invention of Tradition*, edited by Hobsbawm and Ranger, which appeared in 1983.[12] One immediately recognizes and characterizes cases of change in rituals, or in which the context of rituals shifts, and particularly of the revitalization of rituals, as just so many examples of "invented tradition." Thus I connected examples of the renascence of liturgical and ritual devotions, such as the creation some years ago of an observance for St. Hubert in Muiderberg[13], with this concept.

In this chapter, I wish to set forth, within a short compass, several methodological and historiographic concerns regarding the use of the concept of "invented traditions."

Let me begin with a first observation. Upon deeper reflection – that is to say, after a rereading of Hobsbawm – it seems to me that the term, the concept of "invention of tradition" or "invented tradition" has become

[10] In this connection, I need name only: BELL (1992), in particular Part 6, 118ff; GRIMES (1993), in particular Chapter 1: Reinventing Ritual, 5-22; PLATVOET & VAN DER TOORN (1995), in particular the Introduction, 3-24, and PLATVOET: Ritual in plural and pluralist societies. Instruments for analysis, 25-51.

[11] See POST (1991b), especially pp. 104ff; (1991c); (1991d); FRIJHOFF (1991); WEGMAN (1994), especially p. 22; POST (1995d).

[12] HOBSBAWM & RANGER (1983).

[13] See POST (1991d).

rather far removed from its original setting and significance. I see two dimensions in this narrowing of use. It involves, on the one side, the thrust of unmasking or demythologizing, and on the other side on that of manipulation from above. In both cases, the emphasis is placed on "invented" or "invention," and not on the tradition or ritual, let alone on the functions and meanings of inventions of this sort. "Invention of tradition" thus receives a rather pejorative context, and was and is used to call up both the idea of artificially developed myths and the falsification of history, as well as that of manipulation. That is not real; this is absolutely not that old; we go scrounging around in history without any acquaintance with the real state of affairs; as in the Boniface cultus which has recently been reborn again in its full "traditional" (?) glory in Dokkum, people are going to the wrong place and flocking around the wrong spring. Many frankly admit to the pleasure they get from reading anthropologists, sociologists, European ethnologists, historians and theologians who unmask "invented traditions."[14]

The other aspect is that of manipulation. No, "invention of tradition" doesn't just happen; it is systematically directed from above, and the notion of a "plot" is called up, with all sorts of hidden, or open, agendas and strategies.

I will, for the time being, leave out of consideration other equally vague and associated forms of appropriation of Hobsbawm and Ranger's terminology, such as those generated when it coalesces with parallel and closely related established concepts such as mythologization, the process of creating mental images, folklorism/folklorization, revitalization, musealization, etc.[15]

[14] See FRIJHOFF (1991).

[15] For the diffuse usage of the "invention [of tradition]" terminology in the general sense, see the long tradition of the use of such "invention" terminology in French, German and English, among other languages, that runs through to this very day. I would distinguish three lines within it. First, there is a literal meaning ("The Invention of Printing," of eyeglasses, etc.). Subsequently, there is a more imaginative use ("L'invention de l'architecture Romane," du quotidien, etc.). One variation on this is again a more suggestive use such as has particularly occurred after and on the basis of Hobsbawm and Ranger's collection (for instance, R. WAGNER: *The Invention of Culture* (Chicago, 1981); W. SOLLORS (ed.): *The Invention of Ethnicity* (Oxford 1989); R. BENDIX: Tourism and Cultural Displays. Inventing Traditions for Whom?, in *Journal of American Folklore* 102,404 (1989) 131-146; LYNN HUNT (ed.): *The Invention of Pornography: Obscenity and the Origins of Modernity, 1500-1800* (New York: Zone Books 1993); P. BURKE: The Invention of Leisure in Early Modern Europe, in *Past and Present* 146 (1995) 136-150;

This leads me to the question: in using the terminology in this broad and quite generalized way, do we place ourselves in the tradition of the collection edited by Eric Hobsbawm and Terence Ranger, or could it be said that we are ourselves engaged in an academic/theoretical – to continue the pejorative use of the term which we have just sketched – "invention of tradition"? Rereading Hobsbawm brought me to the conclusion that we are often still only touching upon the surface of the term. But what of the content? I will make no secret of the fact that in my rereading of Hobsbawm is, to a large degree, self-critical[16], and to an important extent was inspired by a recent book by Catherine Bell, *Ritual Theory, Ritual Practice*, in which Hobsbawm's work is given a place in an unbiased way.[17]

3. Hobsbawm and Inventing Traditions

Rarely has an academic collection had such repercussions as *The Invention of Tradition*, which appeared in 1983 as the report of a symposium organized by the journal *Past and Present*, in the series *Past and Present*

see also l'invention de l'école, de l'Europe, du social, etc.). These three lines represent roughly the terrain which lies between the extremes of "create" and "invent/fabricate." In German-speaking areas, in ethnological circles writers often work with a sort of triple field of "Invention," "Innovation" and "Diffusion" which is used to typify processes of cultural change. In *Groniek. Historisch Tijdschrift* 124, March (1995), devoted to "national myths," M. Gijswijt-Hofstra speaks of the overlap and competition between the terms mythologization, conceptualization and "invented tradition" (see 35, note 1). In her opening paragraph about the myth of Dutch tolerance, she very correctly points out that demythologizing can not and may not be the only thing that historians have to worry about: they must also give attention to the development, use and functions of the myth (35). On this matter, see also Raedts (1990a), which, revised and enriched with references to the literature, also appeared as Raedts (1990b). See now Raedts (1995). Finally, it is also of interest to note the appearance of the term "reinvention": S. Wright: "Heritage" and Critical History in the Reinvention of Mining Festivals in North-east England, in Boissevain (1992) 20-42, and particularly the influential ethnological collection, Dell Hymes (ed.): *Reinventing Anthropology* (New York 1969). See also Chapter 1: Reinventing Ritual, in Grimes (1993) 5-22 and Gerholm (1988). In the context of of Hobsbawm's work in the field of economic and social history, also see in particular: G. Shackle: *The Years of High Theory: Invention and Tradition in Economic Thought 1926-1939* (Cambridge 1967).

[16] See Post (1991a).

[17] Bell (1992) especially Part 6, 118-168. She does, as so many others, however, consistently spell Hobsbawm as Hobsbawn.

Publications, from the Cambridge University Press, followed a year later by a paperback edition. The collection immediately ran through many reprintings. In retrospect, it was actually primarily its provision of the concept or model of "invention of tradition" to which so many people in so many places responded. That can be seen, for instance, in the fact that the book is cited only in general, or that citations are taken only from Hobsbawm's programmatic introduction. The other essays are seldom if ever quoted.[18]

The collection comprises seven essays. As noted, Hobsbawm provided a theoretical introduction on the concept of "inventing traditions," and a closing essay on "Mass-Producing Traditions in Europe, 1870-1914," which, along with the introduction, contains important theoretical contributions.[19] The other contributions are concerned with the appeal to the past and tradition-forming in national and regional contexts in Wales, Scotland, Victorian India and colonial Africa. The collection has about it a strongly British air, although Hobsbawm, in his own contributions, is also concerned with Switzerland, Germany and America. It is, I think, important to keep this context in mind, and particularly the orientation toward the process of nation-forming, a theme with which Hobsbawm occupied himself to an increasing degree after he became Professor Emeritus in 1982.

The other contributors are established scholars, all of whom present thought-provoking essays. Hugh Trevor-Roper's essay caused some stir in the historical world, and especially in circles dealing with Scottish studies. His central claim is that the whole concept of a distinct Highland culture and tradition is a retrospective innovation. Trevor-Roper deals with the roots of the Scottish identity and revival in the 18th and 19th centuries and reveals the fraudulent identity of clans and kilts. Some specialists, however, show that the reconstruction of the Highland tradition as simply an Irish overflow underestimates the autonomy of

[18] HOBSBAWM & RANGER (1983). Contents: E. HOBSBAWM: Introduction: Inventing Traditions, 1-14; H. TREVOR-ROPER: The Invention of Tradition: The Highland Tradition of Scotland, 15-42; P. MORGAN: From a Death to a View: The Hunt for the Welsh Past in the Romantic Period, 43-100; D. CANNADINE: The Context, Performance and Meaning of Ritual: the British Monarchy and the "Invention of Tradition", c. 1820-1977, 101-164; B.S. COHN: Representing Authority in British India, 165-210; T. RANGER: The Invention of Tradition in Colonial Africa, 211-262; E. HOBSBAWM: Mass-Producing Traditions: Europe, 1870-1914, 263-308.

[19] HOBSBAWM: Mass-Producing Traditions, 263-308; see especially Questions and Perspectives, Section IV, 303-308.

the Highland tradition and sets too much store on the romantic inventions.[20] Prys Morgan's essay deals in more or less the same way with the Welsh tradition. David Cannadine studies the royal ritual and traces a fundamental change in the public image of the British monarchy in the later Victorian period. Here, too, some reviews take a critical look at the highly selective and misleading use of the evidence.[21] Bernard S. Cohn and Terence Ranger focus on the image and adaptation of authority in British India and East Africa. Cohn shows how a European model and ritual is used in India. Ranger, co-editor of the collection of essays, who studied at the University of Oxford, and was professor of African and modern history at the University of Manchester in the years 1974-1987, is a specialist in race relations and noted authority on Africa. In his paper he demonstrates how in East Africa British authorities invented a native monarchical tradition.

The unity of the book depends highly on the British focus on the one hand and on the general concept of inventing traditions on the other. The essays by Trevor-Roper, Morgan, Cannadine, Cohn and Ranger are elaborate case studies, illustrations and applications of the new perspectives of the central concept of "inventing traditions." Only Hobsbawm deals with this general concept from the theoretical point of view. His introduction is not an introduction to the six essays, it is first of all an introduction of "inventing tradition."

For further consideration of the use and background of the concept of "invention of tradition," we are justified in first directing sole attention to Hobsbawm himself, as he determined the shape of the collection, and, specifically, worked out the theoretical background for the concept of "invention of tradition."

Eric Hobsbawm

On the face of it, it is, after all, somewhat surprising to note that the concept of invention of tradition only now is becoming connected with the figure of the British historian Eric John Ernest Hobsbawm (b. 1917).[22]

[20] R.E. QUINAULT, in *History. The Journal of the Historical Association* 69 (1984) 67. See also: R. NYE, in *The Journal of Modern History* 57 (1985) 720-722, esp. 720.

[21] R.F. QUINAULT, in *History. The Journal of the Historical Association* 69 (1984) 67.

[22] It is impossible here to give a full biographical and bibliographical overview of Hobsbawm and his work. Some data has been brought together in an appendix to this chapter. Through the remainder of this text, for complete bibliographical citations on Hobsbawm's work, the reader is referred to this appendix.

Particularly examining his rich oeuvre we can not other than remark that the collection in question from 1983 still stands somewhat alone among this works. Hobsbawm is especially an authority in the field of economic and social history, and is considered as a great authority on revolutionary movements in general, and Marxism in particular.

After a thesis on Fabianism (1950)[23], he specialized at King's College, Cambridge, in the history of revolutionary and social movements, particularly those of the 19th century. There are a number of dynamic lines in his work that we encounter again in the rubrics of the bibliographical survey that McClelland compiled for the period prior to April, 1982.[24] First and foremost is the current of large-scale synthetical projects.[25] Next to these stand monographs examining certain elements from economic and social history. Great Britain – the monarchy! – in the 19th and 20th century, and what is termed *unofficial history* are central in these (*Primitive Rebels*, 1959; *Bandits*, 1969). Third, there are his often very deeply engaged political essays and lectures.[26] Fourth, there are the collections, lectures and essays on themes or subthemes, often starting from one of the main themes discussed above, which he explores through lectures, seminars or workshops. Reference must here be made to, among others, physical culture, sexuality, agrarian history and, particularly also in the period of *Invention of Tradition*, the process by which nations are formed, nationalism and the ritual processes which accompany it – although the theme of nation-forming can also be accounted among his principle themes.[27]

All in all, a certain development can be seen in his work, from economic to social history. Although his work is not characterized by excessive or explicit interest in theory and method, a familiar characteristic of

[23] HOBSBAWM (1950).

[24] See the appendix with numerous publications.

[25] HOBSBAWM (1962), (1975), (1987); among his "classics" are (1959), (1964), (1969), (1973), and (1990). See further the appendix. See now also: (1994) and (1997).

[26] See his great project concerning the history of Marxism produced in Italy: *Storia del marxismo*, I-V (Turin 1978-1982) (English editions, Brighton and University of Indiana Press, Bloomington). In this connection, see also his involvement with *History Workshop*, where not only "innovative" historians but particularly also engaged (socialist and feminist) researchers sought and found a platform. In the meantime, *History Workshop*, which in 1982 changed its subtitle from *Journal for Socialist Historians* to *Journal of Socialist and Feminist Historians*, has grown into a renowned historical journal published by the Oxford University Press.

[27] See HOBSBAWM (1990).

Anglo-Saxon practice of history, it is still striking how, with a certain regularity, reflections on methodological and historiographic aspects do appear in his oeuvre.[28] It is also striking that in work which does not bear the immediate stamp of social-economic history, he brings in numerical data with certain zeal, as can be seen, for instance, in the closing article in the *Invention of Tradition* collection.[29]

Considered against this background, the collection which he compiled together with Ranger seems somewhat peripheral to his work. I would, however, want to somewhat put this impression into perspective – a nuance which is also exemplified in the title of a second festschrift presented to him in 1984, *The Power of the Past*. As it happens, through the notion of the ways in which we call upon tradition and how we involve ourselves with the past, and the functions of that involvement, there certainly is a connection with the main current of economic and social-historical concerns in Hobsbawm's work, and with the subthemes such as revolutionary and other movements for change, nation-forming, nationalism and identity which we have already enumerated.[30] In this connection, I would also suggest that we must pay particular attention to the conference, "The Sense of the Past and History," organized in 1970 by *Past and Present*. There Hobsbawm presented a paper on the social function of the past. To my mind, this paper, as it was published two years later in *Past and Present*, contains the outline of that which he more than ten years later would bring together under the nomenclature of "invention of tradition." It would decidedly be worth the effort to lay this paper, in which the term "tradition" has yet almost no role at all to play[31], next to Hobsbawm's contribution to the 1983 collection, and to consider, for instance, how in 1970-72, in the context of questions and

[28] See, for instance, HOBSBAWM (1971) and (1972). Often these reflections on methods of the practice of history occur indirectly, in reaction to new developments and books. It was in this way, for instance, that he considered the ideas of the *Annales*. See the appendix, the first rubric from McClelland. See now also: (1997).

[29] See HOBSBAWM: Mass-Producing Traditions, with its numerical data concerning sport and postage stamps, among other topics (Table 1, p. 281, "Historical stamps before 1914"; nota bene: a similar use of postage stamps as data is to be found in Frijhoff's essay, FRIJHOFF (1991) 128ff. For this quantifying conception, see also HOBSBAWM: Mass-Producing Traditions, 294, 296, 298.

[30] See HOBSBAWM (1990) and (1972), and the appendix.

[31] In HOBSBAWM (1972), "tradition" and "traditional" are primarily used as adjectives to characterize forms of social organization, i.e., "tradition-bound and ritualized societies," or "traditional society." See particularly 4ff.

notes about processes of social change and the appeal to the past, through the triad of "innovation." "restoration" and "fabricated history," the roots of the body of ideas which he later would bring together around the concept of "invention of tradition" were laid.[32] Within the compass of this chapter, however, I can only point others toward this task and encourage that it be undertaken.

Hobsbawm stands in the tradition of Anglo-Saxon "social history," as it has been shaped, and is still being shaped from Oxford and Cambridge, in the journal *Past and Present*, among others. Elsewhere, in a wholly different connection, I have tried to give a sketch of this tradition through the figure of John Bossy.[33] I see undeniable parallels between Hobsbawm and Bossy: apart from the important platform of the influential journal *Past and Present*, I am thinking of the great power at synthesis (see Bossy's great work on the history of English Catholicism[34]) they share, the breadth and innovative character of their œuvres, but also of their being completely rooted and remaining in the Anglo-Saxon tradition of research. One would seek in vain for great inter- or multidisciplinary awareness in Hobsbawm, at least explicitly. One look at his footnotes is sufficient. This is all the more telling if we realize that the collection *The Invention of Tradition* appeared at the moment when the debate around what is termed "folklorism," or culture in tension between tradition and modernity, was raging in German cultural studies.[35] Only one older study in European ethnology (by Braun, from 1965) is cited by Hobsbawm in this connection.[36]

Although he had, as was already indicated in 1970-72, previously somewhat explored the territory from his enormous familiarity with the sources and knowledge of the period – the 18th, 19th and early 20th century – he still was entering into relatively new terrain, as he had done elsewhere the research fields of iconography and gender, for instance.[37] In this case he directed his attention to rituals and symbolism, among other topics, and thus entered the terrain of "ritual studies" with its key

[32] See HOBSBAWM (1972), particularly Sections II (6ff) and III (10ff).

[33] POST (1990a) and (1990b).

[34] BOSSY (1975).

[35] Of the extensive literature concerning folklorism/folklorization, revitalization, etc., I will here list only SALOMONSSON (1984); ASSION (1986); BAUSINGER (1988); VAN DER KOOI (1990); BAUSINGER (1991); KÖSTLIN (1991); NISSEN (1994); POST (1995b).

[36] BRAUN (1965). See HOBSBAWM: Introduction, 6ff.

[37] See, for instance, HOBSBAWM (1978).

concepts such as tradition, continuity and change, as they, and other concepts, receive their form in certain segments of the social sciences.[38]

What is further interesting about this collection is that Hobsbawm reserves space for theoretical and programmatic passages, and also for summing up previous assessments. Presenting one study as an example is not sufficient, nor is the obligatory perfunctory introduction. No, although there are a number of critical comments which are possible here (see below), the concepts employed are spelled out, to a certain degree, and the results explained, amplified, and directions for further research are indicated. It is also explicitly indicated why the theme of "invented traditions" is of importance for historical research, an explicit legitimation for taking up the theme.[39] In these remarks, I am referring not only to the Introduction to the collection, but also to the final article in the book, on "Mass-Producing Traditions," and particularly there section IV.

In closing, what is striking about Hobsbawm's contribution is the tentative tone that sounds through the collection. The collection appears primarily intended as an impetus to further research: "In any case, the object of this book is to encourage the study of a relatively new subject, and any pretence to treat it other than in a tentative manner would be out of place."[40] He considers the need for inter- or multidisciplinary work important: "Finally, the study of the invention of tradition is interdisciplinary. It is a field of study which brings together historians, social anthropologists and a variety of other workers in the human sciences, and cannot adequately be pursued without such collaboration."[41] It is nevertheless interesting in this connection to see how on the other hand Hobsbawm often feels his inadequacy in approaching certain themes. Thus he displays some jealousy toward Rudolf Braun, whom we have already mentioned, who produced a study of Swiss nationalism which Hobsbawm terms brilliant (Braun having enjoyed training in European ethnology)[42], and he also regards fields such as art history, anthropology and liturgical studies in a special light. It is clearly a position of great deference: "The difficulty is not only one of sources but also of

[38] In the context of Hobsbawm's work, one must think particularly of Durkheim, Van Gennep and Turner.

[39] HOBSBAWM: Introduction, 12ff.

[40] HOBSBAWM: Mass-Producing Traditions, 303.

[41] HOBSBAWM: Introduction, 14. See also 4 and elsewhere.

[42] HOBSBAWM: Introduction, 6ff, with reference to the study by BRAUN (1965).

techniques, though there are available both esoteric [sic] disciplines specializing in symbolism and ritual, such as heraldry and the study of liturgy, as well as Warburgian historic disciplines for the study of such objects. Unfortunately neither are usually familiar to historians of the industrial era."[43]

Ritual, Tradition and Identity

If we look further at the theoretical framework surrounding the concept of "inventing traditions," we see that there are three closely connected ideas which are central, standing out against the background of involvement with the past and the appeal to that which has gone before ("material from the past," "ancient materials").

What is important and at least relatively new in the collection is, in the first place, the attention for and approach to cultural processes specifically via rituals: "Inventing traditions, it is assumed here, is essentially a process of formalization and ritualization, characterized by reference to the past, if only by imposing repetition. The actual process of creating such ritual and symbolic complexes has not been adequately studied by historians."[44] Among historians and others in the human sciences, that heuristic principle has since become common property now, and in a number of instances has rightly led them to settle into the insight that ritual is, par excellence, the appropriate means for approaching culture.

Hobsbawm analyzed and posed questions regarding past cultures through ritualizing processes, and in so doing has specifically had an eye for the historical dimension of ritual activities. For him, it is essentially a matter of the construction of tradition. For the time being, I would thus want to argue for the replacement of "inventing" by the more neutral "construction" or "creation," terms which, for that matter, Hobsbawm himself also repeatedly employs alongside "innovation" itself in this connection. Through this ritual approach, Hobsbawm places himself in a long tradition of theoretical reflections in "ritual studies," as a discipline in both social sciences and religious studies, in which particularly the theme of continuity and change is central.

Through ritual both tradition and the field of tension between continuity and change come into view. On the one side there is the dimension of

[43] HOBSBAWM: Introduction, 4.
[44] HOBSBAWM: Introduction, 4.

continuity that, through their ritual activities, gives people direction and something to hold onto, but on the other side there is change: traditions change in structure and interpretation, and it is specifically interesting to see how this dimension of change is often not recognized, or is even denied, by those who are themselves involved.

Through his use of the paired concepts of ritual and tradition, Hobsbawm places himself in a very definite academic/theoretical context in which two main currents can be distinguished. First, there is the current that proceeds from the proposition that within culture or cultural systems, "tradition" is that which is immutable. Next to it there is the current which suggests that within tradition one can, as it were, speak of an internal conflict: within tradition, change and continuity meet one another (see the work of J.C. Heesterman (1985) with the title, so meaningful in this connection, *The Inner Conflict of Tradition*).[45] Here tradition is understood as a paradox: on the one side there is a timeless order, unchanging, an established structure; on the other, the changing context which is always forcing the tradition to adaptations and compromises.

We must place Hobsbawm in the first, rather conservative current; here, in his attitude with regard to tradition, he is "traditional." For Hobsbawm – and it would be interesting to determine if, and to what degree this was true of his fellow authors as well – tradition is "a set of fixed activities and values," inherited and handed down from the past. He brings in the contextual dimension, the change, by expressly distinguishing "tradition" from "custom."[46] I will here offer no exposition of the difference between "tradition" and "custom," but only indicate how completely "custom" is connected with oral culture and "tradition" with written and literary culture in the "traditional" track within ritual studies and ethnology. "Custom" is flexible and pragmatic, whereas tradition, primarily anchored in literary culture, is, rather, immutable and is sustained and determined by often unpragmatic conventions and routine. Hobsbawm employs here the comparison with the ritual of English jurisprudence: "custom" is what the judges do, tradition is the wig, robe

[45] HEESTERMAN (1985); see also BELL (1992) 119ff.

[46] Grimes argues at this point (a) that Hobsbawm denies the flexible, adaptive aspects of tradition, and (b) that Hobsbawm regards the invention of tradition only as "a symptom or as an ideology-perpetuating tool of political establishments and revolutions." (GRIMES (1993) 10). See recently BERKEY (1995), where in pages 47-50 Hobsbawm's distinction between "tradition" and "custom" is taken over.

and other formal paraphernalia and ritual practices that surround the actual judicial pronouncements.[47] In this, he connects himself with older, and in the meantime to a great degree superceded, ethnological studies with regard to the oral and written dimensions of culture. Thus, in Hobsbawm's work in 1983, we encounter the important underlying antithesis of "literary tradition" and "oral custom."

This now dated academic theoretical context aside, Hobsbawm offers us a double insight. First, ritual can be considered as a more or less fixed expression of tradition or "custom," and second, within ritual there is always a sensitivity for changing circumstances.

What is important and new in Hobsbawm is that he now, as a historian, in the collection, takes the way in which actual "fixed traditions" or "flexible customs" are constructed in rites as his point of departure. In this process, the collection also acquires an important comparative and multidisciplinary dimension.

Through case studies – as we have said, mostly from 19th and 20th century Great Britain or, also, the United States, Germany or France – a picture of how "ritual invents tradition" is sketched and analyzed, how in changing historical contexts a sort of legitimized continuity with the past is created in order to indeed experience "tradition" as "fixed." It is precisely in this stability and invariability, in this permanent connection with the past which is sought, constructed and fostered, that the power and authority of tradition lies.

Therefore Hobsbawm is investigating the cultural construction of history and is not occupied with the unmasking of invented pasts or with laying bare manipulations, but with research into the construction, creation or innovation of traditions.[48]

Apart from that, from the heuristic perspective Hobsbawm here clearly accents a number of points. The initial broad effort which he announced is tailored by zooming in on the process itself of creating traditions, without attention for what happens subsequently (i.e., the chance of

[47] HOBSBAWM: Introduction, 2ff.

[48] It is interesting, though, in this connection to see how Hobsbawm and the other authors in the collection deal with the terminology around "inventing traditions." Some use quotation marks, a number of adjectives are used in order to give a term a certain meaning in a certain situation ("genuine," for instance, or "fixed"), but also all sorts of counterparts are introduced, such as those used by Hobsbawm: creation, innovation, construction, and in specific cases, if the changes are central, "appropriation." See now: FRIJHOFF (1997b).

"survival," definite establishment or disappearance). Two citations will indicate this:

> "The term "invented tradition" is used in a broad, but not imprecise sense. It concludes both "traditions" actually invented, constructed and formally instituted and those emerging in a less easily traceable manner within a brief and dateable period – a matter of a few years perhaps – and establishing themselves with great rapidity."[49]

> "It is evident that not all [traditions] are equally permanent, but it is their appearance and establishment rather than their chances of survival which are our primary concern."[50]

He also does not display very much interest in the adaption process whereby old models are employed for new purposes, even though these processes could still be considered as examples of innovations and, strictly speaking, would also fall under the definition of "invented tradition" given previously. Here too a brief quotation is fitting: "'Invented tradition' is taken to mean a set of practices, normally governed by overtly or tacitly accepted rules and of a ritual or symbolic nature, which seek to inculcate certain values and norms of behaviour by repetition, which automatically implies continuity with the past."[51] Rather his interest moves toward new types, "made to order" for new situations: "More interesting, from our point of view, is the use of ancient materials to construct invented traditions of a novel type for quite novel purposes."[52] Finally, his orientation is primarily toward the period since the industrial revolution.[53]

It subsequently comes to appear that the construction of tradition is an extremely complex process. Numerous elements, language, authorities, many interests and specifically also functions come very literally into play here. Above all, Hobsbawm argues that in the construction of tradition, the functional and ritual dimension of demarcation, of profiling the identity of a group, is central. Identity is created, celebrated and expressed through ritual and the traditions constructed within it. We can therefore say, of course, that Hobsbawm's work turns around the construction of identity. In this, it is interesting to see how he also

[49] HOBSBAWM: Introduction, 1.
[50] HOBSBAWM: Introduction, 1.
[51] HOBSBAWM: Introduction, 1.
[52] HOBSBAWM: Introduction, 6.
[53] HOBSBAWM: Introduction, 9ff.

makes use of a concept which has since become popular, or even fashionable, through the work of De Certeau, Chartier and others: "appropriation."[54] Identity is created by appropriating collective images from the past, and thus constructing what is termed "authoritative precedent." That is a constant process, a continuing creative process of production and reproduction, precisely because it is also a matter of rituals that are always celebrated anew, presented, and thus must be reinterpreted (see here the important note on "ritual and performance").[55] With regard to identities, Hobsbawm directs his attention specifically to public rituals through which regions and nations construct their often new identities.[56] It is precisely in this context that his interpretation of "fixed tradition," geared as it is to these circumstances, comes into its own, and he goes in search of the functions of the newly created traditions. In the context of the nationalism which has been his own research interest, he sees these functions being in both the social and the political sphere.[57]

Through this indirect process, despite his static conception of tradition, Hobsbawm comes around to the continuous dynamic and change of ritual repertoires; also, the appeal to the past must be made increasingly effective, and that happens through continual innovation and appropriation.

4. Drawing a Balance

Thus far my rereading of Hobsbawm. Before moving on to a more recent position of Hobsbawm's that indirectly touches on the question of "inventing traditions," by way of drawing a balance I would first like to list several aspects of the really very well-defined and contextually determined content of this origin of the model of "invention of tradition":

[54] For the general use of "appropriation" in cultural studies, see: De Certeau (1984); Chartier (1988); Burke (1992) 97ff; Rooijakkers (1992) 254-283. See now: Frijhoff (1997b).

[55] For this very important matter in ritual studies, of what is termed performance, see Bell (1992) 123ff; see also explicitly in the Hobsbawm and Ranger collection itself, Cannadine (1983). See further Kelleher (1993), and also the work of Ronald L. Grimes.

[56] See also Hobsbawm (1990b).

[57] See, in summary, Hobsbawm: Mass-Producing Traditions, 303.

– First there is the to my mind not unimportant insight that to a certain extent in its inception "inventing traditions" can be regarded as equal to construction, creation and innovation (in which the emphasis lies on the *novus*!) of traditions, and that it is not first of all the elements of invention, unmasking (of "myth-forming"), authenticity or manipulation which are brought in. It is not primarily a matter of a model that enables us to assay the quality of traditions, although Hobsbawm certainly does repeatedly made a distinction between "genuine" and "invented traditions" (see below).[58]

– Next, a very precisely adapted and classic understanding of tradition appears to be concealed in the concept. It is primarily a matter of "fixed traditions," of something to hold onto through the immutable.

– To a certain extent Hobsbawm himself also wrestles with the theoretical framework around "invented traditions." That can be seen not only in the distinction he introduces between "tradition" and "custom," but also in a number of other oppositions that he employs in order to make clear to the reader precisely what he has in mind. Thus he distinguishes "real" and "invented past," "old" and "new traditions," "old" and "new types of invented traditions," "genuine" and "invented traditions," etc. It seems to me that this wrestling with juxtapositions and contrapositions involves characterizing "his" invented traditions with respect to two parallel cultural and ritual processes: namely the revitalizing of traditions and the tenacious existence of traditions. In both cases one can speak of adaptability. For Hobsbawm, "invented tradition" is characterized primarily by a situation of discontinuity: something new is created, it is a ritualizing process that takes place in a vacuum. Therefore his concept fits well with the first of the processes mentioned above, that of revitalizing or "defending" traditions, because in these cases there is such a break, while it does not fit well with old traditions tenaciously continuing to exist.

Here a number of critical observations are possible. The first is the question of whether authors who introduce or "use" Hobsbawm's work in this respect (such as, for instance, Bell, whom we have mentioned) take the specific aspect of his work sufficiently into account. Further, I ask myself if this strictly presented distinction between old and new

[58] For a study in which an attempt is made to develop an armamentarium for the measure of the quality of traditions on the basis of continuity and discontinuity, see GERNDT (1973), in particular 198-202; summarized in POST (1991b) 111ff.

traditions can be adequately maintained: is there not always rather a process of innovation in ritual repertoires? A citation from Hobsbawm's introduction may somewhat clarify and illustrate this point: "Indeed, the very appearance of movements for the defence or revival of traditions, "traditionalist" or otherwise, indicates such break. Such movements, common among intellectuals since the Romantics, can never develop or even preserve a living past (except conceivably by setting up human natural sanctuaries for isolated corners of archaic life), but must become "invented tradition". On the other hand the strength and adaptability of genuine traditions is not to be confused with the "invention of tradition". Where the old ways are alive, traditions need be neither revived nor invented."[59]

Critical notes of this sort are, to my mind, also applicable when Hobsbawm not only works diachronically but also comparatively. Thus he makes comparisons with "traditional cultures," based on "his" invented traditions of the 19th and 20th century, and moreover, he makes pronouncements about the degree in which in certain periods identity-conferring rituals and traditions of this sort had a place in society and to the sort of relationship in which they stood with regard to what he calls "old traditions," "In the private lives of most people, and in the self-contained lives of small sub-cultural groups, even the invented traditions of the nineteenth and twentieth centuries occupied or occupy a much smaller place than old traditions do in, say, old agrarian societies."[60]

However, we shall let the matter rest at this point, and only remark that in addition to processes of change in rituals, especially the delicate distinction between "real and artificial traditions," which since the folklorism debate has by now been put into its proper perspective, plays an important and complicated role here.[61]

– Further, the concept "invention of tradition" is to no small degree supported both by the approach of continuity and change, as well by that of the interplay of ritual, tradition and identity.

– In Hobsbawm's work, the model was really applied in the field of secular public rituals, rituals of what can be called "civil religion" (although Hobsbawm himself uses the term "civic"[62]), through which regions and nations profile themselves.

59 HOBSBAWM: Introduction, 7ff.
60 HOBSBAWM: Introduction, 11.
61 For the debate over folklorism, see note 35, above.
62 See, among others, HOBSBAWM: Mass-Producing Traditions, 269.

5. Hobsbawm 1993

Before a closer examination of the reception of this tradition-aspect in Hobsbawm's work, and with it, in addition to making up a final balance, to devote some attention to its future prospects, there is still a brief note which has bearing on Hobsbawm's own development after 1983.[63] I am not referring to the recently published – and last? – part of the *Age* series, *The Age of Extremes* (1994), but to a lecture given in 1993. In 1993 Hobsbawm opened the new University of Central Europe in Budapest with an address entitled "History is what priests and educators make of it." A Dutch translation (perhaps also edited) of the speech was printed on the Forum page of *De Volkskrant* (Amsterdam).[64] At first examination, the address appears to be somewhat at odds with that which I have formulated in the critical remarks in this chapter around the use of the concept of "inventing traditions."

After an autobiographical introduction and a presentation and characterization of the diverse ideological and economic models which have replaced one another in Central and Eastern Europe, he sketches what he sees as the dangerous situation in Eastern and Central Europe. Dissatisfaction and disappointment have always been the soil in which social dangers can take root and thrive, he believes: "In the last analysis, then, the peoples of Eastern and Central Europe will continue to live in countries which are disappointed in their past, which apparently are to a high degree disappointed in their present, and which are uncertain of their future."

From this diagnosis, he next points out to his audience of university staff and students that the work of the academic, and specifically that of the historian, is, after all, precisely history, the raw material for ethnic, nationalistic and fundamentalist ideologies. He then introduces once again the "invention of history," but now very explicitly in the sense of myth-forming and manipulation, in short, misuse. In this context of the rise of intolerant ideologies and their misuse of history, notwithstanding the fashion of anti-positivist postmodernism, Hobsbawm calls for a separation

[63] For a broader overview of the reception of Hobsbawm's work, the reader is referred to Post (1995d).

[64] *De Volkskrant* (Amsterdam) 4 December 1993, Forum page. I have not been able to determine whether the address bore this same title when it was given in Budapest; it could be that the title is a headline composed by the *De Volkskrant*'s editors, just as there could have been editorial changes made at other points.

between fact and fiction, and makes a passionate plea for intellectuals to resist against the construction of national, ethnic and other myths.

Three things strike me in this – aside from the specific context of the address and the fact it is a decade later – precisely in the light of that which we have argued above from the 1983 collection. The first is the way in which he, in his address, avoids the word "tradition" (even as he does, for that matter, the word ritual; one single time he does mention "collective tradition" in what seems to me a favourable light), now speaking rather of history, the past and memory. Further, he now certainly places the element of misuse in the foreground in a very definite context, although without denying that an unambiguous use of history and the past is impossible, but he does this primarily through terms such as "myths of legitimation" and "fabrications." The term "identity" also occurs in this connection, but then has primarily a political connotation, in the sense of identity politics. Hobsbawm, as an engaged and personally involved (Jewish) historian, here makes a stirring plea for minorities, in a very normative and criteriological way elaborates one element of how we deal with the past, and links his vision very closely with the work of European ethnologists such as Niedermüller.[65] In contrast to the 1983 collection, he now does this however with little or no attention to the rituals through which identities are constructed, this again in painful contrast to Niedermüller.

6. Beyond Hobsbawm, or Dealing with the Past

In closing, we want to briefly devote some attention, as was announced earlier, to the reception Hobsbawm received in the broader framework of cultural, ritual and liturgical studies, in the course of which, in addition to drawing up a final balance, something of a future perspective can be offered. Also, connected with that, by way of conclusion we will take up a question that Hobsbawm himself also poses at the end of the 1983 collection.

Reception and Prospects

In summary, after the foregoing discussion, it can now be concluded that, in spite of the way in which the term "invention of tradition" has been lavishly bandied about, the content of the complex interplay of the

[65] NIEDERMÜLLER (1991).

triad of change, rite and tradition has seldom if ever come to the fore. Generally it remains superficial, the concept being used as a signal, a threadbare reference to myth-forming, unmasking and manipulation.

Generally – but not all the time. In the history of its reception, I also find another use of Hobsbawm's terminology, equally a signal. It is not so much the putative authenticity and manipulation of traditions and references to the past to which this use of "invented tradition" points. No, even as for Hobsbawm himself, reference is made to the changing involvement with the past and the continual construction of traditions. Only here one can say that there has been a broadening of the perspective: in place of a rather specific content of tradition, the authors work more openly around the term "past" and "appeal to the past." We have moved beyond Hobsbawm and his concept of "inventing tradition"; he has been put into perspective in the good sense of the word, which is to say related to a series of closely related analytical tools which have since been developed. It is not a rigid, elaborated programme with a fixed, circumscribed frame of meaning, but an eclectic palette of directions for research that all revolve around how we deal with the past.

In a general sense, I am referring first here to the fact that to an increasing degree people have recognized the diffuse character, the multiple layers, the varying imputed content and also the dissynchronisms of both the past and tradition, as well as identity. Frijhoff and Wegman, each in his own way, elaborated on the multi-layered nature of "the past" through a three-level system.[66] In this connection, students, not in the last place those of the theory and philosophy of history[67], ultimately have come to the insight that every way of dealing with the past is necessarily a construction, an "invention of tradition." This was also true in the past. Further, I would point to the stream of publications on the subject of remembering and forgetting, around collective and individual memory, and their connections with the construction of identity.[68] Fruitful work has also taken place concerning image and self-image, and the processes by which images are created, in which it is also striking how considerable attention is being paid recently to ritual construction of regional and national identities and to the "lieux et rituels de mémoire,"

[66] See FRIJHOFF (1991) and (1992c); for Wegman, see WEGMAN (1994).

[67] See LORENTZ (1990), with its references to the work of Ankersmit and Lübbe's work in the philosophy of history; see also BLAAS (1993), which is primarily critical with regard to Ankersmit. See now: JONKER (1996).

[68] See the collection BÖNISCH-BREDNICH & BREDNICH (1989).

even as there was in Hobsbawm.[69] Especially for historians in this field of research Hobsbawm's concept has functioned as an eye-opener, through which one does not have to subsequently remain stuck at the level of the real and fake, but can ask questions about the function of ways of dealing with the past, one's own or that of others. For instance, he also set researchers on the trail of the liturgical use of "the myth of the Middle Ages," a myth which acted to legitimize Church politics and architectural styles (i.e., neo-Gothic).[70] Here, though, it is striking how often in addition to "invented tradition" authors employ the term "myth," and sometimes thereby tend toward the other line, discussed earlier, of demythologizing, rather than following in the tradition of Hobsbawm and devoting full attention to the process of construction itself and the functions which play a role in it.

To an increasing degree, an important impulse comes from research into the ritual presentation of "invented traditions," the often theatrical "performances." In what tradition do these stand? I also see possibilities for explorations with regard to such concepts as musealization, already mentioned in an earlier note, and the aestheticizing of our culture, both of which could yield considerable fruit. In this connection one can also point to the importance of comparative research within the framework of liturgical studies regarding the themes of liturgy and drama and liturgy and theatre.[71]

7. Conclusion: Planned or Spontaneous?

In closing I wish to return to Hobsbawm's 1983 collection and Dokkum in order to briefly elaborate on and illustrate the aspect of malleability.

[69] From the stream of such publications, see, among others, GRIJZENHOUT (1989); BANK (1990); generally, also, NORA (1984-1992); FRIJHOFF (1992b); DEN BOER & FRIJHOFF (1993) with a section "Invention of traditions," 163-252.

[70] In regard to the neo-Gothic in The Netherlands, for a good overview see VAN LEEUWEN (1989), as well as his dissertation on the restoration projects of P. Cuypers, VAN LEEUWEN (1995). In this connection, see also the work of Auke van der Woud, VAN DER WOUD (1990), but with it see the critical comments in FRIJHOFF (1992b), in particular note 45, and also Van der Woud's inaugural lecture: VAN DER WOUD (1993).

[71] For "musealization" (of [popular] culture), among others; see note 35 and: GERNDT (1973); ZACHARIAS (1990); STURM (1990); LÜBBE (1983a); (1983b); (1989); ELSHOUT (1990); DE JONG (1992a); (1992b); (1994); POST (1991b); (1991c); (1991d); (1994a); (1994d); (1995a); (1995b). For play and theatre: SPEELMAN (1993) and TURNER (1992). See also in this book the Chapters 4, 9,11 and 12.

Sufficient attention has already been devoted to the aspect of the shaping of myths in my previous remarks.

The research programme with regard to how we deal with the past and call upon what has gone before, based upon Hobsbawm and sketched out here, in many respects dovetails well with the last pages of the 1983 collection. There Hobsbawm considers a number of open ends in his work, raising questions and perspectives for further research.[72] His final question touches on an important aspect of *inventing* or *creating, producing* or *constructing traditions* – one which we already encountered in the discussion of the images evoked by the terminology – and lends itself easily to being illustrated through the Dokkum case. In conclusion, Hobsbawm poses precisely the question of the relation between *invention* and *spontaneous generation* in the process of constructing traditions and identities. The question, then, is of the relations among planning, mutability, manipulability and growth. After all, by the nature of language, the whole concept of *invention*, construction, creation, production, innovation, etc., bears within itself the notion of mutability, and certainly does so against the background of the concept's most important function, namely the creation of social, religious and political identities and loyalties. Hobsbawm puts this into perspective. He rejects any notion of an historical "conspiracy theory": like taste and fashion, tradition and trends are only mutable and open to manipulation within certain boundaries.

It is precisely this interaction of planning and spontaneity that we also encounter in a most fascinating way in the context of how Dokkum has dealt with history. As is the case in the origin or growth of many devotions, there is indeed what is qualified as a miracle there. The tradition and identity created, or to be created, become as it were a theophany, confirmed, legitimized and propagated from outside the process, an apparently spontaneous and uncontrollable demarcation of the tradition. In essence, the same question is valid for the miracle as well: namely, to what extent are miracles spontaneous occurrences, or are they, as it were, induced by circumstances? In the case of Dokkum, the miraculous healing of the little girl was unmistakably the primary catalyst for the recent process of revitalization for the St. Boniface tradition. But at the same time, the case of Dokkum demonstrates how this miracle was rooted in a certain way of dealing with the past. Or, to formulate it still

[72] HOBSBAWM: Mass-Producing Traditions, 303ff, in particular 307.

more pregnantly: the miracle was called up out of a museal and ritual approach to a submerged Boniface tradition which was slowly awakening and coming to life again.

Nefthys's parents were not God-fearing pilgrims, but sympathetic, chance visitors who filled their Sunday afternoon with a visit to the historic complex around the spring. There, from the sidelines, they heard the pastor giving a tour to a colleague from Germany, almost as a museum guide, in the course of it telling the story of the spring, as it had been handed down. In a spontaneous act, the parents threw themselves into the story, playing it out in an anamnestic form of living history. And behold: the tradition came to life! This miracle story began to function as an origin narrative for a new, or renewed tradition regarding the spring, which, seen from a diachronic perspective, stands as another in a series of revitalizations, as we saw in the introduction.

Viewed further, from the perspective of Hobsbawm's work, Dokkum thus brings to light an extremely complex process of traditions in varying contexts. Essentially, for Hobsbawm and the researchers who have been briefly mentioned here who stand in his tradition, what matters is the investigation of the creation, construction and innovation of traditions. Ultimately, according to Hobsbawm, it is not only the task of the student of culture to discover and reconstruct the process by which rituals change through involvement with the past, but also to attempt to understand that process in terms of changing contexts, which is to say, to understand why the need for change arose, and arises, and what patterns are involved. For this task, working in a multidisciplinary, diachronic and comparative manner is indispensable.

APPENDIX

Some Bibliographical Data Regarding E.J. Hobsbawm (b. 1917)

By way of an overview of the most important works by Hobsbawm, we offer here a selected bibliography. The selection was influenced by three factors. First, we wanted to sketch the development of Hobsbawm's fields of interest; second, we wished to indicate his main works and their place in his development; and third, to list works that directly or indirectly are connected with the collection which is our central topic here. To the best of my knowledge, no complete bibliography is, at present, available. One can fruitfully consult a very complete bibliography which runs through April, 1982, which is included in the first of the two festschrifte with which Hobsbawm was honoured. This bibliographic overview was compiled by KEITH McCLELLAND with the cooperation of Hobsbawm and his wife Marlene, and is to be found in: R. SAMUEL and G. STEDMAN JONES (eds.): *Culture, Ideology and Politics: Essays for Eric Hobsbawm* (= History Workshop Series) (London 1982) 332-363. In addition to books and articles, the bibliography includes his journalistic work for newspapers and magazines (except for letters to the editor and contributions to discussions), reviews and work published under pseudonyms. The bibliography is arranged thematically, and thus (although it does somewhat obscure the development of his interests) gives a good insight into the subjects of concentration in his work. I have chosen here for a chronological overview.

The second collection of essays which was offered to Hobsbawm two years later is less generally historical and methodological in its scheme, and moreover, P. THANE, G. CROSSICK and R. FLOUD (eds.): *The Power of the Past: Essays for Eric Hobsbawm* (Cambridge etc. 1984), contains no bibliography. It does, however, have a valuable essay by E.D. GENOVESE: The Politics of Class Struggle in the History of Society: An Appraisal of the Work of Eric Hobsbawm, 13-36.

Selected Bibliography of E. Hobsbawm

1948 [1974]
Ed., *Labour's Turning Point, 1880-1900: Extracts from Contemporary Sources* (Brighton 1948; 2nd ed. 1974).

1950
Fabianism and the Fabians (1884-1919) (Cambridge 1950). [Thesis, King's College, Cambridge].

1959 [1971]
Primitive Rebels: Studies in Archaic Forms of Social Movement in the 19th and 20th Centuries (Manchester 1959; 3rd ed. 1971).

1959 [1961, 1989]
"FRANCIS NEWTON" (E.J. HOBSBAWM): *The Jazz Scene* (London 1989; originally 1959, 1961) [see now 1993].
1962
The Age of Revolution: Europe, 1789-1848 (= History of Civilization) (London 1962).
1964 [a]
Labouring Men: Studies in the History of Labour (New York 1964).
1964 [b]
With R. GLASS and others (ed. and contributions): *London: Aspects of Change* (London 1964) [Edited by the Centre for Urban Studies, Report No. 3].
1965
(Editor, with introduction) K. MARX: *Pre-Capitalist Economic Formations* (New York 1965) [Trans. by J. COHEN, introduction by E. HOBSBAWM].
1968 [1969ss.]
Industry and Empire: An Economic History of Britain since 1750 (London, 1968) [see: *Industry and Empire: From 1750 to the Present Day* (= M. POSTAN, C. HILL & E. HOBSBAWM (eds.): *The Pelican Economic History of Britain* (Harmondsworth 1969ff), Part 3).
1969 [1981, 1985]
Bandits (London 1969; 2nd ed. 1981; Harmondsworth, Penguin 1985; rev. ed. (based on 2nd ed.), New York, 1981).
1969 [1985]
With G. RUDE: *Captain Swing: A Social History of the Great English Uprising* (London 1969; Harmondsworth 1985).
1971
From Social History to the History of Society, in *Daedalus* 100 (1971) 20-45.
1972
The Social Function of the Past: Some Questions, in *Past and Present* 55 (1972) 3-17.
1973
Revolutionaries: Contemporary Essays (London 1973).
1975 [1977]
The Age of Capital, 1848-1875 (= History of Civilization) (London 1975; 2nd ed. 1977).
1978-1982
Series ("Progetto di E. Hobsbawm"): *Storia del marxismo* (Turin 1978-1982) [English editions: Brighton and Bloomington: Indiana University Press. 4 vols.].
1978 [a]
Sexe, symboles, vêtements et socialisme (Maison de sciences de l'homme: Paris, 1978) [= offprint from *Actes de la recherche en sciences sociales* 23; = Man and Woman in Socialist Iconography, in *History Workshop* IV (Autumn 1978) 121-138].

1978 [b]

With T. NAIRN and others (eds. and contributions): *Nationalismus und Marxismus: Anstoß zu einer notwendige Debatte* (Berlin 1978).

1981

With M. JACQUES & Fr. MULHERN (eds.): *The Forward March of Labour Halted?* (London 1981).

1983

With T. RANGER (eds.): *The Invention of Tradition* (= Past and Present Publications) (Cambridge 1983) [The collection has been reprinted many times; the precise number of reprintings can not be established because of the many forms in which the Cambridge University Press has reissued it. The book is still available today (1995) as a Canto Book. Contributions by HOBSBAWM: Introduction: Inventing Traditions, 1-14, and Mass-Producing Traditions: Europe, 1870-1914, 263-308].

1984

Workers: Worlds of Labor (New York 1984) [British edition under title *Worlds of Labour: Further Studies in the History of Labour* (London 1984)].

1987 [1989]

The Age of Empire, 1875-1914 (= History of Civilization) (London 1987; New York 1989).

1988

With W. KULA and others (eds.): *Peasants in History: Essays in Honour of Daniel Thorner* (Oxford University Press: Calcutta 1988).

1989

Politics for a Rational Left: Political Writing 1977-1988 (London 1989).

1990 [a]

Echoes of the Marseillaise: Two Centuries Look Back on the French Revolution (= Mason Welch Gross Lecture Series) (London/New Brunswick 1990).

1990 [b]

Nations and Nationalism Since 1780: Programme, Myth, Reality (Cambridge 1990) [Given as the 1985 Wiles Lectures at Queen's University, Belfast.].

1993

The Jazz Scene (London 1993) [Reprint, now under his own name; see 1959].

1994 [1995]

The Age of Extremes: The Short Twentieth Century, 1914-1991 (London 1994). [American edition entitled *The Age of Extremes, 1914-1991* (New York 1995).

1997

On History (London 1997).

4. THE MIRACLE OF DOKKUM AND OTHER ACCOUNTS OF DISTANCE AND ENGAGEMENT

A COMPARISON OF LOCAL PASTORAL INTERACTION AT HOLY PLACES[1]

> "The experiences that constitute apparitions and that attract attention to them are best expressed in stories. The more time one spends with the reports of such experiences, the more the sense of this axiom becomes clear."[2]

1. Opening: A Farewell

On September 17, 1993, the pastor of Dokkum, the place of pilgrimage associated with St. Boniface in the north of The Netherlands, addressed the parish council and the parish meeting in an open letter with an appendix. For some time the pastor had not been well, and, though it pained him to take the step, he felt the time had come to lay aside his pastoral duties.

The appendix is a copy of a letter which the pastor had written the day before to Ype and Janny B. of Sneek. As is also the case in several subsequent and more comprehensive open letters – the longest of which runs 16 pages – the pastor seems to look back on his nine years in Dokkum in an engaged, personal manner. The central point that all these letters have in common is how events in the period since July 29, 1990, the date of a miraculous healing which happened after an immersion in

[1] P. Post: Het wonder van Dokkum en andere verhalen van afstand en betrokkenheid: lokale pastorale interactie op heilige plaatsen, in M. van Uden, J. Pieper & P. Post (eds.): *Oude sporen, nieuwe wegen: ontwikkelingen in bedevaartonderzoek* (= UTP-Katernen, 17) (Baarn 1995) 107-132. The article is an elaboration of a lecture presented at the symposium "Bedevaart en pelgrimage. Tussen traditie en moderniteit," January 21, 1994, at the University for Theology and Pastoral Care at Heerlen. My thanks to Herman Peters, MA, for his generous cooperation, and to Peter Jan Margry, MA, for his critique of an earlier version.

[2] Zimdars-Swartz (1991) 25.

St. Boniface's Spring, changed the pastor's life. In the appendix directed to the B. family, he states it in this way:

> "I've been here for nine years now, and I have the sense that these years have been a great train of miracles big and small. From my perspective, these are not miracles to be taken up into the Church's official register, nor which need to be investigated by medical doctors. There is no pen gifted enough to describe them: so many miracles of love, friendship and care. Greatest of all is the miracle of a history as rich as that of Dokkum so suddenly being rescued from oblivion, a history which I hope will again come to be fully known, bestowing peace, harmony and salvation on human life and all creation.
> How difficult too those early days were, surrounding your extraordinary visit to the chapel of St. Boniface and St. Boniface's Spring on July 29, 1990 [...] Looking back, I am immensely thankful to have been a witness to your experience with Nephtis at St. Boniface's Spring. The source of my joy is your experience of redemption; of that you may be sure!"

Drawing up a balance for his pastorate in Dokkum, now that he must withdraw from active service for health reasons, he repeatedly refers to what has come to be called the miracle of Dokkum, the healing of the B.'s young daughter.

I suspect that this farewell has a lot to do with the flowering of Dokkum as a place of pilgrimage, and the role that the pastor had begun to play in that process. The key event in this was the miracle of Dokkum, which had, as one might expect, caused considerable commotion through the widely scattered Catholic population of that part of the northern Netherlands in the summer of 1990, and particularly, also, in the life of the local pastor.

Here you can see the framework for this chapter: an intuitive diagnosis and many questions, which especially focus on the role of the local pastor. How was it that things were able to happen as they did? Can one say that this was a unique case? Or does what happened here fit into a more general pattern which can also found elsewhere, in the past or today, where a holy place is suddenly revitalized, or a new one arises?

In this chapter, I shall report on a first exploration of this pilgrimage material. The tone of my remarks will be impressionistic. The chapter will primarily be an account of the tension between distance and engagement, a story, particularly, by which I hope to arrive at a new and fruitful perspective for future pilgrimage studies. I will begin with the latter, with the possible perspective, or better, perspectives.

2. Research Perspectives

2.1. General: A Consideration of Miracles, and Diachronic and Comparative Research

In a general sense, the perspectives that I am considering arise out of a survey of recent developments in international pilgrimage studies which I edited in 1994. This involved, first, a consideration of accounts of miracles, healings and appearances, and second, a review of the perspectives of diachronic and comparative study.[3]

A good example of the way in which these two perspectives (which ultimately differ in nature) come together is the book *Encountering Mary*, by Sandra Zimdars-Swartz,[4] dealing with miraculous appearances by Mary in the 19th and 20th centuries. Accounts of miracles, in this case appearances by Mary, are the point of departure for the study; this makes the use of diachronic and comparative perspectives perfectly fitting. It is a multi-layered book. Many accounts of miracles and appearances are presented in relationship to one another, revealing surprising connections. But it is the source material which is especially rich and complex. It is particularly in the presentation of these often very diverse source materials that the author's organizational and critical talents are revealed. Ever and again she returns to her starting point, the stories: the familiar and complex genre of miracle stories and origin-legends, reports of appearances and healings. Zimdars-Swartz confronts, emendates and questions these stories with contextual data, creating a fascinating interplay of "pious fiction and profane facts," as the author herself puts it. Working out from the accounts, which often involve their original narrator in an intensely personal way, the author draws circles of increasing diameter, in which attention is directed particularly on the biographical background of the individuals who experienced the visions, on the mediators, and on others who were directly or indirectly involved. To a lesser extent, and always in close relation to the biographical contexts and the accounts, the author draws in the ecclesiastical, social and political context in the course of her summary and analysis. In this respect, her accent differs from that of, for instance, William Christian Jr., and Thomas Kselman.[5]

[3] See Post (1994b); see also Chapters 1 ans 2 in this book.

[4] Zimdars-Swartz (1991).

[5] For these contextual approaches, see the introduction of the Zimdars-Swartz (1991) 1-21, and the introduction to Chapter 1, 25-27, and especially also the annotated

2.2. Local Interaction

Reading and rereading this book by Zimdars-Swartz, with the case of Dokkum in the back of my mind, led me to the insight that the two research perspectives mentioned could also be applied to the phenomenon of "local interaction." In choosing this term, I am thinking primarily of the local pastoral, parish perspective. This is a perspective which implies that in research, attention will not be directed entirely on the pilgrims, their experiences and motivations. Nor is it a perspective which focuses on the holy place itself, or the journey to it. No, it is a perspective which is directed toward the world around the holy place, the village, the landscape, or in a more limited sense, toward the preexisting pastoral/parochial infrastructure. In doing this, in essence my attention is being focused first on the "supply side," as this takes shape through the "cultural mediator" who is present there, acting as intermediary, i.e., the local pastor or pastoral staff. In relation to the miracle stories or origin-accounts mentioned, the research perspectives which I have outlined only very generally here would focus on the first phase of the sometimes very protracted interactions among the parish, the pastor or pastors, and the newly introduced devotion or devotions.

I am aware that in doing this, only a very limited segment of the local interaction is being considered. A number of other variants and ways in which this perspective of local interaction could be developed are also possible and imaginable, through which other local forces could be taken into consideration. One could also consciously choose to examine the situation in and around the holy place. Or another approach which would be possible would not look primarily at the holy place, but at the situation in the pilgrims' parishes. This is a neglected, but very promising field of investigation that is really very rarely encountered in pilgrimage research. It is for this reason that I am looking forward to the dissertation by Hersbach concerning pilgrims from the western section of the province of North Holland.[6] My proposal here, however, is entirely oriented to the interaction surrounding the holy place, the place where the miracle story is rooted and where the new devotional repertoire takes shape.

bibliographical survey in the Appendix on pp. 271-278. See further the survey POST (1994b). From the work of W. Christian, Jr., and T. Kselman, we would here list: CHRISTIAN (1981a); (1981b); (1989) and particularly (1989); (1991); (1992); cf. now also: (1996); KSELMAN (1983).

[6] HERSBACH (1994).

But even if limited to the parish and holy place, this is a very complex unit. There are multiple layers in the parish context itself: among different groups in the parish community, the reactions to a miracle, healing, appearance, stigmatization, etc., can vary, and are often very different, or even complete opposites. In addition to taking this complexity and dynamic into account, full attention must also be given to the dynamic of time: it is always the case that, among the actors and sponsors involved, developments take place which can be quite varied and out of synchronization with one another. It is precisely this process of development in the interaction between new devotional elements and the preexisting established structures which the researcher must further clarify and describe. As has been said before, in this process attention must in the first instance be directed to the interplay in the very first stages of the process out of which the new devotion arises, and subsequently broaden out to include the eventual establishment and design of the new or revitalized devotion.

In summary, attention given to the miracle (or the account of it) and the general perspective of diachronic and comparative analysis should be concentrated on and translated into the following question: What sort of interaction takes place between the new or revitalized devotional activities and the local parish context in and around the holy place? I suggest that for the initial efforts, focusing on the role of the local pastor or pastorate offers us a good, and more important, a practicable way of narrowing down this question.

2.3. A New Perspective?

Without entering into an extensive historiographic excursus, it is fitting to take notice of the fact that researchers have previously been active in this area. It is not entirely unexplored terrain.

A number of productive explorations have been made for the early Christian, Byzantine and mediaeval period, in which, via the physical and ritual pilgrimage culture, attention has principally been devoted to what Reekmans termed the "Siedlungsbildung" from pilgrimage sites, i.e., locations which not only grow into devotional but also, often, cultural centres, in interaction with local elements.[7]

There also exist studies for 19th and 20th century Europe which have utilized this perspective of local interaction. Among others can be listed

[7] See REEKMANS (1980). See now also: *Akten* (1995).

the work of Mart Bax, which indeed places pilgrimage devotion against the background of conflicting power blocs, and in which it is precisely the preexisting local parish context, also in combination with the accounts of the miracles and the founding of the sites, which is studied.[8] Still, however, for Bax local interaction only enters into the discussion in a relative sense, since he always relates it to the much broader perspective of power blocs and the process of the formation of the state. Further reflection indicates that the process of interaction at a fundamental level and the role of the local pastor are not central here.

Christopher McKevitt, however, certainly did work in the direction which I advocate here. He investigated exactly this interaction in the devotional centre of the Padre Pio cultus, San Giovanni Rotondo, in southern Italy. The report of his research can be found in the collection by Eade and Sallnow.[9] In his fieldwork he came upon surprising discoveries which again underscore precisely the complexity inherent in our research question above. Thus, he found that at first sight everything in San Giovanni Rotondo pointed to a division between the village life down below, and the life on the mountain above – and even beyond the city – which was centred around the Padre Pio cultus. But after a longer period of fieldwork in the village and on the mountain, it began to appear that the interaction between village culture and the pilgrimage culture was really not what it appeared: nearly all residents of the village had an image of Padre Pio hanging somewhere in their home, and at important celebrations the parishioners were seen to be present in the monastery church, the devotional centre for the cultus, on the mountain.

2.4. A Word about Sources and Methods

Finally, I would like to add two methodological notes to the brief statement of the research question which has been made above. First, there is a problem of sources. As is so often the case (or perhaps, in cultural studies, is even *always* the case), we will have to work with source material which is extremely varied and diverse, using one element of it to supplement another. Each of these sources will present us with problems

[8] See the literature list included in PIEPER, POST & VAN UDEN (1994) 277f; as a summary of Bax's approach: BAX (1988); for a critical discussion of the assumptions underlying Bax's work, a.o.: P. POST: in *Antropologische Verkenningen* 10,1 (1991) 71f; see for other works of BAX the bibliography in this book.

[9] McKEVITT (1991).

of its own. Among these sources would be, for instance, the material infrastructure, changes in the size and layout of the town or city, and the design of the holy place; also the ritual devotional repertoire, and, most important, the accounts we discussed above. In particular, it is the moment to which the cultus traces its origins which is surrounded by and embodied in stories. Holy places exist thanks to, in and through narratives. Stories from a number of genres, each with their own patterns, are represented here. Accounts of personal experiences on the part of those directly involved, what are termed "personal narratives," are of central importance;[10] these develop and are disseminated in a number of ways, eventually appearing as interviews, press releases, and later still as sometimes propagandistic "true life" religious narratives, with high hagiographic and promotional content, designed to recruit believers.

For research into the recent past, and in the present, there is also fieldwork of the sort performed by McKevitt. Here too there are a number of problems which must be taken into account. The researcher is dependent on spokespersons and informants; observations are contingent on having been in the right place at the right time; and finally, the value of the researcher's report depends on having achieved the right balance between objectivity and involvement.

Because we generally have to reconstruct the situation at the beginning of the process by which a holy place and its devotional culture arises and develops, it is then important to be able to be as close to the process as possible, in terms of time and place. The research acquires enormous added value through this.

The best ethnographic and ethnological studies often owe their value to the fact that the researchers, at a certain moment in a certain place, thought it worth their while to analyze occurrences going on around them. Direct involvement must then be paired with scientific objectivity. We are not only speaking here of contingency, but also of a certain scientific attitude which will recognize a process as a unique and valuable example, as the source for a real local micro-history that can productively be subjected to the diachronic and comparative research design discussed above. Here, studies based on concrete examples will be better guides for us than theoretical discussions will.[11]

[10] For this narrative genre, see the literature cited in POST (1992b) and (1994a) particularly note 18. See also POST (1994b) = Chapter 9 in this book.

[11] The work of Cl. Geertz is the classic example with regard to this theme in fieldwork in cultural studies and local description in a general cultural studies framework: see

William Christian Jr. fully exploited the chance he was offered when he came from America to live and work in Spain and found himself in the midst of the development and effects of phenomena; in Tenerife in the Canary Islands he did the same on a somewhat smaller scale by watching over his backyard fence and taking the efforts to cure two-year-old neighbour girl's serious brain tumor as his point of departure for research.[12]

In all of this one should especially note how it was possible to begin the research immediately, something for which there appears to be little room in existing research design. It was not coincidence that Christian worked as an independent researcher, funding his study entirely from his own pocket. But most important is to observe the constantly shifting balance between objectivity and involvement, between engagement and detachment. For better or worse, it seems to me that a telling example here is the figure of the Mariologist René Laurentin. Starting out as a critical scientific researcher with an exegetical/theological background, and studying numerous manifestations including Lourdes, he developed into a propagandist for Marian appearances, a mouthpiece for and interpreter of the message, to become, as at Medjugorje, a component of the devotional process itself, a not to be underestimated factor among the influences which led to the establishment and rise of that place of pilgrimage.

Following these methodological notes I will now return to the issues surrounding local interaction which I previously set forth, and to the case study of Dokkum. Since 1990 I have had the opportunity to follow the founding, and what at first sight appears to be the sudden and unexpected blossoming, of a devotional culture there.

3. The Case of Dokkum

3.1. The Miracle of Dokkum

In the farewell letter and its appendix mentioned in the introduction, the pastor of Dokkum alluded to the miraculous occurrence which took place at the height of the summer in 1990, and which has since come to be known as the "Miracle of Dokkum," and is generally regarded as

GEERTZ (1973) and (1985). For the same in a more general setting, see Frijhoff's text, FRIJHOFF (1992a).

[12] See CHRISTIAN (1991); see also note 5.

being the decisive catalyst for the sensational growth of Dokkum as the city of St. Boniface on a number of levels. I will not go into these various levels and contexts any deeper here, but for that merely refer the reader to the first sketch and analysis of that topic in the festschrift compiled in 1993 in honour of A. Blijlevens on his retirement.[13] Rather, I will focus my attention on the miracle, and the role of the pastor, and only give a brief account of the events.

First of all, the healing. I will present the version in which the pastoral perspective predominates, cited from the *Reformatorisch Dagblad*. An article in that newspaper on October 10, 1991, recounts the "miracle" from the perspective of the pastor in this way:

> It all began on July 29 last year. Pastor P., of the Dokkum parish with its 1300 souls, was giving a tour of the St. Boniface chapel to his colleague from Oberhausen on that Sunday afternoon. "A young couple with a child were also there," says P. "I didn't know them, but greeted them, 'The Lord be with you.' At that moment I didn't realize what these words would mean for them."
>
> While P. was showing his German colleague an exhibit on the life of the missionary saint and explaining it to him, the couple walked to the spring across from the chapel and immersed the child in the water. "I saw it happen, but it really didn't leave any lasting impression on me," explains P., "and thus I didn't pay any more attention to it."
>
> All that changed when two days later the pastor at Dokkum received a phone call from Ype B., a chiropractor in Sneek. He identified himself as the father of the child. "B. told me that his nine-month-old daughter had suffered from persistent pertussis, but that since Sunday afternoon she had been cured. For him, it was beyond dispute that the miracle had been the result of the healing power of the water." P. listened to the story, "but I was speechless."
>
> In the meantime, B. had passed the story on to the press. "Not to draw attention to himself, but the couple were so impressed by what had happened that they wanted others to know about it," says P. From that moment, the phone at the rectory at Dokkum began ringing off the hook. "It caused me many sleepless nights and crying fits," the pastor acknowledges. "I was deeply moved."[14]

[13] For the growth of Dokkum as a pilgrimage site, with extensive documentation and list of sources, see POST (1993).

[14] *Reformatorisch Dagblad* October 10, 1991; the "breakthrough" in interest in the "miracle" and in Dokkum as the city of Boniface appears particularly attributable to the

Initially both the pastor and the parish community reacted cooly, although what happened that Sunday afternoon had occurred right under the pastor's nose. Actually, during the rounds of the chapel they frequently made, almost like museum guides, neither of the two pastors paid much attention to what was going on around them. The first reactions to the miracle were also non-committal. The earliest reactions from the pastor, parish council and diocesan officials in Groningen were all guarded. This distance clearly contrasted with the engagement of the couple. The B. family from Sneek, a chiropractor and a naturopath, moving in New Age circles, parents of the girl who had been cured, pressed the pastor to publicize the healing. They wanted to share news about the healing – a salutary act which after all could also happen to others – with the public. Ype B. was already proposing that Dokkum could grow into "a new Lourdes." He suggested this to the pastor, but the pastor was still reserved; the most he wanted to do was place a notice of the young couple's peculiar experience (the pastor very deliberately declined to call it a "miracle") in one of the forthcoming issues of the parish newsletter. Disgruntled, B. made contact with the *Telegraaf*, a Dutch national newspaper, which immediately sent a reporter and ran an article about the miracle. That opened the floodgates. From all sides there was interest, for the first time in ages, in the spring, in St. Boniface, and for Dokkum as the city of Boniface. Pilgrims and the merely curious streamed in, their presence making demands on the dilapidated infrastructure of the spring and grounds; by 1993, more than 20,000 a year were coming. New healings were reported, which the pastor recorded in a sort of logbook. Pastor P. also began to make regular reports to the bishop on developments.

In the period immediately after "the miracle," several rather reserved official statements were made by the parish council and by Bishop Möller of Groningen. However, at all levels, the pivotal role was played by the local pastor, who, as he himself says, had had new duties thrust upon him by events. He continued to be involved in all the events, whether these had to do with the museal activities that arose from initiatives by a dynamic young curator at the regional museum for whom Boniface became the cutting edge of his museum's development, or with the

report of the "miracle" in *De Telegraaf*, August 9, 1990; see [H. PETERS (ed.)]: *Rondom de Bonifatiusbron. Dokkum 1990-1991*, part 1 (Dokkum 1993) 1-3. For a version from the perspective of the B. family, see *Haagse Post*, August 25, 1990, 25.

"Dokkum promotion" of the local and regional tourist industry and local merchants. In all of this, it is striking how integrated and harmonious the interaction between the blooming spring and Boniface devotion on the one side, and parish life on the other was. Thus, for instance, right up to the present, the parish liturgy and the pilgrimage liturgy go hand in hand. To date, the high point of the developments since that Sunday afternoon in 1990, here only reported fragmentarily, has been the complete reconstruction of the pilgrimage complex, now in use after its consecration by the Bishop of Groningen.

If we now zoom in on the local pastor and his role in all of this, I believe it is possible to chart an interesting trajectory from distance to engagement. The pastor became increasingly more involved with, and even in the thrall of Boniface and the spring. For our purposes, however, we need go no deeper into the rich dossier regarding this case study of the revitalization of a holy place.

4. A Comparison: La Salette

I began to read, to collect material for a sort of *pèlerinage comparé* around this first case, and in doing so looked particularly to other accounts of the process by which a miracle led to the establishment of a holy place, and in which, directly or indirectly, the role of the local clergy was an element. As an example, I wish to briefly present one often cited case, in order to then close with several tentative comparative notes and a synthesis.

From the series – to which others could be added – of La Salette, Lourdes, Banneux, Beauraing, Moresnet, Holset, Wittem, Glastonbury, etc., I chose La Salette. As is rather generally acknowledged, the appearance of Mary at La Salette stands at the beginning of a coherent chain of manifestations and Marian holy places.[15] Thus, for instance, it is impossible to understand and see Lourdes apart from La Salette.

On Saturday, September 19, 1846, two young cowherds reported an appearance. Although each was in the service of a different employer,

[15] For a summary regarding La Salette, see Zimdars-Swartz (1991) 27-42, and particularly studies by Stern, of which we will list only the following in this connection: Stern (1972); (1980); (1984). The work of Kselman is indispensable for the contextual analysis of miracle stories of this type. Particularly recommended here is Kselman (1983). I also consulted Caseau (1942) and Estienne (1965).

both had been tending cattle in an alpine meadow near La Salette, in the French Alps, not far from Grenoble. They were François-Mélanie Mathieu (called Mélanie), 14, employed by Baptiste Pra, and Pierre-Maximin Giraud (called Maximin), 11, working for a farmer named Selme, from La Salette. They reported meeting a beautiful woman on a mountainous meadow, at an altitude of about 1770 metres, in the vicinity of a pass reached from Corps. They did not recognize the "beautiful woman" as Mary; they told their story and "outsiders" had to point out to them that it perhaps could well have been Mary (this is a familiar "topos" in accounts of appearances of Mary in the 19th and 20th century). Mary appeared to the children in the meadow, during which, among other spots, she took up a position of a rock outcrop. Subsequently, larger and smaller pieces of rock, taken from the place where she appeared, also play an important role in the account; these pieces of stone were treasured, shown to the curious in a local cafe, broken into smaller pieces and distributed as religious souvenirs, and for some, the face of Christ appeared in them. Later the rocks become secondary in the narrative, and interest – devotional and otherwise – came more and more to be concentrated around the spring near La Salette that seemed to rise at the place where the children had met the "beautiful woman." It was particularly the healings by agency of this water that, together with the role of the local parish clergy and the press (which, as in Dokkum, proved a factor of great importance), which were of decisive importance in spreading La Salette's reputation. The case is fascinating, with many conflicts, miracles, and legal proceedings in ecclesiastical and civil courts; in short, here too we have the genesis of a holy place in which interaction with the local culture plays an important role.

I wish now, however, to concentrate on that local interaction process, and within that, particularly on the role of the local clergy, and leave the broader ecclesiastical and political context, and also what have been termed the "secrets of La Salette,"[16] out of consideration. The available written source material in particular offers a good overview of the role and the reactions of the pastors involved, who each in their own way tried to appropriate the miracle. Thus, we for instance have available the written records of interviews which the Abbé François Lagier, a man

[16] Zimdars-Swartz devotes a separate and extensive discussion to what have been termed the "secrets," which are particularly connected with person of Mélanie; see ZIMDARS-SWARTZ (1991) Chapter 4, 165ff.

from the region and pastor of Saint-Pierre-de-Cherennes, carried out with the children in 1847, and also the correspondence of Pastor Mélin, of Corps, with Mgr. De Bruillard, Bishop of Grenoble.

The honour of first reporting the miracle, in this case the appearance of the "beautiful woman," fell not to the local or regional ecclesiastics, but to the children's two employers. Sunday, the day after it happened, the story was told to the local parish priest of La Salette, Abbé Jacques Perrin. He was very deeply impressed by the account, and took it as the theme for his Sunday morning sermon. When his superiors heard of this, they intervened, and from the higher echelons it was made clear that what was expected was distance, not involvement or promotion. Two weeks after the sermon in question, the pastor was replaced by Louis Perrin, who, despite the same last name, was not related.

In the home base of Maximin's father, the nearby village of Corps, the pastor, Pierre Mélin, was also seized by the story. He kept his bishop informed of further events, and in the course of his reports he was hardly able to conceal his enthusiasm. Thus, among other things, he wrote of how ever increasing numbers of people from his parish were attending the Sunday services, and how the Sabbath rest was being respected more than before. It is striking how he, in his letters, emphasizes to the bishop that he himself has done nothing, and shall do nothing, to spread the story; the story seems to be spreading of its own accord. In this context he writes of "rapports naïves." In fact the pastor played a very sizeable role in the processes surrounding the appearance. Zimdars-Swartz delicately terms him "a sort of administrator of the supernatural."[17]

The source of the first conflict was the rock on which Mary appeared. By now, parts of the rock had been taken to Corps, because of the connection with Maximin. But now the new pastor at La Salette asserted his rights. He forced the village and parish of Corps to return the rock – or at least the greatest part of it – to La Salette. It was at this point that the rock disappeared from the story, and the spring assumed its importance. Pastor Mélin was closely involved with the first miraculous healing. An acquaintance of his, a woman from Corps, was healed after drinking water from the spring which had been brought to Corps in a bottle. Mélin reported numerous healings to the bishop in Grenoble. It is thanks to these reports from Mélin that we know just how quickly developments followed one on another. Especially the healings lead to a

[17] ZIMDARS-SWARTZ (1991) 33.

strong growth in interest. Already, between the eighth and tenth weeks after the appearance, large groups of pilgrims were arriving in Corps and La Salette; Mélin also received many letters, and after ten weeks there appears a first note of desperation in his reports: the parish is being overwhelmed with pilgrims, sometimes as many as 1400 per week going up the mountain. It is impossible for him to find shelter for all of them.

After 1847, a heated discussion arose in the French press about the Church's appropriation of the miracle. In the meantime two investigative committees, appointed by Bishop De Bruillard and composed of professors from the diocesan seminary, among others, had set to work, and the same ecclesiastic had warned his clergy "not to become too deeply involved in the cult around the appearance." The reports of the commissions were extremely cautious, and posed a number of very critical questions, but despite the doubts and opposition, on September 19, 1851, the bishop approved the devotion at the place where the appearance had taken place and at the same time he permitted the publication of the account of the appearance. The crowds now become so massive that the devotion exceeds all parish lines: separate facilities are constructed, the road to the pass is improved, and the landscape itself is reshaped for devotional/liturgical ends. A large neo-Romanesque basilica rises on the spot (built 1851-1879; parts of the rock outcrop are preserved in the sacristy down to the present day), and around the spring and the chapel of the Fontaine de la Vierge a sort of processional park with groups of statues is laid out. Corps and La Salette are both overshadowed by the new devotional infrastructure of Notre Dame de la Salette.

5. Some Provisional Comparative Notes

Fully conscious of their provisional and incomplete nature, by way of striking a balance the following notes can be gathered from accounts of this sort and interactions on the local level.

5.1. The Scale of Harmony and Conflict, Engagement and Distance

Interactions involving the local pastor are important in many respects for the development "from miracle to holy place." In general, the reactions of local clergy vary from distancing themselves totally to engagement. One place will see an almost hostile interaction between the new, rising devotions and the local parish setting, as initially at Lourdes. In another there will be a direct, promotional involvement, as in the case of the visionary Rosa of San Damiano.[18]

One might arrange the reactions schematically on a scale. At the one end would be the engaged pastor. In the most extreme case, this would be a miracle, healing, appearance or stigmata which happens to the local pastor himself, so that he is thus, as it were, perfectly congruent with the devotional attraction. To my knowledge, history does not record this often. It would appear that there is always an interaction with the pre- existing local parochial culture: occasionally when regular clergy are involved in the origin narratives, it is either a case of pastors who only after their death become a focus for devotion (Mgr. Bekkers, Alphons Ariëns), or new clergy who arrive "from outside," sometimes bringing with them pastoral tasks, often on the basis of their devotional aura (see the case of Padre Pio in San Giovanni Rotondo in Southern Italy). But most often the pastor's engagement is expressed in his acting as a "broker," an intermediary or promoter, as did Mélin in the history of La Salette.

In the middle of the scale there is a more neutral attitude, which can run from curiosity through critical distance.

Entirely at the opposite end of our scale is a distancing which finally all too often takes the character of active opposition. The well-known case of Lourdes can in this respect be a model for many miracle and appearance accounts: the local clergy as a counter force. There is doubt, unbelief, denial, scorn, skepticism, and last but not least, opposition.

Behind this rather static scale, focused as it is on the person of the local pastor and ecclesiastical structures, there is ultimately a dynamic and multi-layered interaction process that always must be placed in various contexts: the pastor is always the intermediary between the local parish and higher institutional levels in the Church hierarchy. In this capacity he is also addressed by those who receive the visions, by Mr. B. in the story of Dokkum, by the employers of the young shepherds at La Salette. Sometimes, indeed, within the account of the miracle itself there is a reference to contact with the local parish priest. For instance, this is explicitly so in the case of Lourdes: "Go to the priests and say...," Mary instructed Bernadette Soubirous in 1858.[19]

[18] For an overview and summary, see ZIMDARS-SWARTZ (1991) Chapter 2, 92-123.

[19] For a summary of Lourdes, see ZIMDARS-SWARTZ (1991) 43-66, and particularly early works by R. Laurentin: LAURENTIN (1957); (1962a); (1962b); (1962c); (1963); (1979).

Furthermore, the interaction process includes reassignments, disciplinary measures, arguments, and, especially, a possible development of the local pastor's attitude. As has already been emphasized, one must always take into account the dynamics and developments of the situation. Regarding this process, I would immediately note that I know hardly any examples in which the local pastor jumps significantly from one position to another on the scale discussed here.

It is precisely in this connection that Dokkum seems to me to be an unusual case. By looking at shifts on the scale from distance to engagement, we can also come to a better understanding of the specifics of a case. To my reading, the dossier lets us see how the pastor there, in the course of three years, moved along the scale from distance to engagement. I will return to that point briefly in my conclusion, but now, by way of developing this admittedly very general hypothesis of a typology of local pastoral interaction, I wish to turn my attention to a number of elements that play an especially meaningful role in the process.

5.2. The Narrative Dimension: "Script" and "Scenario"

First of all, I would draw the reader's attention to a not unimportant narrative component in the whole, which for the sake of brevity I will characterize with the TV and film term "script" or "scenario."[20] The course of the interaction, and especially the reactions of the local pastors involved, appears in part to be dictated by already existing parallel origin or growth accounts, in the same way as holy places actually come into being and continue to exist by the grace of myths and rites. To my mind, what is particularly important in this connection is the controlling force which stories can exercise: consciously or unconsciously, the actors involved seem to deal with them as though they were scenarios or scripts, modern *exempla* that direct their own actions.

I found a parallel phenomenon among the pilgrims who maintain a diary or record of their travels on long pilgrimages, such as, for instance, to Santiago de Compostela, and later, after their return, edit and publish these accounts. As is also found in the case of many other kinds of what are termed "personal narratives," it would appear that other travel accounts and diaries clearly serve an exemplary function for the shaping of these new accounts.[21]

[20] For literature, see note 10, above.

[21] See note 10, above.

The position of the pastor on the scale appears to no small degree to be dependent upon a sort of prescribed or expected reaction pattern that is based upon such a script or scenario. People recognize the situation instantaneously and connect it with parallel stories, which begin to fulfill a function as a kind of script. As far as that goes, this does not happen just for the pastor involved; in Dokkum, Mr. B. immediately drew the comparison with Lourdes. But it is particularly among clergy that one encounters knowledge of miracle and origin-accounts like those of La Salette, Lourdes, etc., in so far as they have bearing on the reactions of ecclesiastical figures. Such scenarios seem to be almost "preprogrammed," as it were, for many of those involved. For the pastor, it would appear that the scenario which speaks from these stories particularly points in the direction of critical distance, while keeping the bishop responsible informed is also a standard detail.

It would be interesting to further investigate this narrative aspect: which elements, from which stories, play a role? Examining at the personality structure of the pastors involved could also be an interesting theme demanding attention.[22]

5.3. Infrastructure: Material Culture of Pilgrimage

A subsequent point is the connection between the scale of distance and involvement on the part of the pastor and the eventual shaping of the interaction between devotional and parochial regimes, in terms of material and ritual infrastructures (to once again fall back on ethnological jargon). It is precisely this aspect of the genesis of a place of pilgrimage which I consider to be of great importance, for here we touch on the core of many theological, liturgical and religious reflections and discussions, questions surrounding the inculturation of Christian rites, and also the shaping of what I would label "liturgical landscapes."[23] In short, I am referring to the material culture, the material, infrastructural consequences and alterations in connection with the devotional incentive which arises so suddenly. Although generally it is only after some years that the design

[22] I am here thinking of explorations such as E. Drewermann carried out with the aid of what are termed "psychograms": see E. DREWERMANN: *Kleriker. Psychogramm eines Ideals* (Olten 1990). Recently the historian J. Art, from Ghent, made a bold attempt to apply this psychological approach in church history: see ART (1994); (1997) esp. 41ff; (1998).

[23] Here I would refer the reader to a splendid and little-noted book: LANE (1988). Cf. Chapter 12 of this book with more recent literature.

achieves a monumental status, such as, for instance, the refurbishment of the spring and park at Dokkum, costing over Dfl. 200,000, or the basilica and garden park at La Salette, already, from its very first stirrings, this material infrastructure plays an important role in the interaction process. The rising flow of interest, and more specifically of people, presses its demands and takes its toll. At first there is improvisation, marked by the scale of distance and engagement discussed above. The pastor sets himself up as a coordinator, offers the parish structures and facilities as a devotional infrastructure, or stands back from participation, warns his parishioners against it and blocks them from becoming engaged in the growing devotional culture.

This interaction can issue into various types of devotional organization that are, in particular, defined by the eventual growth and bloom of the newly introduced devotional culture. Here too, a scale can be drawn up, similar to that which we proposed above for the reactions of the local pastor. Both scales show a certain relationship, and the divisions of the scales correspond to a certain extent.

At the one end there is the double liturgy. This is by far the most frequent result, and corresponds to what we designated as the position of neutrality and distance on the scale of pastoral responses. An independent, parallel organization, oriented to the devotion and pilgrimage and supported by its own staff, arises next to, and separate from, the local parish structures, or sometimes at a somewhat greater distance; it has its own material and ritual repertoire, adapted for its own purposes. Generally monastic orders play a role in this. This is also to say, large scale; the double liturgy is to be found at sites which draw considerable numbers of visitors the whole year round. Sometimes the pilgrimage liturgy begins to compete with provisions for local pastoral work, and the pilgrimage centre takes on a local and regional pastoral function. But the form that this takes, again, is always that of the double liturgy. Double liturgy is, beyond this, found on a much wider scale in liturgical history. I am referring, for instance, to double churches, that in many respects still present us with unsolved riddles, from which people have derived double liturgy in one form or another,[24] and also to the solution double

[24] With respect to the interesting phenomenon of double basilicas or double churches, which are more likely to receive attention from (Christian) archaeology than from the perspective of liturgical studies, we here cite only ZOVATTO (1964), and the literature listed in ANDRESEN (1971) 28 sub 5.

liturgy offers to the conflicts which arise from the interaction between forms of chapter liturgies and parochial worship services in a number of places. The construction of the church of St. Jan directly next to that of St. Servaas in Maastricht was a direct consequence of this process.[25]

It is also interesting to note how sometimes, in the miracle narrative itself, concern has already been expressed about, and direction given for the ritual and material structures. For instance, there are calls for building a chapel, or having one built, or the request is made for processions and other such activities.

At the other end of the scale, there is the integrated structure, which appears to correspond with the engaged pastor. Countless modalities are then possible: the structure of a double liturgy may be introduced one or two times a year, creating a harmonious combination of parochial and pilgrimage organization, so that a further, dormant infrastructure comes into ritual life with the help of the parish. Another possibility is that the local parish community makes its church space available as the basis for the pilgrimage liturgy. This formula is found particularly in the smaller sites of regional significance.

But rarely is there that total integration, such as has until now been maintained at Dokkum, in which, to my mind, we are once again confronted with the special nature of this example. Until recently, under the inspired leadership of the local pastor, who in the course of time since the miracle became increasingly more engaged, a form of total integration of parish and pilgrimage liturgy has been sustained. Descriptions and evaluations of this combination of liturgy and pastoral function differ, according to the standpoint and perspective assumed by the viewer. Coming from outside, people are taken up into a parish liturgy which has grown beyond its origins in the parish church; as a parishioner, one takes part in a liturgy which has expanded outside the parish church because of the devotional context: the parish gathers around the spring. The boundaries between parishioner and pilgrim appear to blurr, at least

[25] The church of St. Jan, in Maastricht (The Netherlands, province Limburg), was built in the 12th century and renovated in the 14th, after the double liturgy of parish and chapter continued to be a source of conflict, despite a division of the church which assigned the east choir for the chapter liturgy and the west choir for the parish liturgy.

A related form of double liturgy is what is termed the *simultaneum*, the use of the same church space for protestant and Roman Catholic worship services. W. Munier, in particular, has written on this topic. I here list only MUNIER (1981); (1982a); (1982b); (1985).

from the perspective of the worship experience offered; the pilgrim is a parishioner, and the parishioner a pilgrim.

In summary: in the case of the material, ritual infrastructure, too, there is a sort of scale of interaction between parish and pilgrimage, with on the one side the extreme of total double liturgy, and on the other that of total integration, a scale that, as we have said, is closely connected with that discussed previously which reflected the pastoral interaction. Perhaps one could say that this liturgical, infrastructural ritual scale is to some degree the translation of the original scale of parish interaction, which was connected with the person and story, into the eventual ritual design.

The greatest challenge is now to be able to create a typology for this interaction and the diverse liturgical designs that we are able to distinguish within this combination. What are the characteristics of a specific pilgrimage liturgy, and what are the characteristics of the devotional ritual and material culture of other liturgical forms, in particular those which are found in parishes? I am thinking here, for instance, of the role of open air liturgy.[26]

5.4. Intermezzo

Several points of analysis and synthesis still remain on my list: the role of the press and media, the aspect of tourism, which correctly is receiving increasing attention in research on pilgrimage,[27] the role of the laity. There are also modern elements such as the phenomenon, encountered with increasing frequency, of the appropriation of places of pilgrimage by individuals associated with what can, in a vague and unnuanced way, be denoted as "New Age" circles. A good example of this is Glastonbury, in Southern England, with its miraculous spring around which elements of Celtic, Christian and New Age traditions come together.[28] In this

[26] Valuable building blocks for such a typology can be found in the recent dissertation by H. Evers: EVERS (1994). For open air liturgy, see further NEVILLE (1987) 28ff, Chapter II. See also NEVILLE & WESTERHOFF (1978). See Chapter 12.

[27] THEILMANN (1986); BENDIX (1989). The theme of tourism likewise permeates Morinis's collection: MORINIS (1992), particularly in the contribution by Cohen: COHEN (1992).

[28] For Glastonbury, see the well-documented survey by Marion Bowman: BOWMAN (1993), and the chaotic and confusing MICHELL (1990) From the enormous boom in primarily "criteriological" literature about New Age spirituality, I will here list only the

connection it can be said to be striking that at Dokkum, except for the personal views of the B. family, to my knowledge there has been no evidence of a New Age appropriation or borrowing of its significance. Does the "script" of the original founding narratives involving Boniface, who Christianized the Germans and their nature religion through his miracles and signs, perhaps play a role in this? After all, at the very least these stories could be called confrontational, and definitely not an ideal narrative basis for the integration of Christian myths and rites with the forms of New Age nature beliefs. Apart from that, it is interesting to see how it is precisely elsewhere in Friesland at the moment that attempts have been made for some time now by one pastor to connect elements of the Germanic/Frisian tradition with the Christian tradition.[29]

I can not elaborate on these issues here, but do wish to discuss just two more points of importance: the contextual dimension and the mystic dimension.

5.5. Surface and Undercurrents: Event and Context

There are always two movements in the local interaction process discussed above, each with its own nature and tempo. There is what could be called an undercurrent, that bears the productive context, which is rarely or never explicitly present in the story. Next to it, or better expressed, above it there is the level of event, of the miracle and the occurrences surrounding it. Both currents hang together, but for a proper understanding it is precisely the undercurrent that is important. Often the undercurrent is ignored, for instance because it would (or potentially might) contradict or unmask the miraculous character of the occurrences. It is in this area that the academically trained researcher studying pilgrimage has special responsibility. He or she must place the events, the stories, in the light of the contextual framework of forces around them, in which local,

special issue, of *Religieuze bewegingen in Nederland* (nr. 18 (1989) VU-Uitgeverij Amsterdam), the survey research by J. de Hart (see, among others, DE HART (1993a); (1993b), and the special issue of *Praktische Theologie*: VAN DEN HOOGEN & JONKER (1993); a good survey and status quaestionis concerning the character and context of the "New Age movement" offers: HANEGRAAFF (1996) and: MOERLAND & VAN OTTERLOO (1996); see also Chapter 11 in this book.

[29] I am here referring to the activities of the pastor at Balk, J. van der Wal; in relation to this see also the recent book by G. Noort, NOORT (1993) (reviewed by VAN DER WAL in *Friesch Dagblad* January 5, 1994).

regional, national, geographic, social, economic, cultural, ecclesiastical, theological, spiritual and psychological forces will play a role.

I published just such an attempt to chart the field of forces and provide contextual analysis, in the case of Dokkum. This places the revitalization of this place of pilgrimage into perspective. Within the complex field of forces, strategies for building up the parish and church and encouraging cultural tourism are the central themes, against a backdrop of a local culture moving from living entity to artifact, rising interest in local and regional culture and constructions of identity, and changes in the way our society deals with the past and nature. Harmoniously, the pastor and parish on one side, and those involved in the local and regional tourist industry on the other side, respected and "used" each other's contribution. As an enthusiastic and "converted" cultural intermediary, the pastor fulfilled a key role in this process.[30]

5.6. The Mystic Dimension

Finally, I want to draw the reader's attention to what I will term the "mystic dimension." By now the theories and models developed by Victor Turner have been rather generally critically discussed or even dismissed.[31] There is one aspect of his work which I, for one, still do not wish to let go of just yet. It is not well recognized that Turner showed particular interest in the individual, mystical dimension of pilgrimage; in this connection, he speaks of pilgrimage as "exteriorized mysticism."[32] For him, pilgrimage touched upon the very heart of religious experience, and is ultimately a mystical affair. The basic human activity which defines pilgrimage, the devotional going and coming back, is entirely and totally geared to this: through a complex whole of rituals involving dedication and stepping outside the ordinary course of life, and an infrastructure created around them, one works toward mystical experience, and then away from it. Perhaps we have here a key for understanding the double liturgies noted earlier: pilgrimage liturgy thus aims at a fundamentally different, mystical dimension of experience than does parish liturgy, and therefore requires its own shape and local roots.

[30] For a summary of this, see the article POST (1993).

[31] See POST (1994b) 273.

[32] See TURNER & TURNER (1978); see also the elaboration of this idea in MCKEVITT (1991).

6. Conclusion: Upsetting the Balance

Here we reach the conclusion of this, my first exploration of a new presentation of the questions around pilgrimage. Working on these notes has in any case afforded me more insight into the case of Dokkum in general, and the role of the pastor there in particular. I sense a certain pattern. For instance, I now see why the pastor, suddenly, after three years, turns directly to the B. family: distance has now turned around into engagement. I have a better understanding of the background of why logbooks are no longer kept and dossiers of newspaper cuttings are no longer assembled and circulated – these are after all genres which imply a certain distance – and why engaged, poetic, almost mystic personal narratives were later the expression chosen. I can also now see the peculiarity – and perhaps also the "tragedy" – of the Dokkum case, which is linked to the interaction between the miracle and miracle story from which it arose and local pastoral reactions, to the development that the pastor went through, a process which through our scale can be sketched as development from initial distance to the extreme of mystical, naive engagement. The pastor has become part of the process. Indeed, as the pastor of the parish, he in particular has also become a pilgrim, but a very exceptional one. After all, he does not come and go as is it is fitting for a pilgrim to do. He can not move on through forms of distance-creating double liturgy or by returning from the holy place. No, he is always there, always involved in the holy place. He has become a part of the mystic process of religious experience itself, and in doing so, the balance between engagement and distance has been permanently upset. No person can bear *staying* on the Mount of Transfiguration, and it was not without reason that Jesus refused the suggestion of the engaged, naive enthusiast Peter that they set up booths to dwell there in the full glare of mystic light.[33]

[33] See Mt. 17, 1-13; Mc. 9, 2-13; Lc. 9, 28-36.

Fig. 1. Wittem (The Netherlands, prov. Limburg), cloister and pilgrimage complex (photo: P. Post).

Fig. 2. Wittem (The Netherlands, prov. Limburg), statue of St. Gerard Majella (from a postcard).

Fig. 3. Wittem (The Netherlands, prov. Limburg), cult statue of St. Gerard Majella (photo: P. Post).

Fig. 4. Wittem (The Netherlands, prov. Limburg), cult statue of St. Gerard Majella (photo: coll. P. Post).

Fig. 5. Wittem (The Netherlands, prov. Limburg), procession in the cloister garden (photo: P. Post).

Fig. 6. Wittem (The Netherlands, prov. Limburg), café St. Gerardus, near the cloister and pilgrimage complex (photo: P. Post).

Fig. 7. Banneux, Banneux-Notre-Dame (Belgium) (photo: P.J. Margry, 1993).

Fig. 8. Banneux, Banneux-Notre-Dame (Belgium) (photo: P.J. Margry, 1993).

Fig. 9. Dokkum (The Netherlands, prov. Friesland), aerial photograph, St. Boniface spring and processional park, c. 1928 (collection: P. Post).

Fig. 10. Dokkum (The Netherlands, prov. Friesland), "Restored" processional park, 1994 (photo: P. Post).

Fig. 11. Dokkum (The Netherlands, prov. Friesland), 12th station of the cross in restored park (photo: P. Post).

Fig. 12. Dokkum (The Netherlands, prov. Friesland), St. Boniface Chapel (photo: P.J. Margry).

Fig. 13. "Dokkum: 'n moordstad" (City of his death) (postcard ca. 1990; coll. P. Post).

Fig. 14. Dokkum (The Netherlands, prov. Friesland), St. Boniface Chapel (photo: coll. P. Post).

Fig. 15. Dokkum (The Netherlands, prov. Friesland), statue of St. Boniface in the Boniface Chapel (photo: coll. P. Post).

Fig. 16. Dokkum (The Netherlands, prov. Friesland), pastor Herman Peters by the spring of St. Boniface, 1993 (photo: coll. P. Post).

Fig. 17. Dokkum (The Netherlands, prov. Friesland), redesigned basin by the Boniface Chapel and park, 1995 (photo: coll. P. Post).

Fig. 18. Dokkum (The Netherlands, prov. Friesland), programma of the St. Boniface Pilgrimage in 1983; in the background, pilgrims in the Boniface Chapel, August 21, 1983 (photo: P.J. Margry).

Fig. 19. La Salette (France), pilgrimage complex of Notre-Dame de la Salette (from a 1960s postcard; coll. P.J. Margry).

Fig. 20. La Salette (France), pilgrimage complex of Notre-Dame de la Salette (from a 1960s postcard; coll. P.J. Margry).

Fig. 21. La Salette (France), pilgrimage complex of Notre-Dame de la Salette (from a 1960s postcard; coll. P.J. Margry).

Fig. 22. La Salette (France), procession near the pilgrimage complex (from a 1960s postcard; coll. P.J. Margry).

PART II

THE MODERN PILGRIM: EXPERIENCES, MOTIVES AND EFFECTS

5. TRANSFORMATION AND CONFIRMATION

INTERVIEWS WITH PILGRIMS TO WITTEM AND LOURDES[1]

1. Introduction

As mentioned in chapter 1, within the framework of the "Christian Pilgrimage" research programme two surveys were carried out in 1985 among pilgrims to Wittem and Lourdes respectively. In 1987 a similar survey was carried out among pilgrims to Banneux.[2] The aims of these preliminary investigations were to gain initial insights into the area that was to be researched and subsequently to design questionnaires for use in a large-scale investigation among pilgrims to Lourdes.

From the outset we accepted, however, that collecting quantitative data concerning pilgrimages is limited and that consequently additional interviews with pilgrims were to be conducted. These interviews were used to check the results of the pilot studies with an emphasis on the in-depth study of the material that had been obtained by the survey.

This chapter deals with some of the qualitative data that have been collected so far. We present interview data from two pilgrims; one who went to Wittem and another one who went to Lourdes. We do not claim to give a wholly representative view of the pilgrim and his or her experiences. Rather these cases illustrate how qualitative data can deepen the already established quantitative findings. Thus, the dynamics and changes, as disclosed by the polls, can be clarified.

For each case we present a short summary of the data gathered in the polls, followed by an account of the interview. This will show how both sorts of data are related to each other and what is the additional contribution of the interview.

[1] First published as: J. Pieper & M. Van Uden: Wallfahrt als Glaubensentwicklung. Wandlung und Festigung, in *Archiv für Religionspsychologie* 20 (1992) 270-283.

[2] Derks (1988); Oosterwijk, Van Uden & Hensgens (1986); Pieper, Oosterwijk & Van Uden (1988); Post & Van Uden (1990); Pieper & Van Uden (1990); Van Uden & PIeper (1988).

In the final paragraph of this contribution we will compare and contrast both cases with each other under the header "transformation versus confirmation."

2. The Selection of the Two Cases

The most important criterion in the selection of the two cases was the extent to which each could serve a model for the two categories of pilgrims that had emerged from the various preliminary researches. The similarity in motivation structure among the older pilgrims to Wittem, Lourdes and Banneux constantly manifested itself in the preliminary researches. This motivation structure was clearly different from that of the younger pilgrims whom we met at Lourdes. Our selection of interviews was determined by this distinction. We wanted to try to shed more light on these two groups: the younger and the older pilgrim. From the cases that were available to us we opted for an older woman who went on a pilgrimage to Wittem and a younger man who went to Lourdes. On the basis of their stories depth can be added to the results of our questionnaire-research.

3. The Pilgrim to Wittem

3.1. Data from the Questionnaire

The interviewee is a 57-year-old married woman, housewife and mother of four children. Since 1982 she has been to Wittem once a year. For almost 40 years she has made an annual pilgrimage to Overdinkel (like Wittem a place in the Netherlands where St. Gerard is venerated). She travels on her own to Overdinkel, but she only goes to Wittem on pre-arranged pilgrimages.

Her parents used to subscribe to "The Sint Gerardusklok" (a magazine). Looking back on her pilgrimage to Wittem, she mentioned in the questionnaire that it was a beautiful day. She also stated that the trip by bus was pleasant (rosaries were said, which greatly appealed to her), but it had taken too long, which had unfortunately made her late for the celebration of the Eucharist. She considered the procession to be the most important part of the day and she also appreciated the benediction.

From her entries in the questionnaire it appeared that the interviewee agreed to all the items that refer to "comfort in family problems," "God and a better world" and "St. Gerard as source of help." On the other hand, it appeared that she rejected all motives that suggest recreational and social/ traditional reasons. Her answer to an open question about her motivation to undertake a pilgrimage was: "thanks for favours and further help received." Taken with her other answers, the favours and help do not appear to be concentrated on the small-scale family distress (comfort in family problems), but also on "world distress" (God and a better world) which transcends the individual level. The respondent mainly turned to St. Gerard in search of help and support, but she also agreed to all the motives that refer to the support of the Blessed Virgin Mary.

Furthermore it can be concluded from her questionnaire that she was a weekly church-goer who did not feel however particularly loyal towards her parish and was not active in it. She read a good deal about religion, watched TV-programmes on this subject and listened to religious radio programmes, but only occasionally talked to other people about her faith.

3.2. The Interview

The interview primarily concentrated on her motivation to go to Wittem each year. The explanation she offered was largely a confirmation of the impression gathered from the written information, but added further qualifications. At the core of her motivation to go on a pilgrimage is "gratitude;" to be more exact, gratitude that her children had no trouble finding good jobs. In this respect the interview, more than the survey, gives the impression that small-scale family distress is more at the centre of her motivation. The serious world distress – which seemed to be a motive in the survey, was not broached at all in the interview. Recreational motives appear to be completely absent: "it is, of course, an excursion, it takes you out of your daily routine, it is nice, but that's not why you do it." Her motivation does not seem to have changed since 1982 (her first trip to Wittem): "I always go because I'm grateful. There's always something to be grateful for. Gratitude makes me feel happy and cheerful. This makes it a beautiful day for me."

Although she had subscribed to "The Sint Gerardusklok" magazine for many years, and had gone on pilgrimages to Overdinkel for almost forty years, she only took up going to Wittem once a year some five years ago. Whereas she always went to Overdinkel together with her husband, she goes to Wittem together with a friend ("my husband doesn't really like those long coach trips"). To the question why she suddenly decided to go to Wittem some years ago, she answered: "I had always wanted to go to Wittem, but I didn't know how to. It's much too far to take the car or go by train. I had discussed it with my husband a couple of times, and then I spotted something about Wittem in the parish magazine, complete with an address where you could apply. I phoned and it appeared that there was still room enough in the coach, and then my friend and I decided to give it a try." Apparently there was no specific reason in 1982 to travel to Wittem that year. It was a long time desire, and more or less accidentally she had been offered the opportunity to fulfil this wish. There does not seem to be much difference between her motivation to go to Overdinkel and her motivation to go to Wittem. The only difference was that it is easier to accomplish the pilgrimage to Overdinkel (not so far away, she can go there on her bike) and has closer links with family tradition.

What makes her go to Wittem? The same that makes her go to Overdinkel, i.e. the special atmosphere because it is an open-air religious happening. "There's a great atmosphere, especially in the garden. Like at Overdinkel, the mass is celebrated outside. In all weathers, beautiful. Processions, special intentions, singing. I like it best in the open air... Each time it's a beautiful day. Particularly the benediction in the garden, although it isn't always outside because of the weather. The open air, the scenery, the sunshining through the trees. This is the climax of the day for me. The day is great already, but this makes it absolutely perfect."

She also keeps in touch with Wittem, apart from her yearly pilgrimage, through her subscription to "The Sint Gerardusklok", and by occasionally phoning to have a candle lit: "If there's something bothering me, I may phone. After all, I always put something in the offertory box for the 'East-Holland candle,' so I may demand something in return." Again her "if something's bothering me" mainly seems to refer to small-scale family distress: "For example when my granddaughter had to take her driving-test. It doesn't work, mind you, because she has failed six times already, but I ring without fail. I don't think it's a matter of 'Let's give them a ring and it will be taken care of,' but it makes me feel confident and, anyway, it's the only thing that I can do."

As well as her motivation to go on pilgrimages and the way she experiences them, other matters were discussed during the interview, among them the belief – in particular the disbelief – of the younger generation (especially of her own children). Answering the question if young people also go to Wittem, she said: "Every year you meet the same group in the coach. Regular customers. Lots of women, few youngsters, and the young people don't come a second time. It's a pity, though, that more young people don't join us. My children came to Overdinkel a number of times, but when they got older, they didn't want to know about it anymore. They enjoyed it, but they have lost interest. A pity, but I don't insist anymore. I know better now. I'm resigned to it. I don't want any tension in the home. I raised my children to be Catholics, but they hardly ever go to church now. One of them said 'I still believe,' but if you never go to church it obviously doesn't mean a lot any longer. But I don't want to discuss it anymore. Personally I've derived a great deal of support from it, but it's up to them really. I would have liked it if the children would also have got support from it... I go to church every Sunday. I'm not in and out of church all the time, but once a week shouldn't be too much trouble. It's no duty and there's no compulsion, I just feel I have to go. It's just part of the Sunday, I think."

She blames the Catholic religious education for the lack of belief. "They are at a so-called Catholic school, but... if they had received a better Catholic training, the youngsters nowadays would have taken a completely different attitude. As far as this is concerned, parents need the support of the schools."

Finally her attitude towards the Church was discussed, in particular the changes in the Church and the way the bishops act. She appears to take a more critical stand towards the Church than her seemingly traditional belief would lead one to initially believe. She had three main criticisms:

– The Churches cannot bring themselves to offer concrete help to people who are in need of it. "If somebody is in need somewhere today, they'll first talk about it tomorrow, and they'll get there only the day after. You should get there right away."

– The position of women in the Church. She finds it difficult to understand why, in view of the serious shortage of priests, women should not be given a greater opportunity to play an active role in the Church "to take away the pressure from the few priests that are left." "There's no need to allow these women to do everything, just like that, but now that there are so few men, it's something I don't approve of. I can understand that it used to be the exclusive right of men in the past, but I don't get why women will no longer be allowed to preach, when things had finally got to that stage. They should be glad that those women are prepared to do it. I think they act stupidly in these matters. There's no need at all for them to change ancient laws, but now that we have got into this situation, I say 'try to save what there is to save,' and when they refuse to do so, I wonder if they really want to, but then I don't want to get too involved, it wouldn't solve anything anyway."

– From the above it appears that she is not without criticism as far as the Church authorities are concerned, in particular the bishops. Their attitude towards women taking an active part in church work is not the only thing that she is critical of. She feels that the bishops are insufficiently vigilant over the unity in the Church, and that "they throw dust in the pope's eyes." Both of these seem to spring from one fundamental criticism, namely that the bishops are too far removed from the ordinary Church people. "They are above them and stay there; if they met the ordinary folk more frequently, more people would think differently and consequently there would be greater unity in the Church. They should be more lenient. I have the impression that people don't feel comfortable with their leadership. They concentrate too much on "you should do this and you should do that," and then, of course, people leave. Surely, that's no improvement? I fully support supervision, but it should not become too strict. When we were young we were raised with the idea of unity in the Church, but what has become of it?" In this respect the current pope appeals to her more than the bishops. "I appreciate it that this man really wants to know about the problems in the world, but I think it is a pity that he is only shown the nice things about the countries he visits. He really wants to get close to the people, but when he is kept away from them his travelling becomes pointless. The bishops should do as the pope does. Not only seeing the pleasant aspects, but getting really involved with the people."

4. The Pilgrim to Lourdes

4.1. Data from the Questionnaire

The interviewee was a twenty-year-old, unmarried man who had agreed that the following items from the list presented to him applied to him: "to worship God," "because Jesus appeals to me," "learning to pray," "to strengthen my faith," "nice surroundings," "recreation," "renew my strength," "confess my faith along with others," "an appealing atmosphere". The strengthening of his faith played a major role in his motivation to undertake a pilgrimage, as did confessing his faith together with others in inspiring surroundings. However, holiday-like elements also seemed to play a role. This appeared all the more clearly from his answer to an open question about this matter: "being on holiday and enjoying new experiences." Why he wanted to spend his holiday at Lourdes above all other places, did not become clear from the questionnaire.

The journey to Lourdes was the first time this young man took part in a pilgrimage. He did not go to other places of pilgrimage. He attends church services weekly, beyond which he does not seem to be active in the field of religion. To the question what the journey meant to him, he gave an elaborate answer: "I have come to a better understanding of my feelings, I can handle and express them better. I have also learned to "behave" towards the disabled. I found that there are other young people who have the same feelings I have, whereas I first thought to be unique in this respect." It becomes apparent from this answer in an indirect way that the contacts with people of his own age during the journey were of great significance. It appeared directly from his answers to a number of other questions. For example, his answer to the question which part of the pilgrimage had been important to him was "the talks with members of my group and other people." He spent a lot of the time at Lourdes with the same group of people. He put down the following about this in the questionnaire: "Without them the journey would (probably) not have been so unforgettable as it has been. Within one week I got to know their emotional lives (and my own) better than those of my friends I have known for years." This may have to do with a feeling of acceptance that he experienced: "Everybody was accepted for what he was; strangers became friends within one week." From this it is understandable that his answer to the question about what appealed most to him during the pilgrimage was "all people being together; being at one with the sick and disabled."

The above statement suggests that the pilgrimage impressed him favourably, but it was interesting to find that his scores on a number of scales (scales of anxiety and depression) which measered the psycho-social well-being of the pilgrims before and after the pilgrimage indicated that his psycho-social well-being after the pilgrimage is notably worse than before the pilgrimage. The questionnaire does not offer a clear explanation.

4.2. The Interview

Early on in the interview it appeared that the pilgrimage of 1985 had been the first pilgrimage for this young man, but that he subsequently had travelled to Lourdes on three other occasions. At first he talked about this in a matter-of-fact and superficial manner: "Once you have been there... well, then... for a lot of people it is an addiction" and "you just have to go; you really want to do it again," but it soon appears that his repeated participation arises from problems at a deeper level. More than once he talked about the "hangover" he is left with after each pilgrimage, which, for example, forced him to travel to Lourdes twice within three months over the summer of 1987. This hangover was not a trivial matter: "It takes weeks to clear. Especially during the first days I could not talk about it. I brooded a lot about things. I missed those people badly. Of course you do not feel utterly miserable, but still you are not your usual self." He was somewhat ambivalent about the "function" of the hangover: "That hangover may serve a purpose; you do get to know yourself quite well, but I'm also afraid that a lot of people find it so terribly difficult to handle that it backfires. That is the awful part. There are really people who scream for attention. People who get home and there is nobody there."

He did not explicitly state what caused his problems, but some clues can be found in the interview. For example, he says about one of his later pilgrimages: "This has been a very difficult week for me, an emotional week too, there was nothing for it, I had to return quickly... I didn't come back rested. Then I joined again (two months later) and then I was too busy to have time for myself... I really shut out certain things. I didn't want to end up with that hangover. I didn't want to show my emotions so much. But it turned out differently, because afterwards I had a huge hangover." So this deliberate effort to avoid repercussions was not successful either. "Many new people had to be taken care of; they sought you out to talk, but there was hardly time for yourself, you couldn't do anything about your own problems... You are so intensely occupied with these people that you need time in the evening to relax because otherwise you won't be able to keep going that whole week."

It seems that he could not avoid the hangover once the week is over. Even when he tried to escape the confrontation with himself (for example by shutting out his emotions or "fleeing" into his work) he could not get away from it. When he denied his feelings he will suffer repercussions, but when he is completely absorbed by them he does not feel "happy" either, because he will still have to deal with so many emotions afterwards.

This young man was apparently forced so completely to face up to himself during the pilgrimage by the contacts and the talks with persons of his own age that he is not able to deal with all he has learned about himself at Lourdes on his return ("You can be totally yourself. Nobody knows anybody; you have no past. It has changed me enormously... At Lourdes I was confronted with myself; I got to know myself there").

One of the causes of his emotional confusion was the confrontation with other people's misery, even though it had a favourable effect because he realised how happy and grateful the disabled can be despite their distress. It helped to put personal problems in perspective: "There will be a moment that the difference between sick and healthy people disappears. You realise that other things are becoming more important. You wonder "what is the point, really? You begin to appreciate small things more than before... You see so much misery around you that it makes you stronger. Your own problems appear insignificant. The sick are much more cheerful, or cheerful in a different way. They have recharged their batteries. The presence of sick people is the essential part. You cannot really appreciate Lourdes unless there are sick people there. You will not be confronted with certain things inside yourself if there are no sick people present." Thus he arrived at a confrontation with himself through the confrontation with the sick.

Another cause for his incapacity to handle the experiences gained during the pilgrimage lay in the fact that there was nobody to discuss them with afterwards. "I didn't know what to do about myself. I couldn't talk about it with anybody. You long to tell people close to you what it is like, but it's impossible. It's so terribly difficult. They don't understand." Though it may be less of a problem nowadays than after his first pilgrimage ("the feeling of shame has gone"), he still believed that people cannot really understand his experiences at Lourdes. The result is that after each pilgrimage he tried to stay in touch with his fellow-pilgrims. "You really need people who feel the same, because there's no other way to explain things. So, afterwards you talk a lot with each other on the phone. That's one way of getting rid of the hangover, by talking to people who were there too."

A final cause for his hangover could be that after the journey he was suddenly expected to show a behaviour completely different to his behaviour during the journey. The contrast was considerable: "You are back again in cold Holland and life goes on as before... When you have returned you are fed up again with being alone, in addition to this there are the emotional contacts of that week that you remember. After the pilgrimage in 1985 there was nobody at home with whom I could talk about it. I really didn't know what to do about myself." This was a problem for him. "The contact during that trip for youngsters was quite direct. You were forced to be yourself. You are completely yourself at Lourdes and then you come back into this cold world. Here I can't be the person I am at Lourdes and it hits you hard... After a week of helping everybody at Lourdes, you return and you walk through the town, thinking 'all right, then, who can I help?' And then you get those dark and ponderous glances, as if they want to say 'what do you want?'" Apparently he found it a problem getting to know himself better on the journeys to Lourdes, whereas his daily life only offered him restricted opportunities to put this knowledge to good use. To some extent he managed to do so, particularly in his relations with friends, but he found it far more difficult in everyday life because there he was not expected to behave as at Lourdes. Friendships, for that matter, became a lot easier, because his experiences at Lourdes made him feel less unsure about himself. "I make a more confident impression on people... My self-appreciation has increased... Somehow it has become easier for me to make contact. Whereas I found it a bit of a problem to make new friends in the past, I can do it relatively easily nowadays."

From the survey it had appeared that reasons of faith and recreation had played a major part in his motivation to undertake a pilgrimage. From the interview it appears that they had come first in his pilgrimage in 1985, but that a clear shift in motivation took place in his later pilgrimages. To the question what had made him decide to go on his first pilgrimage he answered: "I was persuaded by the parish priest of the village where I lived at the time. We got along well and he knew I hadn't been on holiday yet. He recommended going to Lourdes. At first I didn't want to hear of it, I thought "what am I supposed to do at Lourdes of all places?", but in the end he did persuade me to go. Then, at one stage, I thought "why not, as long as I'm away from it all. I didn't know what to expect... He had said 'it may be fun to go on holiday together with such a large group of young people', but in fact I'm still surprised to have gone at all." But, looking back, it may have been the most attractive aspect of that first trip, for there were more people like him: "Come to think of it, nobody knew why they had joined. Nobody understood what had made them do it, nobody knew what to expect." This had changed now. He has made the trip several times and is one of the more experienced pilgrims. This made his subsequent trips to Lourdes quite different from the first trip. "The first time you take the plunge with a relatively open mind, on the other occasions it was obviously my duty to be of assistance to others. My regular work is pretty superficial and there you can have really meaningful relations with other people, especially with elderly people in wheelchairs or people who are ill, this is a beautiful experience... That first time I didn't know how to behave towards those people either, now I handle things in a more grown-up way." The shift in his motivation was demonstrated when he said "that first time was merely a holiday, the other times I explicitly went to look after other people." The later pilgrimages were far less non-committal. It seemed out of the question that he would still – as in 1985 – agree to "curiosity" as a motive. He knew what to expect from his later pilgrimages and his motivation was based on this expectation.

It is likely that his "having to go" was mainly connected with the possibility of establishing deeper personal contacts in his own group during the pilgrimage, contacts that led to a better understanding of himself. The feeling of security in the crowds, separated from the rest of the world, and the security of his own group in those crowds played an important part in all this. "The sheer numbers of people are impressive, everybody is on the same wavelength, the scenery is wonderful, the people are quiet, no sullen people, all countries and nations are represented. It's a sort of Utopia. There's no contact with the outside world, you are left with your own problems and those of the people around you, when you sit down on a seat you end up chatting to somebody in no time. The problems of the world, the worries of every day have gone, there's nothing to worry about, you can be yourself... and in those large crowds your own group is the centre, it's with those people that you discuss your experiences. It's wonderful to share those feelings... It's very nice, the atmosphere in the group is tremendous. You get to know an awful lot of people, quickly and thoroughly, not superficially. That first time we spent hours talking. We were very serious about everything, yet we sometimes rolled about laughing. That was wonderful, an ideal mix."

Nevertheless, the later pilgrimages still contained something of a holiday-element: "I may go to relax, but always come back exhausted." He feels that, unlike the younger generation, elderly people go because of "purely" religious motives, but he cannot clearly explain what he meant by this. "Many people merely go to venerate Mary, but the elderly, who have often heard a great deal about it, also go to see what it's like and to see things from the past." To him Mary did not mean much, although he had to admit that this veneration creates a very special atmosphere at Lourdes, a sort of quiet atmosphere that does not miss its effect on him. His trips to Lourdes have clearly affected his religiousness. As far as he is concerned faith, God, Church and pilgrimage are now all linked to his relations with other people. About God he says: "I mainly see God in nature around me and in people. I don't see God as somebody with a beard; it's purely a matter of relations among people. I sense his presence here, literally everywhere. Not always, sometimes He is gone, then I have this feeling of emptiness, but when I get along with people – and nowadays I get along pleasantly with people – I feel His presence. I may feel it when I'm by myself, but frequently when there are people about me." He also wanted to feel this solidarity with people in church: "When I go to church, I must feel something, a certain solidarity with people about me."

The pilgrimages not only made him more conscious of his faith ("I wasn't really interested, but after that trip to Lourdes I paid more attention"), but he felt more at ease in his belief. In this respect he did not evaluate doubt as a negative factor: "When you are in doubt, you take the time to think about things, to say the least. I don't doubt so much the fact that there is "something," as my way of experiencing it. A bit like: what is all right for me to feel, how exactly do I have to believe, and how do I give it a place in my life?" He only dared to face these questions after he had acquired a solid footing in his faith, a fixed point in relation to his feeling certain about the existence of the "something" that provides the foundation for his belief. His pilgrimages have undoubtedly played a part in acquiring this foundation. They started a process in which he could distance himself from the God he was introduced to in church when he was a child, but with whom he could no longer enter into a satisfying relationship. During the pilgrimage he came to realise that contact with God is possible through his contacts with other people. His problem, however, seemed to be that he could only experience this when atmosphere and conditions were conducive. This is the case on pilgrimages, but usually not so in cold Holland. After each trip he tried to integrate his new experiences in his life, with varying degrees of success because people rarely offered him an opportunity to discover God in them. This led to feelings of disillusionment. For this young man pilgrimages seemed to be moments of religious growth, including the "growing pains" that go with it. For him pilgrimages were not moments of quiet and relaxation, on the contrary, they were moments that always acted as watersheds in his faith, including the periods of confusion immediately after the pilgrimages.

5. Comparison and Conclusions

In comparing the respondents, it seems possible to make the following distinction. On the one hand, the pilgrim to Wittem showed a habitual religiousness, in which a pilgrimage is "nothing special," meaning that she saw it as being part of the normal, customary practices of traditional Catholic religious life.[3] On the other hand, there was the young man who was motivated to go Lourdes to deepen his faith (and spend his holidays there). For him, to go on a pilgrimage to Lourdes was certainly not an everyday event. On the contrary, as he put it himself: "I'm still surprised to have gone at all." For him a pilgrimage and the faith behind it, is not a matter of "the way things are," but a matter of coming to terms with the pilgrimage-experiences spiritually and consciously and of making choices. Therefore he found it rather difficult to integrate his experiences as a pilgrim into his daily life. This also explains the deterioration in his psycho-social well-being, as measured by the scales of anxiety and depression immediately after the pilgrimage.

In comparing the interviews in greater detail, we notice that an aspect of religious life is discussed by the older pigrim that is not present in the interview with the young pilgrim to Lourdes, i.e. the worry about the continuity of the religious tradition. The pilgrim to Wittem was disturbed by "the disbelief of the younger generation," more in particular by the disbelief in her own children. It is notable that this disbelief was directly defined by and derived from "no longer going to church." It is

[3] Vergote (1987).

obvious that this older pilgrim associates faith with going to church and she felt that personal faith can only be maintained if it is weekly nourished by the liturgy. For the young pilgrim, going to church on a weekly basis is not an indispensable condition for his religious growth. On the contrary, it was this pilgrimage as a more or less unique event that allowed him to deepen his faith, because it was not part of his daily or weekly routine. The pilgrimage "lifted" him from his normal existence. It made it possible for him to "transcend" and "transform" this existence. During the pilgrimage he was, so to speak, taken out of his daily rut (as he puts it himself: "the daily routine is gone") and even outside himself, so that he could look at his own life from the outside. We think that this is what he meant when he said "you are confronted with yourself."

It is obvious that this "young" pilgrim's faith is less Church-oriented than the older pilgrim's. On the one hand, this offers him the opportunity to interpret his pilgrimages in different terms and in a different – wider – framework, but on the other hand, it also weighs him down with the burden of freedom. For the older pilgrim the traditional meanings are there, in a way they are not for him. We think that this may be a significant explanation for his intense emotional involvement during the pilgrimage and for the hangover afterwards: during the pilgrimage and afterwards he cannot bring his emotions in line with the structure of Catholic traditions. Naturally the older pilgrim cannot do so consciously, either, but she is so steeped in Catholic traditions that she need not make a conscious effort to give meaning to her experiences within this framework. In her case it is an automatic and unconscious process.

However, this does not alter the fact that the pilgrim to Lourdes left a stronger impression than the pilgrim to Wittem of "putting the pilgrimage to good use." In his case the journey led to a real deepening of his faith. But his pilgrimage did not only prove to have been of use as far as his faith is concerned. The young man gained in self-confidence, learned to see himself with other eyes, got to know himself; that is to say his as yet unrealised possibilities as well as his inevitable shortcomings. The feelings of dissatisfaction with this may disappear in due course. It is only then that we will be able to determine – and that he himself will realise – how much the pilgrimage enriched and changed his life.

In the case of the pilgrim to Wittem we find this to a much lesser degree. The pilgrimage did not encroach on her existence. We may go too far in saying that her journey to Wittem had become part of her yearly routine, but she was no longer deeply impressed. For her the journey did not mean pain and confusion, but neither did it mean growth and intense emotions. Some degree of emotionality and joy seemed to result from the pilgrimage when she stated that she experienced a deeper devotion at Wittem (and Overdinkel) than during her weekly churchgoing. But tomorrow is a new day and what was special yesterday has already been relegated to the background. However, this may not necessarily mean that yesterday's happiness has evaporated. This woman seemed to thrive on these short bursts of bliss. Her life is "small-scale," as is her motivation to undertake pilgrimages: gratitude that her children have found jobs, praying that her daughter may pass her driving test. One may not expect big words from her about "confronting yourself", or about "the optimism that drives away your own pessimism." No, just gratitude that daily life is manageable, and that it stays that way. The pilgrimage consolidates the state of things for her, it confirms rather than transforms.

The emerging theme, highlighted by this comparison, centers around the question of whether or not a pilgrimage makes the pilgrim transcend his daily religious routine and as a result puts his life in a new perspective: transformation versus confirmation. In this connection Van der Hart speaks about rites of passage and rites of confirmation.[4] The original term Van Gennep used was "rites de passage."[5] What he had in mind were rituals that mark all sorts of transitions that individuals as well as groups of people have to undergo in their lives. The classic examples are birth, marriage and death. These transitions are often experienced as crises, according to Van der Hart. Some authors speak of the rituals of life's crises. However, according to Van der Hart, rituals that go with crises involving illness (rituals of healing), house-moving and the like, also go under the heading of rites of passage. They are characterised by, among other things, the fact that three stages can be distinguished in these rites: the stages of separation, transition and incorporation. The stage of separation, or the "preliminary" stage, is the phase in which the old situation is abandoned. The transition proper takes place during the phase of "transition", also called the marginal or liminal stage. It is an ambiguous or paradoxical condition. It is often considered as sacred or, to the contrary, as impure. In the final phase of incorporation (the post-liminal

[4] VAN DER HART (1978).
[5] VAN GENNEP (1909).

phase) people make a fresh start on their taking part in social life, but now from a new social and cultural position. When applied to the pilgrim to Lourdes, we may conclude that his case was one of abandoning the home situation and finding himself in a liminal phase during the pilgrimage, which led to a change in faith and identity. The problem, however, lay in the phase of incorporation. His new identity failed to connect with the social and cultural environment from which he started and a smooth integration was not possible. He himself had changed, but his surroundings had not.

Additionaly, from this Van der Hart distinguishes the so-called rites of confirmation. These are rituals that occur with a certain regularity (daily, weekly, annually, etc.). They are tied to one single phase in the cycle of life and are aimed at maintaining the stability of life within this phase. A special form of the ritual of confirmation is the ritual of intensification. Intensification rituals are collective ritual activities of a group, activities, for example, which are connected with the alternation of night and day, or the alternation of the seasons. They affect the group as a whole, not just one particular group member. Our pilgrim who went to Wittem, as well as most of the people who went to Banneux, as described elsewhere in this book, are not dealing with a "transition," but are making an effort to consolidate, to confirm what is there. Therefore their pilgrimages can be characterised as going through a ritual of confirmation. Their faith is not changed, though it is strengthened. Additionaly, their pilgrimage must be seen as a confirmation of their identity as a group: being part of the religious tradition of the Catholic Church.

This view of the pilgrimage as a ritual in two different varieties was, as it were, forced on us by the data collected in the interviews and would never have come to light in a quantitative collection of data only. The interviews afforded us an extra insight into the significance of the written data, as well as modifying our view of "the pilgrimage as a ritual." The suggested combination of quantitative and qualitative methods of research seems to have been vindicated.

6. MODERN PILGRIMAGE TO LOURDES: MOTIVES AND EFFECTS[1]

1. INTRODUCTION

In this chapter the results of an empirical research study on Dutch pilgrims visiting Lourdes are presented. The results show that whilst all pilgrims are close to the Church and to religion, the motivation to go on a pilgrimage differs for older and younger pilgrims. The elders go on the basis of especially religious motives (seeking help and support and a deepening of faith). Younger people go for recreation and to meet other pilgrims. For both groups pilgrimage brings measurable psychological rather than physical benefits.

2. EMPIRICAL RESEARCH

2.1. Preliminary Investigations

A number of surveys were held among pilgrims visiting various shrines. This was carried out within the earlier mentioned context of the research programme "*Christian pilgrimage*." Three preliminary investigations and one main investigation were carried out. Questions were aimed at three phases of pilgrimage. Firstly, the phase preceding the pilgrimage: profiling the pilgrims and their motives for pilgrimage? Secondly, the activities and experiences of the pilgrims at the shrine itself. Thirdly, retrospective, the effects of the pilgrimage. The latter concerning effects related to religious attitude and the physical and psychological well-being of the pilgrims.[2]

[1] First published as: M. VAN UDEN, J. PIEPER & E. HENAU: Modern Pilgrimage and Faith, in *Journal of Empirical Theology* 4 (1991) 32-51.

[2] The choice for these phases in particular (before, during and after) is determined by the fact, that our study of pilgrimage departs from the point of view of a transforming or confirming ritual: VAN GENNEP (1960); VAN UDEN & PIEPER (1989); DERKS, PIEPER & VAN UDEN (1991).

As described in chapter 1 and 5 the first preliminary investigation concerned Dutch pilgrims visiting the southern Dutch Gerardus shrine in Wittem by bus during the summer of 1985.[3] 81, mostly older, participants filled in the questionnaires presented to them partially or entirely. The second preliminary investigation was aimed at an organised train-pilgrimage from Roosendaal (The Netherlands) to Lourdes, in October 1985.[4] 71 people, both young and old, took part in this investigation. The third and last preliminary investigation also used a questionnaire connected with an organised pilgrimage. In the latter investigation pilgrims from four different regions in the Netherlands were researched in September 1987, who were travelling to the Belgian Maria shrine in Banneux.[5] This was the most extensive investigation as there were 273 mostly older respondents.

These preliminary investigations served as a preparation for a large scale main research among Dutch pilgrims visiting Lourdes. The main research took place in 1988/89. This chapter concentrates primarily on the main research, but also draws from the results of the preliminary investigations. Concerning the main research we will limit ourselves to results with regard to (1) profile and (2) motivation of the pilgrims and (3) the effects of the pilgrimage on the physical and psychological well-being. A first analysis of the effects of this pilgrimage on the religious attitudes can be found in Derks.[6] Further analysis of the effects on the religious attitudes is shown in chapter 7 in which data from a control group are used as well.

2.2. Main Research: Realisation and Response

Lourdes is one of the most famous Christian shrines. This small town harbouring 17,000 permanent residents was the goal of 760 official pilgrimages in 1989, with nearly 600,000 pilgrims. The results for 1990 show that the numbers are still growing, no less than 1,030 official pilgrimages were noted, which brought 667,994 pilgrims to Lourdes.[7] The number of non-organised visitors was close to six million.

[3] OOSTERWIJK, VAN UDEN & HENSGENS (1986); VAN UDEN & PIEPER (1988).

[4] PIEPER, OOSTERWIJK & VAN UDEN (1988); PIEPER & VAN UDEN (1990).

[5] PIEPER, POST & VAN UDEN (1990); VAN UDEN & PIEPER (1991b).

[6] DERKS (1990) 179-182.

[7] Data published in *Lourdes – Aujourd'hui. Journal de la Grotte* 142-23 (1990) 5.

In the summer and autumn of 1988 two travel groups from the Netherlands to Lourdes, organized by the National Bureau of Pilgrimages in Den Bosch, were surveyed. In July 1,544 mostly older pilgrims left by train, bus or plane to Lourdes. In October there were 406 mostly younger pilgrims. The latter all travelled by train. Both groups were presented with a questionnaire to be filled in with, among other things, questions on their motives to go on a pilgrimage. 331 (21%) passengers from the July group and 183 (45%) from the October group filled in the questionnaires. In total we had 514 (26%) completed questionnaires.

Considering the poor response the question naturally arises as to the representativeness of the respondents. Through the National Bureau of Pilgrimages we were able to ascertain how the respondents relate to the total group of pilgrims, as far as a number of essential characteristics were concerned. The July or elder pilgrimage was representative of the total group in terms of civil status, occupation, age and physical health. However, there were some differences with regard to two variables. Firstly, more people with a job gave an answer to questions on organisation and course of the pilgrimage (24% among the respondents and 15% among the total group). In addition, the train passengers are overrepresented and the plane passengers are underrepresented. 76% of the total group went by train, compared with 83% of the respondents. 26% went by plane, while only 10% of the participants in the research fall into that category. The October or youth pilgrimage showed no real differences in a comparison of the variables: civil status, occupation, physical health and function of pilgrimage. However younger pilgrims within the group were more likely to participate.

2.3. Profile of the Pilgrim

The questionnaire contained a series of questions aimed at profiling pilgrims. The questions were subdivided into questions on (1) social characteristics, (2) religious characteristics in general and pilgrimage behaviour in particular and (3) attitude towards the Church. In the preliminary investigation we found that two clear groups can be distinguished in the organised pilgrimage ("old": those older than 35 and "young": those who are 35 or younger).[8] So, where the data are useful we will make separate

[8] PIEPER (1988); PIEPER, OOSTERWIJK & VAN UDEN (1988).

mention of both groups. This means that with regard to the main research we have a group of 323 people older than 35 (ranging from 36 to 89 with an average age of 60.5) and a group of 177 people younger than 36 (ranging from 11 to 35 with an average age of 24.6). We will start with an account of the social characteristics.

Social Characteristics

More women than men took part in the pilgrimage in the older group (69% to 31%). The level of education is low. 39% of those researched had only completed primary school and an extra 29% had vocational and technical training for 12 to 16 years-old. 32% of the elders had a higher level of education of which 8% had vocational and technical training for 18+ or university training. The above characteristics are reflected in the employment situation: 40% works at home and the rest are mostly employed in the lower occupational groups. Most pilgrims are married (57%) or have been (widow/widower: 22%; divorced: 3%). As far as political preferences are concerned the CDA (the Christian-Democratic Party: centre right) is by far the favourite (76%). Finally, on the matter of health we can say that it is good (59%) to reasonably good (24%). 12% think twice ("things are O.K.") and only 5% is not satisfied with their own health ("things aren't so good" and "bad").

In the younger group the female participants are in the majority as well (63% to 37%). The level of education is high, especially in comparison with the elders. 32% have completed vocational and technical training for 16 to 18 years-old and 12% fall into the category of higher education. Moreover, nearly half of the younger group is still following some kind of education.Younger pilgrims who already have a job clearly have a higher level of job than the more elder pilgrims.

It is striking that only 2% see themselves as homemakers. Most are unmarried (82%). The political preference is primarily for the CDA (44%). However, there is an amount of aversion or indifference noticeable with regard to politics: 10% has no preference for a political party and 22% has not yet made a choice. The state of health is better than that of the elders. 93% reported feeling good to reasonably good and only 3% reported dissatisfaction with his or her health.

Religious Characteristics and Pilgrimage Behaviour

The answers to the question "to whom is your personal faith mostly aimed?" concentrated on God (35%), Mary (24%) and Jesus (23%) among the elders. 15% of the sample mentions a combination of these three. What is striking is that people with a high attendance of church-services are more aimed at Jesus, while people with a low church attendance are more aimed at God. Respondents with the lowest education (primary school) are clearly more directed to Mary than the rest. The opinion of the pope is important to 67% of them and to 33% of them it is less important to entirely unimportant.

The elder pilgrims are no strangers to the phenomenon of pilgrimage. 63% has been to Lourdes before and 17% have been ten times or more. Other shrines also gain a lot of attention: 57% of the respondents sometimes visit a different shrine. Places often mentioned are: Banneux, Kevelaer, Heiloo, Beauraing, Handel, Scherpenheuvel and Wittem. A quarter of the people were travelling alone on the Lourdes trip which was researched, while the rest travelled together with a partner (34%), member of the family (19%) or friends and acquaintances (22%). One in every four participants is involved in one way or another with the organisation of the trip, either as an organiser (10%), a medical attendant (10%), or as a spiritual guide (3%).

Young people distinguish themselves from the elders on a number of points concerning belief and pilgrimage behaviour. Their personal faith is far more aimed at God (51%) and clearly less so at Mary (10%). The preference for Jesus is about equal to the older group (27%). A combination of God, Jesus and Mary is only mentioned in 4% of the cases. Young people who sometimes go to confession are more aimed at Jesus than those who never go. Besides this, more men are aimed at Jesus than women, who in their turn are more aimed at God in their personal faith. The opinion of the pope clearly carries less weight among the youths: to 28% it is important against 72% where it is not so important to entirely unimportant.

Considering their age it is no surprise to learn that the young people have not built up as much pilgrimage experience. 51% had not been to Lourdes before and "only" 30% visit other shrines as well, like Banneux, Kevelaer, Beauraing, Wittem and Scherpenheuvel. In addition, a number of other shrines were mentioned, which are further away, like Czestochowa, Santiago de Compostela and Medjugorje. In comparison to the elders more travel alone (47%). If travelling in company it is mostly with a member of the family (27%). More than was the case for the elders, people are involved with the organisation (20%) and to a lesser extent with the medical (4%) and spiritual (3%) guidance.

Attitude towards the Church
In general the elder pilgrims are close to the Church. This not only appears from their feeling of affiliation to the community (strong: 60%; some: 33%; none: 7%), but also from a number of behavioural measures. The weekly church attendance is markedly high (83% go church once a week). Four out of ten people researched are involved with the community, especially with regard to visiting the sick on behalf of the church, preparing the liturgy and singing in the church choir. The activities within the community increase the higher the church attendance is and the higher one's education is. Finally, 13% regularly go to confession.

The young people too are strongly involved with the church, perhaps slightly less so than the elders, but certainly more so in comparison to the church involvement of the average Roman Catholic. The sense of affiliation with the community is split up as follows: strong: 35%; some: 46%; none: 19%.[9] The weekly church attendance is very high at 59%.[10] 43% of this group is active within the community, in which the choir attracts a large group of youths (21%). The activity within the community again increases with higher church attendance. The score for confession (5%) cannot said to be very high.

2.4. The Motivation of the Pilgrim

Global Analysis of the Motives
The pilgrims were presented with a list of 42 motive terms in this project, in which they could indicate for each motive whether it applied to their pilgrimage or not. The concrete answers ranged from "yes," "don't know" to "no." As in the preliminary investigations, the answers were calculated separately for the group older than 35 and for the group 35 and younger. The ten most important motives of the elders can be found in table 1, while table 2 shows the youths most important motives.

Six motives occur in the top ten of both the younger and the older group. In each top ten are four motives which are specific to a particular group. In the elder group these are: "on account of the virgin Mary," "to get Mary's intercession," "to implore help or assistance," and "to pray for a better world." In the younger group these are: "to meet others,"

[9] It appears from a recent investigation among youths, who marry in church, that only 19% feel part of the church-community: PIEPER (1988) 38.

[10] This number lies at 16.4% for the average Roman Catholic in 1988 (KASKI: *Journal Een-twee-een* (1988) S 505.

TABLE 1: *The Ten Most Important Motives For Elders*

		"yes"
1.	To give thanks	94%
2.	To pray for those close to me	94
3.	On account of the Virgin Mary	93
4.	To get Mary's intercession	88
5.	To experience my faith among other believers	88
6.	To renew my strength	88
7.	To strengthen my faith	88
8.	To pray for the healing of others	87
9.	To implore help or assistance	86
10.	To pray for a better world	86
		(N= 295-313)

TABLE 2: *The Ten Most Important Motives For Young People*

		"yes"
1.	To meet others	88%
2.	Because of the feeling of affiliation to others	82
3.	To relax	78
4.	To experience my faith among other believers	72
5.	Because of the companionship	71
6.	To pray for those close to me	70
7.	To give thanks	70
8.	To renew my strength	66
9.	To pray for the healing of others	67
10.	To strengthen my faith	62
		(N=171-176)

"because of the affiliation to others," "to relax," and "because of the companionship."

There is a clear difference between the two sub-groups. If we look at the ten most important motives for the elder group we find a striking resemblance to the ten most important motives of the elder pilgrims, who went to Wittem and Banneux.[11] This also applies to the elder Lourdes pilgrims.[12] In this main research the motives the elders set out with

[11] VAN UDEN & PIEPER (1988); VAN UDEN & PIEPER (1991b).

[12] PIEPER, OOSTERWIJK & VAN UDEN (1988).

are primarily of a religious nature as well. Among these motives we can distinguish a) motives that refer (via Mary) to praying for help or support (plea) both for those close to us as well as the world in general and b) motives that refer to religious experience and strengthening. The motive "to give thanks" we take to mean thanks for favours granted, and therefore belongs to the group of motives that refer to pleas for help and support.

The ten most important motives for the younger group are similar to the ten most important motives of the young group in the preliminary investigation at Lourdes. One exception is the motive "out of curiosity". In the preliminary investigation this motive took up a high position (third place), but in this main study it does not make the top ten with a score of 42%. Youths mostly go on a pilgrimage for the contact with other people and the relaxation. Clearly, these are less religious motives than those of the elders. Yet, religious experience and praying for help and support (for the benefit of others in particular) are important secondary motives for youths.

Factor-analytical Findings

Using a factor-analytical procedure the best possible representation was sought for the correlation between the motive descriptions of the main research. The goal was to redefine the 42 motive descriptions to a number of basic motivations. After a number of orientating factor analyses, we chose a principal component analysis with varimax rotation.[13] As there were sufficient respondents, listwise deletion for the missing data was the obvious choice (N=412). The standard criterion of "minimum Eigenvalue" = 1.00 was adhered to. The procedure resulted in an extraction of seven factors covering 32.4%, 10.2%, 4.8%, 3.8%, 3.1%, 2.9% and 2.7% (total 59.8%) respectively of the variation. In the next table the factors are shown. The statistical measures are: the factor loading (minimum 0.40); the % of application per item (motive description) calculated separately for young and old; the reliability coefficient (Cronbach's alpha).[14]

Discussion of the Factors

Factor 1 (Help and assistance) is made up of motives which refer to help and assistance gained through prayer. The help is especially meant for

[13] NIE et al. (1975).

[14] This was done to assess the usability of the factors as scales. As factors 5, 6 and 7 are only made up of two items no alphas are calculated.

others, both people close to us (micro level) as well as the world in general (macro level). The prayer may be directed at Mary, Jesus or God. Coupled to the plea for help is the giving of thanks for favours granted or that are still to be granted.

Factor 2 (Deepening of faith) refers to the experiencing and confession of faith, among other believers in particular. One is aimed at Jesus and God to strengthen one's faith through the confrontation with them. A less strikingly Christian experience of religion also comes to the fore in this factor; "because I experience something of a higher power there." This experiencing of religion is connected to thoughts and reflections on life.

TABLE 3: *The Seven Factors*

	factor loading	*% of application* *young*	*old*
FACTOR 1: HELP AND ASSISTANCE			
– For those close to me	0.75	70%	94%
– Giving thanks	0.72	70	94
– Praying for a better world	0.71	58	86
– Praying for the healing of others	0.71	67	87
– To implore help/assistance	0.67	55	86
– To get Mary's intercession	0.60	40	88
– To implore God's blessing	0.58	28	85
– On account of the Virgin Mary	0.56	58	93
– Finding protection in Jesus	0.53	41	78
– The opportunity for a good prayer	0.52	53	83
– Because I find consolation there	0.45	46	76
alpha= 0.92	average	53%	86%
FACTOR 2: DEEPENING OF FAITH			
– Because Jesus appeals to me	0.72	38%	76%
– Faith among other believers	0.67	72	88
– To meet Christ	0.65	37	73
– To strengthen my faith	0.63	62	88
– To honour God	0.60	46	83
– To be close to God	0.60	47	81
– To testify my faith	0.58	56	83
– To experience a higher power	0.53	39	69
– Because of the chance to reflect	0.50	54	75
– To renew my strength	0.47	66	88
– To think about my life	0.46	51	63
alpha= 0.91	average	52%	79%

	factor loading	% of application young	old
FACTOR 3: HEALING TRADITION			
– Because I made a vow	0.62	12%	31%
– To do penance	0.60	18	51
– It is just a good habit	0.60	05	18
– Because of the poverty in the world	0.60	16	38
– To be healed	0.58	20	37
– To ask for forgiveness	0.57	27	61
– Because of contact with a clergyman	0.54	18	30
– Because I grew up with it	0.53	21	43
alpha= 0.80	average	17%	39%
FACTOR 4: RECREATION			
– To go away for a change	0.81	61%	30%
– Because it is beautifully situated	0.81	46	36
– Because of the beautiful trip	0.79	56	41
– Because of the companionship	0.75	71	36
– To meet others	0.55	88	56
– To relax	0.53	78	58
alpha= 0.84	average	57%	63%
FACTOR 5: PEACE AND QUIET			
– To seek quiet	0.67	55%	58%
– Because it is a haven	0.49	58	69
	average	57%	63%
FACTOR 6: CURIOSITY			
– Out of curiosity	0.68	42%	12%
– A lot of people from my neighbourhood are going too	0.60	17	12
	average	30%	12%
FACTOR 7: GUIDANCE			
– In order to guide someone	0.72	43%	47%
– Because of the affiliation with others	0.64	82	73
	average	62%	60%

Factor 3 (Healing tradition) is not that easy to interpret at face value. It is remarkable that this factor keeps cropping up with nearly the same structure in the preliminary investigations. In our opinion a series of motives come together in this factor, which refer to a belief rooted in religious tradition. This belief is that on the spot of the shrine one may be cured or healed, also in the sense of paying for one's sins. The personal contact with a clergyman is of importance in this, as is the case for confession. Furthermore, a vow is made which is kept in the case of a cure or healing. This religious tradition must be passed on in a child's education to later be experienced as a good habit.

Factor 4 (Recreation) is quite unequivocal. One experiences the pilgrimage as a pleasant and relaxing holiday. One enjoys the journey and the surroundings and the meeting of fellow passengers.

Factor 5 (Peace and quiet) refers to the need for peace and quiet, which the shrine seems to offer.

Factor 6 (Curiosity) shows that there are also people whose motives have not yet crystallised. They are guided by their curiosity about what attracts people, who come from all about, to Lourdes.

Factor 7 (Guidance) can be seen as a focus on others. People go along on a partner's or friends request or in their professional capacity as a pastor or doctor.

In this context it is relevant to point out that we also carried out factor analyses, in which the motives of the younger and elder pilgrims were researched separately. It appears that in general we find the same factor-structure as the analysis in which old and young are taken together. However, an important difference is the fact that motive 42 ("to meet others") unequivocally belongs to the factor "recreation" for elders. The young in contrast, who rate this motive very highly (88%), split it up between the factor "recreation" and a new sub-factor "reflection" as part of the factor "help and assistance." This factor also comprises motives like "so I can think about my life" and "because of the opportunity to reflect." We wish to focus attention on this, because this was also noted in our preliminary Lourdes investigation for the factor "seeking peace and tranquility together." Earlier we wrote: "It is notable that, among the older pilgrims (Wittem and Banneux) meeting others must be seen in the perspective of tourism. In the Lourdes study this item comes… in the factor involving reflection, "seeking peace and tranquility together." It is possible that we are here seeing a transitional area between reflection and recreation, which has to do precisely with encountering others."[15]

In comparison with the factor analyses of the preliminary investigations no new factors came to the fore in the main research. On the contrary, there are systematically repetitive connections. In this sense our main research confirms that which was presented tentatively in the preliminary investigations. If we look to the percentages applicable, then the factors found may be ordered as found in table 4, in which we maintain the distinction between young and old.

TABLE 4: *The Degree to Which the Factors are Applicable to Young and Old*

	young		*old*
1. Recreation	67%	1. Help and assistance	86%
2. Guidance	62	2. Deepening of faith	79
3. Peace and quiet	57	3. Peace and quiet	63
4. Help and assistance	53	4. Guidance	60
5. Deepening of faith	52	5. Recreation	43
6. Curiosity	30	6. Healing tradition	39
7. Healing tradition	17	7. Curiosity	12

In general this table reflects the difference in religious motivation between old and young, as was mentioned earlier. "Help and assistance" and "Deepening of faith" come first and foremost for the elders and though these factors are also of importance to youths they are preceded by "Recreation" and "Guidance." "Recreation" should be seen in the light of what was mentioned earlier for youths. "Curiosity" and "Healing tradition" have relatively low scores for both groups. Contrastingly "curiosity" plays a minor role for youths, but not for elders, while the opposite is true of "healing tradition." Concerning the latter one may talk of a break with tradition among youths.

2.5. Effects on the Physical and Mental Well-Being

We stated earlier that with regards to effects this chapter would be primarily concerned with effects on the physical and mental well-being. From way back Lourdes has had the image of being a place where miraculous cures are possible (the cures not medically explicable officially recognised

[15] PIEPER, POST & VAN UDEN (1990) 196.

are few in number[16]). A share of the visitors come to Lourdes to be cured of a physical ailment. The Dutch National Health Service help to keep this hope alive by (partially) reimbursing patients that are seriously ill with the costs of the trip to Lourdes. The visitors researched by us did not start off on their trip with this as their primary motive (as is patently obvious from the analysis of motivation, in which the factor "healing tradition" applies to only 40% of the elders and 17% of the youths). In connection with this Morris posits that if we speak of effects we should look to psychological effects rather than physical ones.[17] In a small scale investigation (24 respondents) among ill pilgrims he noted a decrease in fear and depression after a visit to Lourdes. In our own research the factor "help and assistance" (which was the most important reason for elders to go the trip) appears to point to the hope for psychological strengthening through pilgrimage.

The changes in physical and psychological well-being were mapped by means of the following measuring instruments: physical well-being was measured by means of the question; "What is your state of health at the moment?" Possible answers were: "good", "reasonably good", "things are O.K.", "things aren't so good," "bad." In the processing of the data the answers were seperated into the categories "physically healthy" (good and reasonably good added together) and "physically unhealthy" (things are O.K., not so good and bad added together).

Psychological well-being was measured with two psychological scales: the ZBV and the Zung. The ZBV is a self-examination questionnaire, which is used to determine the amount of fear present. This questionnaire is the Dutch version of the STAI, Spielbergers "State-Trait Anxiety Inventory."[18] The ZBV is made up of two separate questionnaires with which two distinct concepts of fear can be measured: State Anxiety and Trait Anxiety. As we were more interested in long term effects rather than short term ones, we chose for the Trait Anxiety scale. The scale is made up of 20 statements like "I feel fine" and "I feel nervous and agitated". 10 statements are symptomatically positive and 10 are symptomatically negative in formulation. The alternatives for answering were: "hardly ever," "sometimes," "often" and "nearly always." One can score 1, 2, 3 or 4 points per item. Thus, the range of the entire scale runs from 20 to 80 points. The lower the score, the lower the trait anxiety.

[16] MORRIS (1982); DOWLING (1984).

[17] MORRIS (1982).

[18] VAN DER PLOEG, DEFARES & SPIELBERGER (1980).

The Zung is a self-examination questionnaire used to determine the amount of depression present.[19] The Dutch version of the questionnaire was used.[20] It is made up of 21 items: 8 were symptomatically positive and 13 were symptomatically negative in formulation. Two examples are: "In this period I faced the future with confidence" and "I slept badly in this period". The respondents could choose from the same four answers as in the ZBV. A score of 0, 1, 2 or 3 was given per item, so that the total score may vary between 0 and 63. The lower the score, the lower the tendency to be depressed.

In the two preliminary investigations in Wittem and Lourdes measurements were made just before and just after the pilgrimage, in Banneux no effect measurements were made. The disadvantages of this procedure are that firstly it is hard to determine whether possible effects will last in the long run. Secondly, it is not really possible to point out the active factor because a control group is lacking. "Is it the pilgrimage, becoming familiar with the measuring instrument or are there other factors involved?"[21] Therefore, the following extra measurements were carried out in the main research in Lourdes. The measurements were not only made just before and after the pilgrimage, but also half a year after the pilgrimage. Besides this, a control group was formed. It was made up of a group of youths (N=47) from the southern part of the Netherlands and a group of elders (N=57) from the central Netherlands. Both groups were tested with the same measuring instruments in 1989. Measurements were made just before, just after and half a year after a week's holiday. Thus, we may speak of a non-equivalent control group design.[22] The results of the measurements are presented in tables 5, 6 and 7. The data are solely based on respondents, who participated in all measurements, being either two or three.

The first conclusion we can draw is that physical well-being does not improve through pilgrimage. The main research in particular makes this clear. The physical health drops from 87% to 83%. Any real improvement was not expected, because the majority of those researched were healthy already. Therefore, it is interesting to set the group of people apart, who said in the main research they were going on a pilgrimage to

[19] ZUNG (1965).

[20] For a recent revised Dutch version of the Zung scale see MOOK, KLEIJN & VAN DER PLOEG (1989)(1990).

[21] PIEPER, OOSTERWIJK & VAN UDEN (1988) 169.

[22] CAMPBELL & STANLEY (1966).

TABLE 5: *Changes in Physical Well-being: % "Physical Health"*

	Ist meas.	2nd meas.	3rd meas.
Wittem, 1985 (N=48)	94%	92%	
Lourdes, 1985 (N=50)	92%	96%	
Lourdes, 1988/89 (N=261)	87%	83%	86%
Control group, 1989 (N=34)	91%	94%	91%

TABLE 6: *Changes in Anxiety Level: ZBV Scores*

				t-test	(2-tail)
	Ist	2nd	3rd	p: 1-2	/p: 1-3
Wittem, 1985 (N=26)	36.5	34.5		0.05	
Lourdes, 1985 (N=42)	40.0	36.0		0.01	
Lourdes, 1988/89 (N=262)	37.6	34.6	35.6	0.001	/0.001
Control group, 1989 (N=28)	35.0	35.0	32.9	n.s.	/n.s.

TABLE 7: *Changes in Depression Level: Zung Scores*

				t-test	(2-tail)
	1st	2nd	3rd	p: 1-2	/p: 1-3
Wittem, 1985 (N=26)	17.7	12.8		0.01	
Lourdes, 1985 (N=43)	19.1	13.6		0.001	
Lourdes, 1988/89 (N=258)	14.1	13.2	14.6	n.s.	/n.s.
Control group, 1989 (N=28)	14.5	12.6	13.6	n.s.	/n.s.

be cured (N=55), for further study. This group scores 76%, 65% and 75% consecutively. So, for this group of which we have the most expectations regarding an improvement of physical well-being, we see a deterioration rather than any progress.

A second conclusion is that the anxiety level drops through participation in a pilgrimage. The drop is statistically significant in both the preliminary investigations as well as the main research. Certainly in the main research the drop is highly significant (t-value: 6.32, $p<0.001$[23]). In the third measurement we see that to a large extent the drop has not been impaired. The difference between the first and the third measurement

[23] The large number of respondents plays an important role here.

are also statistically significant (t-value: 3.68, p <0.001). The control group in contrast does not show any significant differences in anxiety level. This points to the possibility that some special effect can be ascribed to the pilgrimage concerning the reduction of feelings of anxiety.

The degree of depression as a third point does drop significantly in the preliminary investigations, but not in the main research (t-value: 1.65, p= n.s.). Depression sooner drops by taking a holiday (drop from 14.5 to 12.6, not statistically significant). An explanation for this inconsistency may be sought in the possibility of self-selection. It appears from the data on the situation at the outset, that depression is relatively high in the two preliminary investigations in comparison to the main research. Especially in the case of the Lourdes investigation. In this investigation the response was very high in comparison to the main research (64% versus 26%). The high response was due to the fact that we personally got respondents on the train to participate in the investigation. The main research was far more anonymous in its operation. It is quite possible that less depressed people decided to participate in the research, so that there is little room for any drop. Therefore, we see that the second measurement of depression hardly differs between the preliminary and the main research. This is because the people from the preliminary investigation (with the high initial scores) drop to the level of the respondents from the main research. Further support of this presupposition is derived from the fact that pilgrims with a high level of depression in the main research (N=67) do show a significant drop. This goes for both the second as well the third measurement. The Zung scores for this group are as follows: 1) 27.3; 2) 21.7; 3) 23.8 (t-value measurement 1 versus measurement 2: 4.42, p<0.001; t-value measurement 1 versus measurement 3: 2.63, p=0.01). With regard to depression we may conclude that though the pilgrimage has no general anti-depressing effect, it does work for people who start out with a high level of depression. We must add that such a mechanism also could apply to the control group. Concerning depression this need not be a matter of surplus value through pilgrimage. However, on the basis of the small number of respondents in the control group, there was no statistically reliable division to be made between those depressed and those very depressed.

In summary, no positive effects (far sooner negative ones) are found for the physical well-being, but they are found for the psychological well-being. Especially for the reduction of feelings of anxiety. Here, a pilgrimage works better than a holiday.

7. LOURDES: A PLACE OF RELIGIOUS TRANSFORMATIONS?[1]

1. Introduction

In the contribution of the psychology of religion to the research programme, "Christian pilgrimage", pilgrimage is studied as a ritual that can cause physical, mental and religious changes in the pilgrims' conditions. As pointed out in earlier chapters this contribution has dealt with four quantitative inquiries of pilgrims in various settings: three pre-researches (Wittem in The Netherlands, Banneux in Belgium, Lourdes in France) and one main-research (Lourdes again). As pilgrimage is studied for its transforming possibilities, these inquiries are focussed on three phases in pilgrimage as a whole: before, during and after. The first phase is an analysis of the pilgrims' conditions preceding the pilgrimage: their profile and motives. The second phase is an analysis of their actual activities and experiences at the place of pilgrimage. Finally, the third phase is an analysis of the measurable effects after the pilgrimage, concerning pilgrims' religious attitudes and their physical and mental well-being.

This chapter is primarily based on the main research. It is limited to results concerning the effects on the pilgrims' religious attitudes. In doing so an elaboration on the pilgrims' profile and motives and on the pilgrims' activities and experiences at the place of pilgrimage will be necessary.[2]

2. Pilgrimage as a Transforming Ritual: Antropological Notions

"Les Rites de Passage" by the French ethnologist Arnold van Gennep, published in 1909, has created a framework within which the study of

[1] First published as: J. Pieper & M. van Uden: Lourdes: A Place of Religious Transformations? in *The International Journal for the Psychology of Religion* 4 (1994) 91-104.

[2] Detailed results with respect to the profile and motives of the pilgrims are presented in chapter 6. See also: Pieper, Post & van Uden (1990); Pieper & van Uden (1991) and van Uden, Pieper & Henau (1991). The two latter articles present results of the effects on physical and mental well-being as well.

the transforming power of rituals has come about.[3] When Van Gennep speaks of rituals of transition, he refers to rituals that mark various kinds of transitions that individuals and groups meet throughout their lives. He deals with transitions of territory and status. Classic examples of the latter are birth, marriage, and death. For an individual these transitions often have the nature of crisis. Therefore Van der Hart speaks of rituals of "life-crisis."[4] He also classifies rituals that accompany crises over illness (healing-rituals), removal etc., as rituals of transition. As for their structure, rituals of transition are characterised by a sequence of three phases: separation, transition and incorporation (or aggregation). In the phase of separation, also called the preliminal phase, there is a separation, a release from the old situation. In the phase of transition, also called the marginal or liminal phase, the actual transition takes place, in an ambiguous or paradoxical situation. It is often seen as holy or, to the contrary, as impure. In the concluding phase of incorporation (the post-liminal phase) people participate again in their social life, but in a new social and cultural position.[5]

In the book, "Image and pilgrimage in Christian culture," which he wrote together with his wife Edith, Victor Turner applied this sequence to pilgrimage, in which his attention is focussed mainly on the middle, liminal phase. "Pilgrimage has some of the liminal phase attributes in passage rites: release from mundane structure; homogenization of status; simplicity of dress and behavior; communitas, both on the journey, and as a characteristic of the goal, which is in itself a source of communitas, healing and renewal; ordeal; reflection on the meaning of religious and cultural core-values; ritualized reenactment of correspondences between a religious paradigm and shared human experiences; movement from a mundane center to a sacred periphery which suddenly, transiently, becomes central for the individual, an axis mundi of his faith; movement in general (as against stasis), symbolizing the uncapturability and temporal transience of communitas; individuality posed against the

[3] Van Gennep (1909).

[4] Van der Hart (1984).

[5] The psychological anthropologist Wallace expands this sequence with a phase preceding the ritual and a phase following the ritual (Canda 1988). In the pre-ritual phase are learning-processes that familiarize individuals with a perception of the procedure and the result of the ritual in the existing culture. In the fifth phase, following the ritual, a lasting memory of the adornments, amulets, mascots (for instance, the water of Lourdes) that are handed out during the ritual, produce a continuous effect of the one-off event.

institutionalized milieu; and so forth."[6] Turner mainly stresses the experience of "communitas," the feeling of solidarity between people, as a sort of universal brotherhood that trespasses daily social demarcations, as a central characteristic of the liminal phase.[7]

An interesting part of Turner's description is: "ritualized reenactment of correspondences between a religious paradigm and shared human experiences." Van der Hart also dealt with these matters, claiming that there is always one complex of myth – in which, in Turner's words, a religious paradigm is expressed – and ritual.[8] In this complex of myth and ritual, the negative experiences of an individual can be expressed within the context of the myth. The myth becomes the medium through which human experiences can be symbolically shaped and altered. By participating in the ritual, changes, presented in the myth, are followed by changes at a subjective level. At this point we trace a cognitive reorganisation on the basis of the fact that individual questions are mirrored by collective answers.[9]

3. Attribution-Theoretical Point of View

A theory that is able to explain this process of change of perspective psychologically is attribution-theory, which holds that people confronted with non-daily, peculiar events and experiences (that can come about for instance during a pilgrimage) will look for interpretations for these events and experiences.[10] These interpretations or attributions can be retrospective, referring to the cause of the events ("causal attributions"), or proactive, referring to the events' significance for the future ("attributions of

[6] Turner & Turner (1978) 253-254.

[7] Turner (1973) (1974); Deflem (1991).

[8] Van Der Hart (1981).

[9] Wallace views "ritual as a means of rapid relearning. It shifts a person powerfully and efficiently from one mental construct of self and world, called "mazeway," to another." (Canda 1988) 209.

[10] Of course there are also other, non-cognitive psychological (psychodynamic and anthropological) explanations possible as regards the impact of this state of liminality. For example Turner (1977) 40 points at the experimental, creative, "ludic" aspects of liminality: "In liminality, new ways of acting, new combinations of symbols, are tried out, to be discarded or accepted." Ross & Ross (1983) suggest a correspondence between liminal qualities and the relation between mother and child in the pre-oedipal period.

meaning").[11] This is our starting-point in trying to understand the transforming power of rituals. We are primarily interested in the occurence of religious attributions, that refer to the influence of God and religion, during a pilgrimage. According to Spilka, Shaver & Kirkpatrick this depends on three variables.[12]

(1) The characteristics of the attributor: to what extent are pilgrims generally, in accordance with their religious past-history, liable to use religious attributions?

(2) The characteristics of the event: to what extent does participation in the pilgrimage generate religious attributions? Do sub-events, related to the pilgrimage, hold an impulse to look for explanations that include God or religious faith?

(3) The context of the attributor: to what extent are religious attributions presented from outside during a pilgrimage, that could be taken over.[13]

Applied to a pilgrimage to Lourdes, the following "screenplay" could be outlined. Pilgrims, who in comparison with the average Catholic population are close to faith and the Church,[14] go on a pilgrimage from an everyday starting-point. Judging from several analyses of motives, it appears that pilgrims make the journey with specific expectations, hoping to be helped and relieved, to deepen their faith and they are looking for intense contacts with fellow-pilgrims (mainly the case with those who are young).[15]

The pilgrimage itself has features of liminality: chaos at the place of pilgrimage, overpowering impressions, sensory overload, a feeling of community and togetherness, intense contacts between the sick, invalids and the healthy and so on. All these non-daily, exceptional events and experiences will lead to attributional activity.

Furthermore, at the place of pilgrimage and even earlier, during the journey, pilgrims are confronted with a Christian frame of interpreting reality. Phenomena such as stories about Bernadette and Mary, references to Jesus and God, collective prayer, participation in liturgical celebrations, Corpus Christi procession, etc. can be pointed at. Osterrieth expresses this as follows: "During the journey, the pilgrim displayed religious zeal. Mostly, he went to pray at the sanctuaries encountered along the way.

[11] BULMAN & WORTMAN (1977).

[12] SPILKA, SHAVER & KIRKPATRICK (1985).

[13] SPILKA et AL. also mention a fourth factor: the context of the event.

[14] PIEPER & VAN UDEN (1991). See Chapter 6.

[15] PIEPER, POST & VAN UDEN (1990); PIEPER & VAN UDEN (1991).

He seized the chance to receive the sacraments, to collect indulgences, to hear hagiographic tales, to listen to sermons, to touch the relics, and to implore saints for intercession. The pilgrim exposed himself to the sacred."[16] It is true that this is a description of a mediaeval pilgrimage, but the present-day Lourdes pilgrimages still immerse the pilgrim (at least to some degree) in the world of Christian ideas.

To summarize, these people have a well-developed religious frame of interpretation at their disposal, undergo non-daily, peculiar events and experiences and are intensively confronted with the Christian interpretation of life. Judging from this account it is legitimate to accept pilgrimage as an event that evokes religious attributions.

In the research on Lourdes-pilgrims, a number of questions were included to evaluate the previous account. These questions can give answers about:

(1) The religious profile and motives of the pilgrims.

(2) The extent to which during their pilgrimage they have experiences of a non-daily, extraordinary nature.

(3) The extent to which they are confronted with the Christian tradition.

(4a) The extent to which they use religious attributions during the pilgrimage, compared with the previous period.

If we assume that the pilgrimage leads to religious attributions at least to sóme degree, the question is to what extent a one-off change of perspective will leave lasting traces on the pilgrims' religious attributional style in general, with traces of this change of perspective after the pilgrimage. Only in this case can we really speak of transformation. So the research also included questions focussed on:

(4b) The extent to which the pilgrimage has a permanent influence on the use of religious interpretations or attributions.

4. Method

As explained in chapter 6, in the second half of 1988 two groups travelling from the Netherlands to Lourdes (France), organized by the "National Bureau of Pilgrimage" at Den Bosch, were researched. In July, 1544 for the most part older pilgrims went to Lourdes by train, bus or airplane.

[16] Osterrieth (1989) 152.

In October, 406 mostly younger pilgrims went to Lourdes by train. Both groups received a questionnaire before, immediately after, and half a year after their travel, filled out by 331 (21%) of the pilgrims from the July-group and 183 (45%) of the October-group. So we received 514 (26%) completed questionnaires, from the first measurement. At the second 453 pilgrims filled out the questionnaire, and at the third only 266.

With such a low response-rate the question of randomness has to be asked. As we checked, however, our groups of respondents did not differ drastically with respect to essential social characteristics, like civil status, job, age and physical health, from the total group of departed pilgrims.[17]

5. Results

5.1. Religious Profile and Motivation of the Pilgrim

Results with regard to religious profile and motivation have been presented in the previous chapter. The data were analysed for old (> 35 years) and young separately. Those groups have a different religious profile and different motives for going on a pilgrimage, which can be summarized as follows.[18] Both older and younger pilgrims felt close to God and attended church weekly. The older pilgrims, however, felt somewhat closer to Mary and Jesus, than did the younger.

The central motivation of the older pilgrims is religious, praying to Mary, Jesus and God for help and support, and deepening their faith by adressing themselves to God and Jesus. Those religious motives are important for the younger pilgrims too, but they were preceded by "recreation" and "guidance" (meaning to guide someone, like a friend or a handicapped person).

5.2. Pilgrimage as an Unusual Event

To measure the degree of "unusualness," we asked the pilgrims to judge a number of pilgrimage-related situations and experiences in terms of their importance. Twenty items were presented with three possible answers: "important to me," "not so important to me" and "not applicable to me." These twenty items were based on information from the

[17] Pieper & Van Uden (1991).

[18] Pieper (1988).

pre-researches (questionnaires and interviews) and naturalistic observation in several places of pilgrimage, Lourdes included. Table 1 shows how important ("important to me") the items were judged, with the answers of younger and older pilgrims presented separately.

TABLE 1: *Experiences and Events: Degree of Rated Importance*

	% important	
	old	*young*
1. Helping each other	96%	96%
2. The atmosphere of joy in Lourdes	95	87
3. My feeling of togetherness with others	94	93
4. The contact between the sick and healthy people	91	96
5. Doing things together with others	91	96
6. Gaining new strength	90	78
7. Praying for the healing of others	90	68
8. Being together with so many others	90	88
9. Expressing and experiencing faith together	90	68
10. The opportunity for reflection	85	63
11. Enjoying silence and tranquillity	83	76
12. The confrontation with the misery of others	82	76
13. The pleasant atmosphere in Lourdes	81	88
14. The total acceptance by others	80	83
15. Enjoying the beautiful environment	80	82
16. Being absorbed in prayer	79	57
17. Diverting myself	71	75
18. Sharing my feelings with others	67	74
19. To experience the relativity of my problems	66	59
20. Praying for my own healing	45	28

We see that almost all the situations and experiences were important during the pilgrimage for a majority of the pilgrims.

The item with the highest support for both the older and younger pilgrims was "helping each other" (96%). For the younger pilgrims "contact between the sick and healthy people" and "doing things together with others" also scored 96%. For the older pilgrims, the second highest score was for "the atmosphere of joy in Lourdes" (95%). The item least important for both groups was "praying for my own healing" (45% old and 28%

young). We earlier emphasized that people do not go primarily on a pilgrimage for their own physical healing.[19]

Remarkable also is the fact that the agreement of the older pilgrims is in general higher than that of the younger pilgrims, except for situations and experiences that point to the recreational or "meeting others"-aspect of the pilgrimage. In these cases the younger pilgrims scored higher.

A factor-analysis offered more insight into the interdependency of the various experiences, with six factors extracted, which included all 20 items (table 2).[20]

TABLE 2: *Six Kinds of Experiences and Events*

FACTOR 1: CONTACT BETWEEN SICK AND HEALTHY PEOPLE	*factor-loading*	*% important*	
		old	young
exp9: Helping each other	0.64	96	96
exp7: Contact between sick and healthy people	0.62	91	96
exp2: Confrontation with the misery of others	0.61	81	76
average % "important to me"		90	89
FACTOR 2: TOGETHERNESS			
exp4: Feeling of togetherness with others	0.73	94	93
exp18: Doing things together with others	0.67	91	96
exp19: Total acceptance by others	0.57	80	83
average		88	91
FACTOR 3: FAITH COMMUNITY			
exp15: Atmosphere of joy in Lourdes	0.66	95	87
exp13: Praying for the healing of others	0.64	90	68
exp6: Expressing and experiencing faith together	0.56	90	68
exp14: Being together with so many others	0.56	90	88
average		91	78

[19] PIEPER & VAN UDEN (1991). See Chapter 6.

[20] After a few orienting analyses, we eventually chose a principal-component analysis with varimax rotation (NIE et al. 1975). The options "missing pairwise" and "mineigen= 1.00" were chosen. Six factors were extracted. These factors respectively accounted for 21.7%, 10.0%, 7.6%, 6.7%, 5.2% and 5.0%, in total 56.2% of the variance. The total number of respondents was 453.

FACTOR 4: RECREATION			
exp5: Enjoying the beautiful environment	0.71	80	82
exp17: The pleasant atmosphere in Lourdes	0.69	81	88
exp20: Diverting myself	0.49	71	75
average		77	82
FACTOR 5: INTROSPECTION			
exp8: The opportunity for reflection	0.79	85	63
exp1: Being absorbed in prayer	0.78	79	57
exp12: Enjoying silence and tranquillity	0.42	83	76
average		82	65
FACTOR 6: RECOVERY			
exp10: Experiencing the relativity of my problems	0.67	66	59
exp16: Praying for my own healing	0.62	45	28
exp3: Gaining new strength	0.53	90	78
exp11: Sharing my feelings with others	0.48	67	74
average		67	60

The factors, "Contact between sick and healthy people," "Togetherness" and "Faith community" in our opinion indicate the communitas-feature of pilgrimage. They are the three highest scoring (average % "important to me") factors for the older pilgrims and two of them are the highest scoring factors for the younger pilgrims too. So, these factors especially represent the experiences of the pilgrim. But the other factors are also of importance to the majority of pilgrims to Lourdes. The least is the factor "Recovery," with the item "Praying for my own healing," the lowest scoring item.

The factor "Introspection" with items referring to reflection, prayer and silence, shows the biggest discrepancy in support (17%) between the older and younger pilgrim. Older respondents judge these matters to be more important during the pilgrimage than do the younger ones, which is also true for the factor "Faith community," with a difference of 13% between older and younger pilgrims.

5.3. Confrontation with Religious (Christian) Interpretations

To see to what extent people are confronted with a religious (Christian) frame of interpretation, we asked the respondents what kinds of religious activities they participated in during the pilgrimage. Fifteen activities, selected out of naturalistic observation in Lourdes, were presented. Table 3 shows the results, presented separately again for older and younger respondents. "Applicable" means that the respondent participated in the activity.

TABLE 3: *Participating in Religious Activities*

	% "applicable"	
	old	*young*
1. Visiting the Cave	100%	100%
2. The light-procession	98	95
3. The singing of hymns	98	99
4. Sacramental-procession	94	80
5. The lighting of candles	94	93
6. The farewell celebration	91	93
7. Blessing of personal objects	76	55
8. Blessing and anointing the sick	75	84
9. Celebration of penance	70	36
10. Way of the Cross	65	83
11. Visiting the "houses of Bernadette"	62	62
12. Benediction	42	18
13. Conversation with a chaplain or priest	42	45
14. Diaporama (slide show of Bernadette)	28	66
15. The walk to Bartres (a place near Lourdes, where Bernadette lived for some time)	13	9

From this table we see that the majority of pilgrims take part in those activities, although "Benediction," "Conversation with a chaplain or priest" and "The walk to Bartres" scored low for younger and older pilgrims. For the older respondents this is also true for the "Diaporama (slide show of Bernadette)" and for the younger, the "Celebration of penance."

It is important to note that not only do most people engage in these activities, but they are also positively evaluated. The older pilgrims vary in these positive evaluations of the various activities from 76% to 99%, and the younger vary from 62% to 96%. Only the "Celebration of penance" did not appeal to the younger pilgrims with only 36% positive evaluations.

5.4. Religious Interpretations

Although there are a few existing scales for measuring religious attributions we did not use them because they are exclusively focussed on God as a causal agent.[21] We did formulate items to measure whether "God", "Jesus," "Mary," a "higher power" (religious attributions) and "fellow man" (as a non-religious attribution) were influential in the lives of the pilgrims. The possible answers for each item, (for example: "I experience Mary's intercession") were: "strongly," "a little" and "not." This part of the questionnaire was filled out before, after and half a year after the pilgrimage to research whether the meaning of God, Jesus, Mary, a "higher power" or "fellow man" increased during the pilgrimage and if so, whether this increased meaning was linked "only" to the event of "pilgrimage" or had a longer lasting trace.

In table 4 the results are presented. A t-test (two-tailed) shows the significance of the differences between a) the first and the second and b) the first and the third measurement.

TABLE 4: *Religious Interpretations Before, During and After Pilgrimage*

(1) In my daily life ....(first measurement)
(2) During the pilgrimage ....(second measurement)
(3) In my daily life ....(third measurement)

A. Younger than 36 years of age and filling out all three measurements (N=95)

	% strongly	*t-values*[22]	
	1 2 3	*1-2*	*/1-3*
1. The feeling of togetherness with others gives meaning to my life	70/82/79	2.69**	/ 1.82
2. The meeting with my fellow-man gives meaning to my life	68/78/73	1.14	/ 0.62
3. I experience that a higher power exists	46/45/42	-0.70	/-1.21
4. I experience Jesus as a model for my life	44/44/41	0.74	/-1.94
5. I am aware of an all-embracing reality	41/48/39	1.32	/ 0.00

[21] RITZEMA & YOUNG (1983); PARGAMENT et al. (1988).

[22] The t-test was performed on the scores "strongly (1)", "a little (2)" and "not (3)." To make it easier to read, the table only shows the percentage "strongly."

6. I reflect on the meaning of my life	40/56/48	2.39**	/ 1.79
7. I experience that God is near to me	36/44/42	1.48	/ 1.06
8. I experience God's guidance in my life	30/34/26	0.97	/-1.15
9. I experience Jesus' protection	29/33/26	-0.14	/-0.65
10. I experience God's righteousness	29/30/30	0.80	/ 1.41
11. I find comfort with Mary	24/38/21	3.02**	/-0.62
12. I experience that Jesus' suffering gives meaning to my life	20/37/24	3.49***	/ 1.65
13. I experience Mary's intercession	19/25/17	1.21	/-0.96
14. I experience that Mary helps me in a miraculous way	18/19/15	1.18	/-0.86

B. Older than 35 years of age and filling out all three measurements (N=161)

	% strongly	*t-values*	
	1 2 3	*1-2*	*/1-3*
1. I experience that a higher power exists	86/84/82	-1.49	/-2.30*
2. The feeling of togetherness with others gives meaning to my life	83/83/73	0.30	/-2.17*
3. The meeting with my fellow-man gives meaning to my life	76/81/66	1.21	/-2.96**
4. I find comfort with Mary	67/78/63	3.14**	/-0.67
5. I experience Jesus' protection	67/61/64	-1.64	/-0.67
6. I experience Jesus as a model for my life	66/64/63	0.38	/-0.31
7. I experience God's guidance in my life	61/66/62	1.59	/ 0.00
8. I experience that God is near to me	60/65/59	1.16	/ 0.15
9. I experience Mary's intercession	60/72/61	2.64**	/ 0.00
10. I reflect on the meaning of my life	59/66/60	2.21*	/ 0.69
11. I experience that Jesus' suffering gives meaning to my life	58/57/56	-0.14	/-0.40
12. I am aware of an all-embracing reality	57/69/59	2.21*	/ 0.48
13. I experience that Mary helps me in a miraculous way	55/63/56	1.80	/ 0.13
14. I experience God's righteousness	55/57/60	-0.65	/ 0.45

*: significant at 0.05 level
**: significant at 0.01 level
***: significant at 0.001 level

Comparing measurements 1 and 2 for the younger pilgrims more of them said that during the pilgrimage "Jesus' suffering gives meaning to my life," "reflected on the meaning of their life," found more "comfort with Mary" and experienced "the feeling of togetherness with others giving meaning to my life," than before the pilgrimage. In an atmosphere of religious-existential reflection Mary, Jesus and "fellow-man" became more important sources of interpretation than before the pilgrimage.

Regarding the older pilgrims, we see a significant increase in the items: "I am aware of an all-embracing reality," "I experience Mary's intercession," "I find comfort with Mary," and "I reflect on the meaning of my life." We find here a deepening of religious-existential reflection, in which Mary plays a dominant role.

Comparing the first and the third measurement we did not find a single item whith a significant increase, so that half a year after the pilgrimage the original situation seems to have returned. As regards the older pilgrims we might even speak of the decreased importance of "meeting with my fellow-man gives meaning to my life" and the "feeling of togetherness with others gives meaning to my life" as a source of meaning-giving. They also experience the existence of a higher power to a lesser degree.

Our questionnaire also included standardized religious attitude-scales ("means," "end," "quest" and "non-religiosity").[23] Evaluating the answers on those scales Derks concluded similarly that even such an impressive phenomenon as a pilgrimage to Lourdes hardly influences the religious attitudes of the pilgrim.[24] Half a year after the pilgrimage the scores on the attitude-scales did not show significant changes in comparison with the situation before the pilgrimage.

6. DISCUSSION

The pilgrims we investigated are close to faith and the Church. Their motives for making a pilgrimage are primarily (for the older ones) or at least to a large extent (for the younger ones) of a religious nature.

Secondly, pilgrimage is an event in which the pilgrims undergo impressive experiences. Especially the contact between the sick and the healthy,

[23] Those scales were constructed by DERKS (1990) as a reformulation of the scales developed by BATSON & VENTIS (1982).

[24] DERKS (1990).

the feeling of togetherness, and expressing faith together are very important during the pilgrimage.

Thirdly pilgrimage involves a deep confrontation with the Christian frame of reference, since the activities, the pilgrims participated in, integrated them with the story of Lourdes and its Christian context.

So it is not surprising that visiting Lourdes leads to a religious/existential reflection on life, in which more than in daily life influence is attributed to Jesus, Mary and fellow man. So, religious interpretations increase. A control group of older and younger people on holiday (n=42), filling out the same questions, showed no increase in religious interpretations during their journey. On the contrary the scores on several items showed a significant decline.

Furthermore, no lasting effects were found. Religious interpretations and attitudes were not transformed permanently. Half a year after the pilgrimage the influence attributed to Jesus, Mary and fellow man on their life was the same as before and the religious attitudes of the participants were not changed. Although pilgrimages influence people, they do not lead to a permanent transformation of attributional style. How can this be explained?

A possible explanation could be that pilgrimage today is less explicitly liminal. Turner and Turner themselves speak of a "liminoid" or "quasi-liminal" phenomenon.[25] Moreover, the intensity of the communitas-feelings during the liminal phase could be relativized. Turner distinguishes "existential or spontaneous communitas" from "normative communitas": "under the influence of time, the need to mobilize and organize resources, and the necessity for social control among the members of the group.... existential communitas is organized into a pervading social system."[26] Pilgrimage belongs to this less extreme "normative" communitas. Other authors doubt whether pilgrimage includes communitas at all.[27] It is said that social demarcations are as sharp during pilgrimage as in daily life. This could indicate that events and circumstances during a pilgrimage deviate from daily patterns less drastically than anticipated, and that, as a result, the need to look for (religious) explanations could be less and the explanations that are made could be less "im-pressive." Furthermore, in terms of the three phases of a ritual (see 2), after pilgrimage there is

[25] Turner & Turner (1978).
[26] Turner (1969) 132.
[27] Bilu (1989); Sallnow (1981).

hardly any sign of a phase of incorporation. In the case of the pilgrims returning from Lourdes one cannot speak of occupying a new social and cultural position. No wonder that the changes in the liminal phase do not linger on. The changes of religious perspective are place-bound.

A second explanation considers the characteristics of the pilgrims. Before their pilgrimage they already were close to God, faith and the Church, especially the older ones. So there is, in general, little room for religious transformation. Elswhere we made a distinction between "rite of passage" and "rite of confirmation."[28] In a rite of confirmation there is no transformation from a non-religious position to a religious one, but the already existing belief in God and the Church becomes affirmed and strengthened. We think that for most of the pilgrims (especially the older ones) pilgrimage is such a "rite of confirmation." The already existing bonds with the catholic tradition are tightened. In this respect we can point at the fact that 63% of the older pilgrims were in Lourdes before, and that 57% of them also visit other places of pilgrimage. For the younger ones these figures are 49% and 30%. Only for a few (especially younger) pilgrims pilgrimage can work as a rite of transformation. To trace these people our effect-measurements are too rude. The statistical mean filters out the few cases where a profound religious transformation could have occured. In further research on Santiago de Compostela as a follow-up to the present Lourdes-research we are applying new qualitative research-methods. In this Santiago-research, analyses of diaries should be able to trace the process of transformation more close (see chapter 8). In these analyses we have to look at the central motivational processes behind attributional activity: meaning-giving, control and self-esteem.[29] A context-bound change of religious attribution only will become part of the characteristics of the attributor if the new attributions are essential for maintaining or enhancing self-esteem, maintaining effective control over events and experiences or understanding events in terms of a coherent meaning-belief system.

[28] PIEPER & VAN UDEN (1992).

[29] SPILKA, SHAVER & KIRKPATRICK (1985).

8. PILGRIMS TO SANTIAGO

A CASE-STUDY OF THEIR SPIRITUAL EXPERIENCES[1]

1. INTRODUCTION

Pilgrimage, as reported earlier has beneficial effects on the well-being of the participants.[2] The effects of going to Lourdes on the spiritual level were shown in chapter 7.[3] We noted there that in order to get more insight into spiritual experiences and changes during piligrimage we needed extra research instruments.

In this chapter we will present some results of research into spiritual experiences during and after a pilgrimage to Santiago de Compostela in Spain.[4] We wanted to establish the experiences and changes of the pilgrims on their way to Santiago.

2. DESIGN OF THE RESEARCH

In looking for changing spiritual experiences one can use various instruments: interviews, questionnaires, analyses of diaries or participant observations.[5] Our presentation is based on working with "trigger-words." The method has some resemblance to the sentence completion test. In our research we gathered several concepts (or trigger words) potentially meaningful for pilgrims walking to Santiago de Compostela. After consultation with pilgrims and analysis of pilgrims-diaries we selected the following twenty concepts: walking, backpack, stamp, sun, encounter, evening, water, tiredness, wind, landscape, night, road, getting mail,

[1] First published as: M. VAN UDEN & J. PIEPER: Pilgrims to Santiago. A case-study of their spiritual experiences, in *Studies in Spirituality 6* (1996) 276-288.

[2] PIEPER & VAN UDEN (1991); VAN UDEN, PIEPER & HENAU (1991); See also chapter 6.

[3] See also PIEPER & VAN UDEN (1994).

[4] See also PIEPER & VAN UDEN (1995).

[5] See also RODING (1991a); (1991b); DE JONG (1994).

monuments, feet, earth, prayer, staff, morning and tent. We also added an "optional-subject."

This list was presented to five people, two men and three women, who walked from southern Holland to Santiago de Compostela in Spain. We time sampled reactions in the form of free associations at the following points along the walk: (a) before departure; (b) in Vézelay; (c) in Roncesvalles; (d) in Santiago; (e) back home; (f) two years after. In this way we hoped to gain insight into the spiritual-existential experiences and the possible changes of (spiritual) values of the pilgrimage. The pilgrims returned their completed list to the researchers at each timepoint. Respondents did not have access to their former reactions, therefore each reaction was relatively fresh. Our selection of the twenty words implied that filling in did not take much time and therefore created less resistance than filling out an elaborate questionnaire. We hoped that this research-method, rather than a structured pre/post test, would allow us to come closer to the emotional level of the pilgrim. We also thought that in this way we could force the respondents to concentrate their reactions from the often elaborate diary-form into a compact response to a given stimulus. This method could also enhance comparisons between respondents. Our research had a double aim: to explore spiritual-existential experiences and changes on the one hand, and to investigate whether our research-instrument was adequate to this purpose, on the other.

3. Historical Background

The chosen measuring-points must be seen against their historical backgrounds. At the end of the first millennium the pilgrimage to the grave of the apostle Saint James in Santiago de Compostela in Spain started. During the Middle Ages Santiago, together with Jerusalem and Rome, expanded into one of the most important places of pilgrimage in the Christian tradition. At the beginning of the twelfth century a definite route was established, called "el Camino de Santiago." The pilgrim-priest Aymeric Picaud already mentioned this route in the twelfth century "Codex Calixtinus." The "Camino" has four French cities as a starting point: Arles, Le Puy, Orléans and Vézelay. Our group of pilgrims started the Camino from Vézelay, which is the second measuring-point during the journey. From Vézelay they walked to Saint-Jean-Pied-de-Port at the foot of the Pyrenees. From there they passed the Pyrenees to the village of Roncesvalles (third measuring-point). The fourth measuring point was Santiago de Compostela, the end of the pilgrimage.

4. The Respondents and Their Journey

The Respondents

Mrs. C. took the initiative to go on this pilgrimage. She put an ad in the newspaper, asking readers to contact her if they wanted to make a pilgrimage, as part of a group, on foot from the Netherlands to Santiago. She also defined some selection criteria, such as age (older than 60) and having retired from work. Seven people responded, of whom four decided to go ahead. Before their departure from the Netherlands the group, three women and two men, met several times. It was then decided that Mr. E would accompany the journey by car. Mr. E agreed to drive ahead of the group to the day's destination, arrange a place for the night and do some shopping. He would then leave the car, walk in the direction of the group and accompany the group, on foot, back to the day's destination.

The Journey

On the sixth of April 1990 the group started its journey on foot from the south of the Netherlands to Santiago de Compostela. In Belgium and France they spent the nights in their own tents and in Spain in "refugios", houses especially built for pilgrims. Only one night was spent in a hotel. Until their arrival in Vézelay on April 30th the group had walked frequently in the rain. From May the sun started to shine and the winter clothing was sent back to Holland. The sun had a positive effect on the mood of the pilgrims. Clothes could more easily be dried after washing and camping-facilities were more readily available. This was quite important because of the toilet-facilities, until that time a lot of irritating improvising had to be done. Each day the pilgrims walked about 25 to 30 kilometers.

The daily routine was as follows: getting up at 6 a.m., getting dressed and washed, packing the tent, having breakfast, and reading the Scriptures. At 8.00 a.m. the pilgrims set off and, after 10 kilometers, had a coffee break. After another 10 kilometers they had lunch and took a short nap. After the last 5 to 10 kilometers they looked for a sleeping-place.

The tents were pitched, they had dinner, did their laundry and planned the journey for the next day. They then read something about the spirituality of the pilgrim and prepared their sandwiches for the next day. At 9.00 p.m. the pilgrims went to sleep.

During their journey the pilgrims realized that the collective prayer was not successfully. Answering letters from home also became stressful and the weekly obligation of Mrs. C. to report on a radio-program put quite some pressure on the group. Finally tensions and irritations among the pilgrims began to develop. These tensions were among the causes for the two men, after passing the Pyrenees, and under pressure from the three women, deciding to end their journey and return to the Netherlands. A German couple with a car took over the transportation-task of Mr. E. In Spain the walking was more difficult than in France, the roads were worse and the temperature higher (30 degrees Celsius). Finding a sleeping-place in a refugio was often a problem and the atmosphere between the pilgrims in the refugio's was not really positive. Even fights between them took place. After 105 days, on the 19th July, shortly before the feast of St. James, the three women arrived at Santiago de Compostela.

5. Analysis of the Material

The measurements took place at six moments in time (before the journey, in Vézelay, Roncesvalles, Santiago de Compostela, back home and two years after returning home). From Mrs. A. we have five responses to each trigger-word (she was too exhausted to fill in the list in Santiago de Compostela). From Mrs. B. and C. we collected six responses to each trigger-word. As Mr. D. and E. stopped their journey prematurely, their reactions are incomplete. Mr. D. filled in his responses at four measuring-points (before the trip, in Vézelay, Roncesvalles and two years after returning). From Mr. E. we gathered reactions at three measuring-points (Vézelay, Roncesvalles and two years after).

The first step in processing the material was to group those trigger-words that belonged together. We devised the following five groups (other combinations are also possible).

Group 1: Encounter and Prayer.
Group 2: Road, Walking, Monuments, Feet and Tiredness.
Group 3: Morning, Evening and Night.

Group 4: Sun, Water, Wind, Earth and Landscape.
Group 5: Backpack, Stamp, Wind, Staff, Tent and "Getting Mail."
Leaving the "optional-subject."

Our next step was to examine reactions to each trigger word for each individual and over the various measuring-points. In this way one could follow the reactions of a certain pilgrim along the way at each trigger-word. This enabled us to look for possible changes in the experience of the pilgrim. By making comparisons within a certain group we could also trace trends within these groups.

After this first analysis the material of each respondent was interpreted by three researchers. They asked themselves the following questions:

(1) Which words trigger deep spiritual-existential experiences and how can these experiences be described?
(2) Which words indicate spiritual-existential changes and how can these changes be described?
(3) At what measuring-points in time do these possible changes take place?

In this exploratory phase of the research the questions were formulated as broadly and openly as possible in order to give room for as many answers as possible. We do not yet have valid scales by which we can measure whether an experience is deep and moving and on the basis of which we can conclude whether one can speak of a spiritual-existential transformation. The reliability was enhanced by means of a so-called interrater-procedure. Independently three researchers (a clinical psychologist, a psychologist of religion and a theologian) looked for answers to the formulated questions. After that a critical discussion took place. This resulted in a "preliminary consensus-interpretation." Finally this was handed out for correction to the participant of the journey. These corrections were integrated into the final version.

6. The Case of Mrs. B.

In this chapter we will confine ourselves to the results of one case. The case needed to be free from potential bias, so Mrs. C. who organized the pilgrimage and knew the aims of the research could not be used. Mrs. B. was selected, a Roman Catholic who worked in health and education, with experience of working in the Third World. First we will present some raw, grouped material as it was noted during the journey by Mrs. B. to give an impression of the sort of material our approach yielded. After that we will deal with the consensus-interpretation, the result of critical discussion among the researchers, after they had closely read the raw material from the viewpoint of the above-mentioned three, open leading questions.

6.1. Presentation of Some Raw Material of Mrs. B.

Group 1: Encounter and Prayer

– Encounter –
Before the journey: The encounter will be good if I open myself to the others.
Vézelay: One of the most exciting experiences of walking, especially the help you get.
Roncesvalles: Short, but always friendly and helpful.
Santiago de Compostela: Inspiring to meet so many nice people, each with their own life-stories and experiences of the journey.
Back home: Casual encounters with helpful people, whom I will never meet again; meaningful encounters with people, whom I hope to meet again. Highlights for which I am grateful, they gave me a lot.
Two years later: Important to stand still and look at, less driven to the goal of our journey.

– Prayer –
Before the journey: To encourage each other, to become silent in myself, so it gets more room.
Vézelay: I like praying together and it does us good. We include the people back home, without them we would not succeed.
Roncesvalles: Comes from within, maybe I learn how to pray along the way.
Santiago de Compostela: Most of the time without words, when I was alone. With each other: The Lord's Prayer at the start, very inspiring. It is a pity we prayed so little with the group.
Back home: Alone: Often without words. Together: At the start praying the Lord's Prayer was a ritual belonging to the journey. From within; real and often without words. That is a certainty that I want to keep on to.
Two years later: Try to find time and room in my daily life for moments of silence (prayer without words).

Group 5: Backpack, Stamp, Staff, Tent and "Getting Mail"

– Backpack –
Before the journey: How to keep it as light as possible. I always leave things behind that cannot be carried. Still this one is going to weigh heavy.
Vézelay: Still a heavy weight, I will have to leave even more "behind."
Roncesvalles: A burden one never gets used to, but it belongs to the journey.
Santiago de Compostela: Started getting used to it on the Camino. With only the backpack life was better ordered, than with all the superfluous luggage, we had earlier, when the car drove along.
Back home: Putting it on was quite a ritual, before leaving. From a burden it became a part of myself, sticking (literally and symbolically) to my back. How well-ordered life was, walking with only my backpack.
Two years later: How wonderful it is being able to live with so few possessions.

– Stamp –
Before the journey: A symbol of confirmation, will probably need it some time.
Vézelay: Confirmation of: That part is behind us.
Roncesvalles: Almost two pages filled. Names of places, monasteries, campings. At the start of the journey only names, now they are a part of me; I was there.
Santiago de Compostela: Every stamp brought us closer to Santiago.
Back home: Proves now, that I was there.
Two years later: What used to be a confirmation, I now no longer need.

– Staff –
Before the journey: Maybe I will need it. But not from the start.
Vézelay: Symbol, still no useful instrument for me.
Roncesvalles: An aid on small, rocky roads.
Santiago de Compostela: Indispensable for the sloops and the descents. When we had to cross small rivers. I found it difficult to accept that it was used as a clothes-line.
Back home: My support. My third leg, became a part of me. Why did I leave it on the way home in the train. A support, also emotionally.
Two years later: Symbol of holding on, going on.

– *Tent* –
Before the journey: A safe hiding place.
Vézelay: Nice, safe on my own. Very cosy, reading letters by a torch, keeping my diary. Learning not to make a mess and not finding anything.
Roncesvalles: Learned to feel safe inside, when the rain falls on the roof. If you don't put it up well, you will risk a wet floor.
Santiago de Compostela: That hiding place, for retreat, I missed at the Camino.
Back home: Wonderful, small tent. Safe haven, a few moments alone. Safe, alone with myself, not having to do anything for a while.
Two years later: Hiding place on our journey. Happy when I can pick it up now, means being unattached, freedom on the pilgrimage.

– *"Getting Mail"* –
Before the journey: To keep in touch with all those, who sympathize. I just want ordinary stories from home.
Vézelay: Nice, surprised at so much mail. Can't write back to everybody. Must write a careful letter for all. Sometimes no time to read it all carefully!! Gives "push," go on!
Roncesvalles: I am amazed at so many sweet letters from friends. Encouraging. Think of one person, then of the other and pray for them.
Santiago de Compostela: Loyal friends took care for letters at each poste restante address; encouraged me and praised me. I do not know what to do with that.
Back home: Got a lot from loyal family and friends. That was a tremendous support. Nice, safe feeling "friends back home."
Two years later: It means how loyal relations keep a friendship and that in its turn appeals to me.

6.2. Consensus-Interpretation of Mrs. B.

Independently the researchers tried to formulate an answer to the aforementioned questions. Next, those trigger-words that, according to the interpreters, aroused only little moving spiritual-existential experiences, were put aside. As a result, in the following presentation of the consensus-interpretation, the reactions of Mrs. B. to the trigger-words: Feet, Tiredness, Morning, Evening, Night, Sun, Wind, Stamp and "Getting Mail" are missing. The remaining eleven trigger-words were, on the basis of similar associations, put in four groups: Communication (Encounter,

Prayer), Pilgrimating (Road, Walking, Monuments), Nature (Water, Earth, Landscape) and Pilgrim-attributes (Backpack, Staff, Tent). The reactions to the optional-subject will be dealt with at those trigger-words that are relevant to these reactions. The optional-subject mainly produced reactions on the level of (a) the group-process, walking together and the start of frictions among each other, and (b) pilgrimating as a process of being on the road and staying on the road, even afterwards. Of the five original groups of trigger-words, in the case of Mrs. B. only four were relevant. The trigger-words referring to parts of the day (Morning, Evening, Night) did not produce really moving experiences.

A. Communication

In this first category, under the heading of "Communication," we find the triggers "Encounter" and "Prayer." In these two themes various levels of communication are dealt with: among the pilgrims themselves, between the pilgrim and others, and between the pilgrim and God.

Encounter

The experiences in this domain can be described as deep, moving, inspiring and fascinating. In this context we can distinguish between casual, short, but fascinating encounters with friendly and helpful people and deep, moving encounters with nice people with their own life-stories. Until reaching Santiago, the first category dominates, after that and especially back home and two years after there is more room for the second kind of encounter. It seems as if the journey is so energy absorbing, that there remains no time for intense contacts. These only occur after arriving in Santiago. Then the stories among the pilgrims are told. At the optional-subject the encounter within the group is mentioned. At first there was hope for a deepening of communication among each other. However, along the way irritations grew, resulting in a splitting of the group. The two men return home. Back home there is regret at not being able to share with each other the experiences of the pilgrimage.

Prayer

Here we can also distinguish between two kinds of prayer. The collective prayer (every morning: the Lord's Prayer) and the silent, internal prayer without words. Mrs. B. gradually learns to pray in the second manner. This starts at Roncesvalles and she tries to hold on to it from there to two years after. As to the collective prayer she is disappointed: at first it is experienced as positive and inspiring, later on there is disappointment, because there is hardly any collective prayer.

Conclusion

Regarding the category "Communication" we can say that along the measuring-points a deepening of experience has taken place. The encounter becomes more profound, the prayer more intense and more individual. For both trigger-words this is most clear at the measuring-points "back home" and "two years after."

B. Pilgrimating

In this cluster of triggers: "Road," "Walking" and "Monuments" we deal with "Going the way," in the sense of both the physical road and the historical road.

Road

At this word evident shifts in meaning can be determined. From a literal understanding of the road that must be walked, in the physical sense, in Roncesvalles Mrs. B. talks of the historical road, the "Camino" representing the pilgrim-tradition. In Santiago there is the narrowing in meaning because of the grief that not all were able to walk the road till the end. Next, back home and especially two years later, the road becomes a symbol of the path of life. Our respondent is now very consciously making choices. Two years after the pilgrimage Mrs. B. is more in harmony with herself and acts more independently. She carefully reflects on decisions she has to take and asks herself what things she really wants. The optional-subject shows how difficult it often is to hold on to this opening for growth. Daily sorrows force her to a more static existence.

Walking

Also at this trigger-word clear changes in meaning and experience become evident. From an understanding of walking as physical movement, in Vézelay there is the experience of being on the road, in the sense of the experience of space, being unattached and freedom. In Roncesvalles physical movement brings peace with opportunities for reflection, in which "historical" feelings of identification with "predecessors" are found. These last two meanings (that are also interrelated) remain present back home and two years later. I felt free, on the way, Mrs. B. says, and now also I return to myself.

Monuments
The churches, crosses and chapels that are visited along the way activate a strong historical feeling; Mrs. B. feels committed to the thousands of pilgrims before her, and calls herself "somehow" such a real pilgrim. She places herself in the history of these churches and chapels and especially the experience of "empty churches" (secularization) corresponds with her own distance to the church.

Conclusion
In this cluster the pilgrim-tradition of going the way in the literal and symbolic sense is dealt with. The trigger-word "Road" offers the biggest variation, while "Walking" refers more to the physical and "Monuments" more to the historical dimension. In this process Mrs. B. (partially) identifies with the pilgrim-tradition. Looking at the various measuring points it seems as if already during the journey she develops to a symbolic meaning-giving, but only in the phase back home and two years after returning is this explicitly clear.

C. Nature
Under this heading we have put three words: "Water," "Earth" and "Landscape." All these three triggers aroused, more than for example "Sun" and "Wind," moving spiritual-existential experiences in Mrs. B.

Water
In the experience of the pilgrims there are three kinds of water: water from heaven (making you wet), water to wash (purifying) and water to drink (refreshing, thirst-quenching). The journey was a process of physically experiencing the multiple meanings of water. Mrs. B. felt the fundamental human need for water. The necessity to drink, the desire to wash. She learnt to exert herself to find water. She came closer to water. She gained respect, through hardship, for this cosmic element, that she labels as a vital condition.

Earth
At first there is a movement from literally far away (living in an apartment at home) to feeling close to the earth (enjoying the beautiful fields in Vézelay), to experiencing so many colours (in Santiago). Back home this is put in words as follows: felt it under my feet, nearby, used and abused. Two years later: how earthly I am and how far away heaven still

is. In other words, only in looking back at home and especially two years after returning, the symbolic level appears and only then can we speak of a religious perspective: the earthly earth is seen in contrast to heaven, that is still far away. Also during the journey there is a growing consciousness in terms of environmental aspects.

Landscape
The landscape triggers reactions similar to the reactions to the word "Earth." While walking the landscape roots deeper in the experiences. Here also there is a growing consciousness of the environmental aspect: the human impact on nature. Looking back at home Mrs. B. feels close to nature and two years later she speaks of the human participation in God's creation. In other words, after two years there is a more symbolic attribution in which God is seen as creator and people are seen as participating in God's creation.

Conclusion
Nature is a source of spiritual-existential experiences. At these trigger-words literal, single meaning becomes multiplied and symbolic. Especially in looking back this takes the form of a kind of symbolizing trend. In the case of the trigger-words "Earth" and "Landscape" an explicit religious dimension also appears.

D. Pilgrim-attributes
Here we deal with objects that are of great importance during and after the journey and with which the pilgrim develops an emotional tie: "Backpack," "Staff" and "Tent."

Backpack
The backpack evokes experiences of getting rid of redundant possessions, making life more surveyable. It changes from a heavy burden, after leaving behind the redundant luggage, to a part of oneself. In this respect one could speak of a "rite de séparation" in a nutshell. Life becomes more surveyable if it is reduced to its essentials.

Staff
During the journey the functional side of this object dominates: an aid to conquer physical hindrances, even to be used as a laundry-line. Back home Mrs. B. speaks of "became a part of myself" and two years later

of a symbol of "grip" and "anchorage." In other words a clear change in meaning from literal to symbolic.

Tent
The dominating meaning of the tent seems to be its securing function: "for a moment alone." This meaning does not change during the journey. Possibly the group tensions play a role here, making this securing function necessary. Two years later there is an other level of meaning. Then "Tent" also means freedom and unboundness, and so there is a change of meaning in an existential direction.

Conclusion
With all these three objects at first the literal understanding and the "physical" function dominates. Only two years after returning, the symbolic value is elucidated and distinguished. This meaning is always put in "existential" terms: "Backpack" becomes reduction to essentials, "Staff" becomes anchorage and "Tent" becomes symbol of freedom. As we said earlier: this all happens especially after two years, in retrospect.

7. Final Remarks

7.1. Kinds of Experiences and Changes

All in all we can speak of an impressive journey, that especially after two years shows its impact, as can be shown in Mrs. B.'s final remark: "The pilgrimage has added much to my life, deepening it and giving it memories, these now are an integrated part of my life."

More specific one could speak of a kind of "coming closer" on four levels. First of all there is a coming closer to nature: nearer to the earth, the water and the landscape. Mrs. B. feels very close to these elements. They offer man support, refreshment and esthetic pleasure. There is also uneasiness about the destructive human activity regarding nature. Two years after returning the experience of nature is put in a religious perspective. Man is involved in a divine, creative process. A second "coming closer" deals with the pilgrims who travelled before her. Mrs. B. identifies herself – a little – with these historical pilgrims during the journey, especially when confronted with signs of remembrance such as the Camino, churches, crosses and chapels. She is absorbed into the history of this Roman Catholic tradition, but experiences at the same time its partial destruction. Thirdly there is a growing towards, a coming closer to the pilgrim-attributes "Staff," "Tent" and "Backpack." Originally these were objects for use, along the road and afterwards they become symbols (a) for emotional support, (b) for freedom, (c) for simplicity. A fourth and final aspect of the journey deals with coming closer to oneself. We see this in reaction to various trigger-words. "Walking" gives way to exploring oneself; the trigger-word "Tent" leads to safe hiding-places in which you can come to yourself; the trigger-word "Praying" leads to becoming silent in yourself and making room, and the trigger-word "Road" is gradually pictured as going on one's own path of life. Especially this last aspect is two years after returning still present. The pilgrimage has not ended yet: life has become a continuous pilgrimage. Mrs. B. is still on her way. This being "on the way" has almost become a purpose in itself and touches upon what for many is the essence of pilgrimating: letting go, loosening up, leaving behind all your daily sorrows and social commitments.

Finally, a remark on this case in contrast to the other cases. A first analysis of the reactions of the two male respondents, who did not travel the journey till the end, suggested that in these cases the reactions to the triggers, after returning and two years later in retrospect, were rather static. There was no change in the direction of more symbolizing. Further research will have to show in what way this has to do with not completing the journey, the group process or male-female differences.

7.2. Methodological Remarks

How effective was our research-method in measuring spiritual-existential experiences and changes? More than half of our trigger-words exposed these experiences. This does not mean however that the other words were less well-chosen. In other cases they could probably function as a good trigger and lead to relevant associations. The method of spreading the measurements in time also gives interesting results. Various key-words changed in meaning. Remarkably this shift in meaning is often in the direction of a symbolic "understanding" of the words. This symbolizing especially takes place two years after the pilgrimage. During the journey there is little time for reflection. Only from a distance, words can be understood apart from their literal meaning. In other words: Only after a certain time of reflection (two years later) can the deeper meaning of the pilgrimage consciously be phrased.

On the other hand we also have to mention a few limitations of the method. It is not always very clear what is meant by the short, condensed reactions. That is why, the interpretation of the reactions is often complicated. We must also mention the fact that there are no clear-cut criteria available to determine when we can speak of a moving experience and of change, especially of spiritual change. Methodologically we have tried to eliminate this danger of arbitrariness by means of the so-called "interrater-procedure." In future research it will be necessary to include a theoretical frame of reference into the analysis as well. Psychological theories that are relevant in this respect are:

- The psycho-social developmental theory of Erikson[6], especially life-phase eight ("integrity"), is relevant for an interpretation of coming closer to oneself, at the end of the path of life.
- Experiences of contrast[7], especially those triggered by nature can activate (religious) frames of interpretation. In that context attribution-theoretical notions are relevant.
- Taking the role of the pilgrim can give rise to spiritual experiences. In this context we refer to the social role-theory of the Swedish psychologist of religion Sundén.[8]

Finally: apart from research by means of reactions to trigger-words, that can help – as we have shown – the pilgrim to express their experiences, depth-interviews will be necessary to explore the deeper meaning of these experiences for life after the pilgrimage. Only then can we give an answer to the question if and how the pilgrimage is a spiritual experience that makes itself felt in daily life.

[6] ERIKSON (1968).
[7] POST (1994).
[8] SUNDEN (1966).

9. THE MODERN PILGRIM

A STUDY OF CONTEMPORARY PILGRIMS' ACCOUNTS[1]

1. Introduction

> And would I now accompany him to fill in the paperwork? Don Javier is known as a fervent collector of pilgrim statistics. The form on which he wrote my information is designed in a multiple-choice format. Under "reason for trip," for example, the options "religious," "cultural," "friendship," "athletic" and "other" can be checked off. (...) I tell Father Javier that my motives are spiritual and journalistic. He is silent, staring at my stamp card (...) and then at me, trying to work out if I am being completely serious. With a sigh he writes down the two words, his check boxes unattended. "I dislike journalists," he says as he gets up. He walks to the door of his office and opens it for me. Appointment finished. The only question I was able to put to him concerned the growth in the number of pilgrims. Up until 1982 there were at most one hundred registered per year. In 1984 there were five hundred and in 1987 nearly fifteen hundred. 1989 showed signs of a fifty percent increase compared with the previous year.[2]

This anecdote is in the pilgrim's account of the trip home from Santiago de Compostela by the Dutch journalist and sociologist Herman Vuijsje. His account is one of many which have appeared in recent years in the Netherlands and Belgium, as also in the rest of Europe; the diary format is particularly popular for such accounts.

[1] This chapter is a revised version of the Im Thurn Memorial Lecture, delivered in the University of Edinburgh (School of Scottish Studies) on 12 November 1992. This version was published as P. Post: The Modern Pilgrim. A Study of Contemporary Pilgrims' Accounts, in *Ethnologia Europaea* 24,2 (1994) 85-100. A detailed first account of the research appeared along with a co- (or contra-) report, "Een vragende voetnoot" [A questioning footnote] by H. Wegman (Wegman (1992)), as P. Post: Pelgrimsverslagen: verkenning van een genre, in *Jaarboek voor liturgie-onderzoek* 8 (1992) 285-331, a short version as: P. Post: The Modern Pilgrim: a Christian Ritual Between Tradition and Post-Modernity, in *Concilium* (English edition) 266 (1996) 1-9.

[2] Vuijsje (1990) 120.

What is the source of this popularity? This is a complex question. What is the initiative that brings people to undertake such a journey and to write an account of it? What is the motivation for publishing an account of the journey, which is often so personal in nature; and in what form should it be published? There is also a question of reception: Why do these accounts find an audience? Does it have something to do with a fascination with pilgrimage itself, or does it have more to do with a curiosity about the long-distance runner, or with the increasing interest in the genres of (auto)biography and travel literature? Or is it a more general cultural-historical interest that people take in pilgrimage, in writing and in reading?

The opening quotation touches upon the phenomenon of pilgrimage itself. The old pilgrimage routes in Europe are busy these days: thousands upon thousands of usually single and non-affiliated pilgrims spend weeks, even months, on the way towards the traditional goals of pilgrimage such as Rome and Chartres. The old medieval routes to Santiago de Compostela in Spain are far and away the most popular. From all the corners of Europe people walk and cycle to the tomb of St. James, but smaller local and regional goals also seem to share in this European "pilgrimage boom."[3]

Here also a number of questions arise: Is there really a question of a renaissance throughout the entire spectrum of pilgrimage? May we speak further of continuity or discontinuity in the pilgrimage tradition? What is to be said about the "religious content," about motives, effects and functions? What should we think about Father Javier's list of motives? Do people seek holiness and healing, or is it rather a matter of the omnipresent shift of touristic culture to cultural tourism? Finally, we can look for relevant global cultural processes which can serve as fruitful interpretational frameworks. What should we be considering in this regard? The return of religion in a postmodern period? Or rather than this a "culturalization" of religion?

[3] Most accounts are of pilgrimages to Santiago de Compostela. The great majority are privately published accounts. A survey of accounts in Dutch is provided by the Flemish Society of Santiago de Compostela (Library: Abdij Sint Andries, Zevenkerken, Bruges) and the journal *De Pelgrim*, or by the Dutch Society of St. James with its magazine, *De Jacobsstaf.* Outside the Netherlands I know so far only the more "literary" accounts brought out by official publishers such as: NEILLANDS (1985) (account of a bicycle journey starting from Puy); AEBLI (1991); HANBURY-TENISON (1991) (account of a journey on horseback); BENTLEY (1992). See summary giving patterns of types of accounts: POST (1992b) 287f and 292-297.

2. Framework and Organization of This Report

2.1. Theoretical Framework

"Revitalization"

Before giving the framework of the investigation, I shall first draw attention to the stream of "revitalization" literature, chiefly from an ethnological or anthropological angle.[4] Just as in other aspects of pilgrimage, there are unmistakable reports of indications of regeneration and resurgence, indications that make it appropriate, in the theoretical respect, to seek connections with other forms of ritual revitalization processes. Alongside studies by Boissevain on processes of change in the subject area of festival and ritual in Europe, I shall want above all in this connection to utilise the insights and starting points of Salomonsson. In a classic article of 1984, this Scandinavian ethnologist formulated a range of points to take into account in the investigation of revitalization processes which, in this connection, I shall want to sum up under two heads and incorporate in my research. First is the emphasis on the cultural-scientific researcher's need to turn to underlying ideas,[5] and second the thesis that revitalization often goes together with the conferment of new meanings, new functions and new underlying factors and arguments.[6]

A Debate About Pilgrimage

In the following I shall seek to utilise a more tailored form of research into the phenomena of revival, namely research into pilgrimage in the form it has taken in recent years in a number of disciplines.[7]

A good introduction to the broad spectrum of questions and problems of ethnological pilgrimage research in general, is offered, in my opinion, not so much by the numerous articles providing an overview of the field, as by the equally numerous debates and polemical studies. In particular,

[4] Cf. Salomonsson (1984); Boissevain (1991); (1992); (1994); Post (1991b); (1991c), (1993).

[5] Salomonsson (1984) 45: "Thus, it is important for us to get behind the scenes and analyze the motivating forces of the process."

[6] Salomonsson (1984): 46: "The same phenomenon may (...) be taken up anew, but with fresh arguments in a different situation."

[7] Cf. for pilgrimage in general: Theilmann (1986); Dupront (1987); Post & Van Uden (1987); Van Uden & Post (1988); Post (1988b); (1989a); Pieper, Post & Van Uden (1990); Post (1991b); (1991c); Margry & Post (1994) = Chapter 2 in this book.

I am thinking of the fierce discussions which took place in German studies in the seventies and eighties.[8] I will review certain themes, positions and attitudes in this regard, as exemplified by such a debate, as a form of orientation for the kind of research and questions with which this study is concerned. Assion, in a sampling of social sciences orientated "Gegenwartsvolkskunde" (contemporary European ethnology) assesses the contemporary revival of pilgrimage, the renaissance of the traditional pilgrimage, and the rediscovery of the phenomenon in a number of disciplines. This is all firmly set against the background of changing concepts of tourism, given as an important facilitating factor. The renaissance of journeys on foot or on bicycle is of especial interest to him. Assion attempts to characterize and interpret this phenomenon. In doing so, he calls attention to two associated characteristics: a withdrawal from the cult object, the holy and healing centre of the journey, and motivational structures which lie in a derivative social-existential level rather than a primarily religious one. In a general sense, Assion talks of a supportive contrast-experience to which the pilgrim addresses him- or herself. An experience of actual sociability and solidarity, of vocation, is set in contrast to modernity; the pilgrimage is, in short, an oasis, a blank space, in a world permeated by modernity even within the framework of church communities. Assion places these issues in the broader framework of religiosity in the (post)modern world and ties his thesis in with various forms of lay devotion and new religious movements and countercultures. Forms of religious (popular) culture, in this case pilgrimage, are not seen as relics or as expressions of continuity with the past, but as important new forms of religion, as ritual behaviour, the functions of which become clearer when placed in the context of the social-cultural framework of modern society. The internal situation of the Church after Vatican II is completely implicated in this.

Brückner reacted at that time in a strong and engaged manner. Given the general social theoretical background, which he, unlike Assion, does not see as relating European ethnology to the social sciences, but rather to the "natural partner," social history, Brückner opposes the all-too-easily-reached conclusions concerning processes of change in the field of pilgrimage. He denies that there is a sudden increase in attention to the pilgrimage journey as opposed to the goal with its holy site and cult

[8] Cf. Assion (1982/1983); Brückner (1983); Scharfe, Schmolze & Schubert (1985).

objects. He stresses how the journey and the group experience of the pilgrims stood and stands in the centre, how the journey and the goal actually should not be placed in opposition to one another. He treats the motivational structure with the utmost care and reticence. He argues a Marxist inheritance in Assion, according to which popular religion is seen and interpreted as a cry from an oppressed proletariat. Brückner asks for attention to be drawn to the everyday methodology of European ethnology in particular: is the empirical substructure established, for example, through responsible fieldwork or through social scientific case studies? Brückner asks for restraint from researchers, for caution in the employment of various stereotypes and categorizations concerning pilgrimage, and for clear differentiations between participatory elements such as the social aspects, and specific supportive elements. The point of departure for him is that pilgrimage is that which the pilgrims themselves find it to be, that their interpretations must be central. The granting of meaning, and here Brückner and Assion are in accord, must mostly be formulated as an emotional experience. Brückner sees more continuity with the past in present pilgrimage practices, and the success of pilgrimage is explained for him through the success of the traditional, of a received tradition, of a working, always newly actualized, practice.

The main elements of our subject are, in my opinion, strikingly laid out here. I consider that these two points of view can, in fact, be brought into harmony. There are aspects of each with which I would like to associate my discussion. In the case of Assion, I find his questions to be quite to the point, and I would like to test his answers as working hypotheses. In the case of Brückner, I accept his methodological viewpoints, his advice and his warnings, his arguments for the necessity of empirical research, for unbiased and methodical responsibility, especially as regards the quest for the pilgrim's own bestowal of meaning.

Discourses and Appropriations

I want to add an important additional perspective to my theoretical framework. I shall, in fact, to a greater extent than in the forementioned debate, want to lay stress on the differences between the various circuits, "discourses" and appropriations as a way of bringing into the picture the field of force within which rituals develop (afresh). This involves a search for the attributions of meaning (sometimes very diverse) by the participants themselves: the pilgrims (men and women, younger and older) as well as other participants (organisers, spectators, pastors, theologians, the tourist industry, the press). Essentially the controversy described for illustrative purposes is also to a great extent determined by just these different perspectives. Here we touch on an important impulse that in recent times had been profitable introduced to studies in the field of (popular) culture. Following De Certeau, Chartier, Burke and others it was to an increasing extent, and successfully, operated within this perspective of cultural circuits and appropriations and related mutual influence on behaviour.[9] The final analysis of a (revived) ritual should then be seen as the outcome of a synthesis of sometimes very varied ways of dealing with or adapting it. Perhaps more than happened in the debate between Assion and Brückner, it is necessary right from the start of the investigation to keep an eye open also for changes in perspective, changing forms of appropriation and giving of meaning. Besides, in this way full justice can be done to Salomonsson's points.[10]

2.2. Organization of this Chapter

Against these theoretical backgrounds, I propose to give a first "reading" of text and context of a dossier of present-day pilgrims' accounts. In doing so I shall stay in the first instance, very close to the pilgrims' accounts themselves, in order at the end to emerge again more analytically free from the account of the pilgrimage and the questions about function, meaning and change. We will first orientate ourselves by examining the actual sources, then attempt to establish a model of analysis in order finally to interpret the accounts at the textual and contextual levels. We shall then set the interpretation into a broader framework of research into the function and meaning of pilgrimage. I conclude with a number of earlier soundings of religious (popular) culture in which the theme of dealing with the past occupied an important place.[11]

[9] De Certeau (1984); Chartier (1988); Burke (1992); Rooijakkers (1992). See now Frijhoff (1997b).

[10] For an application of these theoretical perspectives I refer not only to the long-standing fruitful multi-disciplinary soundings within the framework of the Dutch research programma, "Christian pilgrimages," but also in succession to a pilgrimage study from the Protestant viewpoint of which I had not been aware before but which inspired me greatly, as an exemplary ethnological investigation, and more one of recent appearance in which historical-anthropological perspectives are applied: Neville (1987); Dekker (1993); Te Boekhorst, Burke & Frijhoff (1992).

[11] Cf. Post (1991b); (1991c); (1991d); (1992b), Post & Pieper (1992a); (1992b).

3. The Corpus of Pilgrim's Accounts and a Model of Analysis

3.1. Introduction to the Corpus

The sources that I wish to consider, (published) accounts of pilgrimages, poured forth abundantly from about 1980 in the Netherlands and Belgium, after their emergence in the late sixties. From the approximately 100 collected Dutch pilgrimage accounts of various natures and types, I have selected six for a thorough examination: a selection which appears purely intuitive at first glance. I list them briefly (translating the Dutch titles):[12]

1. Hans Annink, *A Late Pilgrim Along the Milky Way. A Round Trip From Enschede to Santiago de Compostela: 5500 Kilometres on Foot*, 1980.[13] Hans Annink, after a severe motorcycle accident, resigned his position as a young history teacher, sold all his possessions and undertook in 1977-78 to make the journey on foot from Holland to Santiago de Compostela and back. Parts of his account appeared earlier in the local and regional press of East Netherlands.
2. Loek Bosch, *Pilgrims of Peace: Pilgrimage to Assisi June 7-August 24, 1986* (privately published).[14] Loek Bosch is a young priest in a modern district of a large city. In the summer of 1986 he made the journey on foot from Utrecht to Assisi with two other companions. He returned by bus.
3. Henny Lamers, *Diary of a Pilgrim to Santiago de Compostela*, 1987 (privately published).[15] Henny Lamers was employed by the faculty of astronomy at the State University of Utrecht. He underwent a crisis in both his personal and his professional life, and in 1984 undertook, originally with a friend, to make the journey from Utrecht to Santiago by bicycle.

[12] See for more details: Post (1992b). Also note 1.

[13] Annink (1980); 110pp. Return journey Enschede-Santiago de Compostela in 1977/78; many other diaries refer to this report. Parts of it also appaeared earlier in the local/regional press (East Netherlands). Differs from other reports/journeys is that Annink also came back on foot.

[14] Bosch (1986) (privately published); 138pp. Journey from Utrecht with two other people to Assisi; return by bus.

[15] Lamers (1987) (privately published); 98pp. Utrecht – Santiago de Compostela: a book based on diary accounts.

4. Herman Vuijsje, *Pilgrim Without God*, 1990.[16] We have met him already. Walking the route from Santiago to Amsterdam in 1989, he took a "reversed pilgrimage." Portions of his story appeared earlier in the national press.
5. C. and J. Houdijk, *To the True Jacob: Diary of a Foot Pilgrimage to Santiago de Compostela*, 1990.[17] A middle-aged couple, Cootje and Jan, undertook the journey on foot from southwest Netherlands to Santiago. Their office jobs were temporarily suspended for this purpose. Jan also writes historical novels and makes sketches. The account of their journey was written by both of them, with Jan providing the drawings.
6. Herman Post. *On Foot to Rome: In the Footsteps of Bertus Aafjes*, 1991.[18] A journalist advanced in years, employed by the Catholic Broadcasting Service (Katholieke Radio Omroep), Post used a leave of absence for a journey by foot to Rome, following in the path of the famous Dutch poet Bertus Aafjes, who made the same journey in 1936, and included his experiences in an influential poetry collection in 1944-45.

There is neither time nor space to present these sources in greater detail. I will argue however, that the accounts I have selected do provide us with insight into the broad field of modern pilgrimage accounts.

3.2. Exploration of the Genre: a Model of Analysis

Two Formative Principles

There are two formative principles which establish the foundation for the model of analysis employed in this chapter. These concern the understanding we have of a relative genre, and further a number of points that come to the fore for consideration if we designate the accounts as personal narratives or biographical stories of experience.

[16] VUIJSJE (1990); 234 pp. Accounts of a journey from Santiago de Compostela to Amsterdam (account 1990, journey 1989); the author calls it "a reversed atheistic pilgrimage"; appeared (in parts) earlier in *NRC Handelsblad* (newspaper); see for an interview: *HP / De Tijd* 3,4 (1992) 46-50.

[17] HOUDIJK & HOUDIJK (1990); 269 pp. Journey from Woensdrecht to Santiago de Compostela by the couple, Cootje and Jan Houdijk; the book was written by both of them, and an indication is always given of who wrote the parts in question. Jan was responsible for the drawings. See also interview in: *Op lemen voeten: tijdschrift voor voettochten* 10,3 (1988) (Nijmegen).

[18] H. POST (1991); 134 pp. 4th edition of the book, the 1st by Conserve. Parts of it prepared earlier in columns in the KRO-programma magazine *STUDIO*; the 1st, 2nd and 3rd editions were published by the Schaduw Press, Tilburg 1989.

(a) A Relative Genre

In the introduction I freely used the term "pilgrim's account" as a sort of indication of genre for the set of accounts.[19] The question now arises whether such a term as "pilgrim's account" can indeed serve this purpose. This question of orientation concerning our corpus of accounts is of the highest relevance. Each definition of genre is already a step towards analysis, and is indicative in particular of a relevant context. Now it is almost impossible to demarcate the genre. But on the other hand, this affords us a glimpse of a positive aspect of the use of the term, an advantage that lies likewise in its openness and relativity. The term "pilgrim's account" compels us to begin broadly, to take into account all possible relationships and lines of association with the related materials, that is a broad range from ego-documents or accounts in the first person (telephone, recorded accounts, stories, video, photo album, sketchbook, letters, household books, travel notes, diaries, accounts, memoirs, inscriptions in guest books, etc.), "mediated" accounts (interviews and journalistic accounts) to the edited accounts (travel account, travel short story, poetry collection, photographic book, travel guide, travel stories) and the fictional account ("voyage imaginaire").

(b) Biographical Stories of Experience

As a second formative principle I would like to take a set of methodological insights which enter the field of view when we designate our accounts as biographical stories of experience and thereby seek connections with, in particular, recent developments in literary studies and above all in research into (folk)narratives.[20] I shall list these points of consideration here briefly in order to employ them as a checklist:

1. Reflection on terminology and division of genre.
2. Attention to the narrative context.
3. Interaction of the oral and written traditions.
4. Form and editing.
5. (Responsible) interpretation.

[19] See for the "genre" of the pilgrim's account: HENNIG (1944-1956); SEEMAN (1976); HOWARD (1980); RICHARD (1981); HOLLOWAY (1987); HERBERS (1988).

[20] See for this perspective of the (folk)narrative: LEHMANN (1978); (1980); (1983); PENTIKÄINEN (1978); WARD (1979); RÖHRICH (1988); RÖTTGERS (1988); SCHENDA (1988); DOLBY STAHL (1989); KVIDELAND & KVIDELAND (1990).

Model of Analysis
I considered six pilgrim accounts according to a model of analysis which in schematic form can be described as follows: first there is the orientational research phase (investigation and description of genre); secondly the analysis of text and context, followed by a synthesis or interpretation (function, meaning, contents, message); and then the outcome can be taken up in a further, broader investigation, in our case that of the question of changed or changing function and meaning of pilgrimage.

4. Example of use

4.1. Structure and Narrational Levels

Three levels of the account are to be distinguished: (a) the level of the daily account, of the experiences of the journey; (b) the level of the contemplative pieces framing or interpolated therein, of the perception of the journey; and (c) the level of the unspoken messages, for example concerning the function of the book itself in the life of the narrator or of the group in which the account functions, the level of the "ultimate, primary function(s)/meaning(s)" of the pilgrimage. Each of these levels may now be further analyzed and decoded, using the previously described phases of analysis as a checklist.

The first narrational level is in all the accounts very consistent. Just as with boarding school experiences or extended life stories, the pilgrimage bears with it a set of commonplace elements, which may be regarded as a sort of "script." Intimacy, self-presentation and recognizability go hand in hand with a set model of life. Each account pays consequent attention to the established daily model: rising, seeking the way, losing the way, meetings, eating and drinking, seeking shelter for the night, sleeping, weather, impressions of the landscape.

The surprising – or perhaps better put, that which contrasts with daily routines of home – is emphasized. Through the journeys they have undertaken, these individuals acquire an interest in things at which beforehand they would never have paused to look. The first-person figure of "I" runs (literally) as a sort of Leitmotiv through this trivial level. The story is, as it were, carried by a hero who undergoes a development, a growth, sometimes even a conversion. The resulting "I-report form" underlines this.

Onto this first linear narrative level is tied, or worked in, a series of more representative segments at a second level. At this derivative second level a fixed series of themes, plots or narrative types are also present.

4.2. Themes

In all the accounts, in my opinion, the following contents and themes are dominant:

Departure and Arrival
It is striking that the arrival is, for the most part, briefly and summarily narrated. All of the emphasis is on the pilgrimage, the journey itself. In some cases, such as those of Houdijks and Post, the arrival is something of an anticlimax: "...is this then everything...?"

Encounters
An important role is set aside for encounters en route, and to these encounters are tied elaborations of various sorts. The anecdote dominates here. The account may in certain respects also be read as a linking together of usually unplanned, diverse encounters along the way; there is much attention given to reflection on involvement with other people.

Nature and Occasion of the Pilgrimage
Various experiences on the way provide occasions for digressions, as for example concerning the religious "calibre" of the event (in comparison to a walking tour, in comparison to the past, especially the Middle Ages), above all also concerning the occasions, motives, and effects of the journey undertaken and changes in these regards throughout the journey, etc.

Nature
The constant confrontation with nature during the journey is a dominant theme in all accounts. "Nature" is in them broadly construed. It is a question not only of the experience of the landscape, the changing weather conditions, but also of discoveries in relation to one's own body. Concerning the theme of nature we read digressions which above all verbalise the contrast with the bourgeois existence left behind and sometimes lead to discussions of our estrangement from nature, about nature and the attribution of meaning, milieu, and quality of life coupled with living in harmony with nature. Yet the theme is not as dominant as is

the case in some English-language accounts. I am thinking, for example, of the "green account" by Hanbury-Tenison that concludes with an ecological pleading or manifest.[21] In any case, this association with nature is a "classic" pilgrimage theme. Research shows clearly how important the (emotional and religious) surplus value of the pilgrim is as an "outdoor liturgy." The experience with nature forms an important source of attraction also for the smaller local and regional pilgrimages.[22]

The past
Finally, I would like to take up more explicitly involvement with the past as a theme. The past first of all plays a role in the various cultural/touristic digressions: places-of-interest invite elucidation in the manner of a travel guidebook, invite stories about origins and development. Also laid out or sought is a coupling with a Christian past that is tied up with the religious, personal identity of the author, or with a more general, cultural denominator. We meet here both personal reminiscence and a general cultural thread. Here the dyadic opposition of engagement and distance, or of the actuality of the journey and the general historical framework, plays a part.

The past also frequently functions as a means in bringing better into focus several of the above mentioned points: consider especially motivation, perception, bestowal of meaning, etc.

4.3. Synthesis and Interpretation

On the basis of these observations the researcher proposes further questions concerning the role of the development of the narrator of the story, following norms and values which implicitly and/or explicitly come forward, etc. Three clusters, with the help of which the above mentioned analytical material can be ordered for an analysis of contents, could, in my opinion, be listed as follows: (a) the ritual, the journey, the essence of being a pilgrim; (b) meetings, relations; (c) the past. These three clusters exist as overlapping sets ordered under the supportive and binding denominator of "experience of contrast" and "self-presentation." The "why" of the narrated story is the disseminated and narrated consciousness, lived through the journey undertaken as a series of contrast-experiences,

[21] HANBURY-TENISON (1991).
[22] Cf. NEVILLE (1978): Chapter II 28ff; (1987).

experiences which are fundamentally different from the life experiences that prevailed before the journey. These experiences touch on the quality of life, interaction with nature, with other people and with one's own past that is again embedded in a more general past. The fact that Lamers, Annink, Post, Bosch, Vuijsje and the two Houdijks produced their accounts is a sign of what I am describing here: there is something else at play different from the traditional, possibly routine, organized Lourdes expeditions. They, from the moment that the plan for their pilgrimages took shape, had the feeling of "not running with the crowd," and in many cases the journey undertaken is a ritual with an enormous impact, frequently with the character of a singular rite of passage or even conversion. Those experiences which are judged of greater and broader significance are very personal; the editorial process tries to structure this self-presentation in order that it can be relevant for a broader group of readers or listeners.

5. The Theme of "Involvement with the Past" more Closely Examined

The elements of these syntheses – I am specifically targeting the three clusters, already referred to, of ritual, encounter and bygone days – can now be elaborated in turn and can be set within a broader framework. I intend further to set in a central position the aspect of association with the past. As part of this, (or possibly a case can be made for it on the basis of our exploratory analysis of the pilgrims' accounts), it also appears that (popular) religious rites and symbols are going to constitute a branch of what is well-described as "musealization of culture." If the concept of a "museal pilgrim" is revealed by the account, are we not then on the track of a new modern bestowal of meaning or appropriation? Perhaps it is not really a question of a pilgrimage and is the traditional rite of pilgrimage extracted from its original context; perhaps it is rather a matter of a cultural, ritual framework for the diverse individual forms of presentation of a range of contrasting experiences.

In a more derivative sense, even more closely related aspects in this connection merit our attention: the question of what I term the "proportion" of tradition in this type of pilgrimage. I shall keep this aspect of "the tradition-proportion" for the final conclusions, and just now shall first briefly investigate the traces of "musealization."

5.1. Introduction to the Mechanism of Musealization of Culture

Through musealization a cultural process is traced and typed.[23] This concerns a certain form of involvement with cultural elements, a certain mapping out of human experiences. Objects are primarily in focus here, but I should emphatically also include rites among these, in particular those rites of religious (popular) culture such as pilgrimage.

Musealization involves a hypothetical diagnosis of time or culture, a model of diagnosis that concerns our human experiences. It is a mechanism that requires and deserves a closer differentiation.[24] The concept of musealization presupposes, for example, a double movement: a development of historicization, a certain involvement with the past that among other things is inclined towards regarding cultural elements as purely expressions of a strange, other life; and one of aestheticization, which transforms everything into the pretty, the beautiful, and in the end reduces it all to the mere appearance of beauty. Wolfgang Zacharias has demonstrated both aspects of the musealization process in the death ritual of a Cologne prelate who tagged the crucifix placed on his deathbed with the label "Schlechte Arbeit. 18. Jahrhundert" ("Poor workmanship. 18th C.").[25] He died as he had probably lived: in a museum.

The process of musealization therefore is chiefly concerned with experiential change, called by some loss of experience or reality, with transformed and transforming attempts at signification in a transforming world. The involvement with cultural elements is determined through distance, through viewing, rather than through integration with everyday life.[26]

5.2. Musealization and the pilgrim accounts

In my opinion in the accounts the past functions as an evocation of the totally other; we read of the contrast, the irretrievable contrast with the Medieval pilgrims whose quality of fascination is due precisely to their inaccessibility and otherness. One experiences the journey undertaken

[23] Cf. LÜBBE (1979); (1983); ASSION (1986); VAESSEN (1986); ZACHARIAS (1990); STURM (1990); POST (1991b); FRIJHOFF (1992c); important in this context is also: GERNDT (1972). See now also: KORFF (1994).

[24] ZACHARIAS (1990).

[25] The example quoted of the Cologne prelate is taken from ZACHARIAS (1990) 29 citing B. WALDENFELS: *Stachel des Fremden* (Frankfurt 1990).

[26] Cf. LUKKEN (1991).

in important ways as a journey to the past. One seeks for a way to summon the experiential world of the past; one wishes to connect with the past up to the level of direct experience. This is all summarized in the constantly returning formulation of "becoming a pilgrim."

The manner in which experiences are related in our six pilgrim accounts, insofar as they are concerned with the past, strikes me as evidence that they are involved to a very high level indeed in this mechanism of musealization. Many experiences are seen, as we have noted, in the light of the modern everyday life that those who have undertaken these journeys have left behind for varying lengths of time. This is not an isolated observation of musealization and compenzation, but something which stands in the much broader context of the functions of (popular) religious rituals in the past and today. The pilgrims appear to wrestle with a constant sense of contextual and functional change. In part, I would like to interpret the pilgrims' accounts as an unmistakable sign of the musealization of religious (popular) culture. Much of the contents and the messages which I have outlined in this analysis seem to indicate that an old ritual was performed in the eighties and nineties of this century, but performed in a new context. Due to the shift in context, the consequent experiences constantly become confusing.

An important question for further multidisciplinary research lies in the further designation and analysis of the nature and functions of these experiences. Various compensation theses already associated with the process of musealization are therefore appropriate for consideration in this context, as also in the realm of folklorism ("Folklorismus") which lies so close to that of musealization. And thus, with the theatrical and reassuring reversion to the past, with the exploitative involvement with the past, we stand in the midst of the interesting debate on folklorism that in essence is a reflection of the very nature of the field of European ethnology.

The involvement with the past displayed by our pilgrims, and the indicated shifts in context and function, can cause us to see the "vessel-ritual" of modern pilgrimage as an aspect of musealization: we would then see the pilgrim as an actor in a performed reality; we would make a piece of religious theatre of his journey. The conclusion of this enacted living history, in a complete museal context, is reached by none of the accounts; all seek to root the traditional ritual in his or her daily life and experiences, this forming the balance of the effects they acknowledge; the account takes in many aspects the character of a struggle, but also that of a legitimation. The cultic, ritual, religious component is thus frequently designated as a cultural component.We should, though, be aware that the pilgrims, through their relationship with the traditional "vessel-ritual" of the the pilgrimage, find themselves on the borders of folklorism and theatre. Vuijsje's account refers directly to the consequences of a complete change in context and function through an anecdote:

> Somewhere along the route a host father enthusiastically told me about a group of true pilgrims who had recently passed by. "Twenty Frenchmen, all in classic pilgrim costumes, with staffs and gourds. There were various physicians among them, also journalists and a television producer. They had their baggage in a car driven by a chauffeur." How delighted I would have been to have seen this group arrive at Father Javier's!: "Profession?" "Journalist." "Reason for the journey?" "Just a moment. Once our car is here we can show you our screenplay. In the meantime, could you hold this antique rosary and look towards the camera?" Here are played out the ultimate consequences of all the developments which threaten the authenticity of the Camino ["camino" = the pilgrimage route or road to Santiago (PP)]. Pilgrims as actors in a hyperreality, an enacted reality. The Camino as an artificial evocation of something that, in fact, it no longer is. Javier would never admit this group, because he would thereby become an actor in their street theater. It is now only a question of time before there are turnstiles installed, a life-sized image of the apostle will be mounted on the gable of the cloister and after every mass a well-meant applause will be heard.[27]

6. Pilgrimage Between Tradition and Modernity: Some Concluding Comments

The contribution is admittedly put forward as a first exploration. We have laid stress here on a theoretical framework and on a justified analysis-model. On the basis of tests of the analysis, in the end we still stood specifically by the aspect of the association with the past, insofar as that appears from the accounts, and tried through it to look behind the scenes of the ritual and to consider the extend to which there is talk of a new dimension of appropriation and giving of meaning. This is, it must be repeated, only one of the aspects that deserves to be elaborated; perhaps it is not even the most significant. Further research should step

[27] Vuijsje (1990) 121.

by step take account of the whole field of influence in which the pilgrims are on a journey and give an account of it.

At the end of this exploration, I give some further comments. I do so in order to bring some points from the analysis more sharply into the forefront, and set them alongside the theoretical framework that we presented at the beginning of this contribution. First of all, I link them with the comments we have just made on the involvement with the past.

6.1. A New Pilgrim? Or: the "Proportion" of Tradition

Questions concerning the involvement with the past are essentially contained within the question concerning tradition and modernity[28]: to the degree of change or continuity of the pilgrimage ritual, tradition or fashion, changes in function or motives. Pilgrimage, above all that to Santiago, is seen as an interesting old tradition to which people wish to make a connection. It is therefore, in my opinion, fully a question of continuity and tradition. But on the other hand we saw how Father Javier, shaking his head, broke off his discussion with the modern pilgrim Vuijsje. So there is also discontinuity. Perhaps it is through the concern with the old tradition that these pilgrims are differentiated from other pilgrims. Looking at motives and functions, these pilgrimages over old, traditional paths, leading to old cultural-historical regions deeply rooted in Europe's history, should differentiate themselves fundamentally from traditional bestowals of meaning. Perhaps I have formulated this incorrectly: it may be not the pilgrimages but the pilgrims themselves who should be differentiated. Or: we must attend to various repertoires of behaviour, and above all to various forms of appropriation. A single type of pilgrimage can be appropriated by different people in completely divergent manners. The differences in adaptation are apparent in the opening anecdote: Father Javier and Herman Vuijsje appropriate the journey completely differently. The Father had no place in his extensive question form for the journalistically spiritual "modern" motives of Vuijsje. All the other pilgrims to Santiago, Rome and Assisi also recount similar conflicts piece by piece.

It is consistently apparent that this appropriation is the first matter of importance in these accounts. The past is used, is invoked and deployed; it extends to a sort of "vessel-ritual" that may be filled according to

[28] Cf. BAUSINGER (1991); KÖSTLIN (1991).

individual necessities, a ritual framework as offered by the possibilities of contrasting experiences which may be filled by each pilgrim according to his own insight and, most of all, his own needs.

Now, every ritual fulfils such a "vessel" role to some extent, but this case is to a very high degree one of an open framework, and the "vessel-rituality" itself determines the degree of attraction and the function to a very important extent.

Thus I would in no sense wish to associate the renaissance of this sort of pilgrim account only with various reflections on altered pilgrim behaviour, or on the return to religion, or on the incurable religiosity of humanity. It is a "vessel-ritual" that possesses allure because it is "traditional." Various compensating functions play an unmistakably important role here: the past, a traditional ritual such as pilgrimage, offers a holdfast in a modern, hectic, and most of all ordered and minimally surprising or exciting existence, but also offers a holdfast for an existence which has diminished in quality in regard to identity and interpersonal relations, or that has run amok, or that has become confused. One seeks in the past a holdfast as an orientation towards the future. The journey of searching can possess a clear religious component, but it need not.

This very important factor of the past, of tradition, leads us to the differences from other pilgrimages. We have here a completely new and emerging type of pilgrim and pilgrimage: beside the already noted concern with continuity and tradition, innovation is also involved, in the sense of a principally different function or appropriation. Wolfgang Brückner was right to speak of "the success of the traditional." But in contrast to Brückner I see here a fundamental shift in the signification and adaptation: these are less explicitly religious, and they do not completely cover the contrasting experiences which others sketched with terms such as community and solidarity. Of the complex system of actions that is pilgrimage, in the cases we are now considering only the vague cultural contours of a generally applicable "vessel-ritual" remain. Through a detour to the past, one seeks identity and quality of life through a series of contrast in experiences. Just as in so many other places in the modern world, tradition offers here an island of time and meaning, to use an image that Konrad Köstlin employed.[29] I also see traditional goals such as Lourdes, moreover, as being increasingly taken over in this manner.

[29] KÖSTLIN (1991) 58-61.

6.2. "Pelgrimage" and "Bedevaart" ("Pilgrimage" and "Prayer-Journey"), Elite- and Popular Culture

The material and the analysis we have made of it still raise some important related questions. In the first place, it is possible to speculate on whether (only) specific types of pilgrimage lend themselves to adaptation like those we think we have identified through the accounts, and also whether in connection with this a difference can be established between "elite" and "popular" pilgrimages.[30] In other words: in the pilgrimage accounts, are we seeing an "elite" travelling and writing, or is it still possible to speak of rituals of popular culture? Besides, it may also be the case that the sketched-out musealizing association with the ritual is only appiclable as a compensating adaptation process of the pilgrim "elite."

"Bedevaart" / "Pelgrimage" ("Prayer Journey"/"Pilgrimage")

Through the difference cannot be readily rendered in English, nevertheless closer investigation of the differentiated religious experience indicated by "pelgrimage" and "bedevaart" is of great importance. I draw attention to the long debate over the terminology. The same differences, if it comes to that, appear also in the debate between Assion and Brückner that I have outlined. In the framework of this investigation, however, I consider a resumption of the discussion and the establishing of difficult definitions and demarcations to be superfluous, certainly after the very recent synthesis of Berbée.[31] In this framework I do not wish so much to name the differentiating point of the emphasis on the (long) journey and road, as the aspect of the foreignness and alienation. Whenever we set our accounts within the broader framework of the difference between "bedevaart"/"pelgrimage", the antithesis appears as far as concerns "bedevaart" and the "bedevaartgangers" ("prayer journey goers"), who seldom write accounts, and the unique character of our report-writing "pilgrims" is expressed. The difference in relation to the "bedevaartgangers" ("prayer journey goers") stands out. In the case of "pelgrimage" it is more a matter of personal choice, about the establishment of an attitude to life, about a converting withdrawal from the present existence,

[30] Cf. WEGMAN (1992); POST (1992b).

[31] For the discussion on the terminology "bedevaart" and "pelgrimage" I only mention: BERBÉE (1986); (1987). See also: POST (1992b) and WEGMAN (1992). Sometimes both terms or words are used: cf. for example the Dutch translation of the account of FIENNES (1992).

about alienation: "The pilgrims" accounts should well be examples of the description by more or less learned people of their personally experienced alienation, of the estrangement of the self and of the polite social and ecclesiastical ambience, an estrangement which they convert into reality in the act of the pilgrimage.[32] As far as concerns "bedevaart" it is a matter of a prayer expedition of a religious "people" in which the aspect of alienation and estrangement plays no (or a reduced) role. A closer evaluation of the differences between "pelgrimage" / "bedevaart" certainly gives in this way the possibility of bringing the unique character of our literate "pilgrims" still more sharply into focus. The ritual of pilgrimage can be seen as a counter to the experienced alienation. Historicizing and aestheticizing are in that way forms of compensation in which and through which pilgrims before the present in the past seek a footing with an eye to the future.[33]

Another element that can be tied in with the difference "bedevaart" / "pelgrimage" in an illuminating way is that we said about musealization and association with the past. That seems after all not (or to smaller degree) to be applicable to "bedevaartgangers" ("prayer journey goers"). Perhaps the classical "bedevaart" is a form of (popular) religious tradition, of which the sketched out phenomenon of musealisation still has the least grip.[34]

Nevertheless I want to warn against making the difference between "pelgrimage" and "bedevaart" too pronounced, also as far as concerns dealing with the past. Thus, I see a number of signs which indicate that the mentioned processes of changes in feast and festival also begin to affect the "bedevaart." Just as the massive dichotomy between popular- and elite-culture can be abolished or at least made more relative through working with the concept of changing representations of appropriations, so also in the case of "bedevaart" / "pelgrimage" can a change of perspective perhaps be fruitful. Attention should also be paid in the difference between "bedevaart" / "pelgrimage" to the contrast in appropriation. An individual devotional journey to and from a holy place can then for one (or for a group) be a "bedevaart" and for another (or another group) a "pelgrimage." In source material concerning "bedevaart" and "pelgrimage" it is often possible to discover traces of both in the use of words. Are these parallel and differing forms of terminology perhaps to be seen as markers of differing degrees of appropriation?

[32] WEGMAN (1992) 334f.
[33] WEGMAN (1992) 336.
[34] WEGMAN (1992) 336.

Elite- / Popular Culture?
I should like to make a short annotation in relation to one aspect of the evaluation of the difference "bedevaart" / "pelgrimage" which has already been conveyed in the above. Wegman sees "bedevaart" as an action of "the folk" and "pelgrimage" as belonging to less or more literate people ("elite"). He especially stresses this differentiating point and couples with it the question of whether there is in the pilgrims' accounts no talk of an elite culture and of wether we should not rather investigate the "bedevaart" where we are on the lookout for religious popular culture.[35]

Behind this critical question lurks a difference in the basic assumption which I shall briefly consider. I set the investigation of the pilgrims' accounts, inter alia, within the theoretical framework for what I and others call the rituals of religious (popular) culture. Here a short diversion is appropriate on popular culture and "Volkskunde" or European ethnology as the branch of knowledge which carries out research in that area. From that it might then appear that I gave a somewhat different interpretation to "popular culture" than Wegman and should want to a far less degree than him to work with the dichotomy "folk" and "elite". It is not my concern in the first instance to re-open the question of what is termed the "canon of European ethnology". Rather do I wish to stress, in the tracks of discussions about the diverse forms of cultural concept, that European ethnology is not concerned with a normative but rather with an interactive cultural concept. In the context of discussions about diverse forms of cultural concept, it may be argued that European ethnology employs an interactive rather than a normative conception of culture. The term "popular culture" no longer implies primarily an engagement with specific segments of a society or population (social classes or strata), but with civilization in general, with the way of life in which everyone takes part. Thus the European ethnologist is interested in the broad cultural stream, in the everyday culture of as broad a spectrum of the population as possible, in culture with a small "c", and no longer with the culture of the "kleine Leute". The reconstruction of culture and continuity are also no longer points of departure for ethnological research. European ethnologists direct their attention to the matrix of the culture they study; it is a discipline which studies the formation, meaning and effect of collective cultural phenomena in society; it is a discipline which is in search of the meaning of cultural phenomena in

[35] WEGMAN (1992) 333.

society. Therefore, the changes in and differences between these phenomena over the course of time and in their dissemination, both spatial and social, are the focal points of attention in the field. In this connection, European ethnology becomes strikingly close to cultural scientific research into everyday life just as that, is carried out, for example within the framework of the disciplines of history and anthropology. Like social sciences that are acquainted with "Kultur als Forschungsfeld" (culture as a field of research), European ethnology wants to investigate the everyday culture at the present day from different but mutually complementary points of view; it is a science on the lookout for the functions, meanings and mutual relationships of cultural phenomena. From this perspective, I count the culture of the "bedevaart," as also that of the "pelgrimage," present and past, as lying within the field of ethnological research.

6.3. Tradition and Modernity

In this chapter we came, in my opinion, on the track of a new form of appropriation, by way of pilgrims' accounts. A "traditional" ritual is played out in a new way. I shall conclude with a quotation from such a "modern" pilgrim, to mark the adaptation process between tradition and modernity, including the emphasis laid on the theme of association with the past. In thinking and speaking about the reasons for their journey of pilgrimage, we read in the Houdijk's account the following:

> You are familiar with everything concerning the Romish faith. Then you wish to walk – walk very long and very far. Is there a more beautiful goal than this unknown city in northern Spain, where all of Christianity journeyed a thousand years ago? Add to this that there are a great many historical and cultural monuments preserved along the routes to Santiago. The Romanesque churches that we travel to see are treasure chambers where we too, in imitation of Medieval pilgrims, go to gape in wonder. To feel something of what the beggars and wretches and the punished and the sick and the plague-ridden from far before our time lived through – howbeit that we in our time can never do so fully, in that we cannot share their fears and dreams, and above all that we lack their childlike and blind faith – that is what we wish. Bound with your own past and that of our entire European culture and savoring this solidarity sparsely – each day a little piece – building it up further in your innermost self. Yes, it must be something like this.[36]

[36] HOUDIJK & HOUDIJK (1990) 30f.

Fig. 23. Lourdes (France), Dutch pilgrims (photo: coll. M. van Uden).

Fig. 24. Lourdes (France), Dutch pilgrims (photo: M. van Uden).

Fig. 25. Lourdes (France), Dutch pilgrims (photo: M. van Uden).

Fig. 26. On the way to Santiago, Camino de Santiago (photo: P.J. Margry).

Fig. 27. Santiago de Compostela (Spain), the cathedral from the Paseo de la Alameda (photo: J. van Herwaarden).

Fig. 28. Santiago de Compostela (Spain), the statue of St. James (1694), Puerta Santa, cathedral, Plaza de la Quintana (photo: J. van Herwaarden).

Fig. 29. Santiago de Compostela (Spain), cathedral, portico of the Glory, 12th cent. (coll. P.J. Margry).

Fig. 30. Heiloo (The Netherlands, prov. Noord-Brabant), sale of devotional items, May-month, pilgrimage grounds of Our Lady of Need (Onze Lieve Vrouw ter Nood) (photo: P.J. Margry, 1983).

Fig. 31. Laren (The Netherlands, prov. Noord-Holland), St. Jan's Procession (photo: P. Post, 1993).

Fig. 32. Laren (The Netherlands, prov. Noord-Holland), St. Jan's Procession (photo: P. Post, 1993).

Fig. 33. Laren (The Netherlands, prov. Noord-Holland), processional banners in the St. Janskerkhof during the celebration of the Eucharist (photo: P. Post, 1993).

Fig. 34. Laren (The Netherlands, prov. Noord-Holland), festive arch in a street in Laren on the route of the St. Jan's Procession (photo: P. Post, 1993).

PART III

CONTEXTUAL EXPLORATIONS AND PERSPECTIVES: SACRED PERSON AND PLACE, RITUAL BETWEEN TRADITION AND MODERNITY

10. ON SAINTS

TWO CASE-STUDIES BETWEEN BELIEF AND SUPERSTITION[1]

1. INTRODUCTION

This chapter presents two case-studies to support the argument that the distinction between belief and superstition is difficult to make and is often based on prejudice. Private expressions of popular religion are to be carefully judged from a psychological point of view. A crucial criterion is the question whether, in this specific case, religion helps the individual to cope with his life's tragedy.

Two viewpoints are put forward. We will do this by presenting two cases (Mr. Oakes and Mrs. Thijssen) from the research on the role of religion in the crisis of bereavement.[2]

Both viewpoints deal with the value and function of certain elements of popular religion. The first claims that, from the perspective of the psychology of religion, the distinction between belief and superstition rests on soft assumptions; that is to say, there is only idiosyncratic religiosity in which health promoting and health stagnating tendencies can be pointed out.

The second statement claims that a preference, even a pleading for the collective experience of phenomena from popular religion, like pilgrimage, devalues experience of privatised expressions of belief. Many churchleaders fear that legitimizing this privatizing tendency, popular religion is moving more and more away from the influence of Christian tradition and the atmosphere of established religion. From the viewpoint of psychology of religion we might consider William James' statement that healthy religion is to be recognized by its fruits and not by its roots.[3]

[1] First published as: M. VAN UDEN: On saints. Case-studies between belief and unbelief, in: J. CORVELEYN & D. HUTSEBAUT (eds.) *Belief and Unbelief. Psychological perspectives* (Amsterdam/Atlanta 1994) 175-184.

[2] VAN UDEN (1985).

[3] JAMES (1902).

In other words it is crucial whether religiosity in this case helps to carry one's fate, to deal with the unavoidable and to give meaning to existence.

In the forthcoming, both respondents are presented. In this way the aforementioned statements are illustrated with concrete material.[4]

2. Presentation of the First Case-Study

2.1. Personality Description of Mr. Oakes

Mr. Oakes is 55 years of age. He was born in England and is living in The Netherlands. A year ago he lost his wife of cancer, she was aged 55. They had been married for 31 years and had one son. Mr. Oakes met his wife during the Second World War. Until he was 43 he worked as an upholsterer. He then became ill with heart disease. Two years before the interview, when he was recovering from an operation, cancer was diagnosed in his wife. Six months later she died.

Speaking about his wife Mr. Oakes said: "My wife had a tremendous ability to help people already before I knew her, as a young girl. A tremendous, easy way of dealing with people. She did this purely out of love. I think I will always admire my wife, for everything she was and did, the things I could not do. She was a tremendous independent person. I experienced my marriage as a wonderful thing. The one thing my wife and I terribly regretted was that we didn't get a second child. But for the rest I can only say that in those days I met a wonderful woman. I wouldn't repeat it with anyone else. We had the finest understanding. Nobody can take her place. I miss her most in her company and care. She always arranged everything in a way that was always satisfying for everybody. Her company, that cup of coffee or that glass of milk at the moment you were not thinking about it. Those little things."

In his 53rd year Mr. Oakes was operated on for the second time: "When I got home the misery actually began. I said to my wife that she did not look well. But it is very typical, I was the one who was to die first. At a certain moment my wife said, I think I will be gone before you, I don't feel sick, but I feel something is wrong. Yet I should have seen, that my wife was worse than I... I had expected it for myself but not for my wife. I was really puzzled. Also about the fact that nobody

[4] See also Van Uden (1986) 102-114, Van Uden (1988) 54-66, and Van Uden (1991) 155-162.

showed us the way a little. I never got the chance to talk about it with her. All kinds of things didn't get through to me. That she said: "Keep those pyjamas, I want to wear them when I get buried." She had a destination for everything, she had attached the names on things months before. I dusted these things, but I didn't see the stickers. I just want to say, she had lots of friends and yet I feel she was terribly lonely, she couldn't express it, not even to me. If anyone had said to us that it was an ending case, then maybe we could have done something for the last time. Yes, why couldn't we have gone to Lourdes? It could have happened. It was still possible."

"My wife always arranged the housekeeping, you name it. If anything had to be paid, or arranged, my wife did it all. And I have this idea that still, now that I have to do it all myself, she is in my neighbourhood to see whether I am doing well. When I go to bed at night I still say goodnight to my wife, as if she is there. I have this feeling that in spite of all, and I know it is not true, she is somewhere in my neighbourhood. Because I have never been independent. My wife always did everything. My wife even wrote my letters to my own family in England. I have a lot of good friends from my wife, and me. They say the house is not the same without your wife. If you spoke with my wife for five minutes you were at ease."

Most striking is the way Mr. Oakes idealised his wife. She becomes a kind of proximal saint. He is standing completely in her shadow. He derived his independence from the identity his wife gave him. Their mutual friends are actually his wife's friends. Mrs. Oakes dealt with everything, including the writing of his letters. His wife's death does not intrude into his awareness. Without his wife Mr. Oakes is lost and feels redundant. The feeling of stagnation has been predominant since his wife's death.

2.2. The Religiosity of Mr. Oakes

About his religious background Mr. Oakes said: "I used to be a protestant and I became a catholic when I got married. My mother was originally a catholic and she stayed that way. If there was anything to do in the Catholic Church she would go there. She also went to the protestant church with the children. That didn't matter."

Being asked about a religious story that struck him, Mr. Oakes said: "I can't think of the name. That story in which Our Dear Lord walks that road with the cross. That always impressed me. That torture with that cross. I think we all have to carry our cross. As with us, what we both have gone through. I think that without our faith we would have gone mad. I am convinced of that."

Whilst he was suffering fromt heart disease Mr. Oakes came into contact with the blessed Peerke Donders[5]: "At a certain moment someone got the idea to contact Peerke Donders. In that little wooden church in Tilburg masses were read. Every month a little booklet comes, and I also got a little cross. There are some texts of his and more general texts of certain miracles that have happened. They are written down in that book. And even when my wife and I were very ill, we always read that book. We didn't go to sleep, even when we were too sick to do anything else. It is a kind of novena, during several days each day some short prayer. We spoke a lot about that. These were the things my wife and I did speak about. But in a sense, when my wife needed it, I didn't speak about it with her. Maybe because I thought she was better or would be better."

About his religiosity today Mr. Oakes said: "You keep on praying, to get things clear. I read in my book of Peerke Donders every night. But I always place it on the top of my bedside cabinet, never inside. It is as if sometimes at night I hear the drawer of my wife's cabinet. Those bedside cabinets of mine and hers, used to be closed at the same time, when we finished reading. I am convinced, that it helps me, as it helps everybody. You have to work through these prayers. Have I done right? Is it in the book? You really must think through. When I do that, I try to do it as well as possible."

"Faith is often tested, but there is only one Dear Lord. That is the way I see it. And I think that if you believe, it all comes down to the same thing. Protestant, Catholic or whatever. We all think we do it right. You can pray at home or in bed or in a chair, as well as in church. At night when I go to sleep I say goodnight to my wife, and I always say a few prayers for her. Not from a book that is very typical. In general I pray in English. From a book I pray in the Dutch language. And then, I say it in words, in simple words."

[5] Peerke Donders CssR (1809-1887), cf. *Lexikon für Theologie und Kirche* (3d ed.) Vol. 3, 335; DANKELMAN (1982a); (1982b); FERRERO & SAMPERS (1982); VERHEES (1984). NB: Our use of the term "saint" or "Saint" includes those whose official title is "blessed." Donders is not cannonized, but declared "blessed" in 1982.

"Those changes in religion come a bit fast, but actually I have not changed. Maybe on the outside, but on the inside I have not changed. Neither has my wife. We are, yes, old fashioned. We think, and I still do, the way we used to do things is good for us. Allowing strange ways cannot be done overnight. They can not be reversed, but I think, everybody must use his own intelligence. Everybody will have to answer for that later, if they have done something wrong or right. I think we all will be judged in our own way. If there is a hell or a heaven? I don't know. I believe in Our Dear Lord and I believe that He will reward us all. Punish I don't know, I can't say anything about that."

On the hereafter: "I have this feeling, that if something happens to me, my wife will be waiting for me. And then the whole family will be reunited. I feel my wife around me. Watching over me, or pointing the way so that things go right." Comfort he finds in: "A simple thing you hear in many songs. It is a simple line, that says: "We'll meet again". It is quite simple. I often wonder. I say it often. That we will meet again some time. That is a very important comfort, just a few words."

In Mr. Oakes' religiosity, his somewhat simple good-natured character strikes us. He does not get angry. He can not even imagine a punishing God. That would create too much aggression. Taking positions troubles him. He does not take a stand. Catholic, Protestant or whatever, it does not matter. Mr. Oakes identifies himself with Jesus' way of the cross. This is not surprising; it expresses his feeling of carrying one's burden without rebelling to it. His religiosity perfectly fits this personality structure. Comfort he finds in traditional beliefs that have not been influenced by cultural change. His contact with Peerke Donders as a saint far away but also nearby in the house, is of great importance in his popular religious belief. Praying results in contact with his wife. His belief in a hereafter ("we'll meet again") has, in all its simplicity, transcending power. Religion has given him, this weak figure, a helping hand. Minimal means and optimal results.

3. Presentation of the Second Case-Study

3.1. The Personality Description of Mrs. Thijssen

Mrs. Thijssen is 56 years of age. Two years ago she lost her husband, who was then 52 years old and died suddenly of a cerebral haemorrhage. Mr. Thijssen had been disabled through a heart-attack, six years earlier. Mr. and Mrs. Thijssen had been married for 25 years and had 3 children.

Thinking back to her first years of marriage, Mrs. Thijssen said: "From the beginning I should have dealt with things in a totally different way. But I was always afraid. He was a real dictator. He paralysed me. He was terribly mean with words. Then I couldn't say anything back. I was paralysed. He knew that. And never an apology. And always alone. I had expected a great deal of marriage. He knew everything better than me. Everything I said was nipped in the bud. Nasty things happened in the beginning of our marriage. When I was pregnant, he stood with a knife above me. He put a cigarette on my body. The fear was there. He was sadistic. My son saw this. It can not be erased. He was drinking then, too. He commanded his will in everything. Yes, we didn't fit together at all. I was much too calm, too quiet. Maybe it would have been better if I had protested, but that didn't work. I didn't need an opinion of my own, he knew everything. Our marriage was a big disillusion."

About the last years together: "Then I used to sit alone with him. The children came home and saw how he was sitting. It was kind of sad, he was ashamed that he was at home the whole day. He had just cut off the two hind-legs of his chair so that he could lay back, and couldn't be seen from outside. In this way he could look between the curtain and the window-sill. He had a tape-recorder and a gramophone. The whole day he was taping music. There was nothing else for him to do but to sit with his headphone on. Yes, in a way one could feel sorry for him. The last years he drank each day. Until he was completely senseless. Then I had to drag him upstairs. Yes, that was terrible. He used to drink at home, he didn't go to bars or anything. No, that was the worst, you saw him go down each time in front of your eyes. Beer no longer appealed to him. He started a bottle of Dutch Gin in the early afternoon and the whole bottle would be finished. You couldn't say anything critical to him, you just had to let him drink. You couldn't look at him. One had to watch one's step. Because then he used to hit... Often it only was threats. But they terrified me as well... It was terrible. Therefore I say that it was a relief for me when the good old man died. Yes, the drinking ruined him. From the beginning. Because of the excessive drinking we had to marry. Yes, that is where it all began and where it all ended. By drinking, with drinking, in drinking..."

"I think I am now in the stage of feeling locked up. I have dealt with everything alone. It is a pity having no one to talk things over with. I'll manage. At the moment I am... I would like to be more energetic.

I mean, there are so many groups, but I don't know how to handle such things. I just let it go. I can never see further than my nose."

"My mother used to say, for example when I had a date: "always remember: desire is worse than possession." That was my mother's motto. You can desire something, but once you have it, it is not so great anymore. Another motto: "five minutes of thoughtlessness can make you weep for years". That appeals even more to me."

The thing that strikes most in the case of Mrs. Thijssen is the way she experienced her marriage. For twenty-five years she didn't live her own life. She wonders whether she should not have opposed more to this humiliating husband. She would have liked to be more assertive. Her marriage ended more and more in disillusionment, increased by the drinking habits of her husband. A disillusion she puts in her motto "five minutes of thoughtlessness can make you weep for years." Her basic attitude is: "I just let it go" and "I can never see further than my nose". This attitude undoubtedly determined her marriage. Her husband's death was a relief. The burden of an unhappy marriage is taken from her. Yet loneliness is a problem. Passively she hopes that things will end well.

3.2. The Religiosity of Mrs. Thijssen

With reference to her religious background Mrs. Thijssen is asked about the role of religion in her youth: "Faith had a crucial role. I'd like to go back to those days. You miss quite a lot nowadays. Going to benediction in the evenings and all those special holy days. I loved it all, I remember it with pleasure."

Central in Mrs. Thijssen's religiosity now is her relation to her patron saint. She says: "We went on a pilgrimage to the Black Forest in Germany. I have a patron-saint there, Judas Thaddeus[6], whom I have great admiration for. He had a chapel there. I wanted to go there. Well, we went there and returned as soon as possible. I thought we would never make it home alive. We drove 800 miles non-stop. That isn't normal. He would never spend the night somewhere. No, no, drive today, sleep in the car for a while, and back again. As I say, I didn't live my own life, he arranged everything. Just up and down to the Black Forest. Up and

[6] In modern times Judas has acquired popularity as the "patron of hopeless cases." This patronage is said to have originated because nobody invoked him for anything since his name so closely resembled that of Judas who betrayed the Lord. Consequently he favours even the most desparate situations of his petitioners. Cf. FARMER (1987) 241.

down. Driving without stopping, not even having a cup of coffee on the way. The thermos had to go in the car."

"Still I find a lot of comfort in my belief, in these things without perspective. Just talking, but that is praying too. Not like I do now, but when I really speak to God or to Judas, in this case, I really feel... relieved. You don't get a real direct answer, they don't say this or that will happen, or just have patience. No, you just feel maybe because you talked things over, at least you tried, you feel relieved. You go away and things aren't so negative anymore. You think: God, things will work out. You are more optimistic. Sometimes everything is in the dark. Then you think, God, how will this, or how will that work out? When you look back, you think everything ended well, though".

Sometimes she goes to a little chapel nearby: "There I meet my patron-saint whom I worship. The other day was the feast of Judas Thaddeus, and I went to the chapel in the morning. It was packed with many old nuns. Judas Thaddeus is a patron for hopeless cases, but he doesn't listen very well. Nothing. This patron-saint really is a friend in our family. He goes with every son and daughter. You have to stick to him, you must have faith. Sometimes I am grumbling then and I wonder how long I have been asking for something. "Don't you hear me or what?" Sometimes I think I'm going mad. But still this is the way it goes. I keep my trust. I keep on praying. Through Judas I ask God. So I take him as an intermediary. When I go to bed at night, I have a little booklet with a novena to Judas in it. I pray it every night. Sometimes I think, I'll skip a few prayers. Then I take a book, or the newspapers before I go to sleep, but I can't. I have to. It gives me a feeling that it just isn't right. So I put away the book, and do my prayers first. Sometimes I am rebellious and think not tonight, but still I do it. I don't feel it as an obligation, I can not do without it. I must be able to pray. I don't have to pray in bed. I can pray sitting at a table, or when I am sewing. Those prayers of Judas I know by heart. So that is no problem. If only a Hail Mary or a Our Dear Father and a Hail Mary. Just repeating them, and a short conversation in between, or a question... Just praying, just like that. Then I pray to Judas or to God or Maria. But not especially for them. I am a real believer. Always have been. Nothing hypocritical. I can do without a church now. I only go there when there is really something to do. I can pray now without a church. At first I thought you had to go to a church to pray, but that isn't necessary any more."

In her religiosity Mrs. Thijssen resembles a gentle, somewhat traditional, even simple catholic. With nostalgic pleasure she remembers her religious upbringing. Still this does not go in any depth. Faith stands for talking with her patron-saint in hopeless affairs, Judas Thaddeus. In him she has a partner without conflicts, the partner her husband could not be. To him she can talk without danger about "things without perspective". Her prayer to someone else who will solve things fits her passive attitude. Avoiding conflict, she waits until things pass. Instead of active resistance, she calls upon Judas Thaddeus, and puts all her hope in his hands. By praying to Judas she has an address for her feelings.

4. Review

When we look at the religious stories of both of these cases, some might devalue this religiosity. Saints belong to a somewhat discriminated minority group in popular religion within the official church.

In the case of Mr. Oakes, we saw how the worship of his saint gives structure to a life that takes place in a few inches, in one room, as a matter of speaking, closed to the world. Little things get big meaning: Peerke Donders, a booklet and things like that. Simple lines from a song mediate hope for a meeting hereafter: "We'll meet again, don't know where, don't know when". Mr. Oakes is satisfied despite everything. His little, isolated world is quiet and clear. His mourning has not ended. However, one might wonder whether this will ever be the case when people suffer such a loss. Within the framework of his mourning we must be grateful that in the domain of popular religion, these small privatised means for help are available. On the surface one might say these are minor things, but still they give meaning and make life tolerable.

In the case of Mrs. Thijssen it is also easy to qualify her devotion to her saint as an expression of questionable, magic nature. Such a judgement does not do justice to Mrs. Thijssen's religiosity. For, especially in her prayer to Judas Thaddeus, authentic religious moments appear. Moments in which the transformation from obsessive ritual to a religious ritual is made.[7] When we speak about individual religiosity we must not be tempted to think in exclusive categories. Especially since there has always been prejudice against the value of expressions of popular religion such

[7] Freud (1907).

as the worship of saints, we must ask in concrete cases about the role this religiosity plays in the whole structure of meaning for this individual. Only then is a careful judgement possible and we gain insight into the important coping-function Judas Thaddeus represents for Mrs. Thijssen. Judas Thaddeus mediates a structure to externalize her most primary structure: immobility. As such, this case underlines the close connection between personality and religiosity. Judas Thaddeus can be seen as the perfect choice, the personification of her life-situation. Her feeling of hopelessness becomes tolerable and is lifted up in a religious context, is transcended to a higher level.

One negative aspect in both cases is the fact that the motivation to active change disappears. In both cases one could discuss the question, about the extent to which this faith keeps them passive, functions as an opium, and prevents them from really saying goodbye to their deceased partner. A faith that does not stimulate them to change, but fits both their passivity and immobility. The guilt question about their own role in the process is pacified. In this way the role of religion has two sides: On the one hand it offers a way to survive in life-threatening circumstances. On the other hand it does not challenge to change. Individual religiosity often consists of a mixture of healthy and unhealthy, magic and authentic elements. Sometimes one element dominates, then again the other. Certain expressions of popular religion are located somewhere "between belief and superstition". It is crucial to see what function this religiosity plays for this person. In that sense there only exists "personally fitting" religiosity.

In the case of popular religion we must learn to look with a magnifying-glass so that the inconspicious yet meaningful does not slip through the prejudiced researchers net. Then one discovers that judgements on healthy or unhealthy religiosity, on belief, or superstition are mostly based upon careless exploration of the meaning-giving process of the individual.

11. GOOD TIMES, BAD TIMES: DEVOTIONAL RITUALS BETWEEN TRADITION AND MODERNITY[1]

1. Introduction

1.1. Amsterdam: City of Pilgrimage

The 650th anniversary of the "Miracle of the Blessed Sacrament," which took place in a house on Amsterdam's Kalverstraat in 1345, was observed in 1995. As a result of this sensational miracle involving the Eucharist, Amsterdam became an important pilgrimage destination. In a complex process, through good times and bad times, this medieval devotion developed into an annual silent nocturnal procession through the centre of the metropolis, which is still well attended today.[2]

"Prettig weekend" (Pleasant weekend; a televised preview of cultural events and tourist attractions for the coming weekend) highlighted the pilgrimage on March 17, 1995, the day before the Silent Procession was to take place. In fact, they spotlighted three events: the reportage on the Miracle of Amsterdam and the Silent Procession was sandwiched between items on the Rotterdam Zoo and the Tax Museum.[3]

Though short, the item's structure was refined. It began with an impression of the rough image evoked by modern Amsterdam's street life, accompanied by pop music. The message was clear: this is a city where there is little room for religion and pious devotions. Then, as a

[1] This is an expanded and annotated text of a lecture presented at the symposium held at Amsterdam on March 31, 1995, to mark the 650th anniversary of the Miracle of Amsterdam. I thank P.J. Margry, M.A., for his critical reading of an earlier version of this paper. The article was first published as: P. Post: Goede tijden, slechte tijden: devotionele rituelen tussen traditie en moderniteit, in P.J. Margry (ed.): *Goede en slechte tijden: het Amsterdams Mirakel van Sacrament in historisch perspectief* (Aerdenhout 1995) 62-80.

[2] For a summary, see: Margry (1988); Raedts (1993); Beijne (1995); see now: Margry (1995b), as our note 1; and Margry & Caspers (1997) 134-150.

[3] *Prettig weekend. Programma over uitgaansmogelijkheden* (AVRO), Dutch channel 1, March 17, 1995, 18:57-19:28.

contrast, the Silent Procession was introduced through old black and white images. Next, in a theatrical reprise complete with an enormous communion wafer which floated through them, scenes from the Miracle were evoked for secularized viewers, and the whole issued seamlessly into a cultural/historical visual documentary about the Miracle and an exhibition at the Amstelkring Museum. The final scene closed the circle with the beginning, drawing a parallel from the traditional Silent Procession, through to the modern procession of shoppers in the Kalverstraat and its adjoining streets.

At the close of the whole programme the practical, touristic facts were recapitulated: the stepping-off point and time, the Silent Procession as a weekend attraction, the exhibition with liturgical utensils in the display cases, free entry for those with national museum passes.

In many respects, this piece of modern visual communication is a concise synthesis of my argument. I am no master of the language of television, but in this chapter I certainly can perhaps provide some commentary for the script and scenario.

1.2. Approach

My contribution can be situated somewhere within the wide field of what are called *ritual studies*, but in particular I speak from the theological subdiscipline of liturgical studies. I want to bring the devotions surrounding the Miracle of Amsterdam in general, and in particular the devotional going and coming that is styled "traditional," the *procedere* of the Silent Procession, into confrontation with modernity and current events. I will try to offer a sort of diagnosis of the times. As I have said, the devotion surrounding the Miracle has seen good times and bad times, bloom and oblivion, various rebirths and revitalizations. It is fitting that we ask the question: In what sort season does it ritual find itself now? Are these good times or bad times for it?

1.3. Devotional Ritual

Devotions occupy a particular place within the broad field of ritual or liturgical repertoires. Thus, in what has come to be called the Silent Procession, we are dealing with a very special segment of liturgy, one of the terms for which is "devotional ritual." More than is the case for rituals which take place within the space of a church, it is precisely with regard to this ritual repertoire that appraisals, prognoses and conceptualizations run rampant, not in the least because here we enter into the strange world of religious popular culture.

Without inserting a detailed excursus here concerning what can or should be understood as being included in it, I will list only a few points which, in my view, characterize devotional ritual:[4]

- Devotional rites possess a certain measure of intensity and are directed in part (and to a greater degree than mainstream liturgy) to emotion and empathy.
- Next, devotion refers back to a certain fundamental religious attitude.
- Further, there is a personal, individual, private dimension involved; devotional rites are characterized by a unique interplay of private and public, of individual and collective celebration.
- Mediators, often physical, also play an important role in this; in devotional rites communication with the holy or the holy one is "mediated" through holy places, holy images, miracles, etc.

This is far from an exhaustive, let alone all-inclusive, description. But these characteristics are indicative of the specifics of this liturgical domain.

1.4. Ritual, Time and Culture

As we have said, in this chapter we address the question of the contemporary context of rituals of this sort. Are they still "timely"? Are the times with or against them? Are they good times or bad times? We enter here into an unusually interesting, but also complex area, namely that of ritual, time and culture.[5] After all, in addition to elements which

[4] In a number of contexts one can see evidence of a debate about the content of the concepts of devotion and piety. I will list here only the entry "Vroomheid" in the *Liturgisch Woordenboek* II, cols. 2883-2887, and the survey article DAXELMÜLLER (1988). Further, the ongoing reflection on the term "devotion" with respect to image and ritual are especially important: see VAN OS (1994). For a summary, see (review article) POST (1991a). See also: SCRIBNER (1992).

[5] For the theme of liturgy and time, the reader is particularly referred to an international congress devoted to Liturgical Time held in Paris in 1981 by the Societas Liturgica: for the report of this congress, see: *Studia Liturgica* 14,2-4 (1982); *La Maison-Dieu* 147 (1981); *Liturgisches Jahrbuch* 31 (1981) and 32 (1982). I would specifically cite the contribution by MEYER (1981-1982); for a summary: POST (1981). See further: SCHEER (1992) and WEGMAN (1994). For the theme of ritual/liturgy and culture: our note 18.

determine its structure, such as the design of the ritual, the actors and participants, leaders and celebrants and the spatial context, the temporal aspect also plays an important role in ritual. I am defining time very broadly here, as including the full spectrum from biological and cosmic time through cultural time, as juncture. The rhythm of biological and cosmic time is very important for rites. The cosmic cadence of day and night is often, deliberately and gladly broken through, as are also our biological rhythms of waking and sleeping, speaking (sometimes speaking a lot) and silence. Thus holding a procession in the still of the night is on the same plane with a ritual such as fasting, which breaks through another temporal, bodily rhythm, that of eating and drinking. Liturgy stands or falls with time, in the same way that time also takes aim at the other elements which determine the structure of rites which we have just listed, such as the spatial location and celebrants. Thus time refers to the general rhythms of life, to the experience of time, to short or long duration, to the long or short term, and so ultimately also to that anamnestic tension which is so definitive for liturgy, past and future.

But, as we have also said, there is the question of cultural time too, of the nature of the times in which we live, the good and bad times of our existence. Specifically, it is a matter of the times today, which some have called a bad time for religion and liturgy: modernity, which would appear to challenge or sweep away precisely the tradition of devotional rites.

The approach and the context of this argument is now clear: are these good or bad times for devotional rituals?

1.5. The Chaos of Modernity

I can already say now that there can be no simple answer to this question. Indeed, this question pitches us into the midst of a network of cultural processes, about which observers of culture are more than ever realizing that it is nearly impossible to trace the order we often seek and suppose within them. Times are always both good and bad. Without taking flight into Postmodernist jargon, and presenting chaos as the result of fashionable efforts at deconstruction on the part of postmodern cultural critics, it is nevertheless important to take into account the chaos of our times, the fragmentization, its asynchroneities, inconsistencies and contradictions. It is precisely in the area of religious rituals and attitudes about the sacred and profane that traditional attitudes and configurations have fundamentally changed. Or to put it another way, through new connections

(I borrow the term from a recent postmodern and eclectic discourse by Mary Grey[6]) the sacred is being rediscovered in our culture in a number of places and ways. With regard to the question which we have posed here, it will be productive to fully acknowledge and take the measure of this chaos, rather than cultivating the terminal pessimism of the bad times by, for instance, engaging in a perpetual lamentation about empty churches and the decline of traditional rites and myths.[7]

1.6. Structure

I will now try to evoke for you some of this chaos, some of the fragments and asynchroneities, by following up several aspects of the devotional ritual repertoire, and of the Silent Procession in particular, under five headings. One may wish to consider this as a development of the script that must have lain behind the item in the television programme with which we began our discussion.

2. Asynchroneities, Changes and Shifts in Perspectives

Far better than any theoretical argument could have done, the television report demonstrated how rituals are surrounded by a network of synchroneities and – more to the point – asynchroneities, of contradictions and inconsistencies, and in particular, how this complex network determines the experience, function, perception and meaning of rituals. In relation to the Miracle of Amsterdam and the Silent Procession, under five headings I wish to further elucidate a number of elements which are closely related with one another.

2.1. General: Rites in Crisis

Rather generally, these are spoken of as bad times for Christian rites.[8] A superficial analysis would appear to confirm this diagnosis: every year

[6] See M. Grey: Wankelende grondvesten – opnieuw! Over cultuur en de bevrijding van de theologie, lecture "St. Thomasfeest," Faculty of Theology, Katholieke Universiteit Leuven, Leuven March 7, 1995 (The shaking of the foundations – again! Culture and the liberation of theology). The lecture was published in *Louvain Studies* 20 (1995) 347-361.

[7] A passage from Mary Grey's lecture (see note 6) was the starting point for these, my own differing reflections.

[8] For rites and the crisis in rites in general, see: Lukken (1988); (1984); (1994) in particular Part I, 45-236.

there are fewer people participating in what mainstream ecclesiastical ritual offers. Rather generally, this is blamed on something called "secularization," which has manifested itself since the 1960s. In short, bad times, globally.

At the same time, however, we are receiving all sorts of signals that point to good times. Rites and myths, symbols and signs, the language in which we try to communicate the holy, are also "in;" whether as a part of religious popular culture or in the sphere of New Age practices, there is plenty of interest in rites, and to spare, in myths and rites which seek and give meaning. Further consideration appears to indicate that even in secularization it is not so much that rites and sacred places have disappeared from our world, but rather that they have been relocated. Sacredness, rites and liturgy have in many respects moved: we find them now in other, and often unexpected places. Connections are being established between the profane and sacred dimensions of our existence in new ways. The perspective of emptying pews, mentioned above, is only one part of the story. Many ritual repertoires have, for instance, moved outdoors, outside the walls of church buildings. The times would thus smile on the Silent Procession, because it appears to share in the strongly experienced interest for rituals outside the walls of churches, because it appears to tie into the general interest in the culture of public observances which has developed since the same 1960s and '70s.

It is precisely in the present age that devotional rites seem to be playing a role in the network of new connections between the sacred and profane. Interest in pilgrimages is overflowing: the roads to Santiago de Compostela are busy, but so too are the roads near flourishing holy places such as Dokkum[9] and Heiloo. This is what we could well term the paradox of the crisis for rites: in rites (at least Christian rites) we see both a crisis and a flowering. This paradox is defined, to a not unimportant extent, by the relocation of ritual settings which we have mentioned, through shifts in the zones of the sacred and profane.

This general observation about rites in modern times and the connections between the sacred and profane could be worked out in many ways, given specific focus and nuanced. We could go into the constant

[9] For Dokkum, see: Post (1993). More generally, see: Van Uden, Pieper & Post (1995). See now my lemma "Dokkum" in Margry & Caspers (1997) = Post (1997d). Cf. Chapter 3 and 4 in this book.

interaction between tradition and modernity, or the tension between cultus and culture. In this connection, I want to briefly elucidate several aspects from this scale, always with the chaos of modernity and the specific ritual situation of the Miracle devotion and Silent Procession in mind.

2.2. The Holy One and the Holy

The element of the personal dimension of sacredness is of major importance in this connection of rituals in context. In a number of places in his studies on holiness and holy figures, the historian Peter Brown emphasizes precisely this element.[10] In his view, the revolutionary thing in the praxis of Christian belief lies in the fact that in Christendom the Holy, God Himself, took and takes a human face. In that way, the sacred became a personally defined concept. This has not lost its appeal down to this very day. Indeed, one could even say that we are experiencing a strong rise in interest in saints. Saints are popular again, more and more books of hagiography appear, the old and somewhat forgotten genre of "a saint for every day of the year" is experiencing a rebirth, and many bookstores have a separate shelf for books about saints.[11] The regeneration of holy places would appear to be connected with this: in Dokkum Boniface has been rediscovered, along with Titus Brandsma, and Wittem is sustained by the faces of Gerard Majella and Mary. Especially Mary is being rediscovered at a number of places, and also gives direction to thinking through and living out the *gender specific* consequences of Christianity. At the same time, there are signs of a certain rebirth in the theological subdiscipline of Mariology.[12]

For the devotion surrounding the Miracle and Silent Procession, this predilection for personalized holiness at first may seem an unfavourable characteristic of our times. After all, here in Amsterdam it is a matter of

[10] Listing only two of his most important works: BROWN (1981); (1982). See further, ANGENENDT (1994).

[11] From the extensive catalogue of literature about saints, I will list only the following, including popular and academic items and mature reflections and enthusiasms, to sketch the broad picture: KLANICZAY (1991); GOOSEN (1992); SCHAUBER & SCHINDLER (1992); BARTH (1992); LÄPPLE (1992); VAN EIJK (1993); VAN KEMENADE & SPAPENS (1993); VAN REEN (1994); JÖCKLE (1995). Outstanding as introduction (with bibliography) are, ANGENENDT (1994) and HARNONCOURT & AUF DER MAUR (1994). See also: *La Maison-Dieu* 201 (1995): "Liturgie et sainteté."

[12] See: BEINERT & PETRI (1984); LOGISTER (1995).

a rather abstract, historically-rooted sacred thematic: it is not that the holy receives a face in a particular life recognizable to humans, but in an Eucharistic miracle, in a miraculous Host as a ritual component of "the last sacrament," a *locus sacer* with a hagiography of a very specific nature.

How are we to assess this? Is our age a fitting and favourable time for such a narrative of sacramental salvation and for a ritual that is based on Eucharistic fascination?[13] Does the dominant "personality" of the Eucharistic Christ ultimately play its role in the background or the foreground?

But here too there is another side to the coin. In addition to the tendency to the personalization of the holy which we have mentioned, in our times one can also observe a process of depersonalization of the sacred, once again coexistent and at first glance without competition. Questions might be asked about the real presence of saints in our culture, and about the nature of the interest in the holy which we sketched. Upon further examination, there is much that points to it being the strange traditions and stories that fascinate, rather than personal holiness. Saints supply legends of strange and different times, which like folk tales, legends and fairy tales find a ready audience. They are remnants of a strange past, complete with an old repertoire of folk customs and a literature of incantation boiled down to meteorological proverbs. People choose only certain saints, in arranging them they always follow the civil calendar year, or the seasons, not the liturgical calendar, and they happily add customs and "traditions" to the hagiographic details. To my mind, the popular genre of angelological literature must be regarded in a similar light.[14] Here the question of the sacred is indeed raised within our modernity, but the point is precisely that angels balance on the edge between personal and impersonal. The popularity of angels points unmistakably to a different conclusion, the conclusion that our culture also depersonalizes the sacred. Furthermore, it is striking that the new ritual forms, it is the non- personal categories which play a role, rather than the personal. We can also point to the search for the holy, and for communication with it, which many engage in under New

[13] I have borrowed the term "Eucharistic fascination" from HARTINGER (1992).

[14] As was the case for literature about saints in note 11, I can here give only a global picture of the literature regarding angels by listing a handful of titles. See: BURNHAM (1990); MOOLENBURGH (1990); (1991); VON BRAUCHITSCH (1990); VORGRIMMLER (1991); CAFÉ & INNECCO (1994); FRANKEN-DUPARC (1995). See now: KÖSTLIN (1994).

Age forms. In this connection I would raise the remarkable evolution of Bernard Huijbers who, after having given the new Dutch liturgy shape and melody after Vatican II, took his leave of a personal God in a book, the title of which says it all: *Aan Gij voorbij* (Beyond You).[15] In his recent survey work, *Heilige und Reliquien*, Arnold Angenendt bestows attention on this process.[16] Thus, from a number of sources, to an increasing degree, it would appear that it is not the holy one, but the holy, which is the issue. Angenendt sees this as an inescapable tendency in modernity: after all, when the core of Christian belief about God, namely in His transcendent personality, becomes vague and disappears, what then remains for people in the modern age, acting from their experience of their own finitude, except to search for and explore that which is different, strange and beyond in the otherwise generally unresponsive, but constantly sought-after sacred?

Seen in this context, at first glance it would appear that the times would again be favourable for the cultus of the Silent Procession, not being bound to one person. Here, almost par excellence, we have a tradition telling a strange story from a different and lost age. Yet it would appear that this diagnosis too is perhaps overly optimistic. Again, that has everything to do with the Eucharistic component in the Amsterdam narrative. How does so traditional a mediation of the sacred fit with modernity? That brings me to my third observation.

2.3. Eucharistic Fascination

If I were to sum up the origin, development and reception – in short, the cognitive soil around its roots – of the Silent Procession and the Miracle of Amsterdam in two words, I would choose "Eucharistic fascination." With this characterization, we once again call up questions, changeable diagnoses, contradictions and asynchroneities.

From the negative side, without too much trouble at all we could argue that there appears to be no more room for classical forms of devotion that have surrounded Eucharist. It is precisely through its fascination for the Eucharist that this kind of ritual excludes itself from today's marketplace of ideas. After all, the classical liturgical structure surrounding this fascination has been dismantled or is in decay; children

[15] HUIJBERS (1989).

[16] ANGENENDT (1994) 303ff, particularly 306.

no longer "play mass," there is no homage, no large-scale processing of monstrances under the heavens with shrouded hands any more. Is it not precisely the celebration of the "Selbsthingabe Jesu" in the Eucharist and the concepts connected with it, such as *sacrifice* and *presence*, that have become the most difficult parts of Christian doctrinal heritage? The time appears ripe for fundamental adjustments in old forms of Eucharistic fascination, adjustments that will relate them to a new theology of liturgy.

But here too there are noises from the other side, heard at the same time, but telling a different story. In a recent interview Jan Duin, Dutch liturgical specialist and pastor, observed how Eucharistic fascination is still eminently present.[17] People continue to be fascinated by the Eucharist and Host. "I came to church, and there was no mass!": that is often the reaction to the celebrations of word and communion being held with increasing frequency in Catholic circles because of the lack of priests/celebrants. I can see many signals that point to Eucharistic fascination even within these "substitute celebrations": the Host remains the preeminent locus of the sacred, and it would appear that even in its exclusion the Eucharist continues to define the face of Roman Catholic liturgical repertoire.

This fact fascinates me. What is happening here? Is it more than a nostalgic yearning for the glory-days of Roman Catholicism? It is remarkable chiefly because, as we said, the contextual framework of this Eucharistic fascination and piety has been dismantled and there are hardly even the contours of a new theology of liturgy to be discerned that could provide a new ground for inculturating the *corpus Christi*, although, from the theoretical perspective, there are enough building blocks around, such as new thinking about the nature of signs, symbols, rites and myths and how they work, and about sacramentality as sacramental thought and life. One could also consider here the flourishing interest in the inculturation of Christian rituals[18], and in a theology of liturgy that is again trying to discern the coherence among the three dimensions of the *corpus Christi*. Based on the fundamental confession of the incarnation of God in the world, that belief proceeds from the premise that we can encounter the *corpus Christi* in three ways. Mediaeval theology therefore

[17] Interview with Jan Duin, We zitten nog altijd in een communiecultuur, in *Samen kerk* (published by the Diocese of Haarlem) May 1994, nr. 6, 8f.

[18] See: LUKKEN (1994); (1996); LAMBERTS (1996); VAN TONGEREN (1994); (1997).

speaks of the *triforme corpus Christi*: 1) the *corpus historicum*, 2) *corpus, quod est ecclesia*, and 3) the *corpus sacramentale*. The *corpus Christi* doctrine offered (and perhaps still offers?) the possibility of connecting together the diffusion and fragmentation, the heterogeneity of materializations in many places, persons and situations. But – and here we are close to the roots of the devotion of the Miracle of Amsterdam – a certain form of fascination involving the *corpus Christi*, namely honouring the *corpus sacramentale*, became the only point of crystallization in ever more places and for ever more people, one that ultimately even eclipsed the celebration of the *corpus sanctorum* in the Eucharist through directing attention entirely on the exalted Host. A rereading and redigesting of Henri de Lubac's 1949 standard work on the subject of this *Corpus mysticum*, a study that deals with the theological dimensions of the Church and Eucharist in the Middle Ages, would be productive for further reflection on this point.[19] Then, at the same time, this body of ideas could be brought into connection and confrontation with both the more recent historical studies in this field[20], and with the tension which we have already noted between personal and impersonal dimensions of the sacred, which touch so fundamentally on the basic Christian doctrine of the incarnation.

2.4. Urban Character and Ritual

The next not unimportant aspect of the Miracle devotion and Silent Procession, after the impersonality (in a certain sense) and oddity of the ritual, is the fact that it is a ritual in an urban context. It is not the idyllic backdrop of the countryside that forms the setting, but the metropolis. Here again we encounter changing contexts. Earlier both the city and the celebration enjoyed good times, as recently once more recapitulated by Lipp's sketch.[21] In urban culture – or better, in the heart of "urbanism" ("Urbanität" (German), "urbaniteit" (Dutch)), by which I intend to denote an interplay of social, political and religious processes – devotional rites could also find their place in the tension between the sacred and profane, which was also chiefly defined by the interplay of public

[19] DE LUBAC (1944); for a summary: STOCK (1994) 9-19.

[20] I will here mention only: RUBIN (1991); CASPERS (1992); SNOEK (1989); DUFFY (1992).

[21] See: LIPP (1995).

and private. But times have also changed in the city; it is now precisely the urban, in opposition to the rural, that is hostile to devotion. It is exactly the public nature of the city which has exiled religion and devotions to the private domain, or to rural places outside its bounds. We see its remains in the fragments of the once important ecclesiastical ritual settings, strange museum pieces such as the Gothic clustered column that adorns the Rokin in Amsterdam, amidst the postmodern street furniture.

In this connection, I am happy to be able to refer to an interesting passage in a recently published volume of *Gottesdienst der Kirche*, a German liturgical studies handbook. In the section on the ecclesiastical calendar and feasts of the saints, the Vienna liturgist Hansjörg Auf der Maur (he was for many years a professor in Amsterdam, and in those years lived in the city centre – the heart of Amsterdam with its sacred tracts) sketches the Miracle and the sacred geography, speaks about the surviving "Heilige Weg" as a *via sacra*, and in this context neatly points to the displacement of the sacred (just as the television programme with which we began did): today's Kalverstraat as a modern "Tempelbezirk" for contemporary shopping rituals.[22] It is indeed a phenomenological analysis, for in terms of the organization and conduct that the programme accurately evoked, pedestrian streets in shopping areas of our cities are the modern *viae sacrae*.

Changing times for urban rites. But there is still room and need for rites which mark out the sacred as a counterpoint to the everyday order. For instance, one can point to the flourishing culture of public celebrations. It is certainly still an open question with regard to what kind of experience of the sacred is literally being played out here. The precise background and functions of the ritual will now be the subject of the final and most thorough of my observations.

2.5. The Theatre of the Past

When a silent devotional procession passes through the heart of a city in times such as these, then, we may ask ourselves what is going on in terms of motivations, experience, function and meaning. Research into

[22] AUF DER MAUR (1994) 242: "Noch immer gibt es im Zentrum von Amsterdam, "De Heilige Weg," der einst die Pilger von Süden her über die Leidsestraat zum Ort des im 14. Jh. geschehenen Hostiewunders an der Kalverstraat führte, die heute ein faszinierender tempelbezirk moderner Geschäfts-Sakralität ist."

the various forms of contemporary public devotional rituals shows that there are certain characteristics or signals that point to fundamental changes in the context and in the way they are experienced and perceived by participants.[23] With the aid of these signals, one can attempt to place the ritual involved on a scale of how rituals are perceived and experienced.[24]

Scale of Ritual Experience

The changes in perception and experience to which I referred can be identified with the aid of an imaginary scale of myth, folklore and theatre called up in our minds. At the one end of the scale there is the *mythic phase,* the phase of ideal liturgy, of mythic, collective celebration. In the centre there is the phase of *folklore.* What distinguishes the celebrations here is precisely that they are more staged, presented and viewed. The collective mythic form is here replaced by performance and audience. Sacred dance, for instance, becomes the folk dance at the town festival. Ultimately, at the far end of the scale, it can be entirely embalmed in the *theatre* or *museum.* Distance now is the characteristic. The sung mass or vespers are performed by ensembles specializing in *musica antiqua,* compline by the Spanish monks of Silos winds up on a CD, and OSB is understood as the title of a successful record label, and what was originally a liturgical celebration now requires concert tickets, and is closed by applause...

Signals

Studying the design and development of rituals, and the changes they undergo, will now enable us to track rituals as they move on this scale. At this point it must be noted that changes of context which took place in the past can also be traced by this method, and that one and the same ritual can simultaneously occupy different positions on the scale, depending on the various degrees of appropriation and grants of meaning on the part of actors and participants. I will now briefly list some of the signals that I see, chiefly in devotional rituals, but also elsewhere in celebrations and rituals in general.

[23] For this process of changing contexts, and more particularly for ritual changes and folklorization of liturgy as well as musealization, see: SCRIBNER (1987); NISSEN (1994); GERNDT (1973); ZACHARIAS (1990); STURM (1990); POST (1991c); (1991d); BOISSEVAIN (1991); DEKKER (1993). See also Chapter 9 and 12 in this book.

[24] For this scale, see, among others: LUKKEN (1991).

(a) The ritual is not celebrated or enacted collectively for its own sake any more, or that is hardly ever done, but is chiefly staged and presented by a small group and viewed by others. There is an audience in addition to, or in place of, participants; a row of people along the sidelines watch. This is a signal that I myself, as a viewer, see every year in the Sint-Jans Procession at Laren (Procession on the Feast of Saint John The Baptist); each year the procession becomes smaller and more of an artifact, and the row of viewers greater.

(b) Next, and closely connected with the above, is the signal that the ritual play, the active handling of signs and symbols, is no longer enacted according to the mythic rules. That is to say, it is no longer uninhibited, carried out in all its sensory dimensions, and, most important, without any accompanying commentary or explanation. We are increasingly seeing how rituals are defined not by words *pointing toward*, but by words *about*. Just as music only really exists if it is played, so ritual only exists if it is enacted. But many of our contemporary rites talk about and comment on the ritual act, explain its smallest detail, and even go into its origin and development.

(c) Further, there is the signal of needing to offer a justification, as it were, for what is happening in the ritual within the ritual itself. In this respect, there also exists an assiduous search for legitimization and plausibility through social relevance. For instance, this can take the form of seeking ethical justifications. Although the day of the political evensong and discussion-and-action liturgy lies behind us, there is still the feeling that ritual celebration must somehow be legitimized. Just celebrating, without any practical outcome, appears impossible, or at least more difficult to accept. We are therefore always setting out again in search of a relevant liturgy, worthy of celebration. For instance, here in The Netherlands, we like to see our traditional "palmpaasstokken" (sticks decorated with palm fronds and sweets, carried in procession by children on Palm Sunday) taken around to hospitals or senior citizen's homes afterwards.

Against this background, there is always also a theme, preferably topical and often with moralizing undertones. Viewed liturgically, this is strange: after all, by its placement in the calendar, and through the nature of the celebration itself, liturgy always has a theme already. Themes are a sometimes desperate attempt to anchor liturgy in the world, to make it useful and relevant. But without following Frits Staal at all points in his sketch of ritual actions as "pure actions" and almost disseminating a message of "ritual nihilism," one can still say that at its most profound level, ritual cannot be made relevant by an appeal to "use" or "effect."[25] Its relevance, if you can and may use that word here, consists precisely in its gratuitous and unself-conscious celebratory and festive nature. In short, here again we see an important signal that something has changed in much of our dealings with ritual. It is no longer a self-evident action.

(d) Finally, there are also many signals that point to a change of context which has already taken place, and to a ritual having changed its position on our imaginary scale from myth to theatre. Mythic celebration has landed in the domain of the museum and theatre, via the intermediate stop of folklore as a beautiful old local or national tradition. It is no longer a living tradition, but a ritual that is cherished as a piece of the past. There are no new songs composed for it; there are no new visual statements added to the tradition. It is precisely the language of the past that people cherish; old prints and engravings define how we see it. Celebration has become commemoration, for in addition to the ecclesiastical and domestic arenas, there is also the celebratory space of the museum, the display case, catalogue and documentary. There a new form of sacredness is celebrated. There are the rites of the exhibition, the academic, chiefly historical symposium, the books which discuss and reveal the past.

In a number of places I see devotional liturgy such as pilgrimage and processions undergoing this change of context. Just like other segments of our culture, they are being absorbed into a particular way of dealing with tradition and the past that we try to characterize in professional jargon such as historicizing, aestheticizing and musealization. The search for ethical justifications we mentioned above has been surpassed and replaced by aesthetic justifications. What is good is beautiful; what is beautiful, is good.[26]

The theme of musealization has been developed further, and indeed in the context of rites and religious popular culture, elsewhere.[27] The process touches upon changed and changing attempts to interpret a

[25] STAAL (1979); APOSTEL (1994).

[26] See VUYK (1994).

[27] For literature, see note 23, above, and particularly the work of Zacharias cited there. For the rest, I see the process of musealization somewhat differently, and more broadly than Peter Jan Margry does in his recent contribution dealing with the same theme that forms the subject of this chapter. He separates musealization from the changes in cultural/historical context, while I see that as precisely the point that defines the process of musealization, just as it does aestheticizing. See MARGRY (1995a) sub 5, 187-191.

changed and changing world, with changed and changing points of view lying between the extremes of engagement and distance, aloofness and involvement. How cultural elements (in our case, devotional rituals) are dealt with is in part defined by distance, viewing, rather than through integration and participation in everyday life. For instance, it is a matter of rituals and liturgy being experienced as an old tradition, ever more often being cherished solely and exclusively as monuments, remnants of a "beautiful" but also strange past culture.

This all perhaps ties in too with that which some psychologists and philosophers propose as a diagnosis for our culture: they see our culture as one in which anamnestic celebration (that is, a celebration in which past, present and future are and remain involved with one another) has become difficult, where celebration and ritual at the very most can take on the form of commemoration, and in which, ultimately, going to war is the only remaining celebration and form of a *Moratorium des Alltags*.[28]

We have reached the end of the series of observations surrounding devotional rituals between tradition and modernity. The challenge which remains now is to pose the question of to what extent the signals which I have just now summarized, and particularly the last sketch of our ways of dealing with past culture, apply to the Miracle devotion and the Silent Procession. Is such a change of context also at work here? I have already dropped hints that I recognize these signals at a number of points in Amsterdam. In an indirect way, this chapter itself is also a part of the cultural process of musealization!

3. Conclusion: Silence in the Night

I would close by extracting still two more aspects of the combination of good and bad times, and connecting these with elements which define the image of the Silent Procession, namely, the silence and the nocturnal hour of the ritual enactment. Hidden within its ritual design, which we could characterize as "ascetic," this accommodating procession[29] has indeed its own counterweight to the process of musealization. The middle of the night is not a favourable time for attracting spectators or those

[28] Marquard (1988).

[29] See Margry (1993a); (1993b); (1995b); (1995c).

with historical or folkloristic interests, and the silence throws up a dam against the tendency of ritual to take flight into words about itself. More than other devotional rites, through these aspects of silence and night, the Procession has a built-in counter-force against the fundamental changes in context I have discussed here. Thus, I would view the silence not so much as a socially determined form of cultural behaviour[30], but rather as a ritual design which surmounts the tension between distance and involvement, as well as that between collective and individual ritual. To my mind, it is here particularly that the power of the ritual lies, the vessel which ever again is to be filled with and modified by cultural meaning: the power of silent procession and silent prayer which, since antiquity and the late classical world possessed magical power and ritual inapproachability, as well as a demonstrative power to offend, as Piet van der Horst has demonstrated in his fine essay on silent prayer.[31]

But how this silent power will relate to the other signals of our modernity listed is still unanswered. The accompanying commentaries, the talking about the ritual, swell around it, before it, behind it. The critical question is whether this ultimately is going to penetrate the heart of the ritual action, the ritually designed asceticism of listening.

[30] See MARGRY (1993a) 183, note 34, following Peter Burke.

[31] VAN DER HORST (1994).

12. RITUAL LANDSCAPE: ON OUTDOOR LITURGY

PROCESSIONAL PARKS, PAPAL VISITS, AND POPULAR RITES ASSOCIATED WITH SUDDEN DEATH[1]

1. Introduction: Structure

In this chapter I will be examining ritual landscapes, liturgy which takes place outside of church buildings, and open-air liturgy. The structure will be as follows: first, I will further elaborate what this chapter will involve, and pause to examine some of the central concepts employed, such as *liturgy* and *landscape*. After a general survey and categorization of the forms of liturgy which take place outdoors, three concrete examples will be discussed. For the first illustration and analysis we will turn to the development of the ritual design of the landscape at Dokkum, a Dutch cultic site in Friesland where, according to tradition, St. Boniface and his company were martyred. Subsequently a Papal visit and the design of rituals associated with sudden death will be examined.

Although Roman Catholic liturgy in The Netherlands in the 20th century – indeed with an emphasis on recent and contemporary developments – will always be the primary frame of reference, the liturgical analysis is conceived with broader interests, resonances and applications in mind. The pursuit of a *liturgie comparée*, the heuristic perspective of diachronic and comparative observation which has been so important for liturgical studies since Baumstark,[2] will always be in the background, and occasionally in the foreground as well.

[1] This is a shorter version of P. Post: *Ritueel landschap: over liturgie-buiten. Processie, pausbezoek, danken voor de oogst, plotselinge dood* (= Liturgie in perspectief, 5) (Heeswijk-Dinther 1995). *Ritueel landschap* was presented by the author as his inaugural lecture as Professor of Liturgy and Sacramental Theology in the Theological Faculty Tilburg, on Friday, May 19, 1995. A French version appeared in two parts in *Question liturgiques / Studies in Liturgy*: Paysage rituel: liturgie en plein air (I), in *Questions liturgiques / Studies in Liturgy* 77 (1996) 174-190; Paysage rituel: la liturgie en plein air (II): la visite du pape, action de grâce pour la moisson, rites autour d'une mort subite, *ibidem* 240-256.

[2] See Baumstark (1939); (1953); (1958). Regarding Baumstark and what is termed "comparative liturgical studies," see Post (1995c) esp. 11ff; see also the fine booklet, West (1995) based on West (1988); see also, Cameron-Mowat (1995); Klauser & Killy

2. The Subject: Liturgy and Landscape

2.1. Procession, Liturgy and Ritual Domains

As a beginning, we can productively approach our theme by using processional culture as our point of departure, and stepping off from there. The devotional going and coming of procession is first and foremost a ritual in its general sense, which is to say, a more or less established, formalized pattern of actions in which signs and symbols are arranged in a way which can be repeated.[3] In a more precise sense, a procession is liturgy, which is to say that it is part of "the Christian worship, in the broadest sense of the term. All Christian rituals which one encounters in Christian churches and denominations and in which the faith of the community is expressed in one way or another can be counted as part of this. More concretely, among the things which can be accounted part of liturgy are sacraments, services of the word, and as components of these, the homily or sermon, canonical hours, all celebrations which are connected with the ecclesiastical year, Christian rituals of passage, pilgrimages and processions."[4] Drawing the circle even more closely, for many processional culture is a typical exponent of Roman Catholic liturgy.

I have just utilized a broad and open description of liturgy that in turn corresponds to a broad and open conception of the subject, which repeatedly must be called into question, justified and defended. Indeed, through my choice of liturgy in non-traditional and non-official settings, in a modest way I wish to once again advance the argument for this broad and open conception of the field, and in doing so I am prepared to literally step outside the traditional walls, by showing how the subject must always be rooted in the broader interdisciplinary framework of *ritual studies* and comes to life by the grace of variations of perspective and multidisciplinary alliances.[5]

(1949); Heiming (1949); and see further: *Oriens Christianus* 37 (1953) 2f; *Liturgisch Woordenboek* I, cols. 222f.

[3] For procession, see yet the typology in Wegman (1977). See now: Felbecker (1995). Within the broad field of what are termed *ritual studies*, the shape of theory with regard to ritual is again of great interest. I here list only a handful of studies in this connection: Bell (1992); Grimes (1990); Grimes (1993); Gerholm (1988); Heimbrock (1993); Asad (1993); Humphrey & Laidlaw (1994); Platvoet & Van der Toorn (1995).

[4] See Post (1996b) 22.

[5] Lukken (1993); (1994). See the first lecture also for a survey of developments in Dutch liturgical studies, with bibliography.

At the same time, by directing our attention to processions, we point to an aspect that is essential in liturgy. Liturgy is procession, *procedere*, process, movement, activity, actions, doing. In this respect, it is notable how in the vocabulary of the early church, *procedere* is pre-eminently the term used for the celebration of the liturgy, as is so striking in the report of Egeria's pilgrimage to the Holy Land.[6] There, at the end of the fourth century, liturgy takes place both indoors and outdoors. In his dissertation on the liturgical vocabulary in Egeria, Bastiaensen spends considerable time discussing this dominate place of *procedere*, and attempts to further define the term in the context of the late Hellenistic world.[7] In the course of this, the dynamic of acting in various realms of life comes to the fore: *procedere* means moving from one domain to another, for instance, from the home to the church through the public domain of the street. But there is also the aspect of appearing in public, particularly in relation to late Hellenistic public ceremonies. Thus, in addition to *what*, the questions of *how, when* and particularly *where* automatically come to the fore here as inescapable elements for analysis in liturgical studies.[8]

It is this spatial dimension which I wish to raise as central, space as a part of ritual process and as a component in achieving new perspectives. This is not merely a question of just a roof over some heads, or just ground under the feet.

Subject and frame are domains or "zones" which interact with one another. Such spatial contexts join phenomenological elements, functions and meanings and the element of time in forming a structural element of ritual actions. Working with varying perspectives of this sort is proving increasingly fruitful in a number of places. I am thinking here of studies in the history of liturgy, piety and art, in which with increasing frequency one discovers how rites, books, prayers and artifacts are

[6] MARAVAL (1982); WILKINSON (1973); LEDEGANG (1991).

[7] BASTIAENSEN (1962) II, 26-39.

[8] RICHTER (1995); LUKKEN (1989); MUCK (1986). In this connection, and following upon what we will later have to say about domains and zones, I would also refer to the discussion, particularly in general survey works, of space as an aspect which determines the structure of ritual. See, for instance, HARTINGER (1992) 45-62 sub 1.2.3.; WEGMAN (1991) sub I, 17-45 (including the elements of time, space and people); AUF DER MAUR (1994) 72-357 sub 251, 227-249 (structural manifestations: time, space, ritual forms); ANGENENDT (1994) sub IX, 123-137 (place and time). Though focused on a specific period, the following is also certainly relevant here: DE BLAAUW (1991). See now the bibliography in: POST (1997b) 96-101.

connected with private devotion, at home, as was to be seen for example in the "Art of Devotion" exhibition.[9] But this had already been illuminated in Marrow's work, for instance, and studies concerning the "discovery" or "invention" of the devotional image in the late Middle Ages.[10] I could also list here the international European project *Orte des Alltags*,[11] and Hartinger's perhaps undervalued book *Religion und Brauch.*[12] A 1994 symposium at Tilburg explored ritual repertoires in their spatial domestic context.[13]

Within the domains there are, again, zones with their own accents, actors and rites. Köstlin traces these within the church building,[14] but in the domestic domain there are also zones with an rising degree of private character (kitchen, living room, bedroom). And within a room there is again a more private zone – the cabinet or closet – with its own ritual or repertoire of images (although here "domain" is broadly conceived in the sense of *Raum* or *Bereich*). We must always see that what we are dealing with is an open system, an interaction between domains and the zones mentioned, with an interaction of asynchroneities, contradictions and inconsistencies. The perspective changes each time we enter a new zone, and a new play of appropriations arises. Seeking the peculiar accents that are brought in by each specific domain is a great challenge which lies before us.

As an illustration of the use of this perspective of domains I might, for instance, point to studies involving the Old Testament. Some Psalms should not be connected with contexts of the public cultus, but with private contexts. These speak of "my" God, the concerns of the individual receive greater play, there is a greater sense of presence and more room for apotropaic and prophylactic ritual actions.[15]

[9] See the exhibition *Gebed in schoonheid. Schatten van privé-devotie 1300-1500, Rijksmuseum Amsterdam 26 nov. - 26 febr. 1995*: VAN OS (1994). A good synthesis of the interplay of various domains and diverse functions of religious visual language is found in BELTING (1990). For "domains" or "zones", see also SCRIBNER (1992).

[10] For a summary, see my review article POST (1991a).

[11] HAUPT (1994).

[12] HARTINGER (1992) 83-87 sub 1.2.3. and sub 2.1.3 ("Geistliche" Landschaft).

[13] Cf. symposion *Religie thuis. Religiebeleving in het katholieke huisgezin rond 1900*, Tilburg, December 8, 1994; see POST, NISSEN & CASPERS (1995).

[14] KÖSTLIN (1989), particularly on sacred "zoning," 428-431.

[15] My thanks to Prof. dr. K. Waaijman for this suggestion. See VORLÄNDER (1975); ALBERTZ (1978); SEYBOLD (1978).

This play of domains is also exhibited in liturgical/historical research into Jewish Pesach traditions, in which one can follow the traces of diverse appropriations in various domains, up through early Christian traditions.[16] For example, there are the aspects of roots in the various spheres of thanksgiving and prayerful approaches to the fertility of the earth. Pesach is a celebration that is rooted, on the one side, in a pastoral celebration with the slaughter of a lamb in the spring, and on the other side in an agrarian celebration with the unleavened bread. Both fuse together into a celebration of remembrance for the Exodus: the lamb becomes the paschal lamb, the bread the sign of the hasty departure for the Promised Land. Moreover, the development of Pesach traditions shows evidence of an unfolding from a domestic celebration to a pilgrim celebration centralized in the Temple. Thus, connected with various ritual domains, there is the Palestinian-rabbinical family rite of Exodus 12, with the shepherd, the *passa* as God's passing over, and the cultic Hellenistic-Jewish rite of Israel of Deuteronomy 16, with its context of agriculture and exodus. The first line runs through into the Easter tradition of Asia Minor, of *pascha*, *paschein*, *passio*, and the second into the Alexandrine Easter celebration where *diabasis* forms the underlying element.

This, then, is the background regarding the framework and the use of domains. Before launching into an exploration of the liturgical landscape of outdoor liturgy, we must still pause to consider the concept of *landscape*.

2.2. Landscape

Like *nature*, *landscape* is an extremely vague concept. In our everyday speech, we often tend to use it metaphorically. Landscape enters the liturgist's realm of interest through church architecture, among other ways. If we survey studies in the field of church architecture done since about the mid-1960s, we are immediately struck how in them landscape is discovered through the process of stepping outdoors. A church building, certainly in its Gothic, or particularly in its neo-Gothic form, would

[16] I here cite the extremely complex development of the Passover/Easter celebration only as an example of distinguishing ritual domains. For a short, nuanced sketch of this material, see AUF DER MAUR (1983) 56-83 sub 131, 132, 133; (1980); CANTALAMESSA (1981), in particular *Einleitung* xiii-xliv; WEGMAN (1991) 74-78, 133-137.

seem to be the formative element of landscape par excellence, whether or not that was consciously taken into account in its original design. In The Netherlands, it was the discussion surrounding the demolition of a number of neo-Gothic church buildings which brought this into focus,[17] while elsewhere it was chiefly the place of the churches in the fabric of large cities that initiated reflection on the *genius loci*.[18]

But in place of the expressive and associative use of language around *landscape* or churches in the context of landscape, as my point of departure for this short introduction to the use of the concept I wish to proceed from the attention which has recently been given to the concept of *landscape* across a very broad platform of academic disciplines. In this, I intend to look particularly to those studies which raise the general theme of the sacred, "spiritual landscape" or enter into the phenomenon of *landscape* and *ritual*. From the broad terrain of what might be called "spatial disciplines," I would particularly focus on historical geography, and the disciplines of urban and country planning and landscape/ecological research, concerning open space planning. From the social sciences I might further list sociology, political science and anthropology, and from the humanities, art history and archaeology.

During my attempt to impose some order on the use of *landscape* and at the same time assemble building blocks for a theoretical framework, I have come across a number of studies which, in my opinion, offer relevant points of interest and coordinates for an exploration of *ritual landscape*. In particular, I consulted Neville's model anthropological study, *Kinship and Pilgrimage*, Lane's American study *Landscapes of the Sacred*, with its slant to theology and the philosophy of religion, Bender's rich collection *Landscape: Politics and Perspectives*, and the work by Hartinger cited earlier, *Religion und Brauch*, which stands on the juncture of European ethnology and liturgical studies.[19]

[17] See *'t Gat in de Biltstraat* (1973); regarding the element of landscape, particularly the contribution by DETTINGMEIJER, 27-31. In this connection, see also the landscapes in the beautiful catalogue *Camera Gothica* (1993).

[18] See NEDDENS & WUCHER 1987. See now bibliography in POST (1997b) 100 sub 7.

[19] NEVILLE (1987); LANE (1988); BENDER (1993), and in particular, in this item, BENDER: Introduction, 1-17; and IDEM: Stonehenge – Contested Landscapes (Medieval to Present-Day), 281-305, and K. OLWIG: Sexual Cosmology. Nation and Lanscape at the Conceptual Interstices of Nature and Culture; or, What does Landscape Really Mean?, 307-343; HARTINGER (1992), sub 2.1.3., p. 83-87 on "Geistliche Landschaft", a term that Hartinger borrows from KAPFHAMMER (1989). In addition to these sources, as an indication of the scale of landscape studies and as a sort of basic bibliography for

From these studies, I would want to highlight the following issues, schematically and eclectically, with regard to working with the concept of *landscape*.

Definition
We must first of all wrestle with the definition of *landscape*. At the conclusion of Bender's collection, Olwig offers a synthesis with regard to the semantic development of the work in the various linguistic and cultural traditions, complete with appendices.[20] In addition to documenting numerous striking shifts in meaning and lexical renaissances, it shows how the concepts of *nation*, *nature*, *cultus* and *culture* arise semantically through *landscape*. Through the word *landscape* we come to stand in the midst of the field of cultus and culture, with a range from *worship* to *pastoral concerns*, which is so important for *ritual studies* in general and for liturgical studies in particular.

At the same time, in taking this care to further define the term, the insight comes to the fore that *landscape* is also literally a matter of perspective. *Landscape* depends on the gaze of the viewer, and the standpoint that the viewer takes. Through this dependence on perspective, landscape is also by definition fragmentary, but at the same time also encompassing and inclusive: the component parts are seen, experienced and presented in the field of vision as one great whole.

Most definitions of *landscape* leave room for this aspect of the point of view. In Olwig, among many others in the Bender collection, we find

this exploration, I would also list a series of studies on the themes of *landscape* and *nature*. The subject of Christian holy places is generally not included in these considerations; readers are referred to a recent survey of the literature for that topic, and I will limit myself to including only some supplementary items here (see POST (1994b); GRABER (1976); RITTER (1978); EBERLE (1980); THOMAS (1983); VAN DER WOUD (1987); DUPRONT (1987), here in particular on sacred landscapes 378-394 and 515-524; SCOTT & SIMPSON-HOUSLEY (1991); *Au-delà du paysage moderne* (1991); KRAMER & LUTZ (1992), and herein among others C. CANTAUW-GROSCHEK: Natur aus zweiter Hand. Menschliche Naturaneignung am Beispiel der Ruhrquelle, 101-120; DANIELS (1993); DE MARE & VOS (1993); ROOIJAKKERS (1994), particularly sub 5, p. 205-248; WINGENS (1994); LASH & URRY (1994), particularly Parts 3 and 4; KOMMERS (1994); CARMICHAEL et al. (1994); TWORUSCHKA (1994), particularly A. STOCK: Katholizismus, 9-19 (= STOCK (1994)); SCHAMA (1995); ROYMANS (1995), and a report of the discussion which included contributions by B. BENDER and others on pp. 25-35, and Bibliography on pp. 36-38; see also ANGENENDT (1994), particularly sub IX; MARX (1995); LIPP (1995). See also POST (1996g).

[20] OLWIG (1993).

landscape defined as "a portion of area that the eye can comprehend in a single view, vista, prospect."[21] The third Flemish Congress on Open Space Planning (1980) described landscape as "the visually perceptible part of the earth's surface that extends to the skyline, or to the ultimate horizon. It is perceived as a more or less structured and perhaps differentiated whole. Its components are of both endogenous and exogenous origin, and consist of elements of both biotic and abiotic nature. The perception is dependent on the moment, the standpoint, and the observer's capacity for observation."[22] Two years later, the Study Group for Agricultural Ecological Research was somewhat more concise: "Landscape: a complex of relational systems that together form a recognizable part of the earth's surface, which is made up of and kept in existence by the interaction of living and non-living nature, inclusive of human beings."[23] The introduction to the recent manual *Het Nederlandse landschap* ("The Dutch Landscape") is still more concise, and also more pointed: "By landscape, then, we mean the coherence among relief, ground and soil, water, vegetation and all of the elements introduced by human beings that you see in a certain place. Landscape is thus really an ecosystem that in its external aspects forms a whole."[24]

Experience, Perception, and the Formation of Mental Images

Working from this perspective, there is constant attention to experience, perception and the formation of mental images around *landscape*. This dimension can extend from a religious/mythic experience of the landscape (i.e., the mantle of Gaia or divine body) to processes of aestheticizing and folklorization, and ultimately to the distanced view of landscape as a theatrical setting for life, as the object of touristic *sightseeing*.

This scale of experiences surrounding *landscape* can be further explored through a series of oppositions.

Sacred/Profane

For example, the cultic aspect which we have already mentioned is expressed in sacred or mythic landscapes. Certain parts of the earth are singled out and sacralized: thus "spiritual landscapes" and holy places

[21] OLWIG (1993) 307.

[22] See GYSELS et al. (1993); Introduction 17-33; the definition is cited from p. 17.

[23] Ibidem.

[24] TEUNE & TERLINGEN (1986) 3. See also *Woordenboek der Nederlandsche Taal* (Den Haag/Leiden 1916) 8,1, sub voce "landschap" 1026-1029.

arise through actions (i.e., the graveyard as *locus sacer*) and experiences (i.e., trees, hills, caves and springs as "numinous" sites). In his book Lane seeks to formulate axioms for religious appropriations of the landscape of this sort. In the framework of this introduction and orientation I will mention only the point that "spiritual" or holy landscapes are not made or chosen, but, as it were, force themselves upon us or let themselves be discovered, and that there is always a strange and unexpected interaction between the domains of the sacred and profane, the special and the commonplace.

A whole chain of further oppositions could be tied to this opposition of the sacred and profane. We will take notice of several which arise from the literature we have cited.

Urban/Rural; Universal/Local; Dream-Vision/Reality

In addition to sacred/profane, or also private/public, there is chiefly the opposition of city (or better, urban[25]) and countryside, *landscape* as the natural opposite to citification. Not the least cause evoking this opposition is the continual process of change to which the landscape is increasingly exposed. Landscape is the victim of modernity, but at the same time is a source of inspiration.

One and the same landscape bears a symbolic and ritual arsenal of antitheses within itself: the idyll of the Dutch polder landscape, the Flemish countryside, the coast or mountains. In this way, a location – that is to say, a landscape connected with a specific place and viewpoint – also takes on universal dimensions. Landscape is a place for the projection of dreams and ideals. It could be a matter of the universal image of the ordered garden, the beautiful, idyllic meadow, the paradisiacal garden of the liturgy surrounding the Lamb in the middle panel of the Jan van Eyck's Ghent altarpiece of the Lamb of God.[26] But it could also be the unyielding desert, the primaeval forest, the yet empty land.

Past/Present/Future

As the idyllic garden of peace, *landscape* is an important link in our anamnesis. *Landscape* offers us the symbolic material for representing the paradise of the past and future which lie on either side of our *tempus*

[25] Regarding this, see LIPP (1995).

[26] Jan van Eyck, Central panel, retable of the Lamb of God, Ghent, St. Bavo Cathedral, prior to 1432; see VAN DER MEER (1978) 237-257. See now: SCHMIDT (1995).

interim. Landscapes enable us to deal with the constant tension between past, present and future; they give us something to hold on to in our collective or individual memory. In this respect, landscapes can be romanticized, mobilized, nationalized, regionalized, monumentalized, put on display, frozen as natural parks. But they can also be called to life and revitalized by rituals and narratives. Lane in particular emphasizes that narratives (*storied landscape*) and rites (*landscapes of the sacred*) always play a decisive role in this.[27] Bender illustrates all of this in a probing way in an essay on the history of the Stonehenge landscape: the mythic, ritual roots, the private and public appropriations of these over the course of time, the musealizing in this century, through the current attempts at revitalization through New Age cosmic rites.[28]

In summary, with reference to the rich literature surrounding the concept of *landscape*, it can be asserted that *landscape* is certainly also a concept full of perspectives for ritual and liturgical objectives, and I therefore add my voice to the plea for giving a heuristic value to the concept of *landscape*, as that argument is found in Bender's collection and other places. *Landscape* is a useful concept in a rigorous analysis of culture and ritual because it is a *concept in between*. By definition, in landscape fixed perspectives and positions are broken through and opened up; thus, architectural design of space is included, and not excluded. *Landscape* brings semantically closely related concepts such as *nature*, *culture* and *cultus* into perspective – and into shifting perspectives – as well.

3. Outdoor Liturgy: General Exploration of the Landscape

I will begin by first mapping out the terrain. In this, we can counter the impression that indoor and outdoor liturgy are to a great extent to be seen as mere parallels to liturgy and paraliturgy, and that just as soon as we leave the vestibule of the church we have also stepped outside of Christian liturgy into the strange world of religious popular culture.

I wish to divide the landscape of outdoor liturgy into six parcels, in doing so accepting that there will be fluid boundaries and overlap.

[27] See particularly Lane (1988); Schama (1995).

[28] Bender: Stonehenge (as note 19).

3.1. The Outdoor Component of Indoor Liturgy

In the first place, there are the outdoor elements of liturgy which otherwise predominantly takes place indoors. Indoor liturgy is the norm; as an annex, a bit of derived ritual takes place outside. It is, however, important to note how relative that norm was and is – how, for instance, in the early church outdoor liturgy was once the norm for baptism,[29] and how for a long time marriage was celebrated *in facie ecclesiae*. But in a continuing process of standardization, codification and regimentation, liturgy was brought indoors. Of course, there were also a number of more external factors, such as climate, and particularly in parts of northern Europe, the intervention in public ritual and liturgical repertoire after the second half of the sixteenth century. The stripping of the altars was often followed by the dismantling of the sacred landscape.[30]

In a general sense, there are always two movements to be recognized here. Thus, there is first of all a process in which the Church, with its ritual repertoire, was steadily withdrawing from public life. Liturgy, for the most part, has been forced indoors. But there was also liturgy which was pushed outdoors, or was left there. That ritual either was given the label of paraliturgy, conceived as marginal or stray ends, or was dependent on the main stream of ecclesiastical ritual indoors. One could cite a number of forms of outdoor liturgy during Palm Sunday and Holy Week as examples of such outdoor components, Easter Eve celebrations which begin with a fire outdoors in many places, but also Christmas celebrations which can – and it would appear to a rising degree do – receive an outdoor component.

It is important to recognize how dynamic the relation is between indoors and outdoors. The counter-movement is also particularly interesting, the way in which indoor ecclesiastical liturgy seeks an outdoor component in order to give itself a tie with the outer world. Sometimes, as in The Netherlands in the period of the Catholic emancipation (after 1853), this happens in self-assured and demonstrative ways, and sometimes it even has the characteristics of purification and Christianizing, as in the planting of the cross during popular mission campaigns,[31] but it

[29] See *Didachè* 7,1-3; RORDORFF & TUILIER (1978); KLEINHEYER (1989) 48-50, sub c.

[30] See DUFFY (1992).

[31] See, for example, ROES (1993), in particular, 282f; for a general discussion of popular missions, with bibliography, EVERS & POST (1986) 97ff sub III.10.B.

can also be a more hesitant excursion, as in the case of a small "palmpaas" procession before or after the family mass on Palm Sunday.

3.2. Outdoor Celebrations of Necessity

A second form of outdoor liturgy is in a certain sense a variant of this dependent outdoor liturgy. Under certain circumstances, indoor celebration is impossible. One might think here of a number of peculiar circumstances such as liturgy "in the field" in the context of military combat.[32] The most frequent situation is that of massive celebrations such as those accompanying a Papal visit: because of the large number of participants the indoor liturgy must be moved outdoors, to a public square, a stadium, or an airport.

3.3. "Deliberate" Open-Air Liturgy

I see a "deliberate" open-air liturgy as a third area. A conscious decision is made to celebrate liturgy outdoors, not as a part of a further, dominant indoor liturgy, and not forced by the size of the congregation; rather, celebration in the open air is an essential part of the rite, and from the standpoint of ritual is a determinative part of it. This is the category which will encompass all forms of processions and circumambulations. Often celebrations which have to do with the land, harvest and the vitality of the earth, such as services of thanksgiving for harvest or blessings of livestock, will belong here. We could also list the repertoire of blessings and consecrations, rites concerning land and water. We might further recall the celebrations of the traditional archers' and riflemen's guilds, or liturgy which forms part of the activities of recreational ministries. Particularly in recent years there has been a tendency to very deliberately move forms of indoor liturgy, for instance those surrounding Christmas, outdoors.[33]

[32] To my knowledge, there has been hardly any attention bestowed on liturgy in the context of the various divisions of the military forces from within the broader field of ritual studies or liturgical studies. It is striking that the various chaplains in the military (as, for instance, during the stationing of Dutch forces with the UN contingent in Bosnia) see liturgy as one of their core activities. I am grateful to my colleague, Prof. dr. A. van Iersel, for information on open air liturgy of this type. Dr. Ch. Caspers also alerted me to HUF (1917). Now there is MOOIJ (1998) with some literature.

[33] See, for example, to list only a couple of Dutch examples, the annual Christmas celebration in the open air on Christmas Eve on the ramparts at Naarden, North Holland, and the open-air gathering which takes place in a sheep pen in De Renderklippen,

3.4. Liturgy Connected with Places

Liturgy which has a certain degree of connection with a location, and therefore is taken outside the spatial confines of the parish church, is closely connected with "deliberate" outdoor liturgy. Here we enter the territory of rituals surrounding holy places, liturgy that is pilgrimage, going forth and returning, liturgy undertaken as devotional journey alone or with others, to sites far away or near by.[34] It is also the liturgy of circumambulation, celebratory processions, and processing relics. As is well recognized and has often been described, these liturgies connected with places have a play of indoors and outdoors that is entirely their own.

3.5. Funeral Rites

I want to claim a separate entry for a variant of liturgy which is more or less tied to a location. All sorts of liturgy involving death and burial has the landscape as its setting. This can involve the death of an unusual person, in the *memoria* liturgy for saints, from whom so many places initially draw their sacred character.[35] But it can also involve the deaths of everyday individuals, for example in the first model for the committal ritual which, as rewritten after Vatican II, has two processions which unite three ritual domains – the home of the deceased, the church and the cemetery.[36] In the case of the typically indoor ritual of cremation too, people are increasingly expressing the need for an outdoor component. Fields for spreading ashes and open-air columbaria are now appearing. I would also list here the crosses along roads and in fields which mark and consecrate the landscape of sudden death, liturgies which have to do with death in war and disasters, private and familial forms of memorial liturgy for All Saints, and of course the Stations of the Cross itself as a sort of Ur-form of *procedere*.

between Epe and Heerde in the Veluwe, prov. Gelderland. In both cases, these are Protestant initiatives with a clear evangelistic element. For the broader ritual domain of blessings, see yet the standard work FRANZ (1909), and the rewritten "Benedictionale", *Rituale Romanum. De Benedictionibus*, editio typica 1984. See now also: "Vieringen buiten" 1-2, = *Werkmap Liturgie* 30,3-4 (1996).

[34] See the literature included in note 19.

[35] See, generally, the studies by ANGENENDT (1994) and AUF DER MAUR (1994).

[36] See *Rituale Romanum: Ordo Exsequiarum* (editio typica 1969) primo typo cap. II, 17-27 nos. 35 en 52.

3.6. "Folklorized Liturgy"

I would characterize a final form of outdoor liturgy under the somewhat problematic heading of "folklorized liturgy." With this term I am referring both to Scribner's work, as well as to the abundant ethnological literature surrounding folklorism and folklorization.[37] I will resist the temptation to introduce a theoretical excursus on folklorization and liturgy at this point, and rather content myself with indicating that in "folklorized liturgy" I am designating what is chiefly a fundamental change in the context of ritual and the way it is experienced. What is involved here is liturgy which has undergone or is undergoing a complex process of festive alteration and change of context. To put it very generally, the ritual forsakes the ritual domain, and lands in the realm of the culture of public celebrations, where old traditions which have been handed down to them are appropriated by groups in new ways. This dynamic process coincides very closely with musealization, and also with aestheticization.[38] In addition to alterations in function and meaning, this change in context chiefly brings with it alterations at the level of the way in which the ritual is perceived and experienced. Thus folklorization of liturgy mirrors the scale of the experience and perception of ritual which runs from mythic celebration through folklore to theatre. From an original, primarily mythic celebration, liturgy can turn into folklore and ultimately even become "theatre,"[39] for instance a Requiem Mass performed in a concert hall, or the recreation of a pilgrimage procession at a festival of street theatre.[40]

There are characteristics, ritual signals that indicate this process of folklorization. There is distance, not collective celebration but a performance for viewers, an audience. There is also the presence of explanation, background information. It becomes a spectacle, with rehearsals, scripts and sponsors. It also acquires a justification, a theme, a higher purpose.

[37] SCRIBNER (1987), on *folklorized ritual*, 28f; NISSEN (1994). From the rich library of literature regarding folklorism/folklorization, I will here list BAUSINGER (1988); KÖSTLIN (1991); VAN DER KOOI (1990); POST (1991b); (1991d); BOISSEVAIN (1991); BARON & SPITZER (1992); DEKKER (1993). See also in this book Chapter 9 and 11.

[38] See the concise article by STURM (1990).

[39] For liturgy and theatre, see TURNER (1992); LUKKEN (1991), particularly 138 sub 3 on liturgy and theatre; LUKKEN (1990), particularly 27-30; HARTINGER (1992) 194-222; SPEELMAN (1993); POST & PIEPER (1992a), with bibliography; KOCH (1995). See now the bibliography in POST (1997b) 100 sub 9.

[40] I have in mind specifically a project which was part of *Etcetera La Strada*, a street theatre festival in Amersfoort, province of Utrecht, The Netherlands, July, 1994.

And most of all, there is a certain way of dealing with the past and tradition from which the group derives its place. A folklorized ritual or liturgy is thus "site specific," with a whole spectrum of local, regional and national identity constructions.

The boundaries here are fluid, and it is precisely in the open air that the fluctuating circles of liturgy, *functiones sacrae* and *folklorized ritual* overlap with each other. We have here a multiform and dynamic process. Liturgy can land in this folkloristic "outer world" and become folklore, but folklorizing ritual elements can also penetrate liturgy and change it. Whether there is also something which might be called a process of "liturgizing," through which rites which have become folklore or theatre can be converted (or converted back) into mythic liturgy, I will leave as an open question for now.

As illustrations here I will mention only particular forms of appropriated processions, circumambulations and pilgrimages, liturgical elements in the rituals of guilds (or, going the other direction, the honour guards and banners that have penetrated worship services), and the "palmpaas" processions which, in contrast to the variety mentioned in section 3.1, are organized independently of Palm Sunday observances. I have in mind pageants with a more or less liturgical quality which surround St. Martin or Epiphany, often with children in the leading rolls. I am thinking also of the "manger cultus" which is strongly in the ascendancy in a number of places around Europe, taking place around Christmas in or, much more frequently, outside the church building, of the controversial liturgies marking the festival of the "eco-saint," St. Hubert,[41] and last but not least of the interplay of contacts between carnival and liturgy.[42]

This, then, is the landscape. It is a relevant and unusually varied landscape, the liturgical importance of which is often underestimated – quite unjustly, even if we are looking merely at it quantitatively. In any case, it illuminates an interesting aspect of the much discussed "crisis of rites." As the pews in the churches empty, it is perhaps not so much a matter of a diffuse farewell to churches and liturgy but, if we involve the perspective from outside the church, in at least a part perhaps a movement transferring interest and participation in ritual from indoors to outdoors. The kernel of what people call secularization lies in such shifts and in surprising synchroneitics and asynchroneities. Large numbers

[41] See my article on St. Hubert in Muiderberg, POST (1991d).
[42] WIJERS (1995).

who otherwise remain uncounted attend outdoor liturgies; the profile of this group is to a great extent unknown because indoor liturgy is also the norm for censuses. Pilgrimage sites with an important repertoire of outdoor liturgy are now being brought into the count in a major way. *Bedevaartplaatsen in Nederland* (BIN = Places of Pilgrimage in The Netherlands), the large-scale research and documentation project which intends to inventory and document Dutch pilgrimage sites past and present, now has more than 650 locations in its files.[43] The annual harvest thanksgiving celebrations in the Dutch dioceses of Breda and Den Bosch bring together about 20,000 people for open-air liturgy in fifteen celebrations spread over two weekends. One could also point to the fact that it is particularly the funeral ritual that still regularly brings people in touch with Christian liturgy, and that is a ritual which, as we noted, has an important open-air component and is, at the same time, the only ritual in which (once again speaking of the Dutch situation) one finds an average increase in respect to numbers. The continued decline in the figures for indoor liturgy is well attested; thus the average Dutch parish (which of course does not exist) had an average of 360 participants at services inside the church building in 1993/1994.[44]

I now wish to further explore this landscape by means of three soundings, and in doing so, to enter upon as many of these various parcels as is possible through the selection of soundings. I have chosen a processional park, and the lesser researched rituals connected with Papal visits and rites surrounding a sudden death.

4. Three soundings

4.1. The Processional Park in Dokkum

Rediscovery of a Park in Dokkum

Dokkum, in the province of Friesland, The Netherlands, was reborn as the city of Boniface and as a holy place after a miraculous healing took

[43] See Margry & Post (1994); Volume 1 of the BIN-project: Margry & Caspers (1997); cf. Chapter 2 in this book.

[44] For the statistics from the KAKSI, the basic figures for 1993/1994, see *Informatiebulletin Een-twee-een (Kerkelijke documentatie)* nov. 22,8 (1994) 400f/14f. For the "average" parish, *ibidem*, 739f/3f. See for recent figures: Dekker, De Hart & Peters (1997).

place there in the summer of 1990. In chapters 2 and 4 I have sketched this revitalization. Here, however, my focus is on the ritual landscape at Dokkum, and in particular its processional park and outdoor stations of the cross.[45] In the recent process of revitalization and renovation of the ritual landscape there, this park was the final recipient of attention, and the renovation of the park since September 1992 formed the last phase of the general regeneration of Dokkum as a holy place.

The layout of this processional park near the spring was the first phase in the design of a ritual landscape there in the third decade of this century. The process of reshaping the landscape began in 1925, after the acquisition of land by the Dobbe, just outside the centre of the town. This was accomplished through the construction of a large processional park. The design for the park, with the stations of the cross incorporated into it, was by the architect W. te Riele (1867-1937), who drew his inspiration from similar parks at Brielle, Boxtel and Roermond. The firm Bosgra, from Bergum, carried out the work. For a long period it remained merely a park with avenues and plantings, with the chapel, stations of the cross, the surrounding walls and the crosses existing only on paper. As was also the case elsewhere, people laid out in the open countryside the basis for what should grow into a beautiful, large park. The chapel, designed by H. de Valk, only arose in 1934, and was carefully integrated into the park landscape. Kingmans recently summarized this well: "It is beautifully designed, combining the open and protected, culture and nature (as, for a part, it is paved with sod), church and canopy, consecrated space and rustic appearance that puts one in mind

[45] I thank Pastor Herman Peters and Peter Jan Margry for their assistance on this section. A summary of the revitalization of Dokkum as a holy site, with extensive bibliography, can be found in POST (1993); (1995e). See now POST (1997d), = the lemma "Dokkum" in: MARGRY & CASPERS (1997). See in this book Chapter 3 and 4. For the park, see *Rapport Renovatie Bonifatius-park* (Dokkum 1992); *Een kruisweg voor Dokkum. Pater Titus Brandsma* (Dokkum 1992); H. PETERS: *Bonifatius in Dokkum. Het verhaal van een levende* (Dokkum n.d.) 21; DRAGT et al. (1986) 35 with an aerial photo of the processional park; for other photographs see also DRAGT (1991) 73f; KINGMANS (1994) 37-46, with a reproduction of the original design by Te Riele on page 37. After the first pilgrimage for priests in 1934, the Boniface Foundation was established in 1925, originally as a Confraternity; the processional park was a central element in its official statement of purpose: "To again make Dokkum a true place of pilgrimage, attempting to attain that goal by the purchase of land near the Spring of St. Boniface and creating a processional park on this land, and, if possible, constructing a chapel with a wayside altar and a statue of St. Boniface."

of a grange."[46] In all respects, this park set the tone for the design of a holy place. Only in the years 1936-1949, on the initiative of Titus Brandsma (1881-1945) and Jacq. Maris, was the contract let for construction of the stations of the cross. The construction was completed in 1949, with a memorial plaque for Brandsma in the 12th station.

By the time that the garden had matured over the course of several decades and the ritual liturgical settings were finally all in place, not only had the Second World War (during which trees from the park were sold for making wooden shoes) intervened, but liturgical patterns had changed. During and after the 1960s, interest in the holy place decreased sharply, the stations of the cross were neglected, and the orderly paradise became overgrown. That state of affairs lasted until 1992. After the "miracle of Dokkum" (the purported healing of a young girl after she was immersed in St. Boniface's spring in the summer of 1990), the whole complex was given a general facelift, which ultimately also extended to the park. Beginning in September, 1992, as the final phase in the general renovation of the pilgrimage complex, work on the processional park got under way, trimming and removing trees, rescuing the stations of the cross from the undergrowth and setting everything in order. But, in contrast to the spring and chapel, there was no thought of redesign, but purely of restoration, recovering an historical landscape.

Development of Dutch Processional Culture

The processional park and stations of the cross at Dokkum can be considered as an almost classic example of an element that is nearly always present in the topography of holy places. Phenomenologically, a garden or park is a component invariably present at a holy place. In addition to a central building of an enclosed devotional centre, the spacious open or half-open site for celebrations, there will be a park or garden, often with a spring.[47] The form of the processional park with stations of the cross is typical for the design of these gardens and parks dating from the second half of the 19th century and beginning of the 20th.[48] This important landscape element, so closely connected with processional and pilgrimage

[46] KINGMANS (1994) 39.

[47] POST (1989b); (1990c); AUF DER MAUR (1994) 237-242.

[48] After the rigid geometrical tradition in France, there were now variations on English examples that were intended to come across as whimsical and "natural." See, in general, WIMMER (1989). See also note 19.

liturgy, allows us the opportunity to examine an important aspect of the development of liturgy in the open air in the Dutch situation. As we saw, the procession is an important form of open-air liturgy, and for a long time that ritual was (and still is?) the model or symbol for Roman Catholic worship in the minds of those of other religious persuasions. I am thinking here chiefly of the development which ultimately issued into the recent facelift of the park in the Friesian diaspora.

Processional culture is simply a fallow field. Dutch processional culture, and particularly the ban on processions, and developments surrounding public practice of religion since the 16th century in the tensions between church and state, has now been the subject of research carried out by Peter Jan Margry. For our purposes, we can already now fruitfully draw upon a series of recent, closely connected articles. I will here discuss some of the lines of force which are becoming clear in these studies of public practice of religion, because lineaments of our theme of liturgy in the open air are clearly to be found there. I will leave aside many issues: juridical nuances, the struggle with terms and definitions (i.e., liturgy, devotion, procession, circumambulation, liturgical procession, etc.) found here too on the part of secular authorities and researchers.[49] Instead, my focus will be on sketching a number of developmental phases.

(a) The Landscape That Was Left Behind

In the second half of the 16th century, the colourful, multifaceted open-air liturgy of the Middle Ages in The Netherlands, with, in addition to burials and consecrations of churches, the processional culture with its great circuits through the cities, so prominent in the 15th and 16th centuries, came to an end. This form of public and demonstrative liturgy was banned from the public domain and driven indoors, into the enclosed spaces of church buildings in the ecclesiastical domain, or into homes, in the private sphere. After finishing with church interiors, the Reformers also attacked the infrastructure of open-air liturgy: the crosses, chapels, marked courses for serial devotions and holy places were purged from the landscape. To a large extent, open-air liturgy was written out of the readapted liturgical books, such as the 1625 *Rituale contractum et*

[49] For this sketch of the development of processional culture in The Netherlands, I have relied to a great extent on the following series of studies by MARGRY: (1990); (1993a); (1993b); (1994a); (1994b); (1995a).

abbreviatum (recently reprinted with a commentary), and is absent from the orders of worship prescribed by state authorities.[50] As is often the case, however, we know little about the actual practice. We can, with Margry, make a number of suppositions. To a great extent processions did disappear from the scene as an important and frequently recurring form of open-air liturgy, and the sacred landscape was altered, purified and purged, but people continued to celebrate in the open air, probably less often and less lavishly, some social classes more than others, and more in rural areas than in the city. Chiefly, people continued to visit select places outside the cities and observe rituals there.

We also know, on the basis of a good deal of research, that this liturgical move indoors is rooted in a much longer and broader process of reaction against forms of open-air liturgy, a reaction which had supporters both in the church and outside it, and which runs right down to our own times. Factors such as lack of control outdoors, propaganda, and the connection with excesses in carnival, in the culture of non-liturgical celebration, as well as continuing concern for the liturgical and theological purity of ritual, had long given impetus for alterations and purges. Furthermore, this literal "interiorization" of at least some rites of this sort ran parallel to the process of internalization and individualization in the lives of Dutch believers that Jan van Herwaarden has been able to trace and typify already in the late Middle Ages, and the processional liturgy which ultimately arose after the 16th and 17th century was a typical Dutch ritual compromise which has left its mark on ritual down to this very day, for instance in what is called the Silent Procession in honour of the Sacramental Miracle of Amsterdam.[51] People were restrained in the number of processions and in their liturgical design (small scale, silent, in the evening hours, using little or nothing in liturgical vestments, processional crosses or canopies, preferably held in the relative privacy of parks or gardens). Thus, too, certain processions could be held in the open air rather than others. Prayer or penitential processions, or harvest processions of thanksgiving around fields and pastures such as the *litaniae minores* on Rogation Day, could be continued more easily than demonstratively processing relics, or urban processions

[50] SPIERTZ (1992).

[51] VAN HERWAARDEN (1995); MARGRY (1995a); (1995b). Auf der Maur also discusses Amsterdam as a holy place; see AUF DER MAUR (1994) 242. Cf. MARGRY (1988). Now: MARGRY & CASPERS (1997) 134-150.

for the purpose of commemorating the consecration of churches or memorials. Rural rituals were modest in scale, with at most a crucifix as a liturgical attribute, and were also rooted solidly in daily life, with prayer for good weather and a good harvest, and were thus able to meet a deeply felt need for apotropaic and prophylactic rites.[52] Moreover, on the Protestant side too, people also held days of thanksgiving and prayer.

(b) The Landscape Refurnished (First Revitalization)

It was not so much because of the legislative framework after the religious emancipation of 1795 and the developments in the law which followed upon it, as through the growing self-confidence of the Roman Catholic portion of the population, that the situation changed in the second half of the 19th century. Liturgy, and especially open-air liturgy, was an extremely important factor in this. To an increasing degree, people ritually stepped outdoors, and landscape was discovered once again, appropriated and refurnished. One can rightly speak here of a process of devotionalization: through discovering, revitalizing or creating historical, national holy places, people reintroduced sacred topography to The Netherlands. Margry examines the martyrs' field or fountain land of Brielle (the holy Martyrs of Gorcum) as an illustration of this revitalization, but Dokkum, too, although later, fits perfectly into this process.

The processional park with stations of the cross is an almost invariable ritual-strategic component of that programme of devotionalization. There, open-air celebration could take place under controlled conditions, an acknowledgement of the enclosed space. Thus all over the Dutch landscape there arose gardens and parks with stations of the cross. Naturally these came first at the holy places such as the revitalized Dutch pilgrimage sites of Heiloo, Roermond's Kapel in 't Zand, and Dokkum, but ritual gardens of this sort were also built for schools, cloisters and parish churches. After 1858 a "Lourdes grotto" became an almost necessary part of this landscape too. Quite simply, in this respect since the end of the last century one can speak of an international "Roman Catholic housestyle" in landscape architecture, to be found everywhere. As we have intimated, the construction of parks and gardens was also linked with the then current developments in landscape architecture: winding paths, large trees combined with thickets and grassy fields, and

[52] See POST (1995b) 32-42 sub 4.3; (1996e), Part 2, 244-251 sub 2; (1996c).

the stations of the cross assimilated into the landscape through the use of quarried stone.

Like the architecture of the spaces for celebration, done up in their "neo"-styles, the parks at these national holy places are often redolent of the most refined compromise of interior and exterior, as is the case in Dokkum. They are enclosed, walled gardens, separated from the landscape surrounding them, which on the one hand offer a fitting ritual setting for the public, outdoor oriented processional liturgy, and on the other hand are the setting for the more inward, personal devotional liturgy at the stations of the cross and Lourdes grotto.

(c) Landscape in Decline

Around the 1960s this refined balance between interior and exterior, between liturgy and devotion was totally disrupted by a complex confrontation with modernity. From this date, most of these gardens no longer had a ritual function and fell into disrepair, the stations of the cross becoming overgrown, and the Lourdes grottos were dismantled.

(d) Restored Landscape (Second Revitalization)

A subsequent, and for the time being latest phase was ushered in when some of these holy places were rediscovered in another complex process of revitalization, in the context of a much broader process of ritual change in which it is precisely public, outdoor rituals of this sort (and their settings) which appear to possess a power of fascination. The processional parks and their stations of the cross share in the context of this rediscovery and the reawakening of these holy places to ritual life, but – and this is important to note – attention for them generally comes last, is derivative, and is seldom or never in a ritual sense. Professional nurserymen or conscientious volunteers again create order from the chaos. To my mind, the way in which these ritual parks are being handled (as at Dokkum) is quite peculiar. In contrast to the way that the devotional centre itself – the spring and chapel – is dealt with, it is impossible to conceal that these parks are no longer really ritual landscapes any more. The tensions in the revitalization come to light more clearly here than in any other components of the pilgrimage complex. The factors in play here have relatively little "ritual calibre." The parks, like those by castles and historic country houses, are fixed up, nourished along, have brochures published and lectures held about them, but the stations of the cross play little or no liturgical role. Few if any processions are still held in these parks. Two aspects predominate: the historic (they are landscapes from the past), and the ecological (they are gardens of green, nature, arcadian idylls). In Dokkum, but elsewhere as well, the processional park is now primarily an oasis, a counterpoint to the city, suitable for strolling, thoughtful Sunday afternoon daydreaming, a place for individual introspection. At the most, it is sometimes the site for the rituals performed in memory of Titus Brandsma (1881-1945).[53] In these parks, it is chiefly the factors of the way we deal with the past and with nature which appear to be most clearly responsible for the latest "accommodation" of Dutch processional culture: "deliturgizing."

4.2. The Pope Visits The Netherlands[54]

One kind of open-air liturgy encountered in the media with a certain degree of frequency are the celebrations that take place during papal visits. In the course of his pontificate, the present Pope, John Paul II, a seasoned traveller and pilgrim, has visited many lands on various continents and celebrated liturgies before hundreds, thousands, tens of thousands and even millions, as he did on January 15, 1995, when during his visit to Asia he celebrated the Eucharist in a park in Manilla in the presence of a crowd estimated at between one and two million Philippinos (although some sources placed the number as high as four to five million!).

Papal Liturgy in Den Bosch and Beek

I want to spend a moment examining the papal visit to The Netherlands which took place from May 11 to 15, 1985.[55] The full programme had two high points of open-air liturgy. On Saturday there was the prayer

[53] For this development in the direction of memorial culture, see VAN DER HEIJDEN (1994). In the broader field of research into feast, festival and ritual, this memorial aspect is increasingly in the limelight. With an eye to liturgy, it is important to determine what the "anamnestic" character of these rituals is. For a survey of this feast and festival literature, see SCHILSON (1994).

[54] I thank Mr. C. de Kaper, staff assistant whose responsibilities include the archive of the Dutch Archdiocese of Utrecht, and Mr. A. Waibel, of the Deutsches Liturgisches Institut te Trier, for their assistance on this section.

[55] The literature concerning the Papal Visit to The Netherlands is really limited to a picture book and materials such as newspaper clippings and planning manuals. I would list here *Pauskrant* (1994); *Draaiboek* (1985); *Paus Johannes Paulus II in Nederland* (1985a); *Paus Johannes Paulus II in Nederland* (1985b); VAN BERKEL, VAN RAS & WOUTERS

procession, also announced as the "Maria Vespers Prayer Procession," through the streets of Den Bosch (capital of the province of Noord-Brabant), which was followed by a service of vespers and the consecration of an altar in the restored basilica of St. John there. On Tuesday there was also the celebration of the Eucharist at the airfield at Beek, in the province of Limburg. Examining these forms of papal liturgy in the open air, I believe they are characterized by the following points:

- First of all, there is the perhaps obvious fact that these involve *papal* liturgy. The tension which is always present between universal and local dimensions in this type of liturgy appears to have been resolved in favour of the universal side.
- Furthermore, the open-air celebration appears to be connected with, or even dependent upon, indoor liturgy, although connections were sought with holy places and such traditional forms of outdoor liturgy such as processionals and pilgrimage that were available. The celebration in Beek took place after a visit to the church of St. Servas and the basilica of Our Lady in Maastricht, and the prayer processional in Den Bosch was the procession to the celebration at St. John's basilica.
- Beek and Den Bosch are distinctive here and at other points. As he has on other trips, in Den Bosch the Pope profiled himself as a pilgrim, in a liturgical sense as well. The Den Bosch prayer procession was a traditional form of processional liturgy, a circuit through the streets, dedicated to Mary, on the way to the altar at St. John's. A number of elements come together here, and present us with the particular question of how they are related to one another.

Thus, the theme of pilgrimage is important. The metaphorical use of pilgrimage, being-on-the-way, a pilgrim in this world, is directly connected with the prayer processional and Den Bosch as a pilgrimage site.[56]

But there is also an aspect of being outside the walls of the church, in the world, on the street that is the backdrop for day-to-day life. In the

(1985); HERUER & PRINSEN (1985); SCHEEPMAKER (1985); a brief historical background is offered by *Katholiek Nederland en de paus* (1985).

The archive of the Dutch Papal Visit Foundation is now part of the archive at the Secretariat of the Dutch Archdiocese, Biltstraat 121, Utrecht. Material concerning the liturgical celebrations is to be found in the archive of the NRL (Nationale Raad voor Liturgie (National Commission for Liturgy)), Zeist/Driebergen. Most of the published material, such as the photo books, etc., can be found in the collection of the Catholic Documentation Centre (KDC), Nijmegen.

[56] For the texts, see HERUER & PRINSEN (1985) IV-VI.

homily the aspect of pilgrimage and the connection with everyday life was taken up explicitly. To what extent all kinds of ritual dimensions of appropriation and marking territory (and thus power) play a role here, as they do in the old stations of the Cross liturgies and papal rites in Rome, is thus a not unimportant question at this point.[57]

This public performance can take on the character of an *adventus*, a demonstration in which power is exercised, legitimized and confirmed. But being in the public domain also exposes the Pope to counter-demonstrations. Venturing outside the walls makes one vulnerable, as it appeared on a number of occasions during the visit. Voices raised in challenge can be heard; there are exceptions to the behavioural limits that are generally clearly marked inside church buildings, that are always to be preserved there; there is potentially always the possibility of debate. The place for public honours is in the open – but it is also the place for confrontation.[58]

Here we again encounter, however, the aspect already mentioned, that this is not just a bishop, or an ecclesiastical procession moving through the streets of Den Bosch, but the Pope. Liturgy is perhaps still a prime ritual medium for appearing before ten thousand people, but here *procedere* is for appearing in public (see 2.1, above). This latter aspect is strengthened still more by the fact that every appearance by the Pope is passed on to a mass audience by the media, and in particular, television.

– In Beek, the Pope's appearance involved a massive celebration of the Eucharist at an airfield, on a stage which had been specially designed for the event. The points we have just made in the course of discussing the Den Bosch prayer procession are also valid here. But in this case it is especially striking how the nature of the celebration indicates that it was an indoor ritual held outdoors. This was a celebration which, had it been intended for a smaller number of participants (journalistic sources spoke of "tens of thousands" at Beek), would instead have been held indoors. The celebration itself, the texts, the addresses and homily, the landscape architecture (with the back wall of the altar/stage suggesting

[57] INGERSOLL (1993); WARNEKEN (1991).

[58] It was particularly in Utrecht that the situation became disorderly. That the vulnerability of appearing in the public domain is not something limited to the pope, but also applies to other bishops, can be seen from a situation in Blerick, in the province of Limburg, The Netherlands, when at the "traditional" mass of St. Hubert on Saturday, November 5, 1994, Bishop Wiertz was confronted with catcalls from members of Kids for Animals and Kritisch Faunabeheer, who had demanded that the bishop also bless photographs of dead animals, victims of hunting and road kills.

an apse window, and a reliquary in front of it) all reinforce this image of an order of service for the interior space of a church which has been moved outdoors. This became all the more clear when, during a spell of very bad weather and high wind at Beek, heroic measures were necessary to keep the chalices, patens and hosts in place. This interior perspective was equally pronounced in the liturgy itself. In his welcome speech Bishop Gijsen made special reference to "the construction and furnishing of the beautiful open-air church," while in his homily the Pope particularly emphasized the family, which was presented as a "house church."[59]

– I am not sure to what degree the emphasis on elements referring to the interior of a church on the part of the organizers and leaders was intended to deny or counter the context of other related mass gatherings such as outdoor theatre productions, shows, pop concerts or sports events; for myself, I am quite certain that these contexts played an important role in how this celebration was experienced. In addition to being a papal liturgy with an "indoor" character, it was also, and chiefly, a mass gathering. Spectacle, event, theatre and television culture were defining elements.

– This last aspect is confirmed by the dominant role of stage direction and scripting, no matter how well this was hidden. In many respects, the general rehearsals for mass liturgies of this sort create an atmosphere of scripted or media liturgy.

– Together with this element of spectacle, we can also sense the tendency to the folklorization of liturgy we discussed above. Already, on his very arrival in Brabant, the Pope walked over a carpet of banners (by which Brabant "welcomed the Pope in a traditional way, and paid homage to him"), and during the celebration the folklore of the guild system was on show.

Research in the Liturgy of Papal Visits

If we broaden out our perspective to look beyond these forms of papal liturgy in the open air, it is striking how little attention such visits have received in ritual studies in general, and in liturgical studies in particular. If I leave the rather specific element of television out of consideration, what is left is chiefly the practically oriented literature concerning regulations and protocol, a few scanty analyses by liturgists, and only

[59] For the texts, see HERUER & PRINSEN (1985) XLIX-LII.

one single broader contextual ritual analysis.[60] This literature confirms and supplements the analysis which we have just offered.

A remarkable combination of the concern for regulations and protocol and a more contextual interest in celebrations of this sort is found in an advisory document on large-scale Eucharist celebrations prepared by the Liturgical Institute at Trier in 1988, and not yet, to the best of my knowledge, published.[61] In contrast to literature devoted entirely to protocol, this document tries to do justice to the peculiar context, principally the open-air ambience, of mass celebrations. The document points to a number of aspects of this characteristic trait, although it does so primarily through the questions it raises. What is the image which comes across through this so public of rituals? That of a simple, instrumental, servant church, or of a triumphant, self-confident community? Most important is the question of whether the liturgical celebration must always take the form of a Eucharist. Is that not precisely a form of liturgical gathering intended and suited for indoors? Why not rather opt for services of word and prayer? After introductory remarks and some fundamental liturgical and theological considerations, the document therefore opens with the spatial dimension that defines the deepest experience of the community present.

A still broader perspective is employed by Daniel Dayan in an essay about the travelling Pope and his ritual appearances in a special issue of *Terrain*.[62] Dayan is primarily interested in the Pope's television appearances, but also works out the pilgrimage aspect which we have mentioned. Who is really the pilgrim: the Pope, the crowd present, or the television audience? What is the role of the holy place in open-air rites? What is it

[60] From the relatively few studies on papal visits, I will here list HAHNE (1980a); (1980b); KACZYNSKI (1981); Amt für die Päpstlichen Zeremonien: *Liturgische Normen für einen Pastoralbesuch des Heiligen Vaters im Ausland (außerhalb von Rom)* (n.p., n.d., certainly prior to 1987); *Seminario di studio sulle celebrazioni Pontificie, Cit.d. Vaticano 28-30 Dec. 1987* (published by Uficio per le ceremonie pontificie); EHAM (1987a); (1987b).

[61] *Eucharistiefeiern als Großveranstaltungen. Erfahrungen und Empfehlungen, zusammengestellt vom Liturgischen Institut* (Trier 1988); this document is the outcome of a study day on the theme in Würzburg where, in addition to representatives of German dioceses, Vatican officials were also present. The way the document is constructed revealing: I Vorbemerkungen: 1-4; II Liturgietheologische Aspekte: 5-6; III Architektonische Aspekte: 7-12; IV: Texte und Sprache: 13-17; V Gesang und Musik: 18 23; VI Zeichen und Bewegungsabläufe: 24-26; VII Konzelebration und Kommunionspendung: 27-28; VIII Übertragung in Medien: 29-36.

[62] DAYAN (1990).

precisely which is going on in the standard ritual of kissing the ground on arrival at an airport? Is it an appropriation of the country as a new fatherland, a ritual such as took place in Warsaw on June 2, 1979, when the Pope made a visit to his own fatherland? Is it a rite of *humiliatio*, abasement? Or is it the consecration of a profane landscape? By his own public ritual performances, is the Pope not actually creating cultic sites himself, and thus really fundamentally relativizing the phenomenon of holy places?

In the end, Dayan too characterizes the complex of ritual experiences surrounding papal visits as a *paraître en public*, a double *adventus* full of power and glory which is directed toward the two most important spheres of life outside the space of the church building; through his appearances in the public spaces, he reaches into the domestic sphere by means of television.

4.3. The Landscape of Sudden Death

A Traffic Accident

Not far from my home, on Monday, April 18, 1994, about 8:30 a.m., while he was on his way to the local Roman Catholic elementary school on his bicycle, eleven year old Tom, from Class ("group") Eight, was struck and run over by a lorry. He died a short time later. It was a terrible blow, for his family and friends, but also, especially, for the school. At first, on the day of the accident, the spot was marked by the police; by the following day it was marked by a wooden cross, and many plants and flowers. Parents went to the spot with their children, Tom's classmates and schoolmates. There, while traffic raced through the complicated, busy intersection or waited impatiently for the light to turn green, people said a prayer, or stood silently with tears in their eyes. The following days the flowers were regularly replaced, and more and more permanent plants appeared in the plot of ground beside the road. There were also many narratives about the site: stories about the accident, stories which explained to passers-by why the site along the roadside had become a small garden.

Today almost no one remembers these rituals. The cross and flowers are gone; a handful of plants alone remain. The ritual with the flowers was briefly resurrected in 1995 on All Souls' Day, when suddenly a big bunch of yellow flowers was tied to a nearby traffic sign. The rituals surrounding Tom's death had changed location, to Tom's grave, and to the school, where Tom's class planted a young tree in his memory. They had also moved indoors, with particular mention of Tom in the school mass.

The Tradition of Marked Places

This plot along side a road with its flowers and plants and a cross is just one more addition to a long tradition of "spiritual landscape" which includes field and roadside crosses, crosses marking the sites of murders and "hail crosses" (traditionally erected by Dutch farmers in their fields to protect crops against destruction by hail storms).[63] To anyone with an eye to see it, this ritual landscape is still present in our modern society. There is a standard pattern: the place of sudden death is marked, set apart from its surroundings and sacralized. Through crosses, flowers, rites of gathering, of going and coming, the quick prayer, the sign of the cross, the moment of silence and reflection, it becomes a *locus sacer*. We see it in the case of football disasters in stadiums, such as that in England in April, 1989,[64] in sea disasters, airline crashes such as those in Suriname in July 1989 and in Amsterdam's Bijlmermeer neighbourhood in 1992.[65] We see it in the case of murders and attacks. There was the sea of flowers on the sidewalk in Stockholm after the murder of Olof Palme,[66] and at the memorial sites for Italian judges murdered by the mafia.

But in addition to these, all over Europe there are many small spots with crosses, flowers and plants that do not attract national news media, roadside crosses that mark the victims of our mobility. There has been almost no research done into the topical question of this ritual landscape for sudden death along our roads. Except for a Yugoslavian study, and chiefly journalistic explorations, there is at the most an essay by Konrad Köstlin written from a specifically German perspective, and a recent project involving traffic crosses in Schleswig-Holstein.[67]

[63] See HARTINGER (1992) sub 2.1.3. p. 83-87 and KAPFHAMMER (1989).

[64] See GRAY (1990) = GRAY (1989); DAVIE (1993).

[65] Two memorial sites have arisen in Amsterdam South East, one outdoors and one indoors. Around a tree near the wreck site there is a paved and fenced off garden with all kinds of memorial elements such as crosses, photographs, remnants of toys, etc. Indoors, number 161 in the Kruitberg apartment building has become the "Memorial Room." Now, in 1998, there is a more permament memorial site around "the tree that saw everything".

[66] SCHARFE (1989).

[67] KÖSTLIN (1992); in this connection, see also KÖSTLIN (1989); RAJKOVIC (1988); MICHEL (1987); READER & WALTER (1993), and herein particularly DAVIE (1993) and WALTER (1993); cf. WARNEKEN (1991). See now also: FRANKE, FRIEDRICHS & MEHL (1994).

A couple of notes about this sacred landscape, in which I will draw upon the little garden in memory of Tom, will have to suffice here.

– The first thing that strikes one is how tradition and modernity meet each other here in this open-air practice, as they also do in the harvest thanksgiving celebrations discussed above. Faced with a modern, public (modern death is supposed to happen indoors), sudden and premature (in today's world one generally "dies of old age") traffic fatality (about 1300 per year in The Netherlands), people reach back to old ritual forms. In the search for rites and ground under their feet, they arrive at age-old, classic forms of sacralizing the landscape, by planting a cross, flowers and plants. These forms immediately remind one of the landscape of cemeteries. Indeed, in Dutch people term crosses like this a "second tombstone," although the term "first tombstone" might be more appropriate, as the actual tombstone at the cemetery generally later replaces the cross planted at the death site.[68]

– Furthermore, it is striking how, in addition to the contemporary quality we have sketched for this modern sacralization of the landscape of mourning and death, at the same time there is a parallel musealization of the older forms of this sacralization which still remain, a process taking the form of cataloguing projects and the adoption and restoration of old field and roadside crosses, death markers, hail crosses and grave markers by local and regional historical and heritage associations.[69] Here too we can see the familiar signs of a change of context.

However, equally striking are the regional differences in my files on this subject reveal. This sort of musealization is primarily a phenomenon of the southern Netherlands, while instances of modern roadside crosses are primarily to be collected from the northern provinces. Tentatively, and with all caution, could one suppose that this perhaps reflects an inverse relationship with the source of personal support in still-vital liturgical mourning rituals in the church? For people in the north, is the landscape of grieving perhaps a form of ritual expression for which the ecclesiastical/liturgical context does not (or at least no longer) provides a ritual repertoire in situations like this? In the cases that I have been able

[68] See VAN SCHOONHOVEN (1993).

[69] EGELIE (1980); (1983); THEELEN (1984); EGELIE & VAN WINKEL (1986); LEENAERTS & NOTERMANS (1988); SCHWINKELS et al. (1991); AERTS (1994); *Wegkruisen en veldkapellen* (n.d.; n.p.).

to document, it is indeed striking that often there were no ecclesiastical mourning rituals which took place after the sudden death. Moreover, it is generally not the family that takes the initiative in creating this landscape, but friends, neighbours, classmates and schoolmates – individuals who are involved, but still often left "emptyhanded" alongside the road by ritual, and who then draw upon the stock of surviving rituals to create these landscapes.

– These landscapes are characterized by their transitory nature. On the average, the landscape disappears after a couple of months. The wooden cross is generally not replaced by a permanent form of marker, and only in exceptional cases – especially where a large number have died suddenly, or the death involves particular injustice – will there eventually be a stone, plaque or monument. That is because the grave with its second tombstone, and not the site of the calamity, becomes the focal point for anamnesis. The fact that the initiative lies, as we have said, not with the family, but with a form of group culture, and is borne by friends from the school, disco, club or neighbourhood, also plays a role in this. What does strike me from my files, however, is that with increasing frequency even in cases of traffic accidents the place is being distinguished in some way for the longer term. I have seen white painted stones appear along the roadside with the date of the accident, and crosses with plastic-covered photographs of the victim are also sometimes maintained for years.

– When all is said and done, however, there is and remains a hesitancy about intervening in the public domain, and sometimes there is also a negative reaction from the side of the authorities. Perhaps this is still a reaction to the previous Dutch history of forbidding public exercises of religion, discussed in the first part of this consideration of outdoor liturgy, in § 4.1, in the course of our examination of the processional park at Dokkum. In part because of that legal and, perhaps more important, mental context, ritual landscape moved to more enclosed spaces such as cemeteries, the home, or the school, where a memorial tree often replaces the flowers and plants along the roadside.

– But there is still a more general background for this reticence, a sign which points to a broader function for this landscape. There is more at stake here than a small part of the grieving process of individuals or a group. Even if only a small proportion of the about 1300 victims of traffic accidents in The Netherlands every year were to be memorialized by a ritual landscape, the berm along our major roads would be changed into one great sacralized landscape! This would also be chiefly a "landscape of guilt." Köstlin remarks on how, were that to happen, a great zone of sorrow and guilt would be introduced into our daily landscape. How would we live with that?

– With this perhaps somewhat strange reflection, we touch another function of this open-air ritual, that of protest and accusation. Although not always connected with a personal and irreparable loss, massive sacralization of our landscape does take place with a certain regularity, for instance in public protest demonstrations. There, in rituals of protest and accusation, masses of people plant crosses as a witness against political killings, torture, cruelty to animals, the clear-cutting of forests and destruction of cultural landscapes – and also against traffic deaths.

Rites which sacralize the landscape are characterized by a tension between relief and legitimization on one side, and protest and accusation on the other. In Tom's case, making the spot a focus of particular care and decorating it with flowers certainly had an important dimension of protest, against road deaths in general, against unsafe conditions at that intersection (about which there are ongoing protest actions), against our acceptance of victims of our mobility and individuality as though they fell to an unavoidable "act of God." In this respect, people found it a relevant and engaged ritual.

– In closing, we can not avoid the question of the "liturgical value" of this ritual landscape. Is this still liturgy? How Christian is the sign of the cross in our society today, for instance? I deliberately included this landscape in my discussion of open-air liturgy so that the discussion might command a broad spectrum stretching from traditional processional liturgy, through liturgies for papal visits, to new rites of this kind, standing at the intersection of tradition and modernity. I would, as of yet, want to be rather cautious in pronouncements about the "liturgical value" of rites of this sort. I have watched parents and their children go to Tom's cross, watched them lay flowers there, watched them pray together there. Procession, and devotion. It is, moreover, important that people who have lost their roots in the rituals that take place inside church buildings here, outside, along the side of the street, are searching for some form of ritual. Seen from this perspective, this landscape is at least relevant for liturgy and liturgical studies, in the sense that all forms of new ritual that arise around key moments in life deserve the attention of liturgists.

5. CONCLUSION

In place of an elaborate synthesis and balance sheet based on these three diverse soundings, I would like to place still one more landscape on our agenda. The voice of those temporary rituals along our modern roads is ultimately drowned out again, lost in the main thrust of obituary notice, funeral and graveyard or crematorium. But sometimes – and in many parts of Europe, still with some regularity – there is also what is called the prayer card, which has nowadays become a memorial card, which in addition to the text on one side, bears an image on the other. It is striking that on these cards, at least in the Dutch situation since the 1960s, landscapes have been the dominant images.[70] We see beautiful landscapes: autumn woods, river landscapes, plowed fields, meadows, polder views. I suspect that we have here something more than a purely decorative representation of the idyllic. Perhaps these landscapes too stand in the tradition of outdoor liturgy that I have tried to evoke in this discussion.

In this connection, we might also refer to the visual arts, particularly those of the southern Netherlands, where we regularly encounter ritual landscapes with pilgrimages and processions.[71] Interpreting visual language of this sort is an extremely complex task, and just throwing around labels like naturalism, expressionism and symbolism is not enough. The images show the idyllic, a delight in the outdoors, but they also show the folklorization of liturgy, or a very critical attitude toward the Church and liturgy. One finds the same in literature.[72] Here too, through ritual and landscape, there is a sometimes paradoxical handling of liturgy between tradition and modernity, between dreamed idyll and critical engagement. As early as 1858, Guido Gezelle's famous poem "Kerkhofblommen" was an exponent of and monument to this process.[73] The central theme is the connection that people experience with their environment through ritual landscape.

[70] For data see the most recent research report in POST (1991c) 126-172, particularly 139 sub 4d. The landscapes first appeared in the period from 1960 to 1969, and then became very popular in the years 1970-70 and 1980-88. They far outstrip the other visual imagery of portrait photos, a cross alone in an otherwise empty space, art reproductions and icons (see table 2, p. 172).

[71] Catalogue, *Religieuze thematiek* (1986), examples: cat.nos. 7, 11, 12, 13, 15, 16, 31.

[72] For this, see VAN ITTERBEEK (1986) 62-77.

[73] See, for example, Guido GEZELLE: Kerkhofblommen, in *Verzameld dichtwerk*, ed. J. BOETS (Antwerpen 1980) I, 253.

But there is also a more radical Christian landscape iconography in which the landscape itself has become the medium for the religious. This line, running from Caspar David Friedrich (1774-1840) through Van Gogh (1853-1890), can indisputably be drawn forward into contemporary visual language. Perhaps this tradition at the same time forms the background for both the landscapes of prayer cards and for many forms of outdoor liturgy, the landscape that our visual language provides for modern devotion.[74]

[74] See MOORE (1989).

Fig. 35. Tilburg (The Netherlands, prov. Noord-Brabant), painting of Peerke Donders in the Peerke Donders Chapel (photo: P.J. Margry).

Fig. 36. Barger Oosterveld (The Netherlands, prov. Drenthe), prayer, blessing and offering of pilgrimage candles midway on the procession honouring St. Gerard Majella, near the wayside altar in the processional park, July 1, 1984 (photo: P.J. Margry).

Fig. 37. Amsterdam (The Netherlands), In March 1988 on the Rokin the "Pillar of the Miracle" was erected, consisting of elements from the medieval chapel of the Holy Site, which was demolished in 1908 (photo: P.J. Margry).

Fig. 38. Amsterdam (The Netherlands), Kalverstraat. The Lipstick store is situated on the site of the former "Holy Corner", the spot where the fireplace in which the Miracle of the Sacrament took place was at that time located (photo: P.J. Margry).

Fig. 39. Panorama of Beek airfield (The Netherlands, prov. Limburg), papal visit, 1985 (photo: Dutch Papal Visit Foundation; ANP).

Fig. 40. Naarden (The Netherlands, prov. Noord-Holland), flower bed at the site of Tom's accident, 1994 (photo: P. Post).

Fig. 41. Amsterdam South East (The Netherlands, prov. Noord-Holland), memorial garden for Bijlmer air crash, 1994 (photo: P. Post).

Fig. 42. Amsterdam South East (The Netherlands, prov. Noord-Holland), memorial garden for Bijlmer air crash, 1994 (photo: P. Post).

Fig. 43. Marker at the site of young woman's fatal accident, beside Provincial Road N 417 between Hilversum and Hollandsche Rading (The Netherlands, prov. Noord-Holland), 1995 (photo: P. Post).

Fig. 44. Marker at the site of young woman's fatal accident, beside Provincial Road N 417 between Hilversum and Hollandsche Rading (The Netherlands, prov. Noord-Holland), 1995 (photo: P. Post).

Fig. 45. Landscape prayer card, 1981 (collection: P. Post).

Fig. 46. Naarden (The Netherlands, prov. Noord-Holland), announcement of an open air Christmas celebration, December, 1996 (photo: P. Post).

BIBLIOGRAPHY

ABÉLÈS, M.: Modern Political Ritual: Ethnography of an Inauguration and a Pilgrimage by President Mitterrand, in *Current Anthropology* 29 (1988) 391-405.

ADAIR, J.: *The Pilgrims' Way. Shrines and Saints in Britain and Ireland* (London 1978).

AEBLI, H.: *Santiago, Santiago... Auf dem Jakobsweg zu Fuß durch Frankreich und Spanien, Ein Bericht* (Stuttgart 1991 (4th ed.)).

AERTS, H.: *Wegkruisen in de voormalige gemeente Heer* (Heer-Maastricht 1994) (Commissie Wegkruisen Parochie St. Petrus Banden).

Akten des XII. Internationalen Kongresses für christliche Archäologie Bonn 1991 (= Jahrbuch Antike und Christentum, Erg. Bd. 22, 102 / Studi di Antichità Cristiana, 52) (Münster/C.d. Vaticano 1995).

ALBERTZ, R.: *Persönliche Frömmigkeit und offizielle Religion* (Stuttgart 1978).

ANDRESEN, C.: *Einführung in die christliche Archäologie* (Die Kirche in ihrer Geschichte Bd. 1, Liefer. B (1.Teil) (Göttingen 1971).

ANGENENDT, A.: *Heilige und Reliquien. Die Geschichte ihres Kultes vom frühen Christentum bis zur Gegenwart* (München 1994).

ANNINK, H.: *Een late pelgrim op de melkweg. Een retourtje Enschede-Santiago de Compostela. 5500 kilometer te voet* (Den Haag 1980).

ANTIER, J.-J.: *Le pèlerinage retrouvé* (Paris 1979).

ANTIER, J.-J.: *De Pelgrimage weer ontdekt. In het Nederlands vertaald, ingeleid en wat de Benelux betreft aangevuld door Th.G.A. Hendriksen, bisschop* (Paris 1979 [Utrecht 1981]).

APOSTEL, L.: Rationaliteit in ritueel en mystiek. Over Frits Staal, in *Ons Erfdeel* 37,3 (1994) 393-404.

ARETZ et al. (eds.): *Der heilige Rock zu Trier: Studien zur Geschichte und Verehrung der Tunika Christi anlässlich der Heilig-Rock-Wallfahrt 1996 im Auftrag des Bischöflichen Generalvikariates* (Trier 1995).

ART, J.: Possibilities and Difficulties in Studying the Place of Religion in Everyday Life in the 19th and Early 20th Century, in L. LAEYENDECKER, J. JANSMA & C. VERHAAR (eds.): *Experiences and Explanations: Historical and Sociological Essays on Religion in Everyday Life* (Leeuwarden 1990) 103-116.

ART, J.: Kerkgeschiedenis na Drewermann, in D.J. WOLFFRAM (ed.): *Om het christelijk karakter der natie. Confessionelen en de modernisering van de maatschappij* (Amsterdam 1994) 179-191.

ART, J.: Mannen als bruiden van de Bruidegom? Enkele verklaringspogingen, in M. DERKS, J. EIJT & M. MONTEIRO (eds.): *Sterven voor de wereld. Een religieus ideaal in meervoud* (= Metamorfosen, 1) (Hilversum 1997) 35-48.

ART, J.: Passie, norm en geschiedenis, in *Handeling L der Koninklijke Zuid-Nederlandse Maatschappij voor Taal- en Letterkunde en Geschiedenis* (1998) 5-18.

ASAD, T.: Towards a Genealogy of the Concept Ritual, in T. ASAD: *Genealogies of Religion. Discipline and Reasons of Power in Christianity and Islam* (Baltimore 1993) 55-79.

ASSION, P.: Der soziale Gehalt aktueller Frömmigkeitsformen. Zur religiösen Volkskunde in der Gegenwart, in *Hessische Blätter für Volks- und Kulturforschung* Bd. 14/15 (1982/1983) (= Materialen zur Volkskultur I, Giessen) 5-17.

ASSION, P.: Historismus, Traditionalismus, Folklorismus. Zur musealisierenden Tendenz der Gegenwartskultur, in U. JEGGLE et al. (eds.): *Volkskultur der Moderne. Probleme und Perspektiven empirischer Kulturforschung* (Reinbeck bei Hamburg 1986) 351-362.

Au-delà du paysage moderne = special issue *Début* 65 (1991) 4-133.

AUF DER MAUR, H.-J.: Het Pascha van de Heer door de kerk gevierd, in *Tijdschrift voor liturgie* 64 (1980) 22-39.

AUF DER MAUR, H.-J.: *Feiern im Rhythmus der Zeit. I: Herrenfeste in Woche und Jahr* (= Gottesdienst der Kirche, Handbuch der Liturgiewissenschaft, 5) (Regensburg 1983).

AUF DER MAUR, H.-J.: *Feiern im Rhythmus der Zeit II/1:* Feste und Gedenktage der Heiligen. (= Gottesdienst der Kirche, Handbuch der Liturgiewissenschaft 6,1) (Regensburg 1994).

AUKES, H.: *Het leven van Titus Brandsma* (Utrecht/Antwerpen 1985 (3d ed.)).

AZIZ, B.N.: Personal Dimensions of the Sacred Journey: What Pilgrims Say, in *Religious Studies* 23 (1987) 103-116.

BANGÓ; J.F.: *Pilgrimaging [c.q. The Pilgrimage] in Hungary* (Wien 1979).

BANK, J.: *Het roemrijk vaderland: het cultureel nationalisme in Nederland in de negentiende eeuw* (= inaugural lecture Leiden) (Den Haag 1990).

BARON, R., & N. SPITZER (eds.): *Public Folklore* (Washington/London 1992).

BARREIROS, C.M.A.: *Nossa Senhora nas Imagens e no seu Culto na Diocese de Braga* (Braga 1931).

BARTH, M.: *Sehnsucht nach den Heiligen?: Verborgene Quellen ökumenischer Spiritualität* (Stuttgart 1992).

BARTOLOTTI, P., & P. BARTOLOTTI: *Guida alle Apparazioni Mariani in Italia* (Milano 1988).

BASTIAENSEN, A.: *Observations sur le vocabulaire liturgique dans l'itinéraire d'Egérie* (Nijmegen 1962).

BATSON, C.D., & W.L. VENTIS: *The Religious Experience. A Social-Psychological Perspective* (New York/Oxford 1982).

BAUMER, I.: *Wallfahrt als Handlungsspiel. Ein Beitrag zum Verständnis religiösen Handelns* (Bern/Frankfurt 1977).

BAUMSTARK, A.: *Liturgie comparée: conférences faites au Prieuré d'Amay, Éd. refondue* (Chevetogne 1939); cf.: *Liturgie comparée: principes et méthodes pour l'étude historique des liturgies chrétiennes* (= 3d ed. by dom B. BOTTE, Chevetogne 1953); = *Comparative liturgy* (London 1958).

BAUSINGER, H.: *Volkskunde. Von der Altertumsforschung zur Kulturanalyse* (Berlin/ Darmstadt 1971).

BAUSINGER, H: Da capo: Folklorismus, in A. LEHMANN & A. KUNTZ (eds.): *Sichtweisen der Volkskunde* (= Lebensformen, 3) (Berlin/Hamburg 1988) 321-328.

BAUSINGER, H.: Tradition und Modernisierung, in *Schweizerisches Archiv für Volkskunde* 87, 1-2 (1991) 5-14.

BAUSINGER, H., K. BEYRER & G. KORFF (eds.): *Reisekultur, von der Pilgerfahrt zum modernen Tourismus* (München 1991).

BAX, M.: "Officieel geloof" en "volksgeloof" in Noord-Brabant. Veranderingen in opvattingen en gedragingen als uitdrukking van rivaliserende clericale regimes, in *Sociologisch tijdschrift* 10 (1984) 621-648.

BAX, M.: The Formation of a Dominant Catholic Regime in Southern Dutch Society, in *Social Compass* 32,1 (1985) 57-72 [a].

BAX, M.: Popular Devotion, Power and Religious Regimes in Catholic Dutch Brabant, in *Ethnology* 24,3 (1985) 215-227 [b].

BAX, M.: *Brabant opnieuw missiegebied? Een veranderend kerkbegrip als gevolg van wijzigende intra-religieuze machtsverhoudingen* (= Antropologische papers, 3) (Amsterdam 1985) [c].

BAX, M.: Rebellion at the Lindenburgh. Southern Dutch Monastic Power Relations in a Developmental Perspective, in *The Netherlands Journal of Sociology* 22,2 (1986) 130-145 [a].

BAX, M.: The Misleading Dichotomy of Religion and Power, in *Sociological Abstracts* 10,6 (1986) 60-81 [b].

BAX, M.: Terug naar donkere tijden? Over het falen van een voorgeschreven kerkelijke orde in hedendaags ruraal Brabant, in G. ROOIJAKKERS & TH. VAN DER ZEE (eds.): *Religieuze volkscultuur. De spanning tussen de voorgeschreven orde en de geleefde praktijk* (Nijmegen 1986) 119-135 [c].

BAX, M.: Religious Regimes and State Formation: Towards a Research Perspective, in *Anthropological Quarterly* 60,1 (1987) 1-13 [a].

BAX, M.: Mariaverschijningen in Medjugorje. Rivaliserende religieuze regimes en staatsvorming, in *Sociologisch tijdschrift* 14 (1987) 195-223 [b].

BAX, M.: *Religieuze regimes in ontwikkeling: verhulde vormen van macht en afhankelijkheid* (Hilversum 1988).

BAX, M.: *De vernedering van een heilige. Religieuze machtspolitiek in een Zuidnederlandse dorpsgemeenschap* (= inaugural lecture VU Amsterdam) (Hilversum 1989).

BAX, M.: *Medjugorje: Religion, Politics and Violence in Rural Bosnia* (= Anthropolocial Studies, 16) (Amsterdam 1995).

BEINERT, W., & H. PETRI: *Handbuch der Marienkunde* (Regensburg 1984).

BEISSEL, S.: *Geschichte der Verehrung Marias im 16. und 17. Jahrhundert. Ein Beitrag zur Religionswissenschaft und Kunstgeschichte* (Freiburg 1910).

BEISSEL, S.: *Wallfahrten zu Unserer Lieben Frau in Legende und Geschichte* (Freiburg 1913).

BEIJNE, G.: Mirakel van Amsterdam: 650 jaar traditie en verbeelding, in A. VAN DEN HOUT, P.J. MARGRY & R. SCHILLEMANS (eds.): *Het Mirakel: 650 jaar Mirakel van Amsterdam (catalogue), 1345-1995* (Aerdenhout 1995) 6-19.

BELL, C.: *Ritual Theory, Ritual Practice* (New York/Oxford 1992).

BELTING, H.: *Bild und Kult. Eine Geschichte des Bildes vor dem Zeitalter der Kunst* (München 1990).

BELZEN, J. VAN, & J. VAN DER LANS (eds.): *Current Issues in the Psychology of Religion* (Amsterdam 1986).

BENDER, B. (ed.): *Landscapes. Politics and Perspectives* (Providence/Oxford 1993).

BENDER, B.: Introduction, in B. BENDER (ed.): *Landscapes. Politics and Perspectives* (Providence/Oxford 1993) 1-17.

BENDER, B.: Stonehenge – Contested Landscapes (Medieval to Present-Day), in B. BENDER, B. (ed.): *Landscapes. Politics and Perspectives* (Providence/Oxford 1993) 281-305.

BENDIX, R.: Tourism and Cultural Displays. Inventing Traditions for Whom?, in *Journal of American Folklore* Vol. 102, no. 404 (1989) 131-146.

BENSA, A.: *Les Saints guérisseurs du Perche Gouët. Espace symbolique du Bocage* (Paris: Institut d'Ethnologie 1978).

BENTLEY, J.: *The Way of Saint-James. A Pilgrimage to Santiago de Compostela* (London 1992).

BERBÉE, P.: "Bedevaart" en "pelgrimstocht" in Nederland. Over oude termen en nieuwe methoden in bedevaartonderzoek, in N. LETTINCK & J. VAN MOOLENBROEK (eds.): *In de schaduw van de eeuwigheid. Tien studies over religie en samenleving in laatmiddeleeuws Nederland aangeboden aan prof. dr. A.H. Bredero* (Utrecht 1986) 167-199.

BERBÉE, P.: Zur Klärung von Sprache und Sache in der Wallfahrtsforschung. Begriffsgeschichtlicher Beitrag zur Diskussion, in *Bayerische Blätter für Volkskunde* 14 (1987) 65-82.

BERGMANN, L.: Wallfahrtstätten am unteren Niederrhein, in *Die Niederrhein* (Neuss 1953) 184-192.

BERKEL, T. VAN, J. RAS, J. WOUTERS (eds.): *De paus in Nederland 1985* (text coordination: L. WIJNANDS, photos: J. BAAN et al.) (Den Bosch 1985).

BERKEY, J.P.: Tradition, Innovation and the Social Construction of Knowledge in the Medieval Islamic Near East, in *Past & Present* 146 (1995) 38-65.

Bibliographie Bedevaart – Pèlerinage – Wallfahrt, Maas-Rijn Rhin-Meuse Rhein-Maas (Köln 1982).

BILU, Y.: The Inner Limits of Communitas: A Covert Dimension of Pilgrimage Experience, in *Ethos* 16 (1988) 302-325.

BLAAS, P.: Esthetische geschiedfilosofie, in *Tijdschrift voor Geschiedenis* 106 (1993) 38-48.

BLAAUW, S. DE: Architecture and Liturgy in Late Antiquity and the Middle Ages, in *Archiv für Liturgiewissenschaft* 33 (1991) 1-34.

BLACKBOURN, D: *Marpingen: Apparitions of the Virgin Mary in Bismarckian Germany* (Oxford 1993).

BLIJLEVENS, A.: Volksreligiositeit en eredienst, in A. BLIJLEVENS, A. BRANTS & E. HENAU (eds.): *Volksreligiositeit: uitnodiging en uitdaging* (= HTP-Studies, 3) (Averbode 1982) 61-84.

BLIJLEVENS, A., A. BRANTS & E. HENAU (eds.): *Volksreligiositeit: uitnodiging en uitdaging* (= HTP-Studies, 3) (Averbode 1982).

BOEKHORST, P. TE, P. BURKE & W. FRIJHOFF (eds.): *Cultuur en maatschappij in Nederland 1500-1850* (Meppel/Amsterdam/Heerlen 1992).

BOER, P. DEN, & W. FRIJHOFF (eds.): *Lieux de mémoire et identités nationales* (Amsterdam 1993).

BÖNISCH-BREDNICH, B., & R. BREDNICH (eds.): *Erinnern und Vergessen; Vorträge des 27. Deutschen Volkskundekongresses* (= Beiträge zur Volkskunde in Niedersachsen, 5; Schriftenreihe der volkskundliche Kommission für Niedersächsen, 6) (Göttingen 1989).

BOISSEVAIN, J. (ed.): *Feestelijke vernieuwing in Nederland?* (= Cahier van het P.J. Meertens-Instituut, 3) (Amsterdam 1991).

BOISSEVAIN, J.: *Revitalizing European Rituals* (London 1992).

BOISSEVAIN, J.: *Over de toekomst van de antropologie van Europa* (Amsterdam 1994).

BOSCH, L.: *Pelgrimeren naar de vrede. Pelgrimstocht naar Assisi 7 juni – 24 aug.* (Utrecht 1986).

BOSSY, J.: *The English Catholic Community, 1570-1840* (London 1975; 1979 (2nd ed.)).

BOUDEWIJNSE, B.: The Conceptualization of Ritual. A History of Its Aspects, in *Jaarboek voor liturgie-onderzoek* 11 (1995) 31-56.

BOWMAN, M.: Drawn to Glastonbury, in I. READER & T. WALTER (eds.): *Pilgrimage and Popular Culture* (London 1993) 29-62.

BRANDENBARG, T. (ed.): *De cultus van de Heilige Moeder Anna en haar familie in de Nederlanden en aangrenzende streken* (Nijmegen 1992).

BRAUCHITSCH, V. VON: *Engel. Eine Anthologie* (Kiel 1990).

BRAUN, R.: *Sozialer und kultureller Wandel in einem ländlichem Industriegebiet im 19. und 20. Jahrhundert* (Zürich 1965).

BREMS, F.J.: *Marien-Wallfahrtstätten in Ostbayern* (München 1988).

BRINGÉUS, N.-A.: *Religion in Everyday Life. Papers Given at a Symposium in Stockholm 1993* (= Konferenser 31, Kungl. Historie och Antikvitets Akademien) (Stockholm 1994).

BROMMER, H. (ed.): *Wallfahrten im Erzbistum Freiburg* (München/Zürich 1990).

BROWN, P.: *The Cult of the Saints, Its Rise and Function in Latin Christianity* (= The Haskell Lectures on History of Religions NS, 2) (Chicago/London 1981).

BROWN, P.: *Society and the Holy* (London 1982).

BRÜCKNER, K.H.: *Marienwallfahrten im Erzbistum Bamberg* (Bamberg 1989).

BRÜCKNER, W.: Wallfahrtforschung im deutschen Sprachgebiet seit 1945, in *Zeitschrift für Volkskunde* 55 (1959) 115-129.

BRÜCKNER, W.: Zur Phänomenologie und Nomenklatur des Wallfahrtswesens und seiner Erforschung. Wörter und Sachen in systematisch-semantischem Zusammenhang, in D. HARMENING et al. (eds.): *Volkskultur und Geschichte. Festgabe für Josef Dünninger zum 65. Geburtstag* (Berlin 1970) 384-424.

BRÜCKNER, W.: *Gnadenbild und Legende. Kultwandel in Dimbach* (Würzburg 1978).

BRÜCKNER, W. (ed.): *Maria Buchen. Eine fränkische Wallfahrt* (Würzburg 1979).

BRÜCKNER, W. (ed.): *Wallfahrt, Pilgerzeichen, Andachtsbild. Aus der Arbeit am Corpuswerk der Wallfahrtstätten Deutschlands: Probleme, Erfahrungen, Anregungen* (Würzburg 1982).

BRÜCKNER, W.: Gemeinschaft – Utopie – Communio. Vom Sinn und Unsinn "sozialer" Interpretation gegenwärtiger Frömmigkeitsformen und ihre empirischen Erfaßbarkeit, in *Bayerische Blätter für Volkskunde* 10 (1983) 181-201.

BRÜCKNER, W.: Popular Culture. Konstrukt, Interpretament, Realität. Anfragen zur historischen Methodologie und Theorienbildung aus der Sicht der mitteleuropäischen Forschung, in *Ethnologia Europaea* 14 (1984) 10-24.

BRÜCKNER, W.: Frömmigkeitsforschung im Schnittpunkt der Disziplinen. Über methodische Vorteile und ideologische Vor-Urteile in den Kulturwissenschaften, in W. BRÜCKNER et al. (eds.): *Volksfrömmigkeitsforschung* (= Ethnologia Bavarica, 13) (Würzburg 1986) 5-37.

BRÜCKNER, W.: Geschichte der Volkskunde. Versuch einer Annäherung für Franzosen, in I. CHIVA & U. JEGGLE (eds.): *Deutsche Volkskunde – Französische Ethnologie. Zwei Standort-Bestimmungen* (Frankfurt a.M. 1987) 105-127.

BRÜCKNER, W.: Zu den modernen Konstrukten "Volksfrömmigkeit" und "Aberglauben", in *Jahrbuch für Volkskunde* NF 16 (1993) 215-220 [a].

BRÜCKNER, W.: Warum eine Baisse der Volkskunde?, in *Bayerische Blätter für Volkskunde* 20 (1993) 84-98 [b].

BÜRGEL, R. (ed.): *Raum und Ritual. Kirchbau und Gottesdienst in theologischer und ästhetischer Sicht* (Göttingen 1995).

BULMAN, R.J., & C.B. WORTMAN: Attributions of Blame and Coping in the "Real World": Severe Accident Victims React to Their Lot, in *Journal of Personality and Social Psychology* 35 (1977) 351-363.

BÜTTNER, M., et al.: *Grundfragen der Religionsgeographie. Mit Fallstudien zum Pilgertourismus* (Berlin 1985).

BUJAK, A., & M.B. YOUNG: *Journeys to Glory* (New York 1976).

BURGERNER, L.: *Die Wallfahrtsorte der katholischen Schweiz*, 2 Vols. (Ingenbohl 1864).

BURKE, P.: *History and Social Theory* (Cambridge 1992).

BURNHAM, S.: *A Book of Angels. Reflections on Angels Past and Present and the True Stories of How They Touch Our Lives* (New York 1990).

CAFÉ, S., & N. INNECCO: *Meditating With the Angels* (York Beach (Maine) 1994).

Camera Gothica. Architecture religieuse gothique dans la photographie européenne du 19e siècle (Anvers 1993).

CAMERON-MOWAT, A.: Anton Baumstark's Comparative Liturgy, in *Questions Liturgiques / Studies in Liturgy* 76,1 (1995) 5-19.

CAMPBELL, D.T., & J.C. STANLEY: *Experimental and Quasi-Experimental Designs for Research* (Chicago 1966).

CANDA, E.R.: Therapeutic Transformation in Ritual, Therapy, and Human Development, in *Journal of Religion and Health* 27 (1988) 205-220.

CANNADINE, D.: The Context, Performance and Meaning of Ritual: The British Monarchy and the "Invention of Tradition", c. 1820-1977, in E. HOBSBAWM & T. RANGER (eds.): *The invention of tradition* (= Past & Present Publications) (Cambridge 1983) 101-164.

CANTALAMESSA, R.: *Ostern in der Alten Kirche* (= Traditio Christiana, IV) (Bern/ Frankfurt a.M./Las Vegas 1981).

CARLEN, L.: *Wallfahrt und Recht im Abendland* (Freiburg 1987).

CARMICHAEL, D., et al. (eds.): *Sacred Sites, Sacred Places* (London 1994).

CASEAU, C.: *Courte notice historique et descriptive sur le pèlerinage de N.-D. de La Salette* (Corps 1942).

CASEL, H., & F. STEIL (eds.): *In Gottes Namen unterwegs. Wallfahrten im Bistum Trier* (Trier 1987).

CASPERS, C., & M. SCHNEIDERS (eds.): *Omnes circumadstantes. Contributions Towards a History of the Role of the People in the Liturgy* (Kampen 1990).

CASPERS, C.: *De eucharistische vroomheid en het feest van sacramentsdag in de Nederlanden tijdens de Late Middeleeuwen*, (= Miscellanea Neerlandica, 5) (Leuven 1992).

CASPERS, C.: "Een stroom van getuigen". Heiligenlevens en heiligenverering in katholiek Nederland circa 1500-circa 2000, in A.B. MULDER-BAKKER & M. CARASSO-KOK (eds.): *Gouden legenden. Heiligenlevens en heiligenverering in de Nederlanden* (Hilversum 1997) 165-179.

CAUBERGHE, J.: *Vroomheid en volksgeloof in Vlaanderen. Folkloristisch Calendarium* (Hasselt 1967).

CERTEAU, M. DE: *The Practice of Everyday Life* (Berkeley/Los Angeles/London 1984).

CHARTIER, R.: *Cultural History Between Practices and Representations* (Cambridge 1988).

CHARTIER, R.: Popular Culture: A Concept Revisited, in *Intellectual History Newsletter* 15 (1993) 3-13.

CHÉLINI, J., & H. BRANTHOMME: *Les chemins de Dieu. Histoire des pèlerinages chrétiens des origines à nos jours* (Paris 1982).

CHÈVRE, G.F.: *Les principaux Sanctuaires de Marie dans la Suisse catholique* (Fribourg 1898).

CHIVA, I., & U. JEGGLE (eds.): *Deutsche Volkskunde – Französische Ethnologie. Zwei Standort-Bestimmungen* (Frankfurt a.M. 1987).

CHRISTIAN Jr., W.: *Apparitions in Late Medieval and Renaissance Spain* (Princeton 1981; 1989 (2nd ed.)) [a].

CHRISTIAN Jr., W.: *Local Religion in Sixteenth Century Spain* (Princeton 1981) [b].

CHRISTIAN Jr., W.: Religious Apparitions and the Cold War in Southern Europe, in E.R. WOLF (ed.): *Religion, Power and Protest in Local Communities; the Northern Shore of the Mediterranean* (Berlin 1984) 239-266.

CHRISTIAN Jr., W.: *Person and God in a Spanish Valley* (Princeton 1989 (rev. ed.)).

CHRISTIAN Jr., W.: Secular and Religious Responses to a Child's Potentially Fatal Illness, in E.R. WOLF (ed.): *Religious Regimes and State Formation: Perspectives From European Ethnology* (Albanay, New York 1991) 163-180 (appeared that same year in *Arxiu d'Etnografia de Catalunya* 7 (1989[1991]) 39-55).

CHRISTIAN Jr., W.: *Moving Crucifixes in Modern Spain* (Princeton 1992).

CHRISTIAN Jr., W.: *Visionaries: the Spanish Republic and the Reign of Christ* (Berkeley 1996).

Codex Iuris Canonici (Vatican City 1983, Dutch ed.: Hilversum/Kevelaer 1983).

COHEN, E.: Pilgrimage and Tourism: Convergence and Divergence, in A. MORINIS (ed.): *Sacred Journeys: The Anthropology of Pilgrimage* (= Contributions to the Study of Anthropology, 7) (Westport (Conn.) 1992) 47-61.

COUTURIER DE CHEFDUBOIS, I.: *Mille pèlerinages de Notre-Dame* (Paris 1954).

COX, H.L.: Volkskundliche Kulturraumforschung im Rhein-Maas-Gebiet (1920-1990), in *Rheinisches Jahrbuch für Volkskunde* 28 (1989/90) 29-67.

DANIELS, S.: *Fields of Vision. Landscape Imagery and National Identity in England and the United States* (Cambridge 1993).

[DANKELMAN, J.:] *De zalige Peerke Donders (1809-1887)* (= Informatiebulletin Een-twee-een, special vol. 10, March 26th 1982) (Utrecht 1982) [a].

DANKELMAN, J.: *Peerke Donders: schering en inslag van zijn leven* (Hilversum 1982) [b].

DAVIE, G.: You'll Never Walk Alone: the Anfield Pilgrimage, in I. READER, T. WALTER (eds.): *Pilgrimage in Popular Culture* (Houndsmills etc. 1993) 201-219.

DAXELMÜLLER, C.: Volksfrömmigkeit, in R.W. BREDNICH (ed.): *Grundriss der Volkskunde. Einführung in die Forschungsfelder der Europäischen Ethnologie* (Berlin 1988) 329-352.

DAXELMÜLLER, C. & M.L. THOMSEN: Mittelalterliches Wallfahrtswesen in Dänemark. Mit einem Kultstätten-Katalog, in *Jahrbuch für Volkskunde*, Neue Folge 1 (1978) 155-204.

DAYAN, D.: Présentation du pape en voyageur. Télévision, expérience rituelle, dramaturgie politique, in *Terrain* (= special issue: "Paraître en public") 15 Oct. (1990) 13-28.

DEFLEM, M.: Ritual, Anti-Structure and Religion: A Discussion of Victor Turner's Processual Symbolic Analysis, in *Journal for the Scientific Study of Religion* 30 (1991) 1-25.

DEJONGHE, M.: *Orbis marianus. Les Madones couronnées à travers le monde, Vol. 1, Les Madones couronnées de Rome* (Paris 1967).

DEKKER, A.J.: *De Volkskundevragenlijsten 1-58 (1934-1988) van het P.J. Meertens-Instituut* (= Publikaties van het P.J. Meertens-Instituut, 12) (Amsterdam 1989) 4-16.

DEKKER, A.J.: De volkskundevragen van het P.J. Meertens-Instituut. Hun doel en hun mogelijkheden en beperkingen als bron, in *Volkskundig Bulletin. Tijdschrift voor Nederlandse cultuurwetenschap* 15 (1989) 60-84.

DEKKER, T., et al. (eds.): *Ausbreitung bürgerlicher Kultur in den Niederlanden und Nordwestdeutschland* (= Beiträge zur Volkskultur in Nordwestdeutschland etc., 74) (Münster 1991).

DEKKER, T.: Paasvuren: een veranderlijke traditie tussen toerisme en lokale identiteit, in *Volkskundig Bulletin. Tijdschrift voor Nederlandse cultuurwetenschap* 19 (1993) 78-104.

DEKKER, G., J. DE HART & J. PETERS: *God in Nederland 1966-1996* (Amsterdam 1997).

DELUMEAU, J.: *Le Christianisme va-t-il mourir?* (Paris 1977).

DELUMEAU, J.: *Rassurer et protéger: le sentiment de sécurité dans l'Occident d'autrefois* (Parijs 1989).

DELUZ, Chr.: Pèlerins à Jérusalem à la fin du Moyen-Age, in *Social Compass, 'Pilgrimage and Modernity'* 36 (1989) 159-173.

DERKS, F.: Religieuze attituden bij bedevaartgangers, in M. VAN UDEN & P. POST (eds.): *Christelijke bedevaarten. Op weg naar heil en heling* (Nijmegen 1988) 171-188.

DERKS, F.: *Religieuze attitudetheorieën* (Nijmegen 1990).

DERKS, F., J. PIEPER & M. VAN UDEN: *Bedevaart: de interviews. Verslag van gesprekken met enkele bedevaartgangers* (Wittem-Lourdes) (= UTP-Rapport) (Heerlen 1989).

DERKS, F., J. PIEPER & M. VAN UDEN: Transformatie en confirmatie. Interviews met bedevaartgangers naar Wittem en Lourdes, in M. VAN UDEN, J. PIEPER & E. HENAU (eds.): *Bij geloof. Over bedevaarten en andere uitingen van volksreligiositeit* (= UTP-Katernen, 11) (Hilversum 1991) 105-123.

DEVLIN, J.: *The Superstitious Mind. French Peasants and the Supernatural in the Nineteenth Century* (New Haven 1987).

DIERKENS A., & J.M. DUVOSQUEL (eds.): *Le culte de saint Hubert au pays de Liège* (Bruxelles 1990).

DINZELBACHER, P., & D.R. BAUER (eds.): *Heiligenverehrung in Geschichte und Gegenwart* (Ostfildern 1990).

DÖRING, A., et al.: *Kurzkataloge der volkstümlichen Kult- und Andachtsstätten der Erzdiözese Freiburg und der Diözesen [Fulda], Limburg, Mainz, Rottenburg-Stuttgart und Speyer* (Würzburg: Institut für Deutsche Philologie 1982).

DOLBY STAHL, S.: *Literary Folkloristics and the Personal Narrative* (Bloomington/Indianapolis 1979).

DONIN, L.: *Die marianische Austria* (Wien 1872).

DOWLING, J.: Lourdes Cures and their Medical Assessment, in *Journal of the Royal Society of Medicine* 77 (1984) 634-638.

Draaiboek aankomst Z.H. Paus Johannes-Paulus II op 11 mei 1985 op het vliegveld Welschap te Veldhoven (Comité Ontvangst Paus Welschap, Veldhoven 1985).

DRAGT, G.: *Dokkum in oude ansichten, deel 2* (Zaltbommel 1991).

DRAGT, I., et al. (eds.): *Dokkum. Beeld van een stad. Twaalf eeuwen stadsleven in woord en beeld* (Drachten/Leeuwarden 1986).

DRIESSEN, H.: Pelgrimage, etnografie en theorie. Een overzicht uit de culturele antropologie, in W. JANSEN & H. DE JONGE (eds.): *Islamitische pelgrimstochten* (Muiderberg 1991) 11-23.

DÜNNINGER, H.: Processio peregrinationis. Volkskundliche Untersuchungen zu einer Geschichte des Wallfahrtswesens im Gebiet der heutigen Diözese Würzburg, in *Würzburger Diözesangeschichtsblätter* 23 (1961) 55-176; 24 (1962) 52-188.

DÜNNINGER, H.: Was ist Wallfahrt? Erneute Aufforderung zur Diskussion um eine Begriffsbestimmung, in *Zeitschrift für Volkskunde* 59 (1963) 221-232.

DÜNNINGER, H.: *Maria siegt in Franken. Die Wallfahrt nach Dettelbach als Bekenntnis* (Würzburg 1979).

DÜNNINGER, H.: Grenzen der Auswertbarkeit von Sekundärliteratur für die Wallfahrtinventarisation, in W. BRÜCKNER (ed.): *Wallfahrt, Pilgerzeichen, Andachtsbild. Aus der Arbeit am Corpuswerk der Wallfahrtstätten Deutschlands: Probleme, Erfahrungen, Anregungen* (Würzburg: Institut für Deutsche Philologie 1982) 172-173.

DÜNNINGER, H.: Sankt Wolfgang in Franken und angrenzenden Regionen. Ein Katalog vorreformatorischer Kirchen, Kapellen und Bildwerke des Heiligen, in *Jahrbuch für Volkskunde* 13 (1990) 211-217.

DUFFY, E.: *The Stripping of the Altars. Traditional Religion in England 1400-1580* (New Haven/London 1992).

DUPRONT, A.: Pèlerinages et lieux sacrés, in *Encyclopaedia Universalis* Vol. XII (Paris 1968) 729-734.

DUPRONT. A.: *Du sacré. Croisades et pèlerinages, images et langages* (= Bibliothèque des Histoires) (Paris 1987).

EADE, J., & M.J. SALLNOW (eds.): *Contesting the Sacred; the Anthropology of Christian Pilgrimage* (Londen/New York 1991).

EBERLE, M.: *Individuum und Landschaft* (Giessen 1980).

Een kruisweg voor Dokkum. Pater Titus Brandsma (Dokkum 1992).

EGELIE, G.: *Wegkruisen in Limburg* (Zutphen 1980).

EGELIE, G.: *Gietijzeren wegkruisen in Limburg: een inventarisatie en aanzet tot interpretatie van de thematiek* (Zutphen 1983).

EGELIE, G., & TH. VAN WINKEL: *Wegkruisen – veldkapellen en andere uitingen van de volksvroomheid in de gemeente Beek* (= Wat Boek os bud, 11) (Beek 1986).

EHAM, M.: Besser als die "Baupläne". Die musikalische Gestaltung der Meßfeiern Papst Johannes Pauls II. bei seinem zweiten Besuch in Deutschland (1), in *Gottesdienst* 21 (1987) 92f [a].

EHAM, M.: Singt Gott in eurem Herzen... Die musikalische Gestaltung der Meßfeiern Papst Johannes Pauls II. bei seinem zweiten Besuch in Deutschland (2), in *Gottesdienst* 21 (1987) 100f [b].

EIJK, I. VAN: *Van Allerheiligen tot Sint Juttemis. Achtergronden van onze feestdagen* (Utrecht/Antwerpen 1993).

ELLWOOD, G.F.: Nicaraguan Pilgrimage, in *Journal for the Study of Religion* 4 (1991) 21-23.

ELSHOUT, D.: Musealisering van de cultuur: het museum als geheugen, in *Kunst en beleid in Nederland* 4 (= Boekmanstudies) (Amsterdam 1990) 35-55 (notes on 195-200).

ERIKSON, E.H.: *Identity, Youth and Crisis* (London 1968) (Dutch ed.: *Identiteit. Jeugd en crisis* (Utrecht 1972)).

ERTL, T.: *Austria Mariana* (2 Vols. Wien 1735).

ESTIENNE, Y.: *Notre-Dame de La Salette* (Genval/Bruxelles/Paris/Château-Richer 1965 (2nd ed.)).

Eucharistiefeiern als Großveranstaltungen. Erfahrungen und Empfehlungen, zusammengestellt vom Liturgischen Institut (Trier 1988).

EVERS, H.: *Pastoraat en bedevaart. Een onderzoek naar het pastorale aanbod in het kader van de devotie tot Sint Gerardus Majella en de bedevaart naar Wittem, met bijzondere aandacht voor het zangrepertoire* ([Etten-Leur] 1993).

EVERS, H., & P. POST: *Historisch repertorium met betrekking tot Wittem als bedevaartoord* (= HTP-Katernen, 2) (Heerlen 1986).

FARMER, D.H.: *The Oxford Dictionary of Saints* (Oxford/New York 1987 (2nd ed.)).

FATUCCHI, A., et al. (eds.): *Atti des convegno internazionale sulla peregrinatio Egeriae [Arrezzo Oct 23-25 1987]* (Arezzo 1990).

FELBECKER, S: *Die Prozession: historische und systematische Untersuchungen zu einer liturgischen Ausdruckshandlung* (= Münsteraner theologische Abhandlungen 39) (Altenberge 1995).

FERRERO, F., & A. SAMPERS (eds.): *Studia Dondersiana* (Roma 1982).

FIENNES, J.: *De bedevaart. Verslag van een pelgrim* (Baarn 1992) (originally: *On Pilgrimage*).

FISCHER, R., & A. STOLL: *Kleines Handbuch österreichischer Marien-Wallfahrtskirchen*, 3 Vols. (Wien 1977/1982).

FISCHER-WOLLPERT, R.: *Wallfahrtstätten im Bistum Mainz* (Zürich 1983).

Le Folklore du Dauphiné (Isère): Étude descriptive et comparée de psychologie populaire, 2 Vols. (Paris 1932-1933).

FRANKE, A., U. FRIEDRICHS & H. MEHL, Unfallkreuze an Schleswig-Holsteins Autostraßen, in *Kieler Blätter zur Volkskunde* 26 (1994) 189-212.

FRANKEN-DUPARC, E.: *Over engelen gesproken* (Chaam 1995).

FRANZ, A.: *Die kirchlichen Benediktionen im Mittelalter*, 2 Vols. (Freiburg i.Br. 1909).

FREITAG, W.: *Volks- und Elitenfrömmigkeit in der frühen Neuzeit. Marienwallfahrten im Fürstentum Münster* (Paderborn 1991).

FREUD, S.: Zwangshandlungen und Religionsübungen (1907), in IDEM: *Gesammelte Werke* Vol. VII (London 1941) 129-139.

FRIJHOFF, W.: *Les pèlerinages dans les Provinces-Unies; ébauche d'inventaire et de problématique de recherches* (Paris 1969; unpubl. univ. essay).

FRIJHOFF, W.: Van "histoire de l'Église" naar "histoire religieuse". De invloed van de "Annales"-groep op de ontwikkeling van de kerkgeschiedenis in Frankrijk en de perspectieven daarvan in Nederland, in *Nederlands Archief voor Kerkgeschiedenis* 61,2 (1981) 113-153.

FRIJHOFF, W. (coordination): Literatuurwijzer, in G. ROOIJAKKERS & TH. VAN DER ZEE (eds.): *Religieuze volkscultuur. De spanning tussen de voorgeschreven orde en de geleefde praktijk* (Nijmegen 1986) 137-171.

FRIJHOFF, W.: Traditie en verleden. Kritische reflecties over het gebruik van verwijzingen naar vroeger, in *Jaarboek voor liturgie-onderzoek* 7 (1991) 125-136.

FRIJHOFF, W.: Inleiding: Historische Antropologie, in P. TE BOEKHORST et al. (eds.): *Cultuur en maatschappij in Nederland 1500-1850. Een historisch-antropologisch perspectief* (Meppel/Heerlen 1992) 11-38 [a].

FRIJHOFF, W.: Het zelfbeeld van de Nederlander in de achttiende eeuw: een inleiding, in *Documentatieblad Werkgroep Achttiende Eeuw* 24,1 (1992) 5-28 [b].

FRIJHOFF, W.: *Ordelijk vergeten. Het museum als geheugen van de gemeenschap* (= Goltziuslezing 1992) (Venlo 1992) [c].

FRIJHOFF, W.: *Volkskunde en cultuurwetenschap: ups en downs van een dialoog* (= Mededelingen der Koninklijke Nederlandse Akademie van Wetenschappen afd. Lett. NR 60, 3 pp. 89-143 / 5-59) (Amsterdam 1997) [a].

FRIJHOFF, W.: Toeëigening: van bezitsdrang naar betekenisgeving, in *Trajecta* 6,2 (1997) 99-118 [b].

GADILLE, J.: Lourdes – un pèlerinage à l'échelle de la catholicité: bilan d'une enquête, in *Social Compass, "Pilgrimage and Modernity"* 36 (1989) 175-186.

GANZ-BLÄTTER, U.: *Andacht und Abenteuer. Berichte europäischer Jerusalem- und Santiago-Pilger (1320-1520)* (Tübingen 1990).

't Gat in de Biltstraat. Neogotiek in Nederland (= *Forum* 24,1 (1973)).

GAULLE, J.M. DE: *Les Sanctuaires les plus célèbres de la sainte Vierge en France*, 2 Vols. (Paris 1869).

GEERTZ, Cl.: *The Interpretation of Cultures. Selected Essays* (New York 1973).

GEERTZ, Cl.: *Local Knowledge. Further Essays in Interpretative Anthropology* (New York 1985).

GENNEP, A. VAN: *The Rites of Passage* (London 1960; original: *Les rites de passage* (Paris 1909)).

GERHOLM, T.: On Ritual: a Postmodernist View, in *Ethnos* 3-4 (1988) 190-203.

GERNDT, H.: *Vierbergelauf. Gegenwart und Geschichte eines Kärntner Brauchs* (= Aus der Forschung und Kunst, 20) (Klagenfurt 1973).

GERNDT, H.: Brauchfunktion und Brauchmotivation der Kärntner Vierbergelauf, in M. SCHARFE (ed.): *Brauchforschung* (Darmstadt 1991) 299-320.

GILS, J. VAN: Von alten Wallahrtsorten im Jülicher Land, in *Heimatkalender [....] Jülich* 9 (1959) 81-86.

GILS, J. VAN: Wallfahrtsorte im Jülicher Land II. Teil, in *Heimatkalender [....] Jülich* 10 (1960) 33-40.

GINZBURG, C.: *Storia notturna. Una decifricazione del sabba* (Torino 1989).

GODDIJN, W., U. SMIT & G. VAN TILLO: *Opnieuw God in Nederland* (Amsterdam 1979).

GOOSEN, L.: *Van Afra tot Zevenslapers: heiligen in religie en kunsten* (Nijmegen 1992).

GRABER, L.H.: *Wilderness as Sacred Space* (Washington 1976).

GRAY, D.: Presidential Address "Bridging the Gap", in *Studia Liturgica* 20 (1990) 1-7 = "Jeter un pont", in *La Maison-Dieu* 179 (1989) 7-14.

GREINACHER, N., & N. METTE (eds.): *Popular Religion*, = special issue *Concilium* (1986).

GRIMES, R.L.: *Ritual Criticism. Case Studies in its Practice, Essays on its Theory* (Columbia 1990).

GRIMES, R.L.: *Reading, Writing, and Ritualizing. Ritual in Fictive, Liturgical, and Public Places* (Washington DC 1993).

GRIMES, R.: *Marying & Burying: Rites of Passage in a Man's Life* (Boulder 1995).

GRIJZENHOUT, F.: *Feesten voor het vaderland: Patriotse en Bataafse feesten 1780-1806* (= Kunst-historische series, 3) (Zwolle, 1989).

GUGITZ, G.: *Österreichs Gnadenstätten in Kult und Brauch. Ein topographisches Handbuch zur religiösen Volkskunde in Fünf Bänden* (Wien 1955-1958).

GUMPPENBERG, W.: *Atlas Marianus (...)* (Ingolstadt 1657).

GYSELS, H. (ed.) & J. BACCAERT, A. BEENHAKKERS, T. CASPERS (cooperation): *De landschappen van Vlaanderen en Zuidelijk Nederland. Een landschapsecologische studie* (Leuven/Apeldoorn 1993).

HABERMAS, R.: *Wallfahrt und Aufruhr. Zur Geschichte des Wunderglaubens in der frühen Neuzeit* (Frankfurt 1991).

HAHNE, W.: Im ganzen erfreulich. Gottesdienste bei der Deutschland-Reise des Papstes (1), in *Gottesdienst* 14 (1980) 180 [a].

HAHNE, W.: Offene Fragen und Wünschen. Gottesdienste bei der Deutschland-Reise des Papstes (2), in Gottesdienst 14 (1980) 189f [b].

HAMON, A.: *Notre Dame de France ou Histoire du Culte de la Sainte Vierge en France, depuis l'origine du christianisme jusqu'à nos jours* (7 Vols.; Paris 1861-1867).

HANSEN, S.: *Die deutschen Wallfahrtsorte. Ein Kunst- und Kulturführer zu über 1000 Gnadenstätten* (Augsburg 1991; 2nd ed. 1993).

HALBERTSMA, H.: Bonifatius' levenseinde in het licht der opgravingen, in *Berichten van de Rijksdienst voor het Oudheidkundig Bodemonderzoek* X-XI (1960/61) 395-444.

HANBURY-TENISON, R.: *Spanish Pilgrimage* (London 1991).

HANEGRAAFF, W.J.: *New Age Religion and Western Culture. Esotericism in the Mirror of Secular Thought* (= Studies in the History of Religions, 72) (Leiden 1996).

HARNONCOURT, Ph., & Hj. AUF DER MAUR: *Feste und Gedenktage der Heiligen. Gottesdienst der Kirche*, in *Feiern im Rhythmus der Zeit II/1* (= Gottesdienst der Kirche, Handbuch der Liturgiewissenschaft, 6,1) (Regensburg 1994).

HART, J. DE: Jongeren en "new Age". Recente cijfers betreffende de betrokkenheid van jong volwassenen bij alternatieve levensbeschouwelijke stromingen, in *Sociale Wetenschappen* 36,1 (1993) 1-23 [a].

HART, J. DE: Bijgeloof – bij geloof? Christelijke religiositeit en "New Age"-stromingen onder Nederlandse jong-volwassenen, in *Tijdschrift voor Theologie* 33,2 (1993) 166-176.

HART, O. VAN DER: *Rituelen in psychotherapie. Overgang en bestendiging* (Deventer 1978; 1984: 2nd and extended ed.).

HART, O. VAN DER: *Afscheidsrituelen in psychotherapie* (Baarn 1981).

HARTINGER, W.: *Religion und Brauch* (Darmstadt 1992).

HAUPT, H.-G. (ed.): *Orte des Alltags. Miniaturen aus der europäischen Kulturgeschichte* (München 1994).

HECKMANS, F.: Niederheinische Pilgerorte und Pilgerfahrte, in *Die Heimat* 8 (1929) 190-198 and 9 (1930) 30-37.

HEESTERMAN, J.C.: *The Inner Conflict of Tradition* (Chicago 1985).

HEIJDEN, J. VAN DER: *Don't Forget Us; We Shall Not Forget You. Vijftig jaar herdenking Slag om Arnhem, een herdenking met betekenis* (Arnhem 1994).

HEIM, W.: *Kleines Wallfahrtsbuch der Schweiz* (Freiburg ca. 1980).

HEIMBROCK, H.-G.: *Gottesdienst: Spielraum des Lebens. Sozial- und kulturwissenschaftliche Analysen zum Ritual in praktisch-theologischem Interesse* (= Theologie & Empirie, 15) (Kampen/Weinheim 1993).

HEIMING, O.: In memoriam Anton Baumstark, in *Tijdschrift voor liturgie* 33 (1949) 161-163.

HEIZMANN, L.: *Die Wallfahrtsorte der Erzdiözese Freiburg in der Legende und Sage* (Tiergarten 1932).

HENDRIKSEN, Th.G.A.: Aanhangsel, in J.J. ANTIER: *De pelgrimage weer ontdekt* (Utrecht 1981) 326-439.

HENNIG, R.: *Terrae incognitae. Eine Zusammenstellung und kritische Bewertung der wichtigsten vorcolumbischen Entdeckungsreisen an Hand in der darüber vorliegenden Originalberichte*, I-IV (Leiden 1944-1956 (2nd ed.)).

HERBERS, Kl. (ed.): *Deutsche Jakobspilger und ihre Berichte* (= Jakobus-Studien, 1) (Tübingen 1988).

HERCHENBACH, W.: *Die heiligen katholischen Gnaden- und Wallfahrtsorte mit den Heiligthümern und Reliquien. Nach geschichtlichen Quellen und Legenden* (Stuttgart-Nürtingen 1893).

HERSBACH, G.: *Westlanders op heilige grond. Rapportage bedevaartenquête Westland 1991* (Amsterdam 1992; research report).

HERSBACH, G.: Westlandse bedevaartgangers als hoeders van het Roomse erfgoed, in J. PIEPER, P. POST & M. VAN UDEN (eds.): *Bedevaart en pelgrimage. Tussen traditie en moderniteit* (= UTP-Katernen, 16) (Baarn 1994) 81-104.

HERUER, H., & G. PRINSEN: *Paus Johannes Paulus II in Nederland* (Katholieke Informatie mei 1985 nr. 3. Photo book with texts of all speeches published by Stichting R.K. Voorlichting Oegstgeest).

HERWAARDEN, J. VAN: Hebben christelijke bedevaarten een status-veranderend effect gehad? Een commentaar op een antropologische beschouwing, in *Tijdschrift voor Geschiedenis* 93 (1980) 247-254.

HERWAARDEN, J. VAN: *Op weg naar Jacobus. Het Boek, de Legende en de Gids voor de Pelgrims naar Santiago de Compostela* (Hilversum 1992).

HERWAARDEN, J. VAN: Beminden wij onze heiligen wel? Enkele beschouwingen over het laatmiddeleeuws geloofsleven in de Nederlanden, in M. VAN UDEN, J. PIEPER & P. POST (eds.): *Oude sporen, nieuwe wegen*. Ontwikkelingen in bedevaartonderzoek (= UTP-Katernen, 17) (Baarn 1995) 135-168.

HIERZENBERGER, G., & O. NEDOMANSKY: *Erscheinungen und Botschaften der Gottesmutter Maria. Vollständige Dokumentation durch zwei Jahrtausende* (Augsburg 1993).

HILHORST, A. (ed.): *De heiligenverering in de eerste eeuwen van het christendom* (Nijmegen 1988).

HOBSBAWM, E.: see selective bibliography, Apendix in Chapter 3.

HOBSBAWM, E., & T. RANGER (eds.): *The Invention of Tradition* (= Past & Present Publications) (Cambridge 1983).

HOLLOWAY, J.B.: *The Pilgrim and the Book: A Study of Dante, Langland, and Chaucer* (= American University Studies Series 4, English language and literature, Vol. 42) (New York etc. 1987).

HOOGEN, A. VAN DEN, & E. JONKER: *De pastorale uitdaging van New Age*, = *Praktische Theologie* 20,4 (1993).

HOPPE, A.: *Des Österreichers Wallfahrtsorte* (Wien 1913).

HORST, P. VAN DER: Silent Prayer in Antiquity, in *Numen* 41 (1994) 1-25.

HOTZ, J.: *Wallfahrtskirchen in Europa* (= Keysers kleine Kulturgeschichte) (München 1983).

HOUDIJK, C., & J. HOUDIJK: *Naar de ware Jacob: dagboek van een voettocht naar Santiago de Compostela* (= Santiago de Compostela bibliotheek, 4) (Schoorl 1990).

HOWARD, D.R.: *Writers and Pilgrims: Medieval Pilgrimage Narratives and Their Posterity* (Berkeley/London 1980).

HÜTTL, L.: *Marianische Wallfahrten im süddeutsch-österreichischen Raum. Analysen von der Reformations- bis zur Aufklärungsepoche* (Köln 1985).

HUF, O.: *Krijgs-gebeden en oorlogs-missen* (= Liturgische Studiën, 2) (Bussum 1917).

HUIJBERS, B.: *Aan Gij voorbij. Het mysterie bezongen* (Hilversum 1989).

HUMPHREY, C., & J. LAIDLAW: *The Archetypal Actions of Ritual. A Theory of Ritual Illustrated by the Jain Rite of Worship* (= Oxford Studies in Social and Cultural Anthropology) (Oxford 1994).

HUYGENS, R.B.C. (ed.): *Magister Gregorius (12e ou 13e siècle) Narracio de mirabilibus urbis Rome* (Leiden 1970).

INGERSOLL, R.: The "possesso"; the Via Papale, and the Stigma of Pope Joan, in H. DE MARE, A. VOS (eds.): *Urban Rituals in Italy and the Netherlands. Historical Contrasts in the Use of Public Space, Architecture and the Urban Environment* (Assen 1993) 39-50.

ITTERBEEK, E. VAN: Raakpunten tussen religieuze literatuur en beeldende kunsten in de Belgische Kunst 1875-1985, in *Religieuze thematiek in de Belgische Kunst 1875-1985* (Brussel 1986) 62-77.

JAMES, W.: *The Varieties of Religious Experience* (Glasgow 1977 (1st ed. 1902)).

JELSMA, A.: *De blaffende hond, aspecten uit het leven van Wynfreth-Bonifatius* (Den Haag 1973).

JÖCKLE, Cl.: *Heiligen van alle tijden: levens, legenden, iconografie* (Baarn 1995).

JÖCKLE, Cl., & K. GRAMER: *Wallfahrtstätten im Bistum Speyer* (Zürich 1983).

JONG, A. DE: Meegaan met pelgrims naar Santiago de Compostela. Verslag van een onderzoeksproject in wording, in J. PIEPER & M. VAN UDEN (eds.): *Bedevaart en pelgrimage. Tussen traditie en moderniteit* (Baarn 1994) 59-79.

JONG, A. DE, & A. SKOUGAARD: De Hindeloper en de Amager kamer: twee voorbeelden van een historisch museumfenomeen, in *De Vrije Fries* LXXII (1992) 88-108 [a].

JONG, A. DE, & A. SKOUGAARD: Early Open-Air Museums: Traditions of Museums About Traditions, in *Museum* 175, XLIV, nr. 3 (1992) (UNESCO Paris) 151-157 [b].

JONG, A. DE: Volkskunde im Freien, in *Ethnologia Europaea* 24,2 (1994) 139-148.

JONKER, E.J.: De betrekkelijkheid van het moderne historische besef, in *Bijdragen en Mededelingen betreffende de Geschiedenis der Nederlanden* 111,1 (1996) 30-46.

KACZYNSKI, R.: Die Meßfeiern mit Papst Johannes Paul II. in Deutschland, in *Liturgisches Jahrbuch* 31 (1981) 97-114.

KALTENBAECK, J.P.: *Die Mariensagen in Oesterreich* (Wien 1845).

KAPFHAMMER, G.: Geistliche Landschaft. Regionale Marginalien zu einem internationalen Phänomen, in I. BAUER, E. HARVOLK & W.A. MAYER (eds.): *Forschungen zur historischen Volkskunde, Festschrift Torsten Gebhard zum 80. Geburtstag* (München 1989) 231-236.

KASCHUBA, W.: Volkskultur: Themen, Publikationen, Perspektiven. Ein Forschungsüberblick aus volkskundlicher Sicht, in *Archiv für Sozialgeschichte* 26 (1986) 361-398.

KASCHUBA, W.: *Volkskultur zwischen feudaler und bürgerlicher Gesellschaft. Zu Geschichte eines Begriffs* (Frankfurt a.M. 1988).

Katholiek Nederland en de paus: 1580-1985 (= catalogue of an exhibition at the Rijksmuseum Het Catharijneconvent Utrecht 1985) (Utrecht 1985).

KELLEHER, M.M.: Hermeneutics in the Study of Liturgical Performance, in *Worship* 67,4 (1993) 292-319.

KEMP, A.C.J. VAN DER: De bedevaarten onzer landgenooten, in *Studiën en bijdragen op het gebied der historische theologie* (1880) 1-103.

KEMENADE, K. VAN, & P. SPAPENS: *365 heiligendagen: folklore, gebruiken, iconografie, legenden, namen, weerspereuken* (Eindhoven 1993).

KENNEDY NEVILLE: See NEVILLE.

KINGMANS, H.: *Op pylgerreis, Uitgave van Stichting Kultuer en Toerisme in Fryslân* (= Monument van de maand, Leeuwarden 9,4 (1994)) 37-46.

KIRSTE, R. et al. (eds.): *Engel, Elemente, Energien* (= Religionen im Gespräch, 2) (Hamburg 1992).

KLANICZAY, C.: *Heilige, Hexen, Vampire: vom Nützen des Übernatürlichen* (Berlin 1991).

KLAUSER, Th., & H.E. KILLY: Anton Baumstark (1872-1948), in *Ephemerides Liturgicae* 63 (1949) 184-207.

KLEINHEYER, B.: *Sakramentliche Feiern I* (= Gottesdienst der Kirche, Handbuch der Liturgiewissenschaft 7,1) (Regensburg 1989).

KLOTZ, U., & B. FIDLER: *Sozialgeschichte regionaler Kultur. Lebenslaufnotizen – Positionsbestimmungen – Bibliographie von Wolfgang Brückner* (Würzburg 1990).

KNIPPENBERG, W.H.Th.: *Kultuurhistorische verkenningen in de Kempen III. Oude pelgrimages vanuit Noord-Brabant* (Oisterwijk: Stg. Brabants Heem 1968).

KOCH, K.: Liturgie und Theater. Theologische Fragmente zu einem vernächlässigten Thema, in *Stimmen der Zeit* 213 (1995) 3-16.

KÖSTLIN, K.: Zu Intention und Praxis religiöser Erinnerung, in B. BÖNISCH-BREDNICH, R.W. BREDNICH & H. GERNDT (eds.): *Erinnern und Vergessen. Vorträge des 27. Deutschen Volkskundekongresses* (= Beiträge zur Volkskunde in Niedersachsen, 5) (Göttingen 1989) 427-440.

KÖSTLIN, K.: Folklorismus und Modernisierung, in *Schweizerisches Archiv für Volkskunde* 87,1-2 (1991) 46-66.

KÖSTLIN, K.: Totengedenken am Straßenrand. Projektstrategie und Forschungsdesign, in *Österreichische Zeitschrift für Volkskunde* XLVI, 95 (1992) 305-320.

KÖSTLIN: Die Wiederkehr der Engel, in N.-A. BRINGÉUS (ed.): *Religion in Everyday Life. Papers Given at a Symposium in Stockholm 1993* (= Konferenser, 31 Kungl. Vitterhets Historie och Antikvitets Akademien) (Stockholm 1994) 79-96.

KÖTTING, B.: *Peregrinatio Religiosa. Wallfahrten in der Antike und das Pilgerwesen in der alten Kirche* (München 1950).

KOLB, K.: *Mariahilf. Mariengenadenstätten Heute. Entstehung, Legende, Bedeutung, Gnadenbild* (Würzburg 1974).

KOLB, K. *Große Wallfahrten in Europa* (Würzburg 1976).

KOLB, K.: *Wallfahrtsland Franken* (Würzburg 1979).

KOLB, K.: *Vom heiligen Blut. Eine Bilddokumentation der Wallfahrt und Verehrung* (Würzburg 1980).

KOMMERS, J.: Mythische geografie. Landschap en wereldbeeld in niet-westerse culturen, in H. DRIESSEN & H. DE JONGE (eds.): *In de ban van betekenis. Proeven van symbolische antropologie* (Nijmegen 1994) 46-69.

KOOI, J. VAN DER: Folklore – volkskunde – folklorisme, in *Volkscultuur. Tijdschrift over tradities en tijdverschijnselen* 7,1 (1990) 69-96.

KORFF, G.: Volkskundliche Frömmigkeits- und Symbolforschung nach 1945, in I. CHIVA & U. JEGGLE (eds.): *Deutsche Volkskunde – Französische Ethnologie. Zwei Standort-Bestimmungen* (Frankfurt a.M. 1987) 244-270.

KORFF, G.: Musealisierung total? Notizen zu einem Trend der die Institution nach der er benannt ist, hinter sich gelassen hat, in K. FÜßMANN, H. GRÜTTER & J. RÜSEN (eds.): *Historische Faszination. Geschichtskultur Heute* (Köln 1994) 129-144.

KRAMER, D., & R. LUTZ (eds.): *Reisen und Alltag. Beiträge zur kulturwissenschaftliche Tourismusforschung* (= Kulturanthropologie-Notizen, 39) (Frankfurt a.M. 1992).

KRISS, R.: *Volkskundliches aus altbayrischen Gnadenstätten. Beiträge zu einer Geographie des Wallfahrtsbrauchtums* (Augsburg 1930; 1953-1955 (2nd ed.) in 2 Vols.; 1956: Vol. 3: Theorie des Wallfahrtwesens).

KRISS, R.: Zur Begriffsbestimmung des Ausdrucks Wallfahrt, in *Österreichisch Zeitschrift für Volkskunde* 66 (1963) 101-107.

KRONENBURG, J.A.F.: *Maria's Heerlijkheid in Nederland. Geschiedkundige Schets van de Vereering der H. Maagd in ons Vaderland, van de eerste tijden tot op onze dagen*, 7 Vols. (Amsterdam 1904-1914) and: [A. Scheepers], *Alphabetisch register op J.A.F. Kronenburgs Maria's Heerlijkheid in Nederland* (Roermond 1931).

KSELMAN, TH.A.: *Miracles & Prophecies in Nineteenth-Century France* (New Brunswick 1983).

KSELMAN, T., & S. KSELMAN: Marian Piety and the Cold War in the United States, in *The Catholic Historical Review* 72 (1986) 403-424.

KVIDELAND, R., & K. KVIDELAND: Christliches Erzählen in norwegischen Erweckungsbewegungen, in H. EBERHART, E. HÖRANDNER & B. PÖTTLER (eds.): *Volksfrömmigkeit* (= Referate der Österreichischen Volkskundetagung 1989 in Graz) (Wien 1990) 219-231.

LÄPPLE, A.: *Deutschland, deine Wallfahrtsorte* (Aschaffenburg 1982).

LÄPPLE, A.: *Reliquien: Verehrung, Geschichte, Kunst* (Augsburg 1990).

LÄPPLE, A.: *Das Hausbuch der Heiligen und Namenspatrone* (München 1992).

LAEYENDECKER, L., J. JANSMA & C. VERHAAR (eds.): *Experiences and Explanations: Historical and Sociological Essays on Religion in Everyday Life* (Leeuwarden 1990).

LAFUENTE, V. DE: *Vie de la Vierge Marie et son histoire de son culte en Espagne* (Barcelona: 1889).

LAMBERTS, J.: Bedevaart en liturgie, in J. PIEPER, P. POST & M. VAN UDEN (eds.): *Bedevaart en pelgrimage. Tussen traditie en moderniteit* (= UTP-Katernen, 16) (Baarn 1994) 201-240.

LAMBERTS, J. (ed.): *Liturgie en inculturatie* (= Nikè-reeks 37) (Leuven/Amersfoort 1996).

LAMBERTS, J.: *Op weg naar heelheid. Over bedevaart en liturgie* (= Nikè-reeks, 39) (Leuven/Amersfoort 1997).

LAMERS, H.: *Dagboek van een pelgrim naar Santiago de Compostela* (Utrecht 1987).

LANE, B.C.: *Landscapes of the Sacred. Geography and Narritive in American Spirituality* (Isaac Hecker Studies in Religion and American Spirituality) (Mahwah NY 1988).

LANTIN, A.: *Scherpenheuvel oord van vrede. Ontstaan van de bedevaartplaats. Beschrijving van koepelkerk en kunstschatten* (Retie 1971).

LAURENTIN, R.: *Lourdes, dossier des documents authentiques, Vol. 1 : Au temps des seize premières apparitions, 11 février – 3 avril 1858* (Paris 1962 (2nd ed.)) [a].

LAURENTIN, R.: *Idem: Vol. 2: Dix-septième apparition, gnoses, faux miracles, fausses visions, la grotte interdite, 4 avril – 14 juin 1858* (Paris 1957).

LAURENTIN, R.: *Lourdes, histoire authentique, Vol. 2: L'enfance de Bernadette et les trois premières apparitions, 7 janvier 1844-18 février 1958* (Paris 1962) [b].

LAURENTIN, R.: *Idem, Vol. 3: La quinzaine des apparitions* (Paris 1962) [c].

LAURENTIN, R.: *Idem, Vol. 4: La quinzaine des apparitions: La quinzaine au jour le jour, première semaine, 19 à 25 février 1858* (Paris 1963).

LAURENTIN, R.: *Bernadette of Lourdes* (Minneapolis 1979).

LASH, S., & J. URRY (eds.): *Economies of Signs and Space* (London 1994).

LEDEGANG, F. (ed.): *Als pelgrim naar het Heilig Land. De pelgrimage van Egeria in de vierde eeuw* (= Christelijke bronnen, 4) (Kampen 1991).

LEENAERTS, B. (text), J. NOTERMANS (photos): *Wandelen langs de Gulpener wegkruisen* (Simpelveld 1988).

LEEUWEN, A. VAN.: De neogotiek, van romantische vorm tot enig ware stijl, in A. JANSEN, A. VAN LEEUWEN & G. VRINS (eds.): *"Arbeyd sere voert tot eere": Hendrik van der Geld, de neogotiek en de Brabantse beeldhouwkunst* (= Bijdragen tot de geschiedenis van het Zuiden van Nederland, LXXX) (Tilburg 1989) 1-42.

LEEUWEN, A. VAN: *De maakbaarheid van het verleden: P.J.H. Cuypers als restauratiearchitect, 1850-1918* (Zwolle 1995).

LEHMANN, A: Erzählen eigener Erlebnisse im Alltag, in *Zeitschrift für Volkskunde* 74 (1978) 198-215.

LEHMANN, A.: Rechtfertigungsgeschichten. Über eine Funktion des Erzählens eigener Erlebnisse im Alltag, in *Fabula* 21 (1980) 56-69.

LEHMANN, A.: *Erzählstruktur und Lebenslauf. Autobiografische Untersuchungen* (Frankfurt a.M./New York 1983).

LEPROUX, M.: *Dévotions et Saints guérisseurs [Charentais]* (Paris 1957).

LIEBERGEN, L. VAN, & G. ROOIJAKKERS (eds.): *Volksdevotie. Beelden van religieuze volkscultuur in Noord-Brabant* (Uden 1990).

Liturgische Normen für einen Pastoralbesuch des Heiligen Vaters im Ausland (außerhalb von Rom) (n.p.; n.d.; certainly prior to 1987) (published by the Amt für die Päpstlichen Zeremonien).

LIPP, W.: Der öffentliche Stadtraum und das religiöse Fest, in R. BÜRGEL (ed.): *Raum und Ritual. Kirchbau und Gottesdienst in theologischer und ästhetischer Sicht* (Göttingen 1995) 11-23.

LOCRIUS, F.: *Maria Augusta Virgo Deipara in VII libros distributa (...)* (Atrecht 1608).

LOGISTER, W.: *Maria, een uitdaging* (Averbode 1995).

LOPEZ, P.: Le pèlerinage à Fatima: une expression du sacré populaire, in *Social Compass, "Pilgrimage and Modernity"* 36 (1989) 187-199.

LORENTZ, C.: *De constructie van het verleden. Een inleiding in de theorie van de geschiedenis* (Meppel 1990 (2nd ed.)).

LUBAC, H. DE: *Corpus mysticum: l'Eucharistie et l'Eglise au Moyen Age. Étude historique* (Paris 1944; 2nd revised ed.: 1949); see, *Corpus mysticum. Kirche und Eucharistie im Mittelalter* (= German edition, prepared by H.U. von Balthasar) (Einsiedeln 1969).

LÜBBE, H.: Erfahrungsverluste und Kompensationen. Zum philosophischen Problem der Erfahrung in der Gegenwärtigen Welt, in *Giessener Universitätsblätter* 12,2 (1979) 42-53.

LÜBBE, H.: Der Fortschritt und das Museum, in *Dilthey Jahrbuch* I (Göttingen 1983) 39-56 [a].

LÜBBE, H: *Zeitverhältnisse. Zur Kulturphilosophie des Fortschritts* (= Herkunft und Zukunft, I) (Graz/Wien/Köln 1983) [b].

LÜBBE, H.: *Die Aufdringlichkeit der Geschichte* (Graz/Wien/Köln 1989).

LUKATIS, I.: Church Meeting and Pilgrimage in Germany, in *Social Compass, "Pilgrimage and Modernity"* 36 (1989) 201-218.

LUKKEN, G.: *De onvervangbare weg van de liturgie* (Hilversum 1984 (2nd ed.)).

LUKKEN, G: *Geen leven zonder rituelen. Antropologische beschouwingen met het oog op de christelijke liturgie* (Hilversum 1988 (3d ed.)).

LUKKEN, G.: Die architektonischen Dimensionen des Rituals, in *Liturgisches Jahrbuch* 39 (1989) 19-36 = in G. LUKKEN: *Per visibilia ad invisibilia. Anthropolical, Theological and Semiotic Studies on the Liturgy and Sacrements*, Collected and Edited by L. VAN TONGEREN & Ch. CASPERS (= Liturgia condenda, 2) (Kampen 1994), 360-374.

LUKKEN, G.: Les transformations du rôle liturgique du peuple: la contribution de la sémiotique à l'histoire de la liturgie, in Ch. CASPERS & M. SCHNEIDERS (eds.): *Omnes circumadstantes. Towards a History of the Role of the People in the Liturgy* (Kampen 1990) 15-30.

LUKKEN, G.: Ritueel en theater, in *Werkmap voor liturgie* 25,3 (1991) 132-140.

LUKKEN, G.: *Ontwikkelingen in de liturgiewetenschap. Balans en perspectief* (= Liturgie in perspectief, 1) (Heeswijk-Dinther 1993).

LUKKEN, G.: *Inculturatie en de toekomst van de liturgie* (= Liturgie in perspectief, 3) (Heeswijk-Dinther 1994).

LUKKEN, G.: *Per visibilia ad invisibilia. Anthropological, Theological, and Semiotic Studies on the Liturgy and the Sacrements.* Collected and Edited by L. VAN TONGEREN & Ch. CASPERS (= Liturgia condenda, 2) (Kampen 1994).

LUKKEN, G.: Inculturatie en liturgie. Theorie en praktijk, in J. LAMBERTS (ed.): *Liturgie en inculturatie* (= Nikè-reeks 37) (Leuven/Amersfoort 1996) 15-56 = Inculturation de la liturgie: théorie et pratique, in *Questions Liturgiques / Studies in Liturgy* 77,1-2 (1996) 10-39.

MCDANNELL, C.: *Material Christianity. Religion and Popular Culture in America* (New Haven etc. 1995).

MACHER, F.: *Wallfahrten im Bistum Passau* (München 1981).

MCKEVITT, CHR.: San Giovanni Rotondo and the Shrine of Padre Pio, in J. EADE & M.J. SALLNOW (eds.): *Contesting the Sacred: The Anthropology of Christian Pilgrimage* (London 1991) 77-97.

MANOIR, H. DE (ed.): *Maria, études sur la sainte Vierge,* 8 Vols. (Paris 1949-1971).

MARAVAL, P. (ed.): *Journal de voyage d'Egérie* (= Sources Chrétiennes, 296) (Paris 1982).

MARAVAL, P.: *Lieux saints et pèlerinages d'Orient. Histoire et géographie des origines à la conquête arabe* (Paris 1985).

MARCUCCI, D.: *Santuari Mariani d'Italia. Storia – fede – arte* (Rome 1983).

MARE, H. DE & A. VOS (eds.): *Urban Rituals in Italy and The Netherlands. Historical Contrasts in the Use of Public Space, Architecture and the Urban Environment* (Assen 1993).

MARGRY, P.J.: *Bedevaartplaatsen in Noord-Brabant* (Eindhoven 1982).

MARGRY, P.J.: *Amsterdam en het Mirakel van het Heilig Sacrament. Van middeleeuwse devotie tot 20e-eeuwse stille omgang* (Amsterdam 1988).

MARGRY, P.J.: Gebed en verbod. Processies en bedevaarten in en om Brabant, in L. VAN LIEBERGEN, G. ROOIJAKKERS (eds.): *Volksdevotie. Beelden van religieuze volkscultuur in Noord-Brabant* (Uden 1990) 41-44.

MARGRY, P.J.: Processie versus stille omgang. Het probleem van de openbare godsdienstuitoefening buiten gebouwen en besloten plaatsen in Holland, in *Historisch Tijdschrift Holland* 25,3-5 (1993) 174-196 (= "Geloof in Holland") [a].

MARGRY, P.J.: Processie-exercities. Strategieën van overheid en kerk bij de beteugeling en de stimulering van processies in Nederland en België,

1815-1825, in M. MONTEIRO, G. ROOIJAKKERS, J. ROSENDAAL (eds.): *De dynamiek van religie en cultuur. Geschiedenis van het Nederlands katholicisme* (Kampen 1993) 60-79 [b].

MARGRY, P.J.: Bedevaartrevival? Bedevaartcultuur in het Bataafs-Franse Nederland (1795-1814), in *Trajecta* 3,3 (1994) 209-232 [a].

MARGRY, P.J.: De creatie van heilige ruimten in negentiende-eeuws Nederland. Het martelveld te Brielle, in J.C. OKKEMA et al. (eds.): *Heidenen, papen, Libertijnen en fijnen. Artikelen over de kerkgeschiedenis van het zuidwestelijke gedeelte van Zuid-Holland van de voorchristelijke tijd tot heden* (= zesde verzameling bijdragen van de Vereniging voor Nederlandse Kerkgeschiedenis) (Delft 1994) 249-276 [b].

MARGRY, P.J.: Accommodatie en innovatie met betrekking tot traditionele rituelen. Bedevaarten en processies in de moderne tijd, in M. VAN UDEN, J. PIEPER, P. POST (eds.): *Oude sporen, nieuwe wegen. Ontwikkelingen in bedevaartonderzoek* (= UTP-Katernen, 17) (Baarn 1995) 169-202 [a].

MARGRY, P.J. (ed.): *Goede en slechte tijden: het Amsterdams Mirakel van Sacrament in historisch perspectief* (Aerdenhout 1995) [b].

MARGRY, P.J.: In Memoriam Miraculi. Jubelfeesten rond het Amsterdams sacramentsmirakel, in A. VAN DEN HOUT, P.J. MARGRY & R. SCHILLEMANS (eds.): *Het Mirakel: 650 jaar Mirakel van Amsterdam (catalogus), 1345-1995* (Aerdenhout 1995) 20-34 [c].

MARGRY, P.J.: De Bene-bedevaart: grensoverschrijdende "begankenis" tussen België en Nederland, in *Volkskunde* 97,3 (1996) 350-361.

MARGRY, P., & CH. CASPERS (eds.): *Bedevaartplaatsen in Nederland*, Vol. 1: *Noord- en Midden-Nederland* (Hilversum/Amsterdam 1997).

MARGRY P.J., & P. POST: Het project "Bedevaartplaatsen in Nederland": een plaatsbepaling, in *Volkskundig Bulletin. Tijdschrift voor Nederlandse cultuurwetenschap* 20,1 (1994) 19-5 = Wallfahrt zwischen Inventarisierung und Analyse. Ein niederländisches Forschungsprojekt in historiographischem und methodologischem Kontext, in *Rheinisch-westfälische Zeitschrift für Volkskunde* 39 (1994[1995]) 27-65 [= Chapter 2 in this book].

Maria's Heiligdommen in Nederland en België (Den Bosch: De Katholieke Illustratie [1881]).

Maria's Heiligdommen in Frankrijk, Duitschland, Oostenrijk, Italië enz. (Den Bosch [1882]).

MARQUARD, O.: Kleine Philosophie des Festes, in U. SCHULTZ (ed.): *Das Fest. Eine kulturgeschichte von der Antike bis zur Gegenwart* (München 1988) 413-420.

MARX, W.: Der sakrale Raum als öffentlicher. Elemente einer Ästhetik religiöser Raumgestaltung, in R. BÜRGEL (ed.): *Raum und Ritual. Kirchbau und Gottesdienst in theologischer und ästhetischer Sicht* (Göttingen 1995) 25-38.

MAYR, L.: *Mariae Stammen Buch. Oder täglicher immer werender Onser Lieben Frauen Calender (...)*, 3 Vols (Dillingen 1655).

MEEKAN, D. (ed.): *Adamnen's De Locis Sanctis* (Dublin 1958).

MEER, F: VAN DER: *Apocalypse. Visioenen uit het Boek der Openbaring in de kunst* (Antwerpen 1978).

MEHLER, L.: *Liebfrauengarten. Geschichtliche Beispiele, Legenden, Sagen. Parabeln und Gleichwisse von der Macht und Güte der allerseligsten Jungfrau und Gottesmutter Maria und ihrer Verehrung* (Regensburg 1864).

MEYER, H.B.: Time and the Liturgy: Anthropological Notes on Liturgical Time, in *Studia Liturgica* 14,2-4 (1982) 4-22 = Zeit und Gottesdienst, in *Liturgisches Jahrbuch* 31 (1981) 193-213.

MEYER, M. DE: *Volkskunde-Atlas voor Nederland en Vlaams-België. Commentaar bij de kaarten 21-29 Volksgeneeskunde, stuipen, hoofdpijn, beschermheiligen en bedevaarten tegen hoofdpijn, beschermheiligen en bedevaarten voor het vee* (Antwerpen/Utrecht 1968).

MICHEL, K.M.: Die Magie des Ortes. Über den Wünsch nach authentischen Gedenkstätten und die Liebe zu Ruinen, in *Die Zeit* 12 Sept. 1987.

MICHELL, J.: *New Light on the Ancient Mystery of Glastonbury* (Glastonbury (Somerset) 1990) = *De geheimen van Glastonbury. Een nieuwe visie op het oude mysterie van Glastonbury, Stonehenge en andere krachtplekken uit de Keltische oudheid* (Utrecht/Antwerpen 1993).

MILES, M.R.: Pilgrimage as a Metaphor in the Nuclear Age, in *Theology Today* 45 (1988) 166-179.

MONTEIRO, M., G. ROOIJAKKERS & J. ROSENDAAL (eds): *De dynamiek van religie en cultuur. Geschiedenis van het Nederlands katholicisme* (Kampen 1993).

MONTEIRO, M., G. ROOIJAKKERS & J. ROSENDAAL (eds.): Van hoogaltaar tot tochtportaal, in M. MONTEIRO, G. ROOIJAKKERS & J. ROSENDAAL (eds.): *De dynamiek van religie en cultuur. Geschiedenis van het Nederlands katholicisme* (Kampen 1994) 9-20.

MOOIJ, J.: Krijgsmacht, in P. OSKAMP & N. SCHUMAN (eds.): *De weg van de liturgie. Tradities, achtergronden, praktijk* (Zoetermeer 1998) 413-414.

MOOK, J., W. CHR. KLEIJN & H.M. VAN DER PLOEG: Depressiviteit als dispositie gemeten met de Zung-schaal. Interne structuur en relaties met angst, boosheid, coping en sociale steun, in *Nederlands Tijdschrift voor Psychologie* 44 (1989) 328-340.

MOOK, J., W. CHR. KLEIJN & H.M. VAN DER PLOEG: Een herziene Nederlandse versie van de Zung-schaal als maat voor dispositionele depressiviteit, in *Tijdschrift voor Psychiatrie* 32 (1990) 253-264.

MOOLENBURGH, C.: *Engelen als beschermers en als helpers der mensheid* (Deventer 1990 5th ed. (orig. 1983)).

MOOLENBURGH, C.: *Een engel op je pad: honderd en een engelervaringen* (Deventer 1991).

MOORE, A.C.: Religion und Landschaft. Die spirituellen Landschaften von Caspar David Friedrich und Colin McCahon, in H. SCHWEBEL & A. MERTIN (eds.): *Bilder und ihre Macht. Zur Verhältnis von Kunst und christlicher Religion* (Stuttgart 1989) 80-95.

MOORSEL, P. VAN: *Willibrord en Bonifatius* (Bussum 1968).

MORINIS, A. (ed.): *Sacred Journeys: the Anthropology of Pilgrimage* (= Contributions to the Study of Anthropology, 7) (Westport (Conn.) 1992).

MORRIS, P.A.: The Effect of Pilgrimage on Anxiety, Depression and Religious Attitude, in *Psychological Medicine* 12 (1982) 291-294.

MUCK, H.: *Der Raum. Baugefüge, Bild und Lebenswelt* (= Wiener Akademie Reihe, 19) (Wien 1986).

MUKERJI, C., & M. SCHUDSON (eds.): *Rethinking Popular Culture. Contemporary Perspectives in Cultural Studies* (Berkeley/Los Angeles/Oxford 1991).

MULDER, A., & T. SCHEER (eds.): *Natuurlijke liturgie* (= Liturgie in perspectief, 6) (Heeswijk-Dinther 1996).

MULDER-BAKKER, A.B., & M. CARASSO-KOK (eds.): *Gouden legenden. Heiligenlevens en heiligenverering in de Nederlanden* (Hilversum 1997).

MUNIER, W.: Limburgse simultaankerken, in *Documentatieblad voor de Nederlandse kerkgeschiedenis van de negentiende eeuw* 9 (1981) 12-15.

MUNIER, W.: Het einde van het simultaneum in de kerk van de HH. Nicolaas en Barbara te Valkenburg, in *Publications de la Société Historique et Archéologique dans le Limbourg* 118 (1982) 285-324 [a].

MUNIER, W.: Problemen bij een gemeenschappelijk gebruik van kerken in het verleden, in *Kosmos + Oekumene* 16 (1982) 265-269 [b].

MUNIER, W.: *De beginfase van het z.g. simultaneum in de kerk van de HH. Nicolaas en Barbara te Valkenburg (1632-1687). Katholieken en protestanten in strijd om een kerkgebouw* (Valkenburg 1985).

NEDDENS, M.C., & W. WUCHER (eds.): *Die Wiederkehr des Genius Loci. Die Kirche im Stadtraum – die Stadt im Kirchenraum* (Wiesbaden/Berlin 1987).

NEILLANDS, R.: *The Road to Compostela: Discovering the Pilgrim's Road* (Ashbourne 1985).

NEVILLE, G. KENNEDY: *Kinship and Pilgrimage. Rituals of Reunion in American Protestant Culture* (New York/Oxford 1987).

NEVILLE, G. KENNEDY & J.H. WESTERHOFF: *Outdoor Worship as a Liturgical Form* (=Learning Through Liturgy) (New York 1978).

NIE, N., et al.: *Statistical Package for the Social Sciences* (New York 1975).

NIEDERER, A.: Volkskundliche Forschungsrichtungen in den deutschsprachigen Ländern, in I. CHIVA & U. JEGGLE (eds.): *Deutsche Volkskunde – Französische Ethnologie. Zwei Standort-Bestimmungen* (Frankfurt a.M. 1987) 44-67.

NIEDERMÜLLER, P.: Die Volkskultur und die Symbolisierung der Gesellschaft: Der Mythos der Nationalkultur in Mitteleuropa, in *Tübinger Korrespondenzblatt* 40 (1991) 27-43.

NIEUWLAND, J.: *"De Friezen gedenken zijn wonderbare daden...". De funktie van wonderen in de Friese kersteningstijd* (= Utrechtse Historische Cahiers, 12 nr. 1) (Utrecht 1991).

NISSEN, P.: *De folkorisering van het onalledaagse* (Tilburg 1994).

NISSEN, P.: Grenzen overschrijden. Bedevaart als rituele handeling, in *Communio* 22,3 (1977) 189-200.

NOLAN, M.L., & S. Nolan: *Christian Pilgrimages in Modern Western Europe* (Chapel Hill 1989).

NOORT, G.: *Germaanse cultuur en christianisatie van Noordwest Europa* (= IIMO Research Publication, 35) (Zoetermeer 1993).

NORA, P. (director): *Les lieux de mémoire* (= Bibliothèque illustrée des histoires) (Paris 1984-1992, 3 Parts, 7 Volumes).

OBERHAUSER, G.: *Wallfahrten und Kultstätten im Saarland. Von der Quellenverehrung zur Marienerscheinung* (Saarbrücken 1992).

OLWIG, K.: Sexual Cosmology. Nation and Landscape at the Conceptual Interstices of Nature and Culture; or, What Does Landscape Really Mean?, in B. BENDER (ed.): *Landscapes. Politics and perspectives* (Providence/Oxford 1993) 307-343.

OOSTERWIJK, J., et al.: *Bedevaartonderzoek Wittem* (UTP-Rapport, Heerlen 1986).

OOSTERWIJK, J., M. VAN UDEN & L. HENSGENS: Pilgrimage: motivation and effects, in J. VAN BELZEN & J.M. VAN DER LANS: *Current Issues in the Psychology of Religion* (Amsterdam 1986) 173-182.

OOSTERWIJK J., et al.: *Steun en ontmoeting. Een onderzoek onder bedevaartgangers naar Lourdes* (UTP-Rapport, Heerlen 1987).

ORSI, R.: *The Madonna of the 115th Street: Faith and Community in Italian Harlem, 1880-1950* (New Haven 1985).

OS, H. VAN (ed.): *The Art of Devotion in the Late Middle Ages in Europe, 1300-1500* (London/Amsterdam 1994); = Dutch ed. *Gebed in schoonheid. Schatten van privé-devotie in Europa 1300-1500* (Amsterdam/London 1994).

OSTERRIETH, A.: Medieval Pilgrimage: Society and Individual Quest, in *Social Compass, "Pilgrimage and Modernity"* 36 (1989) 145-157.

PACE, E., et al. (eds.): *Religion et vie quotidienne. A propos de la 16e Conférence intern. de sociologie des religions, Lausanne 1981, = Social Compass* 28,4 (1981).

PACE, E.: Pilgrimage As Spiritual Journey: An Analysis of Pilgrimage Using the Theory of V. Turner and the Resource Mobilization Approach, in *Social Compass, "Pilgrimage and Modernity"* 36 (1989) 229-244.

PANNET, R.: *Le catholicisme populaire. 30 ans après "La France, pays de mission?"* (Paris 1974 (3d ed.)).

PARGAMENT, K.I., et al.: Religion and the Problem-Solving Process: Three Styles of Coping, in *Journal for the Scientific Study of Religion* 27 (1988) 90-104.

PARKER, C.: *Popular Religion and Modernization in Latin America: A Different Logic* (Maryknoll 1996).

Paus Johannes Paulus II in Nederland: 11-15 mei 1985 (Utrecht 1985, ring binder published by Stichting Pausbezoek Nederland) [a].

Paus Johannes Paulus II in Nederland ([Leiden] Roma [1985]) [b].

Pauskrant: Pausbezoek 1985 (Utrecht 1984) (Stichting Pausbezoek Nederland).

Pèlerinages célèbres aux sanctuaires de Notre-Dame (Brugge 1894).

Pelgrimage. Een historische, antropologische en spirituele belichting van een universeel verschijnsel = themanummer *Concilium* 32,4 (1996).

PENTIKÄINEN, J.: Oral Transmission of Knowledge, in R.M. DORSON (ed.): *Folklore in the Modern World* (Den Haag/Paris 1978) 237-252.

PÉREZ, N.: *El culto mariano en España. Histoire Mariale d'Espagne*, 6 Vols. (Valladolid 1941-1948).

PETERS, H.: *Bonifatius in Dokkum. Het verhaal van een levende* (Dokkum n.d.).

PESCH, D. (ed.): *Wallfahrt im Rheinland* (Köln 1981).

PFISTER, P., & H. RAMISCH: *Marienwallfahrten im Erzbistum München und Freising* (Regensburg 1989).

PIEPER, J.: Bedevaart niet gelijk voor jong en oud, in *Korrel. Driemaandelijks tijdschrift voor catechese en godsdienstonderricht* 10 (1988) 151-159 [a].

PIEPER, J.: *God gezocht en gevonden? Een godsdienstpsychologisch onderzoek rond het kerkelijk huwelijk met pastoraaltheologische consequenties* (Nijmegen 1988) [b].

PIEPER, J., J. OOSTERWIJK & M. VAN UDEN: Bedevaart: steun en ontmoeting, in M. VAN UDEN & P. POST: *Christelijke bedevaarten. Op weg naar heil en heling* (Nijmegen 1988) 159-170.

PIEPER, J., P. POST & M. VAN UDEN: Beweegredenen. Sociaal-wetenschappelijke peilingen naar bedevaartmotieven, in *Volkskundig Bulletin. Tijdschrift voor Nederlandse cultuurwetenschap* 16,2 (1990) 176-202 [= Chapter 1 in this book].

PIEPER, J., P. POST & M. VAN UDEN (eds.): *Bedevaart en pelgrimage tussen traditie en moderniteit* (= UTP-Katernen, 16) (Baarn 1994).

PIEPER, J., & M. VAN UDEN: *Bidden in Banneux. Een onderzoek onder bedevaartgangers naar Banneux* (= UTP-Rapport) (Heerlen 1988).

PIEPER, J., & M. VAN UDEN: Wallfahrt: Hilfe und Begegnung, in *Archiv für Religionspsychologie* 19 (1990) 243-255.

PIEPER, J., & M. VAN UDEN: De huidige Lourdesbedevaart: motieven en effecten, in M. VAN UDEN & J. PIEPER (eds.): *Bedevaart volksreligieus ritueel* (Heerlen 1991) 7-26.

PIEPER, J., & M. VAN UDEN: Wallfahrt als Glaubensentwicklung. Wandlung und Festigung, in *Archiv für Religionspsychologie* 20 (1992) 270-283 [= Chapter 5 in this book].

PIEPER, J., & M. VAN UDEN: Lourdes: A Place of Religious Transformations?, in *International Journal for the Psychology of Religion* 4 (1994) 91-104 [= Chapter 7 in this book].

PIEPER, J., & M. VAN UDEN: Op weg naar Santiago de Compostela. Ervaringen van pelgrims, in M. VAN UDEN, J. PIEPER & P. POST (eds.): *Oude sporen, nieuwe wegen. Ontwikkelingen in bedevaartonderzoek* (= UTP-Katernen, 17) (Baarn 1995) 53-83.

PIETRI, L.: Le pèlerinage martinien de Tours à l'époque de l'évêque Grégoire, in *Actes du XIIIe congrès du Centre d'études sur la spiritualité médiévale* (1971) (Todi 1977) 95-139.

PIETRI, L.: Bâtiments et sanctuaires annexes de la basilique Saint-Martin de Tours à la fin du VIe siècle, in *Revue d'histoire de l'église de France* 62 (1975) 223-224.

PIMENTEL, A.: *História do Culto de Nossa Senhora em Portugal* (Lisboa s.a.).

PLATVOET, J., & K. VAN DER TOORN (eds.): *Pluralism and Identity: Studies in Ritual Behaviour* (= Studies in the history of religions, 67) (Leiden 1995).

PLECHL, P.M.: *Wallfahrt in Österreich* (Wien 1988).

PLOEG, H.M. VAN DER, P.B. DEFARES & C.D. SPIELBERGER: *Handleiding bij de Zelf-Beoordelingsvragenlijst* (Lisse 1980).

PLÖTZ, R.: (ed.): *Europäische Wege der Santiago Pilgerfahrt: Ergebnisse der 2. Tagung der deutschen St. Jakobus Geselschaft, Bamberg 29 sept. bis 2 Okt. 1988* (Tübingen 1990).

PLONGERON, B., & R. PANNET (eds.): *Le christianisme populaire. Les dossiers de l'histoire* (Paris 1976).

POST, H.: *Te voet naar Rome. In het spoor van Bertus Aafjes* (= Rome-bibliotheek, 1) (Schoorl 1991).

POST, P.: Tijd en liturgie, in *Rond de Tafel* nov. (1981) 227-235.

POST, P.: Houvast bij geloven en weerbaar pastoraat. Enkele notities vanuit verleden en heden m.b.t. het complexe pastoraaltheologische waarderingsproces inzake volksreligiositeit, in A. BLIJLEVENS, A. BRANTS & E. HENAU (eds.): *Volksreligiositeit: uitnodiging en uitdaging* (= HTP-Studies, 3) (Averbode 1982) 99-126.

POST, P.: Het liturgische spel: implikaties en voorwaarden vanuit omgang met symbolen, in *Werkmap [voor] liturgie* 20,3 (1986) 157-173.

POST, P.: Iconisering of ontbeelding? Enkele notities over de ontwikkeling van de beeldzijde van bidprentjes met de ikoon als invalshoek, in *Jaarboek voor liturgie-onderzoek* 4 (1988) 235-277 [a].

POST, P.: Onderweg. Tussentijdse notities met betrekking tot bedevaartonderzoek, in M. VAN UDEN en P. POST (eds.): *Christelijke bedevaarten. Op weg naar heil en heling* (Nijmegen 1988) 1-38 [b].

POST, P.: Bedevaart zonder grenzen, in *Tijdschrift voor liturgie* 73 (1989) 135-156 [a].

POST, P.: Raum und Ritus, in *Jaarboek voor liturgie-onderzoek* 5 (1989) 301-321 [b].

POST, P.: "Het suizen van een zachte koelte...". Het weer en christelijke rituelen: terreinverkenning en pleidooi voor wetenschappelijk grensverkeer gethematiseerd via palmzondagriten, in *Volkskundig Bulletin. Tijdschrift voor Nederlandse cultuurwetenschap* 15,2 (1989) 177-200 [c].

POST, P.: John Bossy and the Study of Liturgy, in Ch. CASPERS & M. SCHNEIDERS (eds.): *Omnes circumadstantes: Contributions Towards a History of the Role of the People in Liturgy* (Kampen 1990) 31-50 [a].

POST, P.: Sociale geschiedenis van het christendom volgens John Bossy, in *Volkskundig Bulletin. Tijdschrift voor Nederlandse cultuurwetenschap* 16 (1990) 203-210 [b].

POST, P.: Ruimte voor liturgie: enkele notities over de analyse van heilige plaatsen, in J. VAN LAARHOVEN et al. (eds.): *Munire Ecclesiam. Opstellen over gewone gelovigen* (Maastricht 1990) 343-349 [c].

POST, P.: Beeld en ritueel (= review article), in *Volkskundig Bulletin. Tijdschrift voor Nederlandse cultuurwetenschap* 17,3 (1991) 269-285 [a].

POST, P.: Het verleden in het spel? Volksreligieuze rituelen tussen cultus en cultuur, in *Jaarboek voor liturgie-onderzoek* 7 (1991) 79-124 [b].

POST, P.: Volksreligieuze rituelen tussen cultus en cultuur, in M. VAN UDEN & J. PIEPER (eds.): *Bedevaart als volksreligieus ritueel* (= UTP-Teksten, 16) (Heerlen 1991) 47-76 [c].

POST, P.: Traditie gebruiken. Sint Hubertus in Muiderberg, in M. VAN UDEN, J. PIEPER & E. HENAU (eds.): *Bij geloof. Over bedevaarten en andere uitingen van volksreligiositeit* (= UTP-Katernen, 11) (Hilversum 1991) 191-210 [d].

POST, P.: Ikonographische und ikonologische Erkundungen über aktuelle Entwicklungen der Bildseite niederländischer Totenzettel, in T. DEKKER, P. HÖHER, P. POST & H. SIUTS (eds.): *Ausbreitung bürgerlicher Kultur in den Niederlanden und Nordwestdeutschland* (= Beiträge zur Volkskultur in Nordwestdeutschland herausgegeben von der Volkskundlichen Kommission für Westfalen Landschaftsverband Westfalen-Lippe, Heft 74) (Münster 1991) 126-172 [e].

POST, P.: Beeld, ritueel en kunst. Enkele momenten uit het complexe samenspel van beeld en christelijk ritueel nader belicht, in J. LAMBERTS (ed.): *Liturgie en kunst* (= UTP-Teksten, 29) (Heerlen 1992) 24-48 [a].

POST P.: Pelgrimsverslagen: verkenning van een genre, in *Jaarboek voor liturgie-onderzoek* 8 (1992) 285-331 [b].

POST, P.: De pastor aan de bron: over de opbloei van Dokkum als Bonifatiusstad, in F. JESPERS & E. HENAU (eds.): *Liturgie en kerkopbouw; opstellen aangeboden aan Ad Blijlevens* (Baarn 1993) 240-268.

POST, P.: Pelgrims tussen traditie en moderniteit. Een verkenning van hedendaagse pelgrimsverslagen, in J. PIEPER, P. POST & M. VAN UDEN (eds.): *Bedevaart en pelgrimage* (= UTP-Katernen, 16) (Baarn 1994) 7-37 [a].

POST, P.: Thema's, trends en theorieën in bedevaartonderzoek, in J. PIEPER, P. POST & M. VAN UDEN (eds.): *Bedevaart en pelgrimage tussen traditie en moderniteit* (= UTP-Katernen, 16) (Baarn 1994) 253-302 [b].

POST, P. (coordination): Bibliografie, in PIEPER, J, P. POST & M. VAN UDEN (eds.): *Bedevaart en pelgrimage. Tussen traditie en moderniteit* (= UTP-Katernen, 16) (Baarn 1994) 277-301 [c].

POST, P.: The Modern Pilgrim. A Study of Contemporary Pilgrims' Accounts, in *Ethnologia Europaea* 24 (1994[1995]) 85-100 [d] [= Chapter 9 in this book].

POST, P.: Volkskunde in Nederland. Notities over disciplinaire eigenheid, in T. DEKKER, P. POST & H. ROODENBURG (eds.): *Antiquaren, liefhebbers en professoren. Momenten uit de geschiedenis van de Nederlandse volkskunde,* = *Volkskundig Bulletin. Tijdschrift voor Nederlandse cultuurwetenschap* 20,3 (1994) 229-243 [e].

POST, P.: Belangstelling vergeleken: een actuele plaatsbepaling van de Nederlandse volkskunde, in T. DEKKER, P. POST & H. ROODENBURG (eds.): *Antiquaren, liefhebbers en professoren. Momenten uit de geschiedenis van de Nederlandse volkskunde,* = *Volkskundig Bulletin. Tijdschrift voor Nederlandse cultuurwetenschap* 20,3 (1994) 414-427 [f].

POST, P.: Goede tijden, slechte tijden: devotionele rituelen tussen traditie en moderniteit, in P.J. MARGRY (ed.): *Goede en slechte tijden: het Amsterdamse Mirakel van Sacrament in historisch perspectief* (Aerdenhout 1995) 62-80 [a] [= Chapter 11].

POST, P.: *Ritueel landschap: over liturgie-buiten. Processie, pausbezoek, danken voor de oogst, plotselinge dood* (= Liturgie in perspectief, 5) (Heeswijk-Dinther 1995; inaugurele rede Theologische Faculteit Tilburg) [b].

POST, P.: Zeven notities over rituele verandering, traditie en (vergelijkende) liturgiewetenschap, in *Jaarboek voor liturgie-onderzoek* 11 (1995) 1-30 [c].

POST, P.: De creatie van traditie volgens Eric Hobsbawm, in *Jaarboek voor liturgie-onderzoek* 11 (1995) 77-101 [d].

POST, P.: Het wonder van Dokkum en andere verhalen van afstand en betrokkenheid. Lokale pastorale interactie op heilige plaatsen vergeleken, in M. VAN UDEN, J. PIEPER & P. POST (eds.): *Oude sporen, nieuwe wegen. Ontwikkelingen in bedevaartonderzoek* (= UTP-Katernen, 17) (Baarn 1995) 107-132 [e].

POST, P.: "God kijkt niet op een vierkante meter..." of Hobsbawm herlezen, in C. VAN DER BORGT et al. (eds.): *Constructie van het eigene. Culturele vormen van regionale identiteit in Nederland* (= Publikaties van het P.J. Meertens-Instituut, 25) (Amsterdam 1996) 175-200 [a].

POST, P.: Liturgische beweging en feestcultuur. Een landelijk onderzoeksprogramma, in *Jaarboek voor liturgie-onderzoek* 12 (1996) 21-55 [b].

POST, P.: Een idyllisch feest. Over de natuurthematiek in Brabantse oogstdankvieringen, in A. MULDER & T. SCHEER (eds.): *Natuurlijke liturgie* (= Liturgie in perspectief, 6) (Heeswijk-Dinther 1996) 118-139 [c].

POST, P.: Paysage rituel: liturgie en plein air (I), in *Question Liturgiques / Studies in Liturgy* 77 (1996) 174-190 [d].

POST, P.: Paysage rituel: la liturgie en plein air (II): la visite du pape, action de grâce pour la moisson, rites autour d'une mort subite, in *Questions Liturgiques / Studies in Liturgy* 77 (1996) 240-256 [e].

POST, P.: De moderne pelgrim: (een) christelijk ritueel tussen traditie en (post)-moderniteit, in *Concilium* 4 (1996) 114-125 [f].

POST, P.: Rituals and the Function of the Past: Rereading Eric Hobsbawm, in *Journal of Ritual Studies* 10,2 (1996 [1998]) 85-107 [g].

POST, P.: Katakomben in Valkenburg: religieus landschap tussen folly en museum, in J. OFFERMANS et al. (eds.): *Ontgonnen verleden: opstellen over de geschiedenis van oostelijk Zuid-Limburg aangeboden aan L. Augustus* (= Werken uitgegeven door het Limburgs Geschied- en Oudheidkundig Genootschap, 15) (Maastricht 1996) 417-442 [g].

POST, P.: Liturgische bewegingen: een literatuurbericht, in *Praktische Theologie* 24,1 (1997) 59-80 [a].

POST, P. (ed.): *Een ander huis. Kerkarchitectuur na 2000* (= Liturgie in perspectief, 7) (Baarn 1997) [b].

POST, P.: Alle dagen feest, of: de ritencrisis voorbij. Een verkenning van de markt, in P. POST & W. SPEELMAN (eds.): *De Madonna van Bijenkorf. Bewegingen op de rituele markt* (= Liturgie in perspectief, 9) (Baarn 1997) 11-32 [c].

POST, P.: Dokkum, in P.J. MARGRY & Ch. CASPERS (eds.): *Bedevaartplaatsen in Nederland, Deel 1: Noord- en Midden-Nederland* (Hilversum/Amsterdam 1997) 290-304 and 304-306 [d].

POST, P.: Post-modern Pilgrimage: Christian Ritual between Liturgy and "Topolatry," in A. HOUTMAN, M. POORTHUIS & J. SCHWARTZ (eds.): *Sanctity of Time and Space in Tradition and Modernity* (Leiden 1998) 299-315.

POST, P., & J. KERKHOVEN: Historische kringen in de regio tussen Vecht en Eem en hun periodieken. Een landelijk perspectief, in *Tussen Vecht en Eem* 11 (1993) 153-179.

POST, P., P. NISSEN & C. CASPERS (eds.): *Religie thuis*, = *Trajecta* 4,2 (1995) 95-179 [a].

POST, P., P. NISSEN & C. CASPERS, Religie thuis: religiebeleving in het katholieke huisgezin in Nederland rond 1900, in P. POST, P. NISSEN & C. CASPERS (eds.): *Religie thuis*, = *Trajecta* 4,2 (1995) 95-102 [b].

POST, P., & J. PIEPER: *De palmzondagviering: een landelijke verkenning* (Amsterdam/Kampen 1992) [a].

POST, P., & J. PIEPER: De palmzondagviering. Verslag van een landelijke verkenning, in *Tijdschrift voor liturgie* 76,6 (1992) 365-388 [b].

POST, P., & W. SPEELMAN (eds.): *De Madonna van Bijenkorf. Bewegingen op de rituele markt* (= Liturgie in perspectief, 9) (Baarn 1997).

POST, P., & M. VAN UDEN: *Christelijke bedevaart: verschijningsvorm, functies en pastoraal-theologische implicaties van een volksreligieus fenomeen. Omschrijving van het UTP-onderzoeksprogramma Christelijke bedevaart 1986-1991* (= UTP-Rapport) (Heerlen 1985).

PURCELL, W.: *Pilgrim's England* (London/New York 1981).

QUASTEN, J.: Wallfahrtsorte in Westfalen und am Niederrhein. Zu Geschichte und Brauchtum, in *Volk und Volkstum* 1 (1936) 181-200.

QUELHAS BIGOTE, J.: *O culto de Nossa Senhora na diocese da Guarda* (Lisboa 1948).

RAEDTS, P.: De christelijke Middeleeuwen: ontstaan en gebruik van een mythe, in *Toespraken Academische Zitting* (Utrecht: Katholieke Theologische Universiteit, 1990) 17-30 [a].

RAEDTS, P.: De christelijke middeleeuwen als mythe, in *Tijdschrift voor theologie* 30,2 (1990) 146-158 [b].

RAEDTS, P.: Le Saint Sacrement du Miracle d'Amsterdam: lieu de mémoire de l'identité catholique, in P. DEN BOER & W. FRIJHOFF (eds.): *Lieux de mémoire et identités nationales* (Amsterdam 1993) 237-252.

RAEDTS, P.: *Toerisme in de tijd?: over het nut van Middeleeuwse geschiedenis* (= inaugural lecture Katholieke Universiteit Nijmegen) (Nijmegen 1995).

RAHNER, K., et al. (eds.): *Volksreligion – Religion des Volkes* (Stuttgart etc. 1979).

RAJKOVIC, Z.: Roadside Memorial Signs for Traffic Accident Victims, in *Narodna Umjetnost. Annual of Institute of Folklore Research Zagreb (= special issue)* 2 (1988) 167-178.

READER, I.: From Ascetism to the Package Tour: the Pilgrims Progress in Japan, in *Religion* 17 (1987) 133-148.

READER, I., & T. WALTER (eds.): *Pilgrimage in Popular Culture* (Houndmills 1993).

REEKMANS, L.: Siedlungsbildung bei spätantike Wallfahrtsstätten, in E. DASSMANN & S. SUSO FRANK (eds.): Pietas (Festschrift B. Kötting) (= Jahrbuch für Antike und Christentum Erg. Bd. 8) (Münster 1980) 325-358.

REEN, T. VAN: *Een heidin die het licht zag. Roomse fabels* (Amsterdam 1994).

REIS, J. DOS: *Invocaçôes de Nossa Senhora em Portugal d'Aquém e d'Além-Mara e seu Padroado* (Lisboa 1967).

Religion populaire et réforme liturgique, = *La Maison-Dieu* 122 (1975).

Religieuze thematiek in de Belgische kunst 1875-1985 (Brussel 1986) (catalogue).

RÉMY, J.: Religion, rationalité et dynamique affective. Hypothèses en vue d'interpréter les résurgences de formes religieuses dans une société sécularisée, in *Social Compass* 31 (1984) 221-231.

RÉMY, J.: Pilgrimage and Modernity, in *Social Compass* 36,2 (1989) 139-143 / 145-261.

RENATO, A.V.P.: *Marianischer Gnaden-Fluß, Abgetheilt in 31 Geistliche Bücher (...)* (Mainz 1768).

REUME, A.D.: *Les Vierges miraculeuses de la Belgique* (Bruxelles 1856).

RHO, J., & C. BOVIO: *Marianischer Gnaden- und Wunder-Schatz. Das ist: vilfältige, auch durch scheinbahre Wunderwerck von der seeligsten Jungfrau und Göttlichen Mutter Maria* (2 Vols. Augsburg 1737).

RICHARD, J.: *Les récits de voyages et de pèlerinages* (= Typologie des sources du Moyen Âge occidental, 38) (Turnhout 1981).

RICHTER, Kl.: Liturgisches Handeln und gottesdienstlicher Raum. Eine Verhältnisbestimmung aus katholischer Sicht heute, in R. BÜRGEL (ed.): *Raum und Ritual. Kirchbau und Gottesdienst in theologischer und ästhetischer Sicht* (Göttingen 1995) 57-76.

RITTER, J.: *Landschaft. Zur Funktion des ästhetischen in der modernen Gesellschaft* (Münster 1978).

RITZEMA, R.J., & C. YOUNG: Causal Schemata and the Attribution of Supernatural Causality, in *Journal of Psychology and Theology* 11 (1983) 36-43.

RODING, J.: Hedendaagse pelgrims naar Santiago de Compostela. Over pelgrimage en religieuze identiteit, in M. VAN UDEN, J. PIEPER & E. HENAU (eds.): *Bij geloof. Over bedevaarten en andere uitingen van volksreligiositeit* (= UTP-Katernen, 11) (Heerlen 1991) 83-104 [a].

RODING, J.: Pelgrims naar Santiago, in M. VAN UDEN & J. PIEPER (eds.): *Bedevaart als volksreligieus ritueel* (= UTP-Teksten, 16) (Heerlen 1991) 27-36 [b].

RÖHRICH, L.: Erzählforschung, in R.W. BREDNICH (ed.): *Grundriss der Volkskunde. Einführung in die Forschungsfelder der Europäischen Ethnologie* (Berlin 1988): 353-380.

RÖHRICHT, R., & H. MEISNER: *Deutsche Pilgerreisen nach dem Heiligen Lande* (Berlin 1880).

RÖTTGERS, K.: Die Erzählbarkeit des Lebens, in *BIOS* 1 (1988) 5-18.

ROES, J.: Van grote klok tot milieumissie. Volksmissies en katholieke beweging in Nederland in de 19de en 20ste eeuw, in *Trajecta* 2,3 (1993) 273-294.

ROGIER, L.J.: *Geschiedenis van het katholicisme in Noord-Nederland in de 16e en de 17e eeuw*, II (Amsterdam 1947 (2nd ed.)).

ROOIJAKKERS, G.: Volk en massa als elitaire misleiders. het ideeën-archeologisch pleidooi van Irene Cieraad, in *Volkscultuur* 7,2 (1990) 73-84.

ROOIJKAKKERS, G.: Opereren op het snijpunt van culturen: Middelaars en media in Zuid-Nederland, in P. TE BOEKHORST, P. BURKE & W. FRIJHOFF (eds.): *Cultuur en maatschappij in Nederland 1500-1850* (Meppel/Amsterdam/Heerlen 1992) 245-283.

ROOIJAKKERS, G.: *Rituele repertoires. Volkscultuur in oostelijk Noord-Brabant 1559-1853* (Nijmegen 1994).

ROOIJAKKERS, G. & TH. VAN DER ZEE (eds.): *Religieuze volkscultuur. De spanning tussen de voorgeschreven orde en de geleefde praktijk* (Nijmegen 1986).

RORDORFF, W., & A. TUILIER (eds.): *La doctrine des Douze Apôtres (Didache)* (= Sources Chrétiennes, 248) (Paris 1978).

ROSS, M.E, & C.L. ROSS: Mothers, Infants, and the Psychoanalytic Study of Ritual, in *Signs: Journal of Woman in Culture and Society* 9 (1983) 26-39.

ROYMANS, N.: The Cultural Biography of Urnfields and the Long-Term History of a Mythical Landscape, in *Archaeological Dialogues* 2,1 (1995) 2-24 (= Discussion-Article 1).

RUBIN, M.: *Corpus Christi: The Eucharist in Late Medieval Culture* (Cambridge 1991).

SALLNOW, M.J.: Communitas Reconsidered. The Sociology of Andean Pilgrimage, in *Man* 16 (1981) 163-182.

SALOMONSSON, A.: Some Thoughts On the Concept of Revitalization, in *Ethnologia Scandinavica* (1984) 34-47.

SANCHEZ PEREZ, J.A.: *El cultu Mariano en España* (Madrid 1943).

SANTA MARIA, A. DE: *Sanctuario Mariano, ou Historia das imagens milagrosas de Nossa Senhora veneradas em todo o reino de Portugal e seus dominios* (10 Vols. Lisboa 1707-1723).

Santi e Santuari. Atlante dei personaggi e dei luoghi della fede, 4 Vols. (Milano 1979).

SCHAMA, S.: *Landscape and Memory* (New York 1995).

SCHARFE, M.: Totengedenken; zur Historizität von Brauchtraditionen; das Beispiel Olof Palme 1986, in *Ethnologia Scandinavica* 19 (1989) 142-153.

SCHARFE, M. (ed.): *Brauchforschung* (Darmstadt 1991).

SCHARFE, M., M. SCHMOLZE & G. SCHUBERT (eds.): *Wallfahrt – Tradition und Mode. Empirische Untersuchungen zur Aktualität von Volksfrömmigkeit* (= Untersuchungen des Ludwig-Uhland-Instituts der Universität Tübingen 65. Bd. Tübinger Vereinigung für Volkskunde) (Tübingen 1985).

SCHAUBER, V., & H.M. SCHINDLER: *Heilige und Namenspatrone im Jahreslauf* (Augsburg 1992).

SCHEEPMAKER, N. (text): *De paus in Nederland: 11 t/m 15 mei 1985* (Weesp 1985) (photo book).

SCHEER, A.: Bedenkingen bij het liturgisch jaar, in *Tijdschrift voor liturgie* 76 (1992) 294-309.

SCHEMMANN, Ch.K.: *Wallfahrten im Gebirge. 50 Wanderungen in den Alpen* (München 1991).

SCHENDA, R.: Leser- und Lesestoff-Forschung, in R.W. BREDNICH (ed.): *Grundriss der Volkskunde. Einführung in die Forschungsfelder der Europäischen Ethnologie* (Berlin 1988) 381-398.

SCHILSON, A.: Fest und Feier in anthropologischer und theologischer Sicht, in *Liturgisches Jahrbuch* 44,1 (1994) 4-32.

SCHILSON, A.: Das neue Religiöse und der Gottesdienst. Liturgie vor einer neuen Herausforderung?, in *Liturgisches Jahrbuch* 46,2 (1996) 94-109.

SCHLAFKE, J.: *Wallfahrt im Erzbistum Köln* (Köln 1989).

SCHMIDT: P.: *Het Lam Gods* (Leuven 1995).

SCHOONHOVEN, G. VAN: De tweede zerk. Rouwen op de plek van de ramp is oud ritueel, in *Elsevier* 25.09.1993, p. 32.

SCHOUTENS, S.: *Maria's Brabant of Beschrijving van de Wonderbeelden en merkweerdige Bedevaartplaatsen van Onze-Lieve-Vrouw in Brabant* (Sint-Truiden: Schouberechts-Vanwest 1877).

SCHREIBER, Chr.: *Wallfahrten durchs Deutsche Land. Eine Pilgerfahrt zu Deutschlands heiligen Stätten* (Berlin 1928).

SCHROUBEK, G.R.: Traditionelle Wallfahrts- und Andachtsstätten: zur Frömmigkeitsgeschichte der Diözese Budweis, in K.A. HUBER (ed.): *Festschrift zu zweiten Säkularfeier des Bistums Budweis 1785-1985* (Königstein 1985) 211-278.

SCHULTE STAADE, R. (ed.): *350 Jahre Kevelaer-Wallfahrt, 1642-1992,* 2 Vols. (Kevelaer 1992).

SCHWINKELS, K., et al. (eds.): *Monumentjes van devotie: wegkruisen en veldkapellen in de gemeente Venray* (Venray 1991 (2nd ed.)).

SCOTT, J., & P. SIMPSON-HOUSLEY (eds.): *Sacred Places and Profane Spaces. Essays in the Geographics of Judaism, Christianity and Islam* (= Contributions to the Study of Religion, 30) (Westport 1991).

SCRIBNER, R.: Ritual and Popular Religion in Catholic Germany At the Time of the Reformation, in IDEM: *Popular Culture and Popular Movements in Reformation Germany* (London/Ronceverte 1987) 17-48.

SCRIBNER, R.: Symbolising Bounderies. Defining Space in the Daily Life of Early Modern Germany, in G. BLASCHITZ et al. (ed.): *Symbole des Alltags, Alltag der Symbole* (= Festschrift H. Kühnel) (Graz 1992) 821-841.

SCRIBNER, R.W.: Volksglaube und Volksfrömmigkeit. Begriffe und Historiographie, in H. MOLITOR & H. SMOLINSKY (eds.): *Volksfrömmigkeit in der frühen Neuzeit* (Münster 1994) 121-138.

SCRIBNER, R., & T. JOHNSON (eds.): *Popular Religion in Germany and Central Europe, 1400-1800* (Series: Themes in Focus) (Basingstoke etc. 1996).

SEEMAN, Kl.-D.: *Die altrussische Wallfahrtsliteratur: Theorie und Geschichte eines literarischen Genres* (= Theorie und Geschichte der Literatur und der schönen Künste: Texte und Abhandlungen, Bd. 24) (München 1976).

Seminario di studio sulle celebrazioni Pontificie, Cit.d. Vaticano 28-30 dec. 1987 (published by the Ufficio per le ceremonie pontificie).

SEYBOLD, K.: *Die Wallfahrtspsalmen* (Neukirchen 1978).

SIVRY L. DE, & M. CHAMPAGNAC: *Dictionnaire géographique, historique, descriptif, archéologique des Pèlerinages anciens en modernes et les lieux de dévotion les plus célèbres de l'univers*, 2 Vols. (Parijs 1859).

SLOSSE, R.: *Waar men gaat langs Vlaamse wegen, 2 Vols. [Volksdevotie in West-Vlaanderen en de Westhoek]* (Roeselare [ca.1980]).

SNOEK, G.J.C.: *De eucharistie- en reliekverering in de middeleeuwen. De middeleeuwse eucharistie-devotie en reliekverering in onderlinge samenhang* (Amsterdam 1989) = SNOEK, G.J.C: *Medieval Piety from Relics to the Eucharist: a Process of Mutual Interaction* (= Studies in the History of Christian Thought, 63) (Leiden 1995).

SOERGEL, P.M.: *Wondrous in His saints. Counter-Reformation Propaganda in Bavaria* (Berkeley 1993).

SPEELMAN, W.M.: The Plays of our Culture. A Formal Differentiation Between Theatre and Liturgy, in *Jaarboek voor liturgie-onderzoek* 9 (1993) 65-81.

SPERELLI, A.: *Schutz-Mantel Mariae der Allzeit gebenedeyten Jungfrauen und Mutter Gottes (...) in 52 Wundergeschichten (...)* (Nürnberg 1679).

SPERBER, J.: *Popular Catholicism in Nineteenth Century Germany* (Princeton 1984).

SPIERTZ, F.: Volksreligiositeit: een literatuuroverzicht, in A. BLIJLEVENS, A. BRANTS & E. HENAU (eds.): *Volksreligiositeit: uitnodiging en uitdaging* (= HTP-Studies, 3) (Averbode 1982) 159-189.

SPIERTZ, F.: *De katholieke liturgie in de Noordelijke Nederlanden in de zeventiende en achttiende eeuw, met bijlage: het Rituale Contractum et Abbreviatum van de Noordelijke Nederlanden; tekstkritische uitgave*, 2 Vols. (Nijmegen 1991-1992).

SPILKA, B., P. SHAVER & L.A. KIRKPATRICK: A General Attribution Theory for the Psychology of Religion, in *Journal for the Scientific Study of Religion* 24 (1985) 1-20.

SPINELLUS, P.A.: *Maria Dei Para Thronus Dei. De B. Mariae Virginis Laudibus Praeclarissimis* (Köln 1619).

STAAL, F.: The Meaninglessness of Ritual, in *Numen* 26,1 (1979) 2-22.

STAAL, C., & M. WINGENS: *Bedevaarten in Nederland* (Zutphen 1997).

STAUFFER, A.: Worship and Culture: A Select Bibliography, in *Studia liturgica* 27 (1997) 102-128.

STERN, J.: La Salette: bibliographie – état de la question, in *Ephemerides Mariologicae* 22 (1972) 337-355.

STERN, J.: *La Salette, Documents authetiques: dossiers chronologiques intégrals, Vol. 1: Septembre 1846 – début mars 1847* (Paris 1980).

STERN, J.: *Idem: Vol. 2: Le procès de l'apparition fin mars 1847 – avril 1849* (Paris 1984).

STEINER, P.B.: *Altmünchener Gnadenstätten* (München 1977).

STEINER, P.B.: *Gnadenstätten zwischen München und Landshut* (München 1979).

STEINER, P.B., & G. BRENNINGER: *Gnadenstätten im Erdinger Land* (München 1986).

STOCK, A.: Katholizismus, in U. TWORUSCHKA (ed.): *Heilige Stätten* (Darmstadt 1994) 9-19.

STOCK, A.: *Poetische Dogmatik* 1-4 (Paderborn 1996ss.).

STRUYKER BOUDIER, C. (ed.): *Titus Brandsma. Herzien – herdacht – herschreven* (Baarn 1993).

STURM, E.: Museifizierung und Realitätsverlust. Verwandte Begriffe, in W. ZACHARIAS (ed.): *Zeitphänomen Musealisierung. Das Verschwinden der Gegenwart und die Rekonstruktion der Erinnerung* (Essen 1990) 99-114.

SUNDÉN, H.: *Die Religion und die Rollen* (Berlin 1966).

SWAVING, J.G.: *Galerij van Roomsche Beelden of Beeldenstorm der XIX eeuw* (Dordrecht 1824).

TEUNE, P,. & M. TERLINGEN: *Het Nederlandse landschap* (Den Bosch 1986).

THEELEN, T.: *Veldkapellen en wegkruisen in Velden, Arcen en Lomm* (Zaltbommel 1984).

THEILMANN, J.M.: Medieval Pilgrims and the Origins of Tourism, in J.P. CAMPBELL (ed.): *Popular Culture in the Middle Ages* (Bowling Green 1986 (Ohio)) 100-107.

THIERS, O.: *Bedevaart en kerkeraad. De Amersfoortse vrouwenvaart van 1444 tot 1720* (Hilversum 1994).

THIJS, K.L.: Over bedevaarten in Vlaanderen: van stichtelijke propaganda naar wetenschappelijke interesse, in *Volkskunde* 97,3 (1996) 272-349.

THYSSEN, A.: *Antwerpen vermaard door den Eeredienst van Maria. Geschiedkundige Aanmerkingen over de 500 Mariabeelden in de straten der stad* (Antwerpen 1922 (2nd ed.)).

THOMAS, K.: *Man and the Natural world. Changing Attitudes in England 1500-1800* (London 1983).

TONGEREN, L. VAN (ed.): *Toekomst, toen en nu: beschouwingen over de ontwikkeling en de voortgang van de liturgievernieuwing* (= Liturgie in perspectief, 2) (Heeswijk-Dinther 1994).

TONGEREN, L. VAN: Liturgie in context. De vernieuwing van de liturgie en de voortgang ervan als een continu proces, in *Tijdschrift voor liturgie* 81,3 (1997) 178-198.

TOUW, J.M.: *[Huilt Maria in Brunssum?] Wenende Madonna's. Kritische analyse van een fenomeen toegespitst op het huilende Mariabeeldje van Brunssum* (Herkenbosch 1995).

TURI, A.M.: *Pourquoi la Vierge apparaît aujourd'hui* (Paris 1988).

TURNER, V.: *The Ritual Process. Structure and Anti-Structure* (London 1969).

TURNER, V.: The Center Out There: Pilgrim's Goal, in *History of Religions* 12 (1973) 191-230.

TURNER, V.: Pilgrimage and Communitas, in *Studia Missionalia* 23 (1974) 305-327.

TURNER, V.: Variations on a Theme of Liminality, in S.F. MOORE & B.G. MEYERHOFF (eds.): *Secular Ritual* (Assen/Amsterdam 1977) 36-52.

TURNER, V.: *From Ritual to Theatre. The Human Seriousness of Play* (New York 1992 (2nd ed.)).

TURNER, V., & E. TURNER: *Image and Pilgrimage in Christian Culture. Anthropological Perspectives* (New York/Oxford 1978).

TWORUSCHKA, U. (ed.): *Heilige Stätten* (Darmstadt 1994).

UDEN, M. VAN: *Religie in de crisis van de rouw. Een exploratief onderzoek door middel van diepte-interviews* (Nijmegen 1985).

UDEN, M. VAN: Hoop in hopeloze dagen. Godsdienstpsychologische notities rond een eenmalige bedevaart, in: J. VAN BELZEN & J. VAN DER LANS (eds.): *Rond godsdienst en psychoanalyse* (Kampen 1986) 102-114.

UDEN, M. VAN: *Rouw, religie en ritueel* (Baarn 1988).

UDEN, M. VAN: Over heiligen dichtbij en veraf. Reflecties naar aanleiding van een casus, in M. VAN UDEN, J. PIEPER & E. HENAU: *Bij geloof. Over bedevaarten en andereuitingen van volksreligiositeit* (= UTP-Katernen, 11) (Hilversum 1991) 155-162.

UDEN, M. VAN: On Saints. Case-Studies Between Belief Belief and Unbelief, in J. CORVELEYN & D. HUTSEBAUT (eds.): *Belief and Unbelief. Psychological Perspectives* (Amsterdam/Atlanta 1994) 175-184 [= Chapter 10 in this book].

UDEN, M. VAN, & J. PIEPER: Waarom ter bedevaart? Motievenonderzoek bij bedevaartgangers naar Wittem, in M. VAN UDEN & P. POST (eds.): *Christelijke bedevaarten. Op weg naar heil en heling* (Nijmegen 1988) 145-158.

UDEN, M. VAN, & J. PIEPER: Pilgrimage as a Ritual. Analysis of Motivational Structures, in *Proceedings of the Fourth Symposium on the Psychology of Religion in Europe* (Nijmegen 1989) 288-297.

UDEN, M. VAN, & J. PIEPER: Christian Pilgrimage. Motivational Structures and Ritual Functions, in H.-G. HEIMBROCK & H.B. BOUDEWIJNSE (eds.): *Current Studies on Rituals. Perspectives for the Psychology of Religion* (Amsterdam/Atlanta 1990) 165-176.

UDEN, M. VAN, & J. PIEPER (eds.): *Bedevaart als volksreligieus ritueel* (= UTP-Teksten, 16) (Heerlen 1991) [a].

UDEN, M. VAN, & J. PIEPER: Bidden in Banneux. Motieven en belevingen van bedevaartgangers, in M. VAN UDEN, J. PIEPER & E. HENAU (eds.): *Bij geloof. Over bedevaarten en andere uitingen van volksreligiositeit* (= UTP-Katernen, 11) (Hilversum 1991) 55-79 [b].

UDEN, M. VAN, & J. PIEPER: Lourdes: plaats van religieuze transformatie?, in J. PIEPER, P. POST & M. VAN UDEN (eds.): *Bedevaart en pelgrimage. Tussen traditie en moderniteit* (= UTP-Katernen, 16) (Baarn 1994) 39-57.

UDEN, M. VAN, & J. PIEPER: Pilgrims to Santiago. A Case-Study of Their Spiritual Experiences, in *Studies in Spirituality* 6 (1996) 276-288 [= Chapter 8 in this book].

UDEN, M. VAN, J. PIEPER & E. HENAU (eds.): *Bij geloof. Over bedevaarten en andere uitingen van volksreligiositeit* (= UTP-Katernen, 11) (Hilversum 1991).

UDEN, M. VAN, J. PIEPER & E. HENAU; Modern Pilgrimage and Faith, in *Journal of Empirical Theology* 4 (1991) 32-51 [= Chapter 6 in this book].

UDEN, M. VAN, J. PIEPER & P. POST (eds.): *Oude sporen, nieuwe wegen: ontwikkelingen in bedevaartonderzoek* (= UTP Katernen, 17) (Baarn 1995).

UDEN, M. VAN & P. POST (ed.): *Christelijke bedevaarten. Op weg naar heil en heling* (Nijmegen 1988).

UTZ, H.J.: *Wallfahrten im Bistum Regensburg* (München 1981).

VAESSEN, J.: *Musea in een museale cultuur. De problematische legitimering van het kunstmuseum* (Zeist 1986).

VARGAS UGARTE, R.: *Historia des culto de Maria en Hispanoamerica y de sus imagines y santuarios mas celebrados* (Lima 1931).

VEN, J. VAN DER: De structuur van het religieuze bewustzijn. Verkenning van de spanning tussen religiositeit en kerkelijkheid, in *Tijdschrift voor theologie* 36 (1996) 39-60.

VERGOTE, A.: Volkskatholicisme, in A. VERGOTE: *Het meerstemmig leven. Gedachten over mens en religie* (Kapellen/Kampen 1987) 233-250.

VERHEES, J.: *Peerke Donders: apostel van de melaatsen en de indianen* (= Voorbeelden en voorsprekers, 3) (Brugge 1984).

VERHOEVEN, G.: *Devotie en Negotie. Delft als bedevaartplaats in de late middeleeuwen* (Amsterdam 1992).

VERNOOIJ, A.: *Het rooms-katholieke devotielied in Nederland vanaf 1800* (= Kerkmuziek en liturgie, 4) (Voorburg 1990).

Verslag Symposium "Bedevaarten zonder grens. Nieuw onderzoek naar bedevaartcultuur in Nederland en Vlaanderen", = *Volkskunde* 97,3 (1996) 269-379.

VEUILLOT, L.: *Les Pèlerinages de Suisse* (Tours 1893 (1st ed. ca. 1838)).

Volkskunde zwischen Tradition und Modernisierung, = *Schweizerisches Archiv für Volkskunde* 87, 1-2 (1991).

VORGRIMMLER, H.: *Wiederkehr der Engel? Ein altes Thema neu durchdacht* (Kevelaer 1991).

VOS, J.: Historische antropologie: een plaatsbepaling, in *Tijdschrift voor sociale geschiedenis* 20 (1994) 77-98.

VORLÄNDER, H.: *Mein Gott. Die Vorstellungen vom persönlichen Gott im alten Oriënt und im Alten Testament* (Neukirchen 1975).

VROOM, W.: *In tumulto gosico; over relieken en geuzen in woelige tijden* (Nijmegen 1992).

VUIJSJE, H.: *Pelgrim zonder god* (Amsterdam 1990).

VUYK, K.: *De esthetisering van het wereldbeeld. Over filosofie en kunst* (Kampen 1994).

Wallfahrt und Alltag in Mittelalter und frühe Neuzeit. Internationales Round-Table Gespräch. Krems an der Donau 8. Oktober 1990 (Wien 1992).

WALTER, T.: War Grave Pilgrimage, in READER, I. & T. WALTER (eds.): *Pilgrimage in Popular Culture* (Houndsmills etc. 1993) 29-62.

WARD, D.: The Performance and Perception of Folklore and Literature, in *Fabula* 20 (1979) 256-264.

WARNEKEN, B.J. (ed.): *Massenmedium Straße. Zur Kulturgeschichte der Demonstration* (Frankfurt/New York/Paris 1991).

WASSER, B.: *Nederlandse pelgrims naar het heilig land* (Zutphen 1983).

WASSER, B.: *Pelgrimages. Bedevaartplaatsen van de westerse christenheid* (Nijmegen 1993).

WEBER, H.: Wallfahrten und Prozessionen auf dem Rhein, in *Jahrbuch Kölner Geschichtsverein* 45 (1974) 49-62.

Wegkruisen en veldkapellen in Venlo en Blerick (Venlo z.j.).

WEGMAN, H: "Procedere" und Prozession. Eine Typologie, in *Liturgisches Jahrbuch* 27 (1977) 28-41.

WEGMAN, H.: *Riten en mythen. Liturgie in de geschiedenis van het christendom* (Kampen 1991).

WEGMAN, H.: Een vragende voetnoot, in *Jaarboek voor liturgie-onderzoek* 8 (1992) 333-339.

WEGMAN, H.: Liturgie en lange duur, in L. VAN TONGEREN (ed.): *Toekomst, toen en nu. Beschouwingen over de ontwikkeling en voortgang van de liturgievernieuwing* (= Liturgie in perspectief, 2) (Heeswijk-Dinther 1994) 11-38.

WEST, F.S.: *Anton Baumstark's Comparative Liturgy in Its Intellectual Context* (= Ph.D. Diss. Notre Dame University, 1988).

WEST, F.S.: *The Comparative Liturgy of Anton Baumstark* (Joint Liturgical Studies, 31) (Nottingham 1995).

WICHMANS, A.: *Brabantia Mariana Tripartita* (Antwerpen 1632).

WIEL, C. VAN DE: Des "lieux sacrés" dans le nouveau code de droit canonique (canons 1205-1239), in *Question Liturgiques / Studies in Liturgy* 76 (1995) 106-137.

WIJERS, C.: *Prinsen en clowns in het Limburgse narrenrijk. Het carnaval in Simpelveld en Roermond 1945-1992* (= Publikaties van het P.J. Meertens-Instituut, 22) (Amsterdam 1995).

WILKINSON, J.: *Egeria's Travels. Newly Translated [From the Latin] With Supporting Documents and Notes* (London 1973).

WIMMER, C.A.: *Geschichte der Gartentheorie* (Darmstadt 1989).

WINGENS, M.: Van de handt des heeren geraeckt, Miraculeuze genezingen in bedevaartplaatsen nabij de grenzen van de Republiek, 1600-1800, in W. DE BLÉCOURT et al. (eds.): *Grenzen van genezing; gezondheid, ziekte en genezing in Nederland, zestiende tot begin twintigste eeuw* (Hilversum 1993) 68-87.

WINGENS, M.: *Over de grens. De bedevaart van katholieke Nederlanders in de zeventiende en achttiende eeuw* (Nijmegen 1994).

WOODRUFF, C.E. (ed.): *A XVth Century Guide-book to the Principal Churches of Roma, Compiled c. 1470 by William Brewyn* (London 1933).

WOUD, A. VAN DER: *Het lege land. De ruimtelijke orde in Nederland 1798-1848* (Amsterdam 1987).

WOUD, A. VAN DER: *De Bataafse hut. Verschuivingen in het beeld van de geschiedenis (1750-1850)* (Amsterdam 1990).

WOUD, A. VAN DER: *Onuitsprekelijke schoonheid. Waarheid en karakter in de nederlandse bouwkunst* (= inaugural lecture Vrije Universiteit, Amsterdam) (Groningen, 1993).

WYNANDS, D.P.J.: *Geschichte der Wallfahrten im Bistum Aachen* (Aachen 1986).

WYNANDS, D.P.J.: Zum Kult des Gerlach von Houthem – ein einst auch im Rheinland und Westfalen verehrter Heiliger, *Rheinisch-westfälische Zeitschrift für Volkskunde* 37 (1992) 161-177.

ZACHARIAS, W. (ed.): *Zeitphänomen Musealisierung; das Verschwinden der Gegenwart und die Konstruktion der Erinnerung* (Essen 1990).

ZANELLA, A.: *Atlante Mariano*, 12 Vols. (Verona 1839-1847).

ZEEGERS, H., G. DEKKER, J. PETERS: *God in Nederland* (Amsterdam 1967).

ZENDER, M.: *Räume und Schichten mittelalterlicher Heiligenverehrung in ihrer Bedeutung für die Volkskunde. Die Heiligen des mittleren Maaslandes und der Rheinlande in Kultgeschichte und Kultverbreitung* (Düsseldorf 1959).

ZIKA, C.: Hosts, Processions and Pilgrimages: Controlling the Sacred in Fifteenth-Century Germany, in *Past & Present* 118 (1988) 25-64.

ZIMDARS-SWARTZ, S.L.: *Encountering Mary. Visions of Mary from La Salette to Medjugorje* (New York 1991).

ZOVATTO, P.L.: Il significato della basilica doppia, l'esempio di Aquileia, in *Rivista di storia delle chiesa in Italia* XVII (1964) 357-398.

Zu Fuss, zu Pferd. Wallfahrten im Kreis Ravensburg (Weingarten 1990).

ZUNG, W.K.: A Self-Rating Depression Scale, in *Archives of General Psychiatry* 12 (1965) 63-70.

INDEX

Aachen 51, 75
Aafjes, B. 228
accounts, pilgrims accounts 221-242
aestheticization 234, 277, 278, 288
Africa 98, 99
Alkmaar 40
All Souls' Day 308
Amersfoort 92
Amsterdam 10, 15, 51, 228, 263-279, 300, 309
Angenendt, A. 271
Annink, H. 227, 233
Anthony, St. 41
appearance(s) 123, 125
appropriation 6, 7, 108, 140, 141, 226
Arezzo 51
Ariens, Alphons 135
Arles 206
Arnhem 40
Art, J. 5
Auf der Maur, Hj. 274
Austria 57, 65, 66, 74, 80
Assion, P. 224, 225, 226, 239
Assisi 221-243

Baghwan 25
Bamberg 51, 56
Banneux 9, 10, 13, 14, 19, 27, 29, 39-48, 131, 157, 158, 172, 174, 177, 179, 183, 186, 189
baptism 291
Bastiaensen, A. 283
Baumstark, A. 281
Bausinger, H. 4
Bax, M. 23, 126
Beauraing 131, 177
Béco, Mariette 29
Beek 303-306
Beissel, St. 67
Bekkers, Mgr. 135
Bell, C. 97
Belgium 76
Bender, B. 286, 287, 290
Benelux 71-74
Bensa, A. 71
Berbée, P 72, 77, 239
Bergum 297
Bernadette, see Soubirous
Bijlmer (airplane dissaster) 85, 309
Blijlevens, A. 129
Boissevain, J. 223
Boniface, St. 13, 89-94, 95, 121-152, 281, 296-303
Bonn 56, 69, 71
Bosch, L. 227, 233
Bosgra, fa. 297
Bossy, J. 102
Boxtel 297
Brandsma, Titus 89, 90, 269, 298, 303
Brandsma, Nefthys 91, 94, 116, 122
Braun, R. 102, 103
Breda 296
Brielle 297, 301
Brown, P. 269
Brückner, W. 69, 70, 73, 224-226, 239,
Bruillard, Mgr. De, bishop of Grenoble 133, 134
Budapest 110
Burke, P. 226

Cambridge 100, 102
Cannadine, D. 99
carnival 295
Caspers, C. 16, 59
Cauberg (Valkenburg, Grotto of Lourdes) 40
"Celebration of penance" 198
Certeau, M. de 7, 108, 226
Champagnac, M. 65
Chartier, R. 7, 108, 226

Chartres 222
Christ, see Jesus
Christian, Jr., W. 6, 53, 61, 123, 128
Christmas 292, 295
Church (attitude towards) 161-162, 170, 178, 192, 201, 203
civil religion 110
Codex Callixtinus 206
Codex Iuris Canonici 79, 80
Cohn, B.S. 99
Cologne 75
Comenius 85
communitas 33, 54, 78, 190, 191, 202
confession 178
Corps 132-134
Corpus Christi 79, 192 (-procession), 272, 273
Counter Reformation 64, 76
Cox, H. 4
curiosity 37-39, 43, 46-48, 167, 180, 183, 184
custom 105, 106, 109; see also tradition and custom
Cuyk 73
Czestochowa 177

Dayan, D. 307
Daxelmüller, C. 73
Delft 58
Delumeau, J. 4
Den Bosch (Bois-le-Duc) 40, 174, 193, 296, 303-305
Den Haag (The Hague) 40
Derks, F. 174, 201
Devlin, J. 59
devotional ritual 264, 265
diaries 9, 14, 136
Dokkum 10, 13, 15, 89-94, 95, 96, 114-116, 121-152, 268, 281, 296-303, 311
Donders, Peerke 256, 257
"double liturgy" 138-140
Driessen, H. 55
Dünninger, H. 70
Duin, J. 272
Dupront, A. 56

Eade, J. 54, 55, 62, 78, 126
Egeria 283
Enschede 227
Epiphany 295
Ertl, T. 65
Eucharist 158, 263-279, 307
Eyck, Jan van 289

Fenton, A. 16
folklorization, folklorism 11, 62, 95, 96, 102, 235, 288, 294-296
"folkorized liturgy" 294-296, 313
Franken 78
Freiburg 70, 75
Freising 75
Freitag, W. 56, 59,
Friedrich, C.D. 314
Friesland 141
Frijhoff, W. 5, 7, 59, 72, 113
funeral rites 293

Geertz, Cl. 54
Gelderland 30
Gennep, A. van 8, 71, 171, 189, 190,
Gerard Majella, St. 10, 29, 31, 33, 34, 35, 44, 45, 157-172, 174, 269
Germany 57-59, 69-71, 80, 90, 98, 116
Gezelle, Guido 313
Ginzburg, C. 25
Giraud, see Maximin
Glastonbury 131, 140
Görres Gesellschaft 56
Gogh, V. van 314
Graceland 53
Gray, D. 26
Grenoble 132, 133
Gretser, J. 65
Grey, M. 267
Groningen 130, 131
Gugitz G. 68, 69
Gumppenberg, W. 65

Haarlem 29, 39
Habermas, R. 57
Halbertsma, H. 92, 94
Hanbury-Tenison, R. 232

Handel 177
Hart, O. van der 171, 172, 190, 191
Hartinger, W. 57, 284, 286
Hasselt (Belgium) 40
Heerlen 2, 10, 13, 20, 51, 56, 59
Heesterman, J.C. 105
Heeswijk, A. van 16
Heiloo 177, 268, 301
Hersbach, G. 52, 124,
Herwaarden, J. van 58, 300
Holset 131
Hubert, St. 95, 295
Hobsbawm, E. 13, 94-119,
Holy Land 64, 283
Holy Week 291
Horst, P. van der 279
Houdijk, C. & J. 228, 231, 233, 242
Hillsborough (stadium dissaster, April 1989) 26
Hüttl, L. 59
Huijbers, B. 271
Hungary 74

India 98, 99
interviews 9, 28, 159, 164
invention of tradition 62, 94-116
Islamitic pilgrimage 55
Italy 66

James, W. 253
James, St. 222; see also Santiago de Compostela
Jerusalem 206
Jesus 31-35, 38, 41, 42, 45, 48, 132, 143, 176, 177, 181, 194, 199-202
John The Baptist, St. 276
Joseph, St. 41
Judaism 86
Judas Thaddeus, St. 259-262

Kemp, A. van der 66
Kevelaer 44
Kingmans, H. 297
Kirkpatrick 192
Knippenberg, W. 72
Köstlin, K. 238, 284, 309, 312
Kötting, B. 82
Korff, G. 20
Krems an der Donau 51
Kriss R. 67
Kriss-Rettenbeck, L. 69
Kronenburg, J. 67
Kselman, T. 59, 123
"Kulturraumforschung" 24

Lagier, François 132
Lamers, H. 227, 233,
landscape 281-314, esp. 285-290
Lane, B.C. 286
Laurentin, R. 128
Laren 276
Latin America 3, 4
Leiden 29
Leproux, M. 71
Le Puy 206
Liège 29
"lieux de mémoire" 113
Lipp, W. 273
litaniae minores 300
Locrius, F. 65
London 51, 54
Lourdes 9, 10, 13, 14, 19, 27-30, 35-39, 43-48, 79, 128, 130, 131, 135, 137, 157-203, 205, 233, 238, 301
Lubac, H. de 273
Lukken, G. 8

Maastricht 40, 139, 304
McClelland, K. 100
McKevitt, Chr. 126, 127
Mader, D. 16
Manchester 99
marriage 291
Martyrs of Gorcum 301
Meadow, M. 16
Medjugorje 128, 177
Mélanie, François-Mélanie Mathieu 132
Marian devotion 29, 30, 65, 66, 72
Marian festivals 29
Marian pilgrimage sites 65
Maris, J. 298
Margry, P.J. 15, 299, 300

Martin, St. 295
Mary, Blessed Virgin 31, 34-35, 37-39, 41-43, 45, 48, 58, 131-134, 159, 168, 173-188-203, 269
Mary, "Virgin of the poor" 29
Mathieu, see Mélanie
Maximin, Pierre-Maximin Giraud 132, 133
Meertens Institute (Amsterdam) 49, 76, 87
Mélin, pastor of Corps 133-135
Migne, J.-P. 65
miracle(s) 123, 125,
"Miracle of the Blessed Sacrament" 263-279, 300
"Miracle of Dokkum", 129-131, 296-303; see also Dokkum, Brandsma, St. Boniface, spring of St. Boniface
Möller, J., bishop of Groningen 130, 131
Moresnet 131
Morgan, P. 99
Morinis, A. 55, 61, 63, 64, 78,
Morris, P.A. 185
Muiderberg 95
Munich 56, 69, 75
musealization 11, 96, 114, 233-236, 240, 277, 278, 310

Naarden 85
nature 231, 232,
Neville, G. Kennedy 54, 286
"New Age" 130, 140, 141, 268, 270, 271, 290
Niedermüller, P. 112
Nijmegen 2, 10, 51, 73,
Nolan, M.L. & S. 53, 61, 63,
Notre Dame de La Salette 131-134

Old Testament 284
Olwig, K. 287
open air liturgy 140, 160, 281-314
Oregon 25
Orléans 206
Orthodox Churches (Eastern) 86
Osterrieth, A. 192
outdoor ritual 15, 232, 281-314
Overdinkel 158, 159, 160, 161, 171
Overijssel 30
Oxford 99, 102

Padre Pio 126, 135
Palm Sunday 8 (research project), 276, 291, 292, 295
Palme, Olof 25, 309
Papal visit 15, 281, 292, 296, 303-308
past 113-116, 168, 232, 233, 240
pastor 33-35, 46, 48, 89, 91, 92, 121-143
Peel, the 73
penance 34, 35, 48, 198
Perche-Gouët 71
Perrin, Jacques 133
"personal narratives" 127, 136
Pesach 285
Peter, St. 143
Pfister, P. 75
Picaud, A. 206
Pieper, J. 2, 15
pilgrimage, definition 239-242
place of pilgrimage, definition 77-84
Poland 74
Pope John Paul II 75, 303-308
Portugal 65, 66, 72
Post, H. 228, 231, 233,
Post, P. 2, 15
Pra, B. 132
Presley, Elvis 53
procession 282, 283, 292, 293; see also Silent Procession (Amsterdam), 296-303
Protestant tradition 86
Psalms 284

Rajneeshpuram 25
Ramisch 75
Ranger, T. 94, 99, 101; see also Hobsbawm
Reader, I. 52
Reekmans, L. 125
Rémy, J. 22
revitalization (of rituals, of pilgrimage) 95, 96, 131, 223, 264, 296-303
Riele, W. te 297

ritual landscape 15, 281-314
Roermond 297, 301
Rogation Day 300
Rolduc 40
Rome 72, 206, 221-242, 305
Roncesvalles 206-219
Rooijakkers, G. 7
Roosendaal 35, 174
Rosa of San Damiano 135
Rotterdam 39
Saint-Jean-Pied-de-Port 206
saints 253-262, 269, 270, 293
Saint-Pierre-de-Cherennes 133
Salette, La (Notre-Dame) 10, 13, 131-138
Sallnow, M.J. 54, 55, 62, 78, 126
Salomonsson, A. 223, 226,
San Giovanni Rotondo 126, 135
Santa Maria, A. de 65
Santiago de Compostela 1, 10, 14, 58, 64, 136, 177, 203, 205-219, 221-242, 268
Scharfe, M. 25
Scherpenheuvel 177
Schlafke, J. 75
Schleswig-Holstein 309
Schnell & Steiner, editors 75
Schoutens, S. 66
Scotland 98
Scribner, B. 294
Second Vatican Council 3, 23, 52, 72, 224, 271
"secrets of La Salette" 132
Selme, farmer from La Salette 132
Shaver, P. 192
Silent procession (Amsterdam) 15, 263-279, 300
Silos, monks of 275
Sivry, L. de 65
Sneek 121, 130
Snoek, G. 59
Soergel, P.M. 59
Soubirous, Bernadette 30, 135, 192
Spielberger, C.D. 185
Spilka, B. 192
spring, of St. Boniface, in Dokkum 89-74, 121-152, 296-303
Staal, F. 276
stigmatization 125
Stonehenge 290
sudden death 308-312
Suriname 309
Swaving, J.G. 66
Switzerland 57, 66, 98

Taizé 25
Tenerife (Canary Islands) 128
theatre 114, 294
Thomsen, M.L. 73
Tilburg 10, 256, 284
tourism, touristic aspect of pilgrimage 22, 26, 31, 46, 91, 131, 140, 142, 183, 222
Tours 21
tradition 34
tradition and custom 105, 106, 109
transformation, religious 189-203
Trevor-Roper, H. 98
Trier 307
"trigger words" 14, 205-219
Turner, V. 9, 22, 26, 33, 52, 54-56, 60, 61, 64, 78, 142, 191
Turner, V. and E. 43, 190
Twente 40

Uden, M. van 2, 15
unexpected dead 1
Utrecht 40, 227

Vaals 40
Valentine Paquay, "Holy Little Father Valentine" 40
Valk, H. de 297
Valkenburg 40
Verhoeven, G. 58
Vézelay 206-219
Volendam 29
Vosmeer, Sasbout 90
Vuijsje, H. 221, 228, 233, 236, 237

Wales 98
Walter, T. 52
Warsaw 308
Wegman, H. 8, 113, 241

Wichmans, A. 65
Willibrord, St. 90
Wittem 2, 9, 10, 13, 14, 19, 27, 29-35, 43-48, 131, 157-172, 174, 177, 179, 183, 186, 187, 189, 269
Woodstock 25
Würzburg 57, 69, 70, 81

Zacharias, W. 234
ZBV, self-examination questionnaire 185, 186
Zender, M. 71
Zimdars-Swartz, S. 123, 124, 133
Zung, W.K. 185, 186

NOTES ON THE AUTHORS

Prof.dr. P.G.J. Post (1953) is professor of liturgy and sacramental theology and director of the Liturgical Institute, Tilburg Faculty of Theology (The Netherlands).

Dr. J.Z.T. Pieper (1953) lectures psychology of religion at the Theological Faculty of the University of Nijmegen and the University of Utrecht (The Netherlands).

Prof.dr. M.H.F. van Uden (1952) is professor of clinical psychology of religion at the University of Nijmegen and the Tilburg Faculty of Theology. He also works as a psychotherapist in Heerlen (The Netherlands).

PRINTED ON PERMANENT PAPER • IMPRIME SUR PAPIER PERMANENT • GEDRUKT OP DUURZAAM PAPIER - ISO 9706

ORIENTALISTE, KLEIN DALENSTRAAT 42, B-3020 HERENT